HOW PLATO WRITES

Plato is a philosophical writer of unusual and ingenious versatility. His works engage in argument but are also full of allegory, imagery, myth, paradox, and intertextuality. He astutely characterizes the participants whom he portrays in conversation. Sometimes he composes fictive dialogues in dramatic form, while at other times he does so as narratives. In this book, world-renowned scholar Malcolm Schofield illustrates the variety of the literary resources that Plato deploys to achieve his philosophical purposes. He draws key passages for discussion particularly, but not only, from *Republic* and the less well-known *Laws* and also shows how reconstructing the original historical context of a dialogue and of its assumed readership is essential to understanding Plato's approach. The book will open the eyes of readers of all levels of expertise to Plato's masterly ability as a writer and how an understanding of this is crucial if we are to appreciate his philosophy.

MALCOLM SCHOFIELD is Emeritus Professor of Ancient Philosophy at the University of Cambridge and a fellow of St John's College. He is a fellow of the British Academy and an honorary international member of the American Academy of Arts and Sciences. He is recognized as one of the major scholars in the world currently working on ancient Greek and Roman philosophy. His first book was *An Essay on Anaxagoras* (Cambridge, 1980), he co-authored with G. S. Kirk and J. E. Raven the second edition of *The Presocratic Philosophers* (Cambridge, 1983), and he has co-edited numerous other collaborative volumes, including in 2015 with Catherine Rowett a special Heraclitus issue of the journal *Rhizomata*, and with Tom Griffith a new English edition of Plato's *Laws* (Cambridge, 2016). He now works mostly on Greek and Roman political philosophy. He was co-editor with Christopher Rowe of *The Cambridge History of Greek and Roman Political Thought* (Cambridge, 2000). *The Stoic Idea of the City* (Cambridge, 1991), *Saving the City* (London, 1999), *Plato: Political Philosophy* (Oxford, 2006), and *Cicero: Political Philosophy* (Oxford, 2021) are among his major solo publications.

HOW PLATO WRITES
Perspectives and Problems

MALCOLM SCHOFIELD
University of Cambridge

Shaftesbury Road, Cambridge CB2 8EA, United Kingdom

One Liberty Plaza, 20th Floor, New York, NY 10006, USA

477 Williamstown Road, Port Melbourne, VIC 3207, Australia

314–321, 3rd Floor, Plot 3, Splendor Forum, Jasola District Centre,
New Delhi – 110025, India

103 Penang Road, #05–06/07, Visioncrest Commercial, Singapore 238467

Cambridge University Press is part of Cambridge University Press & Assessment,
a department of the University of Cambridge.

We share the University's mission to contribute to society through the pursuit of
education, learning and research at the highest international levels of excellence.

www.cambridge.org
Information on this title: www.cambridge.org/9781108483087

DOI: 10.1017/9781108672603

© Malcolm Schofield 2023

This publication is in copyright. Subject to statutory exception and to the provisions
of relevant collective licensing agreements, no reproduction of any part may take
place without the written permission of Cambridge University Press & Assessment.

First published 2023

A catalogue record for this publication is available from the British Library.

A Cataloging-in-Publication data record for this book is available from the Library of Congress.

ISBN 978-1-108-48308-7 Hardback

Cambridge University Press & Assessment has no responsibility for the persistence
or accuracy of URLs for external or third-party internet websites referred to in this
publication and does not guarantee that any content on such websites is, or will remain,
accurate or appropriate.

Contents

Preface	*page* vii
Acknowledgements	ix
Introduction	1
PART I APPROACHES TO THE CORPUS	13
1 Plato in His Time and Place	15
2 When and Why Did Plato Write Narrated Dialogues?	42
3 Against System: The Historical Plato in the Mid-Victorian Era	52
PART II ARGUMENT AND DIALOGUE ARCHITECTURE	71
4 Callicles' Return: *Gorgias* 509–22 Reconsidered	73
5 Likeness and Likenesses in the *Parmenides*	96
6 The Elusiveness of Cratylus in the *Cratylus*	118
PART III MYTH AND ALLEGORY IN THE REPUBLIC	137
7 The Noble Lie	139
8 The Cave	163
PART IV PROJECTS, PARADOXES, AND LITERARY REGISTERS IN THE LAWS	181
9 Religion and Philosophy in the *Laws*	183
10 The *Laws'* Two Projects	202

11	Plato, Xenophon, and the Laws of Lycurgus	219
12	Injury, Injustice, and the Involuntary in the *Laws*	240
13	Plato's Marionette	251
14	Paradoxes of Childhood and Play in Heraclitus and Plato	275

References 290
Index 305

Preface

A book about the way Plato writes might perhaps approach the subject systematically, taking different key elements in his writing in turn. This book takes a different tack. It proceeds by way of examples. The topics it covers are chosen in the first instance because they raise problems of interpretation, problems which either have an immediate literary dimension or turn out upon analysis to illustrate Plato's use for philosophical purposes of specific literary forms or devices. Indeed, the spotlight is for the most part on passages or themes in dialogues whose philosophical importance for the projects Plato was undertaking seemed to me to have been in various ways misunderstood or under-appreciated – often because his ways of writing had not been sufficiently pondered. The dialogues in question are *Parmenides* (subject of my doctoral thesis), *Cratylus* (another early preoccupation), *Republic*, *Gorgias*, and especially (a main focus over the last quarter-century) the *Laws*.

All the studies included in the volume were composed as occasional offerings. All but one date to the present millennium. All were written in response to invitations to give lectures or to contribute to collective volumes (often in honour of long-standing friends and colleagues) or themed issues of learned journals. Nonetheless, I hope they mostly share something of a common style and approach, not least because most were designed from the outset to be accessible to relatively wide readerships. They have been given a common format in this volume (with revisions to content where some updating seemed particularly desirable).

I remain grateful for the stimulus of the invitations I was given to compose the essays republished here and take this opportunity to thank Dimitri El Murr in particular, whose initiatives prompted no fewer than four of them. Many friends and colleagues gave me helpful critical comments on earlier versions, and I benefited from the responses of audiences of those first delivered as talks or lectures. These are detailed and acknowledged with gratitude in the fairly widely scattered original publications.

My title will remind some readers of Danielle Allen's 2010 title *Why Plato Wrote*: it is a pleasure to acknowledge the echo.

I thank the Syndics of Cambridge University Press for accepting the book and Michael Sharp, my publisher, for encouragement and facilitation throughout, together with his colleagues Katie Idle and Bethany Johnson, and at one point a crucial intervention. It has been a pleasure to work with Reshma Xavier at Integra and my copy editor Kathleen Fearn. The original proposal for the volume was helpfully scrutinized by three readers for the Press. The book's years of gestation were challenging years for most of us, and I thank especially James Allen, Carol Atack, Rachel Barney, Kirsten Canavan, Emily Gowers, Matthew Schofield, and Frisbee Sheffield for support over this period. Carol, Melissa Lane, and Shaul Tor have given much appreciated encouragement for the project itself in later stages. Melissa kindly read to the reader's profit two successive versions of the Introduction.

Note on Abbreviations

Classical references are abbreviated mostly according to *The Oxford Classical Dictionary* 4th ed. (2012) but otherwise should be readily interpretable.

Acknowledgements

Most chapters in this volume originally appeared in other publications, reprinted here courtesy of their editors and/or publishers with thanks. Presentation has been rendered uniform, and in some cases revisions to the text (mostly light) have been made.

1. 'Plato in his time and place' (from *The Oxford Handbook of Plato*, 2nd ed., ed. G. Fine. Oxford, 2019: 41–64)
2. 'When and why did Plato write narrated dialogues?' (from *Plato, Poet and Philosopher*, eds. E. Moutsopoulos and M. Protopappas-Marneli. Athens, 2013: 87–96)
3. 'Against system: the historical Plato in the mid-Victorian era' (from *For a Skeptical Peripatetic: Festschrift in Honour of John Glucker*, eds. Y. Z. Liebersohn, I. Ludlam, and A. Edelheit. Sankt Augustin, 2017: 344–64)
4. 'Callicles' return: *Gorgias* 509–522 reconsidered' (from *Philosophie Antique* 17 (2017): 7–30)
5. 'Likeness and likenesses in the *Parmenides*' (from *Form and Argument in Late Plato*, eds. C. Gill and M. M. McCabe. Oxford, 1996: 48–78)
6. 'Another two Cratyluses problem' (from *Rereading Ancient Philosophy: Old Chestnuts and Sacred Cows*, eds. V. Harte and R. Woolf. Cambridge, 2017: 181–98)
7. 'The noble lie' (from *The Cambridge Companion to Plato's Republic*, ed. G. R. F. Ferrari. Cambridge, 2007: 138–64)
8. 'Metaspeleology' (from *Maieusis: Essays on Ancient Philosophy in Honour of Myles Burnyeat*, ed. D. Scott. Oxford, 2007: 216–31)
9. 'Religion and philosophy in the *Laws*' (De Vogel lecture, from *Plato's Laws: From Theory into Practice*, eds. S. Scolnicov and L. Brisson. Sankt Augustin, 2003: 1–13)
10. 'The *Laws*' two projects' (from *Plato's Laws: A Critical Guide*, ed. C. Bobonich. Cambridge, 2010: 12–28)

11. 'Plato, Xenophon, and the laws of Lycurgus' (from *Polis* 38 (2021): 450–72)
12. 'Injury, injustice, and the involuntary in the *Laws*' (from *Virtue and Happiness: Essays in Honour of Julia Annas*, ed. R. Kamtekar (*Oxford Studies in Ancient Philosophy*, suppl. vol. 2012). Oxford, 2012: 103–14)
13. 'Plato's marionette' (Michael Frede lecture, from *Rhizomata* 4 (2016): 128–53)
14. 'Paradoxes of childhood and play in Heraclitus and Plato' (J. H. Gray lecture, not previously published)

Introduction

A book entitled 'How Plato writes' might seem a rash enterprise. The topic is multidimensional. Plato wrote a great amount, evidently over many years, with a great variety of subject matter and styles. There are many possible routes into the material. And the point, focus, and hermeneutic and other presuppositions of exploration would appear to be highly contestable. Neoplatonists or Straussians might be confident that they have found keys that unlock the secrets of all Plato's writing. But most readers do not share their confidence.[1] Hence my subtitle: 'Perspectives and problems'. The essays included in this volume offer in an empirical spirit *perspectives* on examples of a good number of key ingredients in Plato's writing, particularly his use of argument and of allegory, images, and myth, of intertextuality, and of paradox, but also his treatment of the interlocutors he portrays in dialogue, his adoption now of narration, now of direct dramatic presentation of the conversations he presents, and his assumed readerships.[2] Sometimes the focus is more on the overall shape of a work, or indeed of the corpus itself. All the essays were prompted by a perception of something *problematic*, either in a passage within a dialogue itself, or as often in the way scholarship had tackled or failed to tackle a topic. One presupposition of my own – not controversial for most readers, I trust – is the assumption that whatever and however he writes, Plato means primarily to be doing philosophy, conceived broadly as the search for wisdom and understanding.

---

[1] This is not to say that there is nothing to learn from Proclus or Strauss – and there are important things that I hope I have learned: see Chapters 5 and 9 below.
[2] These features do not, of course, exhaust the range of literary phenomena inviting consideration. I shall say nothing in this book about (for example) protreptic, or parody and pastiche, on which I comment briefly in discussing *Menexenus* in Schofield and Griffith 2010: xix–xxiii, and virtually nothing about genre in general, for which see the brilliant treatment by Nightingale 1995. Rhetoric (in Chapters 1 and 4) and historical narrative (in Chapter 10) do, however, receive some attention.

As its title indicates, the book focuses especially on *how* Plato writes. But also, not divorced from that, it asks *when* he wrote, over the course of that long life, and *why* he wrote what he did in the way he did when he wrote it. 'Why' and 'when' are harder to tackle, given that the evidence we have – whether from ancient biographical accounts or from analysis of his changing literary style – throws up much that sober scholarship must recognize as in varying degrees uncertain. But the attempt upon those questions needs to be made. My shots at doing so are included as the first two chapters here. These discuss in turn the external historical circumstances which seem likely to have been important for Plato's composing the writings he did when he did (or – to be cautious – may well have done), and the shifting literary priorities which seem likely to have prompted his composing of fictive dialogues sometimes in direct or scripted mode, sometimes as narratives. Both approaches to the writing are inimical to any suggestion that it was designed to give expression to some kind of philosophical system. My third chapter takes a step back, to look at the fierce historically grounded reaction of the two great Victorian Plato scholars George Grote and Benjamin Jowett against interpretations that made such a system out of the dialogues. Grote and Jowett are otherwise perceived as championing diametrically opposed perspectives on Plato, utilitarian versus idealist. But on a Plato systematized, they were united.

Time was (the 1950s and 1960s of my youth) when cutting-edge Plato scholarship – as practised in the English-speaking world – seemed mostly to be about his arguments: exposing their fallacies, inconsistent or hidden premises, ambiguous formulations. The need to 'reconstruct' many of the arguments was often taken for granted. Then scholars started talking about dialogue, drama, character, and genre, sometimes in what Myles Burnyeat (who memorably himself drew attention to the significance of Plato's 'first words')[3] once described as a 'curious alliance between conservative followers of Leo Strauss and radical Postmodernists'.[4] A *via media* or Hegelian-style synthesis is evidently called for. Arguments and philosophical theories advanced in Plato's pages often cannot be studied satisfactorily without consideration of the trajectory of the entire dialogue in which they appear or of its other literary dimensions.

A second group of three essays accordingly presents treatments of arguments and philosophical stances in three very different dialogues – *Gorgias, Parmenides, Cratylus* – whose import (I suggest) has eluded satisfactory interpretation, largely because their function within the overall

---

[3] Burnyeat 1997. [4] Burnyeat 2003: 23.

trajectory of the dialogue has not hitherto been given the attention required. Other aspects of the writing naturally also receive scrutiny. The subtleties and dialectical ingenuity of the detail of a key stretch of argument between Socrates and Callicles late in the *Gorgias*, in defence of a central tenet of Socratic ethics, have seldom before now been much discussed. They become a main focus of Chapter 4. In the *Parmenides*' second Third Man argument, a crucial issue of correct Greek text gets debated. The *Cratylus* chapter makes the characterization of the elusive figure of Cratylus pivot for a reappraisal of that dialogue.

But myth and allegory are elements no less significant in Plato's philosophical writing. As Burnyeat once wrote:[5]

> The dialogues record many confrontations between Opinion and Philosophy, but the refutation of Opinion is less an end in itself than a means of opening our minds to the possibility of an alternative perspective. That is why the dialogues are full of images as well as arguments. Opinion is so deeply rooted in our soul that it tends to be intransigent, blind to alternatives, resistant to argument. An image like the Ship of State in the *Republic*, or the charioteer with his two horses in the *Phaedrus*, can liberate us from the familiar chains of Opinion to the realisation that alternative perspectives are available, which provide novel starting points for argument.

Nowhere is that truer than in the *Republic*. Chapters 7 and 8 explore two celebrated imaginative fictions – the Noble Lie and the Cave – which perform key but unstraightforward roles in the strategic development of the dialogue's philosophical argument, as among other concerns these essays make it their business to show.

The final group of six chapters is devoted to the last and longest of the dialogues, the *Laws*. They widen the exploration of different philosophical dimensions of Plato's writing.[6] Chapter 9 explores the dialogue's imagined readerships. It proposes principally two types of reader as targeted: the intellectually limited (represented by interlocutors from Crete and Sparta), for whom the religious framework of the conversation is designed, constraining the range and the openness of its philosophical questioning; and the practised reader of Plato, who will register intertextual resonances with the *Republic* and the *Statesman*, and recall with understanding their more ambitious philosophical horizons. Chapters 10 and 11 discuss the *Laws*' two

---

[5] Burnyeat 2005: 167.
[6] For those readers of this book who may be relatively unfamiliar with the *Laws*, these essays might provide a further entrée into the dialogue and some of its challenges, expanding upon the introduction prefaced to the English edition of the *Laws* authored by Tom Griffith and myself: Schofield and Griffith 2016.

main projects, approaching them initially via Aristotle's puzzlement about them, and then, via study of intertextuality with Xenophon's *Constitution of the Lacedaemonians*, moving to the dialogue's advocacy of a highly disputable Spartan provenance for the kinds of values that are to be enshrined in the dialogue's programme – more palpably Sparta-inspired – for an ideal form of law-based polity.

We next return to consideration of arguments and imaginative fictions. Chapter 12 tackles the difficult argumentative excursus in Book 9 in which subtle distinctions are drawn in order to reconcile the law's distinction between voluntary and involuntary acts (crucial for penal practice) with the principle (inherited from Socrates) that nobody commits wrongdoing voluntarily. Chapter 13 re-examines Book 1's image of humans as marionettes mostly jerked about by the inflexible pulls of pleasure, pain, and emotion, and how Plato puts it to the surprising work of explaining the self-rule needed for virtue. Finally, Chapter 14 considers yet another ingredient in Platonic writing: paradox.[7] It starts with paradox in the aphorisms of Heraclitus and concludes with a complex passage of Book 7 of the *Laws*. There what is truly serious in human life is no less paradoxically identified, Heraclitus-fashion, as playful activity, conceived as participation in the ordered play of the gods.

*

Time now for some more detail on the content of these essays, and first the three in group one. Chapter 1 presents snapshots of different dialogues (ordered in a widely accepted chronological sequence) in their likely historical compositional contexts. What and how Plato wrote evidently reflected the circumstances in which he was writing and the other writers and thinkers with whom he was engaging. For example, his momentous first visit to Italy and Sicily seems to have made a massive impact on his thinking about politics and philosophy. Having spent time in the ambience of the tyrant Dionysius I in Sicily, he now reconceptualized the power of the Athenian *demos* and its susceptibility to rhetoric as approaching a form of tyranny; and the ideas he encountered in Italy about mathematics, the soul, and the afterlife likewise seem to have exercised a permanent grip on him from then on. In the *Gorgias*, these themes are woven into Plato's writing with a fresh vigour and urgency. By contrast, the prose of the late sextet of dialogues headed by the *Sophist* and *Statesman* reflects the more artificially manicured style pioneered by his rival Isocrates. Those two

---

[7] See also Chapters 7 and 12 in particular.

highly technical dialogues, like the *Parmenides* before them, can have been intended only for a readership primarily of members of his own Academy, the philosophical circle he established perhaps partly in response to Isocrates' foundation of *his* school. Even in the *Laws*, which must have been meant for a wider readership, there are passages which could be fully appreciated only by practised readers of Platonic dialogues (see Chapter 9).

In Chapter 2, by contrast, the focus is on differences in the basic literary form of a dialogue itself. Is what is written expressed as a narrative spoken by some imagined speaker? Or does Plato compose the work like a drama, with scripted parts for characters who are conceived as participating in a directly communicated conversation? This chapter asks: when and why did he adopt the narrative mode? 'When' is easy: not in what scholars take to be his earliest dialogues, focused on Socrates' characteristic stances and mode of philosophical conversation (such as *Ion* or *Crito* or *Laches*), nor in those which on stylometric grounds, above all avoidance of 'hiatus',[8] are standardly identified as his latest productions, but in an intervening period that may be seen as culminating especially in the writing of the *Republic*. 'Why' is less straightforward. One major reason was evidently Plato's desire to describe more complex interactions between his characters than was feasible in dramatically composed dialogues – and not least, to create opportunity for Socrates as narrator to convey his own often ironic reaction to a scene he describes and participates in. But sometimes characters other than Socrates himself are made to undertake the narration, as in *Phaedo*, *Symposium*, and *Parmenides*. I suggest the importance of one feature shared by these dialogues, all of them conveying Plato's own developing ideas and concerns: in these latter three works, he puts in the narrators' mouths explicit claims of veracity and reliability, which by authorial distancing techniques are simultaneously undermined or at least put into question. The purpose? To indicate remoteness from what Socrates himself in fact taught or may have said.

Do the dialogues convey a system or systems of philosophy? Ancient Platonists thought so, and they have had their successors in modern times. Chapter 3 considers the views on the issue held by the two great Victorian Plato scholars George Grote and Benjamin Jowett. Grote and Jowett are often perceived as championing diametrically opposed perspectives on Plato: utilitarian versus idealist. And early judgements on their treatments of him found Jowett much more sensitive to the texture and many registers

---

[8] 'Hiatus' ('gap') denotes a situation where a word ending in a vowel stands before a word beginning with a vowel.

of his writing than was Grote, good at the necessary dry analysis though he was. This chapter argues that no less important is what the two of them had in common: an 'atomist' hermeneutics, in fierce reaction against attempts to make an ahistorical system out of the dialogues. They shared a conviction of the prime importance of scrupulous attention to the texts as historical documents, combined with insistence that giving Plato his place in the history of philosophy and 'in the scale of human improvement' was no less the historian's obligation. It was in the approach to that 'scale' that the utilitarianism of Grote and the idealism of Jowett might have yielded differing assessments. But in practice, their judgements on what counted as progress and what might count as further progress were remarkably similar.

The three subsequent essays included here as a second group are concerned with arguments and theories, the dominating concern of Platonic scholarship in the 1950s and 1960s into the 1970s – and an abiding preoccupation of philosophical readers of Plato. First in this second group of essays comes a chapter on the *Gorgias*, which I take to be a relatively early dialogue (see Chapter 1). Discussion of the confrontation between Socrates and Callicles in the dialogue has hitherto mostly focused on its first two phases: Callicles' statement of his views and Socrates' attempted refutations (481–500), and Socrates' subsequent attempt to substitute his own conception of the good life (501–9). Much less attention has been paid to the final phase (509–22). Yet how could a writer such as Plato not invest with importance such a substantial sequence of concluding argumentation? This is where he stages the most sustained debate in the dialogue between alternative answers – with their consequences – to what has by now proved to be its central question: is committing injustice or falling victim to it the greatest evil? Chapter 4 examines in detail the key moves in that debate, in which Callicles is again tempted by Socrates to participate, after refusing to continue midway through the second phase of the dialectic. It is argued that Plato's aim in this final section of the conversation is to show just why and how Socrates might successfully initiate and sustain intellectual engagement with an intelligent young politician hoping to rise within the Athenian democracy, such as Callicles is portrayed as being. He fails to persuade him. But this is not, as is sometimes supposed, a failure on Socrates' part to communicate the radical import of what he means. It is a matter of what Plato wants us to understand as different fundamental existential commitments.

The classic paradigm and perhaps original example of the argument-focused approach to Plato post-1945 was Gregory Vlastos's famous 1954 article on the Third Man argument in the *Parmenides*.⁹ From that article, the debate it triggered, and the further literature it seeded, much was learned about the logic and metaphysics of the theory of Forms. For much of that debate, scholars paid little attention, however, to the positioning of the Third Man and its possible significance within the sequence of difficulties for the theory that Parmenides is made to develop in the first part of the dialogue. A little later in the sequence, a second version of the Third Man regress is presented. It was often read as essentially identical with the original version in its critical thrust. Chapter 5 of this volume, which deals with this second version, was the earliest of the essays that are included here to be written and originally published. It dates to the mid-1990s (all the others were composed in the present millennium) and appeared as a contribution to a collective volume designed to explore philosophical argumentation in Plato's later dialogues within its literary context – *Form and Argument in Late Plato* – and to make the case for the philosophical importance of such an approach.¹⁰

As Chapter 5 suggests, the prevalent interpretation of the second version of the Third Man was in danger of making that version effectively redundant and failed to do sufficient justice to its regress's focus specifically on the Form of Likeness. Nor was attention given to any relationship with the elaborate dialectical exercise undertaken in Part II of the dialogue. *Like* figures in many of the arguments of Part II, where it is often construed as equivalent to *being qualified in the same way*. What readers of Part II in effect come to recognize is that *like* is a second-order predicate: 'is like' means 'share the same first-order predicate', not 'participates in the Form Likeness'. Part II of the *Parmenides* thereby supplies materials for resisting the regress; and the presentation of likeness as a theme which we are invited to pursue through both parts alerts us to the fact that such materials are available and are pertinent to the business of evaluating Parmenides' critique of Socrates. A general moral: arguments need to be studied within the context and structure of the whole dialogue to which they belong.

The next chapter is likewise focused on how a dialogue as a whole works argumentatively. Chapter 6 considers the puzzling character of Cratylus in the *Cratylus*, Plato's dialogue on the notion of a correct language. At the beginning of the dialogue, he is portrayed as a teasingly mysterious figure, who is then silent for most of its duration. But he adopts a quite different demeanour when he finally joins the conversation towards the end. Now he functions as a mostly reasonable and altogether cooperative respondent,

---

⁹ Vlastos 1954.   ¹⁰ Gill and McCabe 1996.

even if the positions he takes are rigid and extreme. The chapter tackles the interpretative challenge that this puzzle poses for the reader (placed after the *Parmenides* chapter, because the *Cratylus* ends by addressing issues characteristically taken up in later dialogues – wherever its latest version might have fitted in the dialogues' chronological order of composition).[11] Plato uses Cratylus initially to sketch linguistic naturalism in the dogmatic and dialectically unelaborated form in which (I conjecture) it was presented by its original author. Then, after Socrates has made of it a full-scale philosophical theory on his own account, the figure of Cratylus is put to another use. Cratylus now proposes a version of that original naturalist position which is developed as the germ of a full-scale theory in miniature, rival to Socrates' own, incorporating semantic, epistemological, and ontological components and constructed from paradoxical stances generated by a range of previous and contemporary philosophers, including notably the Socratic Antisthenes, a construction of Plato's own. In the end, Cratylus' strange dogmatically expressed doctrine is presented as forcing engagement with an interconnected set of major philosophical issues that came to grip Plato in his later period. That for him seems to be what made Cratylus and his enigmatic persona someone of compelling intellectual interest.

My third grouping is made up of just two essays, which both address Plato's use of myth and allegory at crucial points in the developing argument of the *Republic*. Chapter 7 engages with the Noble Lie of Book 3.[12] 'Noble lie': a paradox, if not quite a contradiction in terms, and emblematic of the focus of this collection as a whole in the multiplicity of the challenges with which Plato's writing here confronts the reader. The paradox comes the more startlingly from an author who writes, in the same dialogue, that a philosopher devoted to knowledge will 'not willingly accept falsehood in any form – hating it, but loving truth'. A distinction had earlier been made between the lie in words and the 'true' lie in the soul. Yet that might not seem to do enough to mitigate the paradox or muffle the shock it administers. Lies are told to be believed – in the soul. Perhaps a further distinction might help: we may suppose that a noble lie is one that, while literally speaking a falsehood, albeit in the occurrence in Book 3 of the *Republic* a socially and politically 'useful' myth, is designed to communicate a deeper *truth*, in this particular case, a useful truth about those 'more important things' that Socrates is made to speak of. As such it is presumably 'not deserving of hatred'. On that basis, there does seem to

---

[11] On revisions apparently made to an original version, see Sedley 2003: 6–16.
[12] Part of the material in this chapter coincides with Chapter 7 (sections 2.3–5) of Schofield 2006.

be room for a lie that is 'noble'. But still, does the philosopher not recoil from accepting falsehood *in any way at all?*

Whether, and if so how, the conundrum can be satisfactorily resolved is a matter for debate, discussed with related issues in this chapter. What is not in doubt is the immediate disconcerting effect upon the reader of that paradox of a 'noble lie' itself. Writing disconcertingly is nothing unusual for Plato. Many of the essays in this book grapple with its philosophical import. For example, following the essay on the *Republic*'s Noble Lie, a treatment is included of the same dialogue's discombobulating Cave allegory (Chapter 8). At the point in the *Republic* at which Socrates launches into his cave narrative, readers are expecting further illumination of the education beyond the first studies outlined in Books 2 and 3 that the trainee philosophers being imagined are to receive. Yet initially a picture is painted of humanity at large, as we are at present, imprisoned in benighted illusion and delusion about our common uneducated condition, as symbolized by our inability to see directly simulacra of real things in the dark of the cave. We are represented as in need of radical intellectual conversion. But no indication of how that might come about is forthcoming. Or not at first. When Plato's Socrates does offer subsequent commentary, it becomes apparent that doing mathematics is his recipe – but by then Plato is apparently assuming that readers are now to think again of the smaller and less blinkered class of trainee philosophers with whose earlier education he has been concerned as the primary subjects of the narrative. By distinguishing these two quite different constructions of the denizens of the cave, Chapter 8 aims not to make the narrative or its import internally consistent, but to make sense of a good deal of its clearly deliberate mysteriousness.[13]

The final group of essays (Chapters 9 to 14) are all concerned with the *Laws*, a dialogue which as an example of philosophical writing presents readers with its own special challenges. Indeed, it has sometimes been suggested that the *Laws* is not truly philosophical or dialogical at all, a view of which I hope this sequence of chapters will play their part in disabusing anyone who might be tempted to think it. The issue is taken up at the start of Chapter 9, which (like Chapter 10, too) discusses the strategies Plato adopts in writing the dialogue and the chief projects he undertakes in it. Chapter 9 proposes that Plato directs the *Laws* to two key readerships. One is the reader inexperienced in philosophy, symbolized in the dialogue in the persons of its elderly Cretan and Spartan speakers in their conversation

---

[13] Schofield 2006: 87, 158–9 did not engage with this problem.

with an Athenian visitor to Crete where (exceptionally) that discussion takes place: a visitor who has some Socratic characteristics, but others which might remind one of the great legislator Solon. The other – in the end, it is suggested, the target chiefly in Plato's sights – is the practised reader of Platonic dialogues, who will register the echoes of the *Republic* and *Statesman* in the *Laws* (and indeed of others among Plato's writings), and who will be capable of more challenging philosophical reflection than is required within the religious framework generally presented as authoritative in the dialogue.

Chapter 10 identifies two distinct theoretical projects undertaken in the *Laws*, one idealizing, the other more pragmatic. The main enterprise is clearly construction of a social and political system that will best enable citizens to achieve virtue and happiness. But a subordinate project, less prominently announced, takes on the task of sketching a formal system of laws invested with coercive force as well as educative import, which will serve to deal with the recalcitrant human nature of those who are resistant to education. Chapter 11 then turns to the key opening passage of Book 1, where the primary job of law making (as explained in Chapter 10) is construed as that of fostering the proper development, conduct, and treatment of human beings at every stage of the life cycle, above all by provision for sound customary practices and the like (with attainment of virtue and happiness the ultimate object). It argues something not well appreciated in previous scholarship: that Plato sees this legislative project as a version of the ideal of the Spartan lawgiver Lycurgus that is recognizable in the pages of Xenophon's *Constitution of the Lacedaemonians*, as contrasted with the militaristic ideology often attributed to the Spartans (an ideology here represented in the views initially expressed by Cleinias the Cretan and endorsed by Megillus the Spartan).

In Chapters 12 and 13, the focus shifts to two particular and memorable passages of the *Laws* in which Plato turns to problems about how the human self is to be conceived, and to associated questions about virtue and humans' responsibility for one's own behaviour – since a law-governed society has to assume that responsibility for action is indeed our own. But as Chapter 12 indicates, it becomes evident in later books of the *Laws* that the dialogue remains committed to a version of Socratic paradox. Book 5 insists that no one who is unjust is so voluntarily. Book 9 then tackles what is presented as a serious threat posed by the paradox to any viable theory of criminal behaviour and its punishment; or as the Athenian puts it, to the distinction drawn 'in every city and by every legislator there has ever been between two sorts of wrongdoing (*adikêmata*), voluntary and involuntary'.

The Athenian's strategy for resisting the threat (as most commentators note) relies on distinguishing between voluntarily harming someone, which requires compensation and often purification, and commission of injustice, which merits punishment, reconceptualized however as treatment for involuntary psychic disease rather than as retribution. The chapter explores the way that this distinction is meant to work, how far it is successful in defusing the problem, and how consistently it is sustained.

Theorizing the self begins in the dialogue as early as Book 1. Few writers on the *Laws* have been able to resist the fascination of the strange image of a marionette – no ordinary marionette – which his Athenian speaker offers there, in explaining the rule over the self that is or should be exercised by reason. That topic – particularly the analysis of the self and of the powerful conflicting impulses to which it is subject – is the concern of Chapter 13. Reason's need to have recourse to law and its resources, as anticipated also in a related section of Book 10 of the *Republic*, is something not in general sufficiently emphasized in previous treatments of the passage, where a significant misconstruction of the Greek has impeded understanding. The final Chapter 14 turns to another paradox in the *Laws* and (fittingly for the closing section of this book) to the dialogue's most explicit diagnosis of the human condition, articulated in a digression in Book 7. Here, Plato's Athenian advances the proposal that what, if anything, is truly serious in human life is playful activity, conceived as participation in the ordered play of the gods. The topic is approached here via a review of Heraclitean paradoxes about children, and especially their play, notably in one of his most enigmatic aphorisms (Fr. 52). There, Heraclitus represents the dynamism that propels and sustains us right through a life as that of a child at play. Both in Heraclitus and in Plato, we can see some anticipation of Johan Huizinga's thesis (in *Homo Ludens*) that in application of the concept of play lies the route to understanding not only children's games and the place of sport in the lives of adults, but all of what may be regarded as the higher forms of culture, not least law and religious ritual. In both, the paradoxical point is made vivid through the characteristic compression and wit – the playfulness – of their writing.

PART I

Approaches to the Corpus

CHAPTER I

Plato in His Time and Place

In this opening chapter, I attempt to situate Plato's philosophizing and literary production in its historical context. The evidence external to the dialogues that such an enterprise can rely on is either scrappy or suspect, or both. So what I offer here is a series of snapshots. They follow a chronological sequence, from Plato's relationship with Socrates and the Athens that executed him; through his momentous first visit to Italy and Sicily and its impact on his thinking about politics and philosophy; to the founding of the Academy, Plato's rivalry with Isocrates, and the birth of the theory of Forms; and ending with the worlds of the late dialogues.

Socrates and the Fifth-Century Enlightenment

As a young man – perhaps as a teenager – Plato became a member of Socrates' intimate circle, something he is careful to indicate himself in both *Apology* (34a) and *Phaedo* (59b). After Socrates' death, a number of those who had belonged to the group started writing fictional dialogues (just how soon we do not know) designed to illustrate his character and personality, along with the distinctive themes and methods of Socratic conversation: Phaedo, Eucleides, Aeschines, for example, and probably Antisthenes, already an intellectual heavyweight and prolific author, represented by Xenophon as quite inseparable from Socrates (*Mem.* 3.11.17). Plato was to compose many more 'Socratic discourses' (*Sôkratikoi logoi*, as Aristotle calls them: *Poet.* 2, 1447b11) than anyone, over a much longer time span – about forty years, if we date *Ion* to the late 390s and *Philebus* to the late 350s. Socrates was with Plato a continuing and dominating obsession. Nearly the entire output of the most powerful and fertile thinker in the entire tradition of Western philosophy is conceived as a homage to Socrates and in re-creation of *his* philosophizing.[1]

---

[1] A full discussion of *Sôkratikoi logoi* and their authors is in Kahn 1996: ch. 1; see also the valuable assessment of the Socratic discourses by Dorion 2011. Brief information on the Socratic authors listed

At the very end of the *Phaedo* and its famous death scene, Plato has Phaedo say: 'That was the way our friend met his end, Echecrates – a man, as we would say, who of all in his time that we had experience of was the best, and certainly wisest and most just' (*Phd.* 118a). Those attributes, as Plato saw it, were the keynotes of Socrates' life as they were of his philosophical conversation. The harmony between the two was evidently what made him irresistibly charismatic for those he captivated. In Plato's case, it was precisely those Socratic preoccupations – justice, the good, knowledge – that formed his notion of the philosophical life. Doing philosophy meant trying to understand how to live the life of a just person: getting rid of illusions about what we know or what we think we want, and coming to see what living well really consists in. That is the manifesto Socrates enunciates in his speech to the jurors in the *Apology* (*Ap.* 28a–33c). That is the theme Plato makes him elaborate and defend on a massive scale in the *Republic*, longest and most complex of all his *Sôkratikoi logoi*.

Fundamental in what he took from Socrates is the idea that philosophy is an *inquiry*, and inquiry best pursued in conversation with someone else.[2] The conversation can be of different sorts and can accommodate flights of fancy, as well as close questioning of an interlocutor about the entailments of any views he may have advanced. Yet even when Plato's Socrates has ideas of his own to propound, they are expressly put forward for others to consider – for acceptance, qualification, or rejection – not as teaching imparted to those in need of instruction by someone secure in the knowledge of truth.[3] No doubt the young Plato was so much in thrall to Socrates that it never seriously occurred to him to think that philosophy ought to be more didactic or authoritarian, or a system of doctrines rather than an activity. In various of the early dialogues, his awareness of an alternative model of what education should be is nonetheless made crystal clear. Over and again, Socrates is represented as clashing with those who take education to be a matter of absorbing a *mathêma*, or body of knowledge, from someone who commands the relevant *tekhnê*, or expertise – as though acquisition of moral understanding could be like learning medicine from a doctor or going to a sculptor to pick up his craft.[4]

---

here is in Zeyl 1997; a fuller survey is provided by Döring 2011. Many insightful comparisons between their treatments of particular topics are offered in Brock 2021. Also useful for the chapter in general are Field 1930 and Nails 2002.

[2] See McCabe 2015.

[3] A classic example is Socrates' introduction of his opinion about the Good in the *Republic* (*Rep.* 6.506b–507a).

[4] This issue is a major preoccupation in, for example, *Laches*, *Protagoras*, and *Meno*. Socrates' classic disavowal of any claim to be a teacher is in *Ap.* 33a–c (he practises examination of those who think they know when they don't).

It is not that the Platonic Socrates rejects the conception of knowledge as *tekhnê*. That conception is omnipresent in the dialogues, from the earliest (like *Ion* and *Hippias Minor*) to late works in which Socrates scarcely figures (notably, *Sophist* and *Statesman*). Indeed, he introduces it into discussion in contexts where a modern reader would be surprised to find it figuring at all. Take, for example, the idea expressed early in Book I of the *Republic* that justice is giving each individual his due, explicated as what is appropriate for him (*Rep.* 1.331e–332d). Socrates compares the *tekhnê* which is called medicine: What does *it* give that is due and appropriate, and to what or whom does it give it? Having obtained an answer to that question and an analogous one about cookery, he frames a parallel question about justice: What would a *tekhnê* have to deliver, and to what or whom, if it were to deserve the name 'justice'? Socrates does not here necessarily assume himself that justice *is* a form of expertise comparable with medicine or cookery. His question is hypothetical in form. But it could not have been articulated as it is except in an intellectual world where there was (i) a strong inclination to suppose that the value in any valuable activity must derive from its being practised knowledgeably, and (ii) an assumption that such knowledge must constitute a *tekhnê*, or form of expertise.

Just such a world came into existence in ancient Greece in the last decades of the fifth century – in other words, precisely during the period in which Plato sets the conversations that take place in his Socratic dialogues. The second half of the century saw an explosion of prose writing on all manner of technical topics, from horsemanship to perspective in painting for the dramatic stage. To this period belong the first surviving medical treatises in the Hippocratic corpus[5] and the first attempt we know of to articulate elements of geometry, by Hippocrates of Chios.[6] In a famous passage of the *Prometheus Bound* ascribed to Aeschylus, the Titan catalogues the skills and crafts he has taught mankind, from astronomy, numerical calculation, and writing to housing, animal husbandry, navigation and medicine, divination and sacrifice, and the knowledge and use of metals. 'In one short word, you may know all at once', he concludes (*PV* 506). 'All *tekhnai* men owe to Prometheus.' This text – perhaps from the 440s – is not the only piece of writing in this period to celebrate the range of *tekhnai* commanded by humans. It reflects growing confidence in human ability to make discoveries and master nature.[7]

---

[5] On the Hippocratic corpus, see Lloyd 1978, with useful bibliography. For general discussion, see Lloyd 1979: ch. 1, and Jouanna 1999.
[6] On Hippocrates of Chios, see Lloyd 1979: 102–15, with more general discussion and bibliographical orientation in Lloyd 1990: ch. 3.
[7] A good survey of these fifth-century developments is in O'Brien 1967: ch. 2. See also Lloyd 1979: ch. 3. The *Prometheus* passage, together with a similar passage from Sophocles' *Antigone* (332–71), is

The Hippocratic author of *On Ancient Medicine*, for example, explains in his opening chapters that medicine has made the discoveries he claims for it by following a principle and a procedure; in fact, in essence, this is just the same procedure that has been followed for generations, as people have gradually learned better what sort of food and drink prepared in what ways suit what sorts of constitution – not usually recognized as a *tekhnê*, to be sure, but a *tekhnê* nonetheless.[8] By the time Plato was writing, such self-consciousness about what it is for a *tekhnê* to be a *tekhnê* had evidently become commonplace. At the beginning of the *Gorgias*, he parodies the mannerisms of writers of guides to this or that *tekhnê* by having Polus (author of such a work – on rhetoric: 462b) declaim (448c): 'Chaerephon, many forms of expertise among people have been discovered by experience from experiences. Experience is what makes our life proceed on the basis of expertise, inexperience on that of chance.'

The period of intellectual revolution I have been describing is often referred to as the age of the Sophists.[9] The polymath Hippias, treated by Plato as one of the leading figures among the Sophists, certainly epitomized something of its spirit in his own person. Astronomy seems to have been his favourite subject, but he was prepared to teach virtually anything, from mathematics, grammar, and music to what we might call antiquarian subjects – although he has some claim to be considered the first historian of philosophy (*Hi. Ma.* 285b–e; cf. *Prot.* 318d–e). The word 'sophist' originally signified (in George Grote's formulation) 'a wise man – a clever man – one who stood prominently before the public as distinguished for intellect or talent of some kind'.[10] Thus Herodotus in the fifth century BC calls the lawgiver Solon, the religious thinker Pythagoras, and the Homeric seer Melampus all sophists (*Histories* 1.29, 2.49, 4.95). 'Sophist' never quite lost this general connotation, but in the pages of Plato, Xenophon, and Isocrates it has come to have a more specific meaning: an expert who would teach you his subject for a fee.[11] Thinkers like Protagoras of Abdera, Prodicus of Keos, and Hippias (from Elis in the Peloponnese), who travelled the Greek world to do just that, were

---

presented in translation by Guthrie 1969: 79–80. The authenticity and date of *Prometheus* are disputed: see Griffith 1977.

[8] There is a major edition of this treatise: Schiefsky 2005. Its defence of medicine as a *technê* has been much discussed. The topic is treated in two studies published at the same time as that edition (which refer to previous bibliography): Barton 2005 and Dunn 2005.

[9] The best guide to the Sophists is Guthrie 1969: part 1. Another view is in Kerferd 1981. Recent treatments are offered by Barney 2006 and by Taylor and Lee 2016.

[10] Grote 1850: 479.   [11] For example, Xen. *Mem.* 1.6.13; Guthrie 1969: 35–40; and Blank 1985.

evidently salient presences in Athens around the time of the beginning of the Peloponnesian War (431 BC).

One of Plato's most elaborate dramatic masterpieces – the *Protagoras* – imagines them all assembled together in Athens shortly before the outbreak of the war. He pits Socrates in debate with Protagoras, initially on the subject of Protagoras' educational manifesto: the Sophist undertook to teach good decision-making, whether in running a household or in the public sphere, where those he taught were to be equipped with an exceptional capacity for the conduct and discussion of the affairs of the city (*Prot.* 318e–319a). How such a grandiose promise was to be honoured is not clear.[12] Much of the Sophists' teaching seems to have been conveyed in sustained set-piece performances. Plato's Protagoras gives an impressive demonstration speech in the dialogue, and Prodicus (whose passion for precise distinctions between near synonyms is frequently satirized by Plato: e.g. *Prot.* 337a–c, 339d–342a, 358d–e; *Charm.* 163a–d; *Crat.* 384a–c) was celebrated for his lecture on the choice of Heracles, portrayed as a paradigmatic figure at a crossroads in life who wins the struggle of virtue over vice (Xen. *Mem.* 2.1.21–34).

Most people, says Plato's Socrates, think that some young men get corrupted by Sophists, and that there are some unprofessional Sophists who do the corrupting (*Rep.* 6.492a). His own line is that the whims of the Athenian people – in the assembly or in the courts, on huge public juries – do much more damage. And while Plato would probably not disagree that some Sophists harmed some individuals, the tone of the *Protagoras* is mostly one of urbane amusement at the antics of the Sophists and their followers, coupled with respect for Protagoras himself. Elsewhere, he has Socrates argue that it is just not credible that someone like Protagoras could have fooled the whole of Greece and got away with making his students more depraved than they were when he took them on, for more than forty years (*Meno* 91e). In short, the suggestion is that the Sophists' reputation for good or ill is much inflated. To be sure, Plato does himself engage with some of the ideas they generated (for example, Protagoras' famous slogan: 'Man is the measure of all things', in the *Theaetetus*).[13] But in the early and middle dialogues, the one important line of thought with a Sophistic pedigree that he confronts (in different versions in the *Gorgias* and Book 2 of the *Republic*) is the antinomian claim that justice is a matter of convention (*nomos*) and will be ignored by anyone strong or adroit enough to pursue self-interest as nature (*phusis*) would dictate – although it is not

---

[12] See the quizzical reflections of Ford 2001.   [13] See Taylor 2019.

clear that any Sophist actually advocated such behaviour.[14] Otherwise, it cannot be said that the Sophists or their teaching loom that large in the dialogues, certainly by comparison with the massive presence of Socrates himself. As W. K. C. Guthrie says, Plato 'was a post-war figure writing in an Athens of different intellectual temper. When he put on to his stage the giants of the Sophistic era, he was recalling them from the dead.'[15]

Philosophy, Politics, and Athens

Socrates' trial and condemnation by an Athenian court in 399 BC, on charges of impiety and immoral influence over young people, was devastating for Plato. It was not just a personal trauma. In his mind, it constituted a confrontation that crystallized the inevitability of conflict between philosophy and politics and their incommensurable assumptions. That issue, with its Socratic resonances, was to become one of central significance in Plato's treatment of the philosopher. It is highlighted at critical junctures in some of the most important dialogues in the corpus. Some particular passages serve to illustrate the point.

Nowhere are the rival claims of politics and philosophy more trenchantly advanced than in the *Gorgias*. The dialogue begins with Socrates' critique of rhetoric, but once Callicles enters the discussion he reciprocates with a politician's critique of philosophy. In his famous monologue, he warns Socrates that philosophy makes a person helpless to defend himself in the public forum: if Socrates were brought before a court and faced with an unprincipled prosecutor, he would end up dead if the death penalty was what the prosecutor wanted (*Gorg.* 485e–486b).[16] This thinly veiled prediction of Socrates' actual fate is then reprised by Socrates himself near the end of the dialogue, where he imagines himself as a doctor prosecuted by a pastry chef before a jury of children – on a charge of ruining their health by his medicines and surgical interventions. The doctor could find nothing to say in such a court in his self-defence (521e–522c). Of course, Socrates *did* speak at his trial. Plato's point is that there was nothing he could have said then that could have begun to persuade the infantile citizenry of a self-indulgent democracy.

---

[14] On Sophistic pedigree, see the surviving fragments of Antiphon's *On Truth*, as presented in, for example, Guthrie 1969: 107–13, or Furley 1989: ch. 6.
[15] Guthrie 1975: 6.
[16] Nietzschean affinities of Callicles' speech are explored in an appendix to the great modern edition of the dialogue: Dodds 1959.

In the *Meno*, Plato actually makes Socrates' chief accuser – Anytus – a participant for a while in the dialogue. Conversation turns to the question of whether, if you want someone to acquire virtue, you should send him to a Sophist for training and instruction. Anytus is outraged at the thought: Sophists corrupt the young – any decent father could do a better job. But when Socrates points out that the great and the good – statesmen like Themistocles, Aristides, Pericles – signally failed to turn out sons of the same calibre, Anytus advises Socrates to watch his tongue and his back, too. In Athens, as elsewhere, it's easier to do harm than good, he adds for good measure (*Meno* 94e). On that note, he leaves. The whole passage is coded commentary on what Plato saw as the incoherent malice motivating the charge of corruption brought against Socrates at his trial.

There is further general reflection on the plight of the philosopher in the city, again evoking the trial, in a famous passage in the Cave analogy in Book 7 of the *Republic*. Socrates imagines a philosopher escaping from the cave, acquiring a true understanding of reality – and then returning into the darkness once more. Such a person would find it hard to reacclimatize. People would think he had damaged his eyesight. And if he tried to free others, they would seize him and kill him if they could. He would make a fool of himself if before reacclimatization he was forced to compete over shadows or images of justice, in the law courts or anywhere else, with those who have never seen justice itself (*Rep.* 7.516e–517e). The theme is replayed once more, and in very similar accents, in the digression about the philosopher in the *Theaetetus*, a passage containing many echoes of the Cave. Philosophers, says Socrates again, will only make fools of themselves if they speak in the law courts (*Tht.* 172c). He goes on to develop – at length and in detail – a contrast between the truly important and the trivial, then to argue the mutual incomprehension with which the philosopher (preoccupied with the one) and the rest of humanity (mired in the other) view each other. The final words of the dialogue make the implicit reference to Socrates' own history all but explicit (210d): 'Now I must go to the King's Porch to meet the indictment that Meletus has brought against me.'

These Athenian texts – obsessively replaying the demise of an Athenian philosopher at the hands of the Athenian democracy – illustrate what Plato took to be the fundamental problem for all politics. But Athens and its democracy exerted over him a compelling fascination. He himself was born into the Athenian aristocracy. And his dialogues communicate an unforgettable sense of the high spirits, variety, and intellectual freedom of Athenian aristocratic life – in the gymnasium, at the symposium, at Sophistic performances, or just in private conversation – as Plato partly remembered and partly imagined them during the years in which his philosophical dramas are represented as being played out – that is, the last third of the fifth century BC. It may seem paradoxical that such a vigorous aristocratic culture flourished – as, of course, did Plato's own writing and thinking – under a democracy.

But, in truth, the Athenian political settlement was always a complex negotiation between mass and elite.[17] In his funeral speech of 429 BC, Pericles, the aristocrat who was the dominant figure in Athenian democratic politics in the 440s and 430s, remarked (in the words Thucydides attributes to him) that in Athens's meritocratic form of democracy 'we have provided for the mind many relaxations from exertions', and again 'we cultivate beauty with economy and philosophy without enervation' (*Hist.* 2.38, 40). Loathe and despise democracy though he did, it is hard to suppose that Plato was altogether unaware that the vitality and range of his own writing owed much to Athenian intellectual life as he experienced it under the democracy during his formative years. Plato's vivid portrait of democracy and the democratic lifestyle in Book 8 of the *Republic* itself (*Rep.* 8.557a–564a) exhibits the colour, energy, and variety that it is officially deprecating, and a kind of intimacy, too, all in marked contrast with the external and chilling account of oligarchy that has just preceded.

One thing Plato certainly communicates is a sense of the precariousness of the world he describes. The dramatic date of the drinking party the inebriated Alcibiades bursts in on in the *Symposium* is deliberately set a few months before the public outcry provoked in 415 BC by events – the mutilation of the herms and the profanation of the mysteries – in which he was implicated (along with many others, including, among those present, Phaedrus, for example, and probably Eryximachus, too), and which were to be the catalyst for his political downfall.[18] The *Charmides*, set early in the Peloponnesian War, ends with some menacing words from Charmides (Plato's uncle) to Socrates. This is doubtless designed to remind us that Charmides, incidentally someone else implicated in the outrages of 415, would be involved with the oligarchic junta of the Thirty Tyrants that seized power briefly in 404 (and took pains to silence Socrates), and which was led by Critias, portrayed as Charmides' mentor in the dialogue.

---

[17] Ober 1989. Plato's own stepfather and guardian, Pyrilampes, was a friend of Pericles, active in the democracy's public life, and called his own son Demos.
[18] Brief accounts are in Price 1999: 82–5 and Rhodes 2006: 157–60. A full treatment is in Furley 1996.

The two generals who figure as main participants in the discussion of the *Laches* – Laches and Nicias – were both dead within a few years of its dramatic date. Nicias' acceptance in the dialogue of divination as a form of knowledge, and Socrates' question about its relation to generalship (*Laches* 195e–196a, 198e–199a), are clearly meant to prefigure the disastrous decision that triggered the final debacle of the Sicilian expedition in 413 BC: Nicias took an eclipse of the moon as a portent requiring delay in departure (Thuc. *Hist.* 7.50). The *Republic*, too, is set at some point in the war's duration. The first two of those mentioned as accosting Socrates as he is leaving the Piraeus at the beginning of the dialogue are Polemarchus and Niceratus. Both were to be executed by the Thirty, who also confiscated the immensely profitable arms factory Polemarchus' father Cephalus – Socrates' first main interlocutor in Book 1 – had built up.[19]

So one could go on. Plato certainly did not think democracy (with the intellectual world it sustained at Athens) was the only system of government liable to collapse under the pressure of its own contradictory dynamic: witness the saga of regime change sketched brilliantly in Book 8 of the *Republic*. But the fragility of the world of the dialogues and of the political system at Athens that supported it is surely an insistent subtext. In the ideal communities delineated in *Republic* and *Laws*, life – including intellectual life – is to be strictly controlled at every point. There will simply be no potential for development of the exuberant proliferation of viewpoints of every kind, and of the social structures enabling debate between them, which makes the dialogues such attractive reading. Presumably, Plato concluded that that was the price that would have to be paid for a secure political order – in key respects, more reminiscent of unintellectual Sparta than of Athens – that would promote virtue and happiness. It was a conclusion perhaps already implicit in the enthusiasm for the Spartan social and political system fashionable among some Athenian aristocrats in his formative years and shared by Socrates and his mother's cousin Critias.

Light from the West

'When I first came to Syracuse, being then about forty years of age . . . ' So writes the author of the Seventh Letter (*Ep.* 7.324a); and whether he really is Plato or not, the letter's evidence that Plato made a first visit to Sicily

---

[19] On these and similar resonances of the Peloponnesian War in Plato, see Gifford 2001. Narratives and analyses of the war are in Hornblower 2003: chs. 12 and 13, and Rhodes 2006: chs. 8–15. A fuller account is in Kagan 2003.

around his fortieth year is more or less universally regarded as reliable. Coupled with the usual dating of Plato's birth to 427 BC (D.L. 3.2), it yields a rough date of 387 for the visit, which on any reckoning must belong somewhere in the early to middle 380s. The letter's narrative focuses on the friendship he formed with the young Dion, brother-in-law of the tyrant of Syracuse, Dionysius I, by way of introduction to Plato's entanglements in Sicilian court politics twenty years later. He does not indicate his motivation in making the voyage west, but the most obvious reason is the one that has been transmitted and often repeated in ancient tradition: Plato was wanting to make contact with the Pythagorean philosophers in South Italy (probably his primary destination), and especially with Archytas in Tarentum.[20]

What was the outcome of that meeting of minds? Here is one way of telling the story[21] – which construes the encounter as a decisive moment with extraordinary impact on the future direction of Plato's thought. To put it in a nutshell, Plato converted to Pythagoreanism: to belief in the immortality of the soul; to a fascination with eschatology and myths of a last judgement; to a conviction that mathematics held the key to understanding the nature of reality; to the idea that politics might, after all, be reshaped by philosophy and philosophers; to the resolve to create in Athens his own community of friends dedicated to the pursuit of philosophy. From the conversion will have flowed much of the energy and vision that fuelled the writing of dialogues such as *Gorgias*, *Meno*, *Phaedo*, and *Republic*. Its most practical consequence was to be the founding of the Academy.

If this book were about a famous philosopher of the modern period, there would probably be well-documented evidence of known date and in quantity supporting the interpretation – which might still, of course, be controversial. For ancient Greek thinkers, biographical facts are in short supply, and hard facts almost non-existent. Diogenes Laertius tells us it was after returning from his travels abroad that the Academy gymnasium and its environs became the seat of his activities (D.L. 3.7). Otherwise, everything is more or less insecure inference. We have no absolute or even

---

[20] The following all give fairly similar variants of this account: Phld. *Acad. Ind.* X.5–11; Cic. *Rep.* 1.16; *Fin.* 5.87; V. Max. 8.7 ext. 3; and Olymp. *in Alc.* 2.86–93. Other variants include Apul. *Pl.* 1.3; D.L. 3.6 (which mentions not Archytas, but Philolaus and Eurytus); and Hier. *Contra Rufinum* 3.40. These and yet further texts on the subject are collected (and translated) in Huffman 2005: 272–4.

[21] For example, Guthrie 1975: 35–8 (with 9 n. 1, 24 n. 2, 284). But the effect of Archytas' personal influence is given greater stress, for example, by Dodds 1959: 26–7, and Vlastos 1991: 128–30. For a more recent discussion, see Huffman 2016.

relative dates for the four dialogues listed immediately above. Issues relating to the chronology of the dialogues are only glanced at in this book: suffice to say here that all modern scholarship that is prepared to attempt a dating puts this quartet in that order and (with some hesitation or disagreement over *Gorgias*) makes their production subsequent to Plato's return from Italy and Sicily. Quite how far Plato's preoccupation with mathematics or philosopher rulers or even eschatology has a major Pythagorean dimension could perhaps be disputed, as could the idea of a Pythagorean pedigree for the foundation of the Academy.[22] And we do not *know* that Plato met Archytas or other Pythagoreans on his visit, or, consequently, that discussions with them had any effect on his thought at all.

So the hypothesis about Plato's development sketched above is undeniably speculative. Nonetheless, it is reasonable speculation designed to give an economical explanation of something that certainly calls for explanation. It is a striking fact (here we *can* speak of fact) that the four dialogues under consideration share a preoccupation with mathematics and the ultimate origin and fate of the soul that is entirely absent from dialogues like *Ion*, *Hippias Minor*, *Euthyphro* and *Laches* (for example), which are paradigmatically Socratic in method and content. What accounts for the difference? A simple answer suggests itself: the newly registered impact on Plato of powerful ideas encountered in an exotic non-Athenian religious and intellectual environment.

From as early as the eighth century BC, the Greeks had been establishing settlements on the coasts of South Italy and Sicily, which more or less rapidly achieved political control over the hinterland and its Indigenous inhabitants, with more gradual cultural penetration. By the fifth century, cities such as Acragas and Syracuse, in Sicily, and Croton and Tarentum, in South Italy, had become among the richest and most powerful in the Greek world; 'sybaritic' derives from the notoriously luxurious Sybaris, a city in South Italy already destroyed in 510 BC. In many respects, the cities of these western Greeks passed through phases of development comparable with those familiar from mainland Greece. In religion, they were more distinctive. The surviving evidence indicates a preoccupation with cults concerned with marriage, death, and the afterlife, often associated with Demeter and Persephone. There are burials indicating that the deceased were initiates into mysteries designed to achieve purification and a safe

---

[22] For example, a Pythagorean model for the Academy is dismissed by Ostwald and Lynch 1994: 604.

passage to a better life in the hereafter, with 'other famous initiates and bacchants', as one gold plate of the late fifth century discovered at Hipponion puts it.[23]

This was the world in which Pythagoras arrived, with Croton his destination, as a refugee from Samos in the eastern Aegean, perhaps somewhere in the decade 535–525 BC. He quickly became a charismatic figure whose life, work, and teaching are now the stuff of impenetrable legend. There is no doubt, however, that the main focus of his teaching was the soul and its place in the cosmic scheme of things – and the practices needed to ensure that, after death and judgement, its journey through an inevitable cycle of reincarnation will bring it eventually to the isles of the blessed. Not only in Croton, but elsewhere in South Italy, too, there formed groups of initiates into the austere Pythagorean way of life, instructed in its doctrines and practices, which encompassed everything from diet (where abstinence from beans was the most famous prohibition) to sacrificial and funerary rites.[24]

At Croton (and probably in other cities), the Pythagoreans acquired considerable political influence around the late sixth and early fifth centuries, although that dominance had long since ended by the time of Plato's visit; according to the fourth-century music theorist Aristoxenus (who came from Tarentum), Pythagoreanism petered out in South Italy (I think he means as a political force), with Archytas the one exception he mentions (Iamb. *VP* 249–51). Archytas seems to have achieved a prominence in democratic Tarentum, at the height of its considerable power, comparable with Pericles' at Athens, and like Pericles as general – probably seven years in succession, but probably also some time after Plato's visit (D.L. 8.79).

The name of Pythagoras is nowadays associated pre-eminently with a famous geometrical theorem about right-angled triangles. But there is no credible ancient evidence connecting him with the idea or practice of mathematics or with the identification or solution of mathematical problems. The pioneers here, as in so many other fields of inquiry, were the eastern Greeks in Asia Minor and the neighbouring islands (the name of Hippocrates of Chios has already been mentioned).[25] What Pythagoras does seem to have pressed is the idea that number and proportion – particularly, in the fundamental

---

[23] For the text of the Hipponion gold plate (and some discussion), see Kirk, Raven, and Schofield 1983: 29–30. On western Greek religion, see Zuntz 1971; Redfield 2003.

[24] For Pythagoras and the Pythagoreans, see Kirk, Raven, and Schofield 1983: ch. 7. The fundamental modern treatment is Burkert 1972; a briefer treatment is in Kahn 2001.

[25] On early Greek mathematics, see Heidel 1940; Burkert 1972: ch. 6; Knorr 1981.

harmonic ratios of 2:1 (the octave), 3:2 (the fifth), and 4:3 (the fourth) – were in some symbolic way the key to understanding the universe.

Mysterious generality started to give way to the new style of mathematical inquiry of the later fifth century in the work of the Pythagorean Philolaus (probably of Croton), who developed a complete mathematical analysis of the diatonic octave, apparently in the context of the theory of cosmic harmony.[26] Archytas, however, is the first Pythagorean known to us who was able to stand comparison with other leading mathematicians of his day. His musical theory was devoted to analysis of scale systems in terms of different means and proportions (arithmetical, geometrical, harmonic) and to physical explanation of pitch expressible in terms of ratios. He was famous for his solution of the problem of finding two mean proportionals to double the cube. Archytas presented the study of music programmatically as the sister science of arithmetic, geometry, and astronomy, as Plato seems to be acknowledging when he refers to this as the Pythagorean view in appropriating it in Book 7 of the *Republic* (*Rep.* 7.530d). And he claimed that 'calculation' was the way to promote justice and political harmony.[27]

So when in a climactic passage of the *Gorgias* (*Gorg.* 507e–508a), utterly unlike anything in Plato before, Socrates reports 'the wise' as saying that 'heaven and earth and gods and men are bound together by community, friendship, orderliness, self-control and justice', which is 'why they call the whole thing a world-order (*kosmos*)', and when he invokes at this point the power of 'geometrical equality', his words are best explained as an echo of the conversations Plato had recently enjoyed with Archytas and other Pythagoreans. When the dialogue concludes with an eschatological myth about the contrasting fates of souls who have lived lives of justice or injustice, this new destination for a Platonic dialogue is again best explained as a reflection of the Pythagoreanism its author had assimilated on his western travels – however much or little the detailed content of the story may owe to Pythagorean models. Most readers sense in *Gorgias* not just a shift in philosophical direction but an insistent and radicalized urgency of tone that was quite novel and perhaps unparalleled in Plato's work. That cannot all be put down to the passion of a new convert to Pythagoreanism, but conversion on his travels might well have been the catalyst.

---

[26] On Philolaus, see Kirk, Raven, and Schofield 1983: ch. 11. Philolaus is discussed more fully in Burkert 1972: ch. 3, and the major edition of Huffman 1993.

[27] Archytas is the subject of a major edition (with introductory essays) by Huffman 2005. A more recent treatment of the debt Plato may have owed to Pythagorean mathematical speculation is offered by Horky 2013.

Critique of Rhetoric and Rivalry with Isocrates

What the *Gorgias* is most urgent about is the choice between philosophy and politics (or politics as it is currently conceived and practised): how radical it is, how much is at stake in making it. That is just the kind of focus we might have expected if the dialogue is the most immediate product of Plato's visit to Italy and Sicily, at any rate, given his reactions to the hedonistic lifestyle and the conception of happiness he found prevailing there (according to the Seventh Letter). *Gorgias* is the first of the dialogues to be preoccupied with tyranny and the tyrant (as the supreme lawless hedonist). Readers have often thought that the passage on the difficulty inherent in friendship with a tyrant (509c–511a) encapsulates Plato's reflections on Dion's relationship with Dionysius I.[28] But there is a sense in which the entire dialogue grapples with the problem of tyranny. It is as though Plato is now viewing Athens – which is foregrounded in Socrates' discussion with Callicles, in particular – through lenses sharpened in Sicily. He looks for tyranny at home, and he finds it in the ambitions of political rhetoric – which, as he portrays it, seeks not the good of city or citizens but the manipulation and control of the populace by flattery, as diagnosed by earlier writers such as Aristophanes and Thucydides. The Seventh Letter presents a Plato already primed for comparative political analysis at the time of his stay in Italy and Sicily. *Gorgias* shows us comparison in operation, as, for example, quite explicitly in the long section on the resemblances between the orator and the tyrant in the conversation with Polus (466a–471d).

The *Gorgias* attacks the credentials both of those who exercise political power by the practice of rhetoric and of those who teach it (whether by performance, like Gorgias, or through handbooks, like Polus). By starting with Gorgias and Polus (the teachers) and finishing with Callicles (the practitioner),[29] Plato makes a point: teaching, even by someone as apparently benign as Gorgias, and practice, with all its corrupting potential, form a dangerous continuum. For while Plato treats the Sophists mostly just as intellectual poseurs, he sees rhetoric as a real force for harm. The message is illustrated in some of the later pages of the dialogue, with what is effectively a counter-history of Athenian imperialism. Here, the greatest of the orators on its political stage – Themistocles, Cimon, Pericles – are accused of making Athens bloated and rotten and of

---

[28] For example, Guthrie 1975: 284 n. 4.
[29] On Gorgias, Polus, and Callicles as historical figures, see Dodds 1959: 6–15; see also Guthrie 1969: 101–7, 192–200, 269–74; Kerferd 1981: ch. 8; and Wardy 1996: chs. 1–3.

deserving the blame for its eventual downfall (*Gorg.* 515b–519a). Plato's anger at the grossness of the deception and self-deception needed to sustain Athenian democratic rhetoric seems to have been fierce in the years after his return from Sicily. In the *Menexenus*, likely to have been written in about 385 BC, he puts in Socrates' mouth a pastiche funeral oration, said to have been learned from Pericles' mistress Aspasia (*Menex.* 235e–236c).[30] By virtue of blatant omissions and distortions, this blandly satirical composition paints a picture of Athens' entire history since the Persian Wars at the beginning of the fifth century right down to the ignominious King's Peace of 386 (some years after Socrates' death, of course) as one of noble and mostly successful endeavour. Rhetoric, we are to understand, is both agent and expression of Athenian political bankruptcy.

There was one specific reason why Plato might well have thought it timely to put the case against rhetoric with all the force he could muster: the Athenian speechwriter Isocrates' decision around 390 BC to start taking pupils, marked by publication of his tract *Against the Sophists*.[31] The *Gorgias* is probably not a critique of Isocrates or *Against the Sophists* in particular,[32] although at least one significant passage (*Gorg.* 463a, on the psychological equipment of the orator) seems to turn Isocrates' specific claims for rhetoric (*Against the Sophists* 17) to its discredit. The dialogue is planned on an altogether grander design, as an assault on rhetoric itself. That is why it is named after Gorgias, the first famous exponent of rhetoric conceived as a *tekhnê*, and why it makes this fifth-century figure the initial target. Plato turns his guns much more narrowly and explicitly on Isocrates in the *Euthydemus*, whose date of composition is disputed, but – echoing or pre-echoing the *Republic*'s distinction between the geometer and astronomer and the dialectician as it does – would probably have been written later than *Gorgias* and *Menexenus*.

The main body of the *Euthydemus* is devoted to a Socratic exposé of the logic-chopping of a later generation of Sophists, here represented by the

---

[30] For the *Menexenus*, see Guthrie 1969: 312–23 and Schofield and Griffith 2010: xviii–xxiii; see also the study of Kahn 1963. There is now a fine modern edition: Sansone 2020.

[31] The writings of Isocrates (436–338 BC) survive and are most conveniently consulted in the three-volume Loeb edition: Norlin 1928 and van Hook 1945. More recent translations with good bibliography are Mirhady and Too 2000, and Papillon 2005. Good brief studies are Ostwald and Lynch 1994: 595–602, and Kennedy 1963: 174–203. Interactions between Isocrates and other Athenian thinkers, above all Plato, in the first half of the fourth century BC are the subject of a valuable if often speculative monograph by Eucken 1983. Thus, Isocrates' account of the Egyptian polity in the *Busiris* is read as a parody of the *Republic* (see also Livingstone 2001).

[32] But it is sometimes so taken, as in, for example, Ostwald and Lynch 1994: 605.

brothers Euthydemus and Dionysodorus. But the frame dialogue is a conversation between Socrates and his old friend Crito, who is represented as having been present for the encounter but out of earshot (*Euthd.* 271a). In the final chapter at the end of the dialogue (304b–307c), Crito relates a conversation he had when leaving with an unnamed person, identified as a clever speechwriter who never appears in court himself, with a high sense of his own wisdom. This description fits Isocrates exactly,[33] and he is portrayed as confusing logic-chopping with philosophy – a fair charge against *Against the Sophists*. Socrates makes a damning assessment. Someone like that occupies the borderland between philosopher and politician – neither one thing nor the other, and inferior to both. However, such people have a huge reputation for wisdom, except among real philosophers – whom it is therefore in their interest (especially when their own pretensions are exposed) to represent as no more significant than the likes of Euthydemus.

The likeliest reason why Plato decided he needed to rebut the insinuation (the *Euthydemus* makes the difference between Socratic philosophizing and logic-chopping crystal clear) is that Isocrates' school was by this time highly successful in training budding politicians in oratory, as, indeed, we know it became. The dialogue does not advertise the contrasting merits of the Academy. In fact, it concludes with an injunction to give serious consideration to philosophy itself and not bother with its practitioners, good or bad. But readers might be expected to draw their own conclusions, alerted, perhaps, by the reference to geometers and astronomers: geometry and astronomy are what Isocrates, at any rate, later represented as the distinctive ingredients in the educational programme of the Academy (*Antidosis* 261–8).

Hard facts about the Academy are unsurprisingly in short supply.[34] We should not conceive of it as a school in any formal sense, with its own property and institutional structures. However, Plato did acquire a house and garden in the vicinity of the gymnasium, where communal meals were probably taken. Did Plato take pupils? If so, not (like Isocrates) for money. Ancient sources sometimes speak of 'companions' (e.g. Plu. *adv. Col.* 1126C). Perhaps we should think of a more or less loosely defined society

---

[33] For example, Thompson 1868: app. 2.
[34] Many accounts of the Academy as an institution in standard works on Plato are rather speculative: not exempt from the charge Guthrie 1975: 19–24. For a corrective, see, for example, Cherniss 1945: ch. 3. A lively and balanced brief treatment is that of Dillon 2003: 1–16.

of friends (recalling the Pythagorean slogan, 'friends share what they have'), with younger adherents learning from the conversation of their seniors. Doubtless, discussion would often be conducted in Socratic question-and-answer mode: in his early *Topics*, Aristotle – a member of the Academy for twenty years – formulated rules for its conduct. But mathematicians were among those attracted to the Academy, with Eudoxus of Cnidos notable among them.[35] While we should not assume that the mathematical curriculum of Book 7 of the *Republic* was in any way replicated in its modus operandi, anecdotes of Plato setting mathematical problems for Eudoxus and others (e.g. What uniform motions will account for the apparently disorderly motions of the planets?)[36] and the interest in it reflected in the dialogues (e.g. *Meno* 82b–87c and *Rep.* 7.529 c–531c) suggest that mathematical questions will, indeed, have figured in the discussions a good deal.

The rivalry between Isocrates and Plato persisted. Isocrates seems to have responded to the *Euthydemus* by granting a distinction between those who (like the Socratic Antisthenes) deny the possibility of falsehood and contradiction,[37] and those who (like Plato's Socrates in the *Protagoras*) claim that all the virtues are a single form of knowledge (see the beginning of his *Helen*, which is of uncertain date). But this is a distinction without a difference: both groups are eristic paradox-mongers. It is much better, he says, to venture reasonable opinions on useful subjects than to have exact knowledge of useless ones. Plato, for his part, returned to a reconsideration of rhetoric in the *Phaedrus*. His Socrates projects a rhetoric reformed by philosophy. That would, indeed, be a *tekhnê*, unlike the rhetoric of current theory and practice: 'the art of speech by one who has gone chasing after opinions, instead of knowing the truth, will be a comical sort of art, in fact no art at all' (*Phdr.* 262c). The dialogue ends with some flattering words from Socrates about the natural powers of the young Isocrates and the

---

[35] Eudoxus was notable for his development of the general theory of proportion expounded in Book 5 of Euclid's *Elements* and for the elaborate theory of concentric spheres he devised to account for the apparently irregular motions of the planets. See further Guthrie 1978: 447–57.

[36] For the evidence, see Riginos 1976: 141–5. On the importance of problems in the development of Greek mathematics, see Knorr 1986.

[37] Antisthenes' intellectual activity spanned the fifth and fourth centuries; his literary output was huge (D.L. 6.15–19), although nearly all of it is lost. While ethics was the main preoccupation, he also engaged in Homeric interpretation and theorizing about language. He seems to have fallen under the influence of both Gorgias and the Sophists, before becoming a devoted Socratic. For him, virtue was sufficient for happiness – all that was needed was the strength of a Socrates (D.L. 6.11). See further Schofield 1998.

promise of philosophy in him if he should become dissatisfied with his current activity (278e–279b) – a backhanded compliment, if ever there was one. But the *Phaedrus* paradoxically begins to exhibit in its prose style more of the deliberate avoidance of hiatus that had been Isocrates' constant trademark – and was clearly beginning to catch on more generally, with Plato himself a total convert in the late dialogues. Isocrates, in fact, had the last word, in his late and autobiographical *Antidosis* (353 BC). Here, he makes the patronizing concession that the sort of 'philosophy' practised by those who occupy themselves with the exactness of geometry and astronomy is just training for the mind, a *preparation* for philosophy – more advanced than what boys do in school but similar in most respects (*Antidosis* 266).

Parmenides, Heracliteanism, and the Theory of Forms

In Chapter 6 of the first book of the *Metaphysics* (which surveys earlier thinkers' views on the first principles of things), Aristotle presents Plato as close to the Pythagoreans in making numbers occupy a key place in metaphysical foundations. He is looking at Platonic ontology through the lens of the late *Philebus* and Plato's oral discussions of the one and the indefinite dyad; more generally, Aristotle's perspective is informed by the Pythagorizing approach to metaphysics that prevailed in the Academy during his membership of it. But unlike Speusippus or Xenocrates, he was intent on stressing that there were important differences between Plato and the Pythagoreans. Above all, as he saw it, the Pythagoreans assimilate numbers and the contents of the sensible world, whereas Plato holds that numbers have an existence separate from sensible things.[38] The first main section of the chapter is accordingly devoted to a narrative explaining how Plato came to 'separate' the Forms (how Forms relate to numbers is deferred until later).

Here is Aristotle's narrative (*Metaph.* A.6, 987a32–b10):

> In his youth, he [Plato] had become familiar first of all with Cratylus and with Heraclitean views to the effect that all perceptible things are always in flux, and there is no knowledge that relates to them. This is a position he

---

[38] There are brief accounts of the work of Speusippus and Xenocrates in Guthrie 1978: 457–83; more extended treatments are in Dillon 2003. Speusippus, Plato's nephew and successor, seemed to have been the more interesting thinker of the two, particularly notable for his hypothesis of different but analogous pairs of principles explaining successive levels of reality (e.g. numbers, magnitudes, soul) – on which, see Dancy 1991: 63–119, 146–78. Xenocrates developed the *Symposium*'s idea of *daimones*, spiritual beings mediating between gods and humans (*Symp.* 202e–203a). Collections of the evidence are Tarán 1981 and Isnardi Parente 1982.

later subscribed to in these terms. Socrates, on the other hand, engaged in discussion of ethics and had nothing to say about the general system of nature. But he was intent on finding out what was universal in this field and was the first to fix his thinking on definitions. Plato followed him in this and subscribed to the position that definition relates to something else, and not to the perceptibles – on the kind of grounds indicated: he thought it impossible for there to be a common definition of any of the perceptibles, since they were always changing. Plato, then, called these kinds of realities 'ideas' and claimed that the perceptibles were something in addition to them and were all spoken of in terms of them – what he said was that by virtue of participation, the many shared their names with the forms.

The gist of Aristotle's account is clear. Plato accepts Socrates' view that knowledge as articulated in definitions must relate to something universal; takes over the Heraclitean view that there can be no such knowledge of perceptibles, because they are always changing – they have no definite or at any rate definable nature; and so posits Forms separate from perceptibles as the realities to which definitions do apply. But while the general thrust of the passage is not in doubt, it prompts questions:

1. What exactly is Aristotle claiming about Plato's relationship with Cratylus?
2. Whatever the claim, is it likely to be true?
3. Was subscription to Heracliteanism really a key component in Plato's motivation for positing Forms?

I shall deal summarily with points 1 and 2 and at greater length with point 3.[39]

1. Aristotle is certainly saying that when Plato was young he got to know Cratylus, and through him the Heraclitean theory of flux. Nevertheless, it is not claimed in so many words that Cratylus was his 'teacher'. Is it being stated or suggested that he got acquainted with Cratylus before joining Socrates' circle? The answer turns on what is meant by 'first of all': first in temporal sequence, or the first point in Aristotle's exposition? I do not think we can be sure, although the second option better fits my sense of the flow of the passage. In any case, the issue will not be of much moment for our purposes.

---

[39] On Cratylus, see Sedley 2003: 16–23. A preoccupation with the flux of the perceptible world is not self-evidently what was fundamental in the philosophy of Heraclitus: for example, Kirk, Raven, and Schofield 1983: ch. 6; Kahn 1979. But Aristotle correctly interprets the way Heracliteanism was construed by Plato.

2. It has been suspected that Aristotle does not really have biographical information at his disposal but is simply extrapolating from the end of Plato's *Cratylus*.[40] There, Cratylus at least ends up a Heraclitean, and Socrates argues against a thoroughgoing Heracliteanism that if there were knowledge, it would have to relate to entities like 'the beautiful itself', which is always such as it is and cannot therefore be in flux (*Crat.* 439b–440e). This passage is surely what Aristotle uses to *interpret* the way Plato came to use the Heracliteanism he learned about from Cratylus.[41] But Aristotle knows things about Cratylus – an obscure figure – not to be found in Plato (e.g. his famous criticism of Heraclitus: you cannot step into the same river even once (*Metaph.* Γ5, 1010a7–15)); he does not actually need the biographical claim for his main purpose – to explain Plato's motivation for positing Forms; and the way he highlights it at the beginning of the passage suggests someone who thinks he has real news to impart. The verdict must be that Aristotle was told it by someone he had reason to think reliable – conceivably, Plato himself.

3. The reason for mentioning Plato's early familiarity with Cratylus and Heracliteanism is evidently its significance in the light of what later transpired. Plato had got to know the Heraclitean theory of flux and to understand its consequences for knowledge when young. But it was only later, when reflecting on Socrates' search for definitions (the focus of the early dialogues), and when puzzling about the nature of knowledge on his own account in consequence, that he came to put the Heracliteanism he had imbibed from Cratylus to philosophical work – in concluding that Forms, not perceptibles, must be the object of knowledge and definition. The key question is whether this is a believable account of the origin of the theory.

Nobody doubts that Plato posited Forms as a consequence of reflection on Socrates' definitional 'What is X?' questions. One of his preferred locutions for referring to a Form is to have Socrates speak of 'the very thing that X is'. That formula is not itself a definition. Instead, it specifies what it is that would be captured by an adequate definition of X if we could find it. In other words, there has to be 'the very thing that X is' if there is to be the kind of definitional knowledge of what all Xs have in common that

---

[40] For example, Kirk 1951 and Kahn 1996: 80–3.
[41] Although if he did, he read somewhat more into Plato's text (even supplemented by, e.g., *Phd.* 78c–e) than it literally contains: see Irwin 1999: 149–52, in a study that explores different ways in which Heraclitean flux is understood by Plato.

Socrates was looking for. That, then, prompts the further question: What *kind* of thing is the very thing that X is?

Well-known texts in the so-called middle dialogues address themselves to this issue (notably, *Symp.* 211a–b; *Phd.* 65d–66a, 74a–c, 78 c–79e). In doing so, they avail themselves of the radical thought – at the core of the argument of the great metaphysical poem of the Presocratic Parmenides of Elea ('much of Plato's philosophy', especially his later philosophy, 'is unimaginable without the towering figure of Parmenides')[42] – that if reality is to be the object of knowledge, then insofar as it is knowable, it must be what it is without qualification: it cannot *not* be in any respect at all (*Rep.* 5.476e–477a). Aristotle does not mention Parmenides in his account of the rationale underlying the theory of Forms (he confines himself to figures with whom Plato had significant early encounters). But Plato's encounter with Parmenides' *thought* was clearly decisive in this context. Parmenides' central argument is that only what is is an intelligible object of thought – use of the expression 'is not' attempts something impossible: specifying not a something but nothing (Fr. 2; cf. Fr. 3, Fr. 6.1–2). He then develops the consequences. Reality cannot come into being or pass away, or change or move, or exhibit any variation or imperfection, since to represent it as subject to any of these processes or conditions would require explicit or implicit use of 'is not' (Fr. 8.1–49). The perceptible world as represented in ordinary human beliefs about reality fails to satisfy these constraints. 'Mortal opinions', as Parmenides calls them, are desperately confused because they roll up 'is' and 'is not' together – they fail to make the critical decision between the two (Fr. 6 and 7; cf. Fr. 8.15–18).[43]

In Book 5 of the *Republic*, Plato follows Parmenides in his characterization of opinion as the mental condition of ordinary people who take what their senses tell them for knowledge (*Rep.* 5.474b–480a). Nonetheless, it sounds from his formulations as though he construes the state of the perceptible world primarily in terms of Heraclitean flux rather than any corresponding Parmenidean category – so that Aristotle may well have been right in construing reflection on Heracliteanism as a key metaphysical

---

[42] Guthrie 1975: 35.
[43] For presentation and discussion of the fragments of Parmenides' poem, see Kirk, Raven, and Schofield 1983: ch. 8. A good brief account is in Sedley 1998. A seminal modern interpretation is Owen 1960. The major edition is Coxon 1986 (2009); see also the text proposed more recently in Palmer 2009: 350–87. Philosophical studies that illuminate Parmenides' influence on Plato are Crystal 1996; Curd 1998: ch. 6.2; and Palmer 1999 (see ch. 4 on the Parmenidean dimension of *Rep.* 5.474b–480a).

ingredient in the motivation for positing Forms. Thus, in the account of the beautiful in the *Symposium*, Diotima begins (211a): 'First, it always is and neither comes to be nor passes away, neither waxes nor wanes'; and there are generic formulations in terms of change or coming to be and passing away in the *Phaedo* (*Phd.* 78c–e) and the *Republic* (*Rep.* 6.485b). The reality with which philosophers are concerned in asking 'What is X?' is specified in these texts by means of a contrast – implicit or explicit – with the Heraclitean flux of the perceptible world.

None of these texts makes the *argument* that there cannot be knowledge of what is in flux, so knowledge has to be concerned with entities – the Forms – quite separate from the coming to be and passing away of perceptible things. For anything like that, we have to wait until the end of the *Cratylus*. On the supposition that (as many scholars think probable) *Cratylus* post-dates the three dialogues just mentioned, we might hypothesize that Plato here acknowledges the debt the metaphysics of those dialogues owes to the Heraclitean view of the perceptible world that he had first got to know in Cratylus' company all those years ago. Perhaps, indeed, it was only belatedly – after writing *Symposium*, *Phaedo*, and *Republic* – that he came to appreciate the importance of his conversations with Cratylus in shaping his approach to questions of metaphysics and epistemology when he turned eventually to tackle them. In general, Cratylus emerges from the *Cratylus* as one of the least impressive thinkers put on stage in the dialogues. It is at least a pleasant thought that Plato used its last couple of pages to flag up what he nonetheless now realized he learned from him

The Academy and the Late Dialogues

The literary and philosophical temper of Plato's late dialogues, as every reader notices, is much changed from the writings that precede them. Their hiatus-free prose can be extraordinarily crabbed and involved; they are comparatively lacking in dramatic life and colour; anonymous and anonymized figures – the Eleatic Visitor (in *Sophist* and *Statesman*), the Athenian Visitor (in the *Laws*) – conduct most of the relatively wooden conversation (Socrates has a lead role only in *Philebus*), while Timaeus (in *Timaeus*) and Critias (in *Critias*) resort to uninterrupted monologue. There is less sense of contextualization of philosophical dialogue within a real world. Dialogues like the *Sophist*, *Statesman*, and *Philebus* (and, earlier, the *Parmenides*) read like texts for the Academy and, indeed, reflect discussion within the Academy.

In the case of the *Sophist* and *Statesman*, the argument for that hypothesis derives almost wholly from their combination of pedagogical and didactic concern to instil understanding of correct dialectical method with forbiddingly abstract or technical content. The *Parmenides* exhibits the same combination, but its preoccupation with the critique and proper interpretation of the theory of Forms locates it within a well-documented debate in the Academy about Forms, to which Eudoxus, Speusippus, Xenocrates, and Aristotle all contributed (neither Aristotle nor Speusippus accepted Plato's theory in any version).[44] Whether Plato wrote the *Parmenides* to initiate debate, or whether he was responding to an incipient or ongoing controversy already launched (as one might conjecture from the dialogue's consideration of the possibility – associated by Aristotle with Eudoxus – that Forms are immanent in particulars: *Metaph.* A9, 991a12–20), we do not know. But he must have intended it primarily for a readership within the Academy. The star example of such a dialogue, however, is the *Philebus*.

Philebus is a heady and often esoteric mixture of ethics, methodology, and metaphysics. The methodology and the ontology – couched as they are in terms of number, ratio, limit, the unlimited – reflect the Pythagorizing turn in Academic metaphysical speculation that is attested particularly in Books M and N of Aristotle's *Metaphysics*. This is especially true for Speusippus, but there is also Pythagorizing in Plato's own 'unwritten doctrines', with which the ontology of the *Philebus* has an apparent affinity.[45] In making pleasure and arguments for and against hedonism the focus of the dialogue's ethical enquiry, Plato was not merely participating in an Academic debate but acting as adjudicator (in fact, the dialogue represents itself as awarding prizes – in rank order – to the most convincing candidates for what determines the goodness of a good life). We know – again primarily from Aristotle – that Eudoxus argued

---

[44] For accounts of the metaphysical issues and positions that preoccupied the early Academy, see Ross 1951: chs. 9–17; Burkert 1972: ch. 1; and Annas 1976. For treatments of the contributions of Speusippus and Xenocrates, see also the literature referred to in n. 38 above; for Eudoxus, consult Guthrie 1978: 452–3 and Schofield 1973; for Aristotle, see Fine 1993.

[45] The music theorist Aristoxenus reports a famously unintelligible lecture by Plato on the Good (*Harmonics* 2.30.16–31.3), which is often connected with Aristotle's reference to 'unwritten doctrines' of Plato (*Phys.* 4.2, 209b11–16). It is generally supposed that these must have included an idea he makes central to Platonic metaphysics in *Metaph.* A6 and debates at length in *Metaph.* M and N: that numbers (identified with Forms) are to be analysed in terms of a formal principle (the one) and a material principle (the large and the small). The Tübingen school of Platonic interpretation sees this as the true centrepiece of Plato's entire philosophy, only hinted at in the dialogues; at the other extreme is the thoroughgoing scepticism of Cherniss 1945: chs. 1 and 2. For a balanced and informative review of the evidence and the controversy (with ample bibliography), see Guthrie 1978: ch. 8.

for hedonism and Speusippus against it. What Aristotle tells us about Eudoxus' hedonism (in Book 10 of the *Nicomachean Ethics*) makes it very probable that it is his account of pleasure as the good that Plato is reproducing for discussion in the *Philebus* (*Phlb.* 20c–21a). Later in the dialogue, various other thinkers who provide ammunition for anti-hedonist conclusions are referred to under designations such as the 'difficult' people (44b–e) or the 'subtle' people (53c). It is tempting to try to strip them of their anonymity (could 'difficulty' be what Speusippus was known for?).[46] But whether identifications can be secured or not, there is no mistaking that Plato here introduces contemporary voices – presumably Academic – into the argument.

How much did Plato's own thinking as evidenced in the late dialogues owe to the other leading philosophers who worked with him in the Academy? Everything we have seen of Plato in this chapter suggests that he was someone whose philosophizing was invariably nourished by engagement with his immediate intellectual and political environment. His originality lies in the versatility and fertility of his response to it. So – to return for a moment to the *Philebus* – the very idea of writing once again about hedonism (already discussed in *Protagoras*, *Gorgias*, and Book 9 of the *Republic*), but within a framework shaped by Pythagorizing metaphysics, would surely never have occurred to him without the stimulus of arguments about these issues in the Academy. The great cosmological project of the *Timaeus* must owe much 'to the research of and discussion with other members of the Academy in the 350s, especially mathematicians and astronomers'.[47] It is possible to suspect the impact of much more specific ideas generated there, too. The *Statesman* makes central to its concept of statesmanship something that might well take the reader of the *Republic* by surprise: the idea that the knowledge required by someone involved in practical activity must be a capacity for measured judgement of what is appropriate and timely – in short, of what is 'removed to the middle from the extremes' (*Statesman* 284b–e). Is this an entirely spontaneous innovation by the elderly Plato? Or is it his appropriation of a theory of virtue as occupying a mean determined by practical knowledge that had already been worked out by the young Aristotle?[48]

The *Laws* in Its Time and Place

The *Laws* was evidently designed for a wider public – although quite what audience or audiences Plato was envisaging is unclear, and some of its writing could be appreciated only by practised readers of the

[46] See Schofield 1971.   [47] Ostwald and Lynch 1994: 609.   [48] Cf. e.g. Schofield 1999b: 39–42.

dialogues.[49] It has sometimes been suggested that its existence bears an intimate relationship with the purposes for which the Academy existed. G. R. Morrow, one of the leading twentieth-century authorities on the dialogue, is one of many distinguished scholars convinced that the Academy was a school for statesmen, which prepared its members for the role 'by the study of Greek law and politics', *inter alia*.[50] T. J. Saunders, another major authority on the *Laws*, believes we can infer from it the sorts of policies and procedures that Academic political 'advisers' would have been taught to recommend to those who consulted them.[51] But while some who had associated with Plato in the Academy did become involved in the politics mostly of their home cities, as might be expected of aristocrats, the case is flimsy for seeing them as emissaries from the Academy primed for their task in the way Morrow and Saunders imagine, or for thinking the Academy had its own political agenda.[52] No doubt, its members talked politics during their stay in the Academy. To judge from the evidence of other late dialogues, however, *philosophical* discussion would have been devoted mostly to questions of metaphysics and ethics and to the dialectical methods appropriate for tackling them.

What seems hard to doubt is that the *Laws* was written with practical intent, as a guide to the principles that should inform the communal life of a well-ordered Greek city and as a blueprint for their detailed implementation on a monumental scale. 'No work of Plato's', said Morrow, 'is more intimately connected with its time and with the world in which it was written than the *Laws*.'[53] This huge dialogue is dense with reference explicit and (more often) implicit to the political and sociocultural institutions and practices of the Greek city-state, and, above all, of Athens itself. In fact, Plato's extensive and intricate legal code is a reworking of contemporary Athenian law, embodying a radical new utilitarian penology based on the Socratic view that, since nobody does wrong willingly, criminality is a disease (*Gorg.* 466d–480d). In consequence, a much more inquisitorial form of procedure before the courts was in his view required, reducing the scope for the rhetoric the *Gorgias* thought so pernicious.

One particularly fascinating dimension of the code is its elaborate and un-Athenian differentiation of penalties for offences, according to whether the perpetrator is a citizen, a slave, a temporary visitor, or a long-term resident alien (a metic). As in Athens (but not Sparta), Plato allows for

---

[49] See Chapter 9 of this volume. [50] Morrow 1960: 5. [51] Saunders 1986.
[52] For example, Brunt 1997; Schofield 2000. [53] Morrow 1960: xxix.

a class of metics: persons like Cephalus in the *Republic*, needed for occupations regarded in the *Laws* as harmful to the soul – notably commerce. But unlike at Athens, their residence is to be subject to a time limit (twenty years). The way their alien status is marked can be illustrated from the highly baroque structure of laws covering assault (*Laws* 9.879b–882c). Mostly, the metics are to be subject to more severe penalties than citizens. Some prominence is given to the rule that if a foreigner whose assault on a citizen can be proven – after an examination that pays proper respect to the god who protects foreigners – to have been designed to insult and humiliate, they are to be subjected to as many strokes of the lash as the blows they inflicted in order to put a stop to 'foreign uppitiness' (*thrasuxenia:* a word, as Saunders points out,[54] that occurs nowhere else and was evidently coined for this occasion). There is no rule covering citizen behaviour of this sort (in Athens, imprisonment and loss of citizen rights was probably the penalty).

Morrow went so far as to describe the society Plato was intent on defining through his legislative template as 'an idealized Athens'.[55] Certainly, there is an explicit preoccupation with Athens (as with Sparta and Persia) in Book 3, where a historical approach is taken to the task of working out what the ideal social and political system would be like. It begins with the flood and the emergence of the first simple post-diluvian communities and ends with a discussion of Athens and Persia as societies that, in the past, combined the three prime desiderata of wisdom, freedom, and friendship by balancing in their system of government a monarchic with a democratic principle. Since the time of Cyrus the Great (in Persia) and, less explicitly, Solon (in Athens), the balance has become fatally disturbed. Persia has degenerated into tyranny, Athens into what Plato calls 'theatocracy': the self-indulgence of a society under the control of the illusion that anybody's judgement is as good as anybody else's.

Thirty years on, Plato here plays new variations on the old analysis of the malaise of Athenian democracy familiar from the *Gorgias*. But the contrast between Solonian Athens and the decline since the days of Marathon has a contemporary flavour. Around the time the *Laws* was being composed, Isocrates was vainly appealing for the reintroduction of what he called 'the democracy bequeathed by our ancestors' in his *Areopagiticus*, written

---

[54] Saunders 1991: 275 n. 45.
[55] Morrow 1960: 592. But he did not underestimate the importance of the Spartan and Cretan model for the ideal city of the *Laws* – it is, after all, to be a closed and tightly controlled society. Uniquely, the dialogue is set not in Athens but in Crete, where the Solonian figure of the Athenian Visitor can find sympathetic, if challenged, recipients for the blueprint he proposes. See Chapters 9–11.

(probably in 355 BC) as a wake-up call to Athens in the aftermath of its second brief attempt to sustain an empire.⁵⁶ In the time of Solon and Cleisthenes, Athens enjoyed a balanced, well-ordered constitutional settlement, which did not as now educate the citizens 'to regard licentiousness as democracy, lawlessness as freedom, outspokenness as equality, and the licence to do these things as happiness' (*Areop.* 20). The *Laws* has a different agenda, but it breathes the same air.

An autobiographical dimension to the *Laws* has often been perceived.⁵⁷ In the 360s, Plato had made two further visits to Sicily, to the court of the young Dionysius II: one probably in 366, very soon after his accession to power after his father's death; the other in 361. Both were undertaken to oblige Dion, who had hopes of influencing the new tyrant and, initially (according to the Seventh Letter), of Plato's turning him into a philosopher ruler (*Ep.* 7.327b–328d). Both were wretched failures, with Dionysius turning out to be a dilettante in philosophy and interested only in using Plato in regional political machinations (again according to the Letter).⁵⁸ The *Laws* notoriously gives no room to the aspiration for rule by philosophers articulated in the *Republic*, and the dialogue insists that absolute power will almost inevitably bring about the moral corruption of anyone who wields it. Although the *Republic* itself has plenty to say about the corruptions of power, and the corruptibility especially of those naturally endowed for philosophy (*Rep.* 6.491a–495b), and although the *Laws* is designed to work out an *approximation* to what the *Republic* always conceived as a scarcely feasible ideal, readers have diagnosed personal disillusionment on Plato's part. It is certainly hard to think that his recent Sicilian experience did not somehow colour his thoughts about tyrants in the *Laws*. At any rate, it is interesting that when in Book 4 he comes to sketch the preconditions that might favour the creation of a well-ordered polity, he specifies a location well inland, far from any port (Syracuse had a great harbour), and a young tyrant prepared to work with a lawgiver – thanks to his 'orderly' character (that sounds ironic to the point of sarcasm).⁵⁹

---

⁵⁶ The political history of the period is a tangled tale: for example, Hornblower 2003: chs. 16 and 17. A helpful brief account of the 'second Athenian confederacy' is available in Hornblower and Spawforth 2012: 1337.
⁵⁷ A classic statement of this interpretation is Vlastos 1973.
⁵⁸ For a historical narrative, see Rhodes 2006, ch. 21.   ⁵⁹ As is argued by Schofield 1999b: 43–50.

CHAPTER 2

When and Why Did Plato Write Narrated Dialogues?

Narrated versus dramatic or direct or (perhaps) scripted dialogues: *Ion* or *Gorgias* (scripted) versus *Charmides* (where Socrates is narrator) or *Parmenides* (with a character called Cephalus – not the elderly man who figures at the beginning of *Republic* – as narrating speaker). *Charmides* and *Parmenides* are pure examples of the narrated genre. But there are others (which invite particular reflection) where, though narration by a single speaker is the dominant element, it is introduced and sometimes interrupted by a scripted frame dialogue between that speaker and a companion: examples are *Phaedo, Symposium, Protagoras,* and (most interestingly of all) *Euthydemus.* The *Theaetetus* starts as if it is going to be a further instance of this type but then tells us it is not going to do narrative. The full list of narrated dialogues is: *Charmides, Lysis, Euthydemus, Phaedo, Symposium, Protagoras, Republic, Parmenides,* to which we can perhaps add Critias' speech about Atlantis in the preface to the *Timaeus* (*Ti.* 20d–25e): narrative *within* a scripted dialogue.

When did Plato compose these narrated dialogues?[1] The list already indicates the answer. They were not among his earliest productions, and they were not among the latest either. None of the stylistically homogeneous late group (*Sophist, Politicus, Timaeus, Critias, Philebus, Laws*) is a narrated dialogue. Nor is the *Phaedrus,* which shares more of their stylistic features than any of the other dialogues and is usually put close to them in chronological sequence; nor, as already mentioned, is the *Theaetetus.* As is or ought to be well known, we have no very secure basis for determining which were the *first* dialogues Plato wrote. But *Ion, Hippias Minor,* and *Crito* are probably the most popular candidates: short, scripted dialogues between Socrates and one other speaker, the first two of them simply constructed (the introduction of the laws of

---

[1] A fuller treatment of my topic is offered in Capra 2003, which does not however have much to say about the 'when?' question. See also the suggestive study of Johnson 1998.

Athens as a third voice in the *Crito* shows Plato already experimenting with dialogue form). In short, narrated dialogues are the preferred mode of Plato's middle period. Indeed, very few scripted dialogues are among those usually identified as middle-period works: *Meno*, perhaps, often thought of as transitional between early and middle period; and *Cratylus*, whose dating is particularly controversial, and where there is stronger evidence of revision of the text than for any other dialogue (see David Sedley's brilliant book of 2003).[2] There is a case for saying Plato started by writing direct or scripted dialogues, at first fairly simple in structure, but with the *Laches* in particular (with five main characters) and the *Gorgias* (also five) more complex. Then he moved into the narrated mode, perhaps exclusively so, in his middle-period phase, which by the way I take to be where the *Protagoras* is to be put (see my English edition with Tom Griffith).[3] But, finally, he abandoned it – once and for all – in the *Theaetetus*, and from then on reverted exclusively to the scripted form of dialogue.

Why did Plato get into writing narrated dialogues when he did? And why did he get out of it when he did? On the exit, there is the evidence Plato himself plants in the preface to the *Theaetetus*. In a strikingly metadialogical moment characteristic of dialogue frames, Eucleides, recipient of Socrates' narrative of the conversation purportedly recorded in the dialogue, tells his interlocutor that he wants to avoid the trouble (*pragmata*) of the 'I said' and 'he agreed', and so on, of narration and so is going for the direct or scripted mode of presentation (*Tht.* 143b–c). Of course, that might not be the real or at any rate the full rationale. One suggestion is that reversion to the direct mode might be a way of signalling an 'authentic' return to presenting something closer to the aporetic and probably more 'historical' Socrates of the earlier scripted dialogues, after a middle-period sequence in which he is often made to develop ideas in a more ambitiously Platonic direction.[4] 'Avoiding the trouble', however, does seem to be the best explanation of why in the *Parmenides*, a dialogue of exceptional narrative complexity, and often taken to be the *Theaetetus*' immediate predecessor and indeed companion in the sequence of dialogues, narration is also abandoned in the elaborate dialectical exercise of the second part of the work: inserting 'I said' and 'he replied' throughout that would indeed have been a bothersome and pointless effort. With works like the *Euthydemus* and the *Symposium*, or again the *Protagoras*, by contrast, there were formal and dramatic potentialities in narrated dialogue that could be exploited in service of the distinctive philosophical and literary

---

[2] Sedley 2003. [3] Schofield and Griffith 2010; see also Kahn 1988b. [4] Sedley 2004: 17.

projects being undertaken in them. These resources are simply not required for working through the gymnastic logic of the second part of the *Parmenides*.[5]

More difficult and probably more interesting is the question of what attracted Plato to start and continue writing narrated dialogues when he did. Particularly given the richness and variety and especially the very different ambitions of the different dialogues composed in the narrated mode, it would be a mistake to expect to be able to identify a single explanation, or even two or three clusters of explanatory factors, by way of answer. Nonetheless some basic taxonomy might be a useful first step. I distinguish a group of dialogues set in the gymnasium or palaestra in which Socrates himself narrates conversations he had with boys or teenagers or young men: *Charmides*, *Lysis*, *Euthydemus*. In *Protagoras* too, after an initial scripted frame dialogue with an unnamed friend, Socrates recounts a characteristically Socratic conversation he had had earlier in the day with a young man named Hippocrates. But that takes place in his own house and on their walk to the house of Callias. Once they encounter there Protagoras and other Sophists, Hippocrates drops out of focus. It is in fact with the *Symposium* that *Protagoras* shares many of its themes and other characteristics, not least considerable overlap in the cast of characters who are present (these are briefly discussed in the Schofield–Griffith edition).[6]

Asking for quite different treatment from the trio mentioned above are dialogues where someone other than Socrates recounts a conversation in which he participated. The major examples are the *Phaedo* and the *Symposium*, but the *Parmenides* too is of this type, and so would the *Theaetetus* have been had Eucleides done what the original readers of the dialogues would presumably by now have been expecting a Platonic narrator to do. Critias' narrative in the *Timaeus*, if we allow ourselves to include it as an example of narrated dialogue, clearly belongs with this group of dialogues. Finally, there is the *Republic*, which stands apart from all the rest when considered as a narrated dialogue, just as it does in so many other dimensions. I start by looking at the first group I have demarcated.

---

[5] There was in principle more scope for drama in the twists and turns of the dialectic of the *Theaetetus*, especially but not only in the long first section on knowledge and perception. Harold Tarrant reports stylometric evidence that the dialogue is marked by some of the stylistic traits characteristic of the narrated form and suggests that some of it may have in fact originally have been written as a narrative (Tarrant 2013). But if so, Plato seems to have decided in the end that the strenuous argumentative project in which the *Theaetetus* almost entirely consists could better or as well be delivered without the extra bother of the devices of narration.

[6] Schofield and Griffith 2010: xxiii–xxv.

The first page or so of the *Charmides* marks it out as a dialogue with an erotic theme, or rather as a dialogue which is going to play with the genre of the erotic dialogue. Socrates heads for the palaestra (in itself, it seems likely, an indication of erotic genre). He is impatient to know about 'the present state of philosophy and about the young men, whether there are any distinguished for wisdom or beauty or both' (*Charm.* 153e). In comes Charmides: accompanied by a retinue of lovers, but in truth the whole company, little boys included, are smitten by his beauty. Socrates at once establishes that he himself is more interested in Charmides' soul. But after the jostling to make room for him on the bench where Socrates and Critias are by now seated, Socrates sees inside his cloak, catches fire, and is quite beside himself (155c–d). Of course, he controls himself, and the dialogue can now proceed to investigate *sôphrosunê* (prudence, judiciousness, temperance),[7] as what the soul needs if Charmides' physical problem (hangovers in the morning) is to be remedied. The openings of the *Lysis* and *Euthydemus* are designed in similar fashion to confirm that they too are to be read as erotic dialogues, or as dialogues which within that framework pursue their philosophical agenda: in the *Lysis*, discussion of *philia*, in the *Euthydemus* educational protreptic, both obviously themes central to the ideology of erotic pursuit.[8]

I have been deploying the notion of *genre* of erotic dialogue. Dialogues on erotic themes were evidently as common and striking a phenomenon in the literary activity of the first Socratic circle as were treatments of such themes in the writings of the early Stoics, something I discussed in chapter 2 of *The Stoic Idea of the City*.[9] In one case – the *Alcibiades* of Aeschines of Sphettos – we are fortunate enough to have available testimonies which preserve both the opening and the closing words of the dialogue. Here is the beginning (*SSR*, VI A 43):[10] 'We were seated on the benches in the Lyceum, where the judges organize the games.' And the ending (the theme has been the limitations of human art, not least in curing the sick) (*SSR*, VI A 53): 'Although I know no science or skill which I could teach anyone to benefit him, nevertheless I thought that in keeping company with Alcibiades I could by the power of love (διὰ τὸ ἐρᾶν) make him better.'

---

[7] Etymologically 'sound-mindedness', which becomes significant for understanding the preoccupation with self-knowledge that dominates the most challenging section of the dialogue. The word connotes a state both of mind and of character, at once an intellectual and an emotional condition.

[8] *Philia* is standardly translated as 'friendship', but there are contexts in which it connotes (for example) parental love or affection; and 'lover' is often the natural choice for the associated adjective *philos*, as in compound formulations such as *philippos* (horse-lover) or *philoinos* (wine-lover).

[9] Schofield 1999a.

[10] *SSR* = *Socratis et Socraticorum Reliquiae*, 4 vols., ed. G. Giannantoni (Naples: Bibliopolis, 1990).

The commonalities with the *Charmides* are obvious: to start with, the setting in the gymnasium and the benches on which Socrates and his companions are sitting; in the final passage, the implication that Alcibiades (like Charmides) is sick and needs a cure, and the suggestion that Socrates might somehow have been able to supply it, coupled with tacit acceptance that if so, he failed. And, of course, Aeschines' *Alcibiades*, like the *Charmides*, was clearly a narrated dialogue, with Socrates himself the narrator. Charles Kahn, in *Plato and the Socratic Dialogue*, takes it that Aeschines originated the erotic dialogue, and with it exploration of the notion of Socratic *eros* (ἔρως); and that in the *Charmides* and *Lysis*, Plato was adopting from him both narrated form and thematic content, elaborating the form, however, by giving Socrates two interlocutors in the *Charmides* and four in the *Lysis*.[11]

Assume it to be a reasonable conjecture that in making the *Charmides* a narrated dialogue, Plato had Aeschines' *Alcibiades* for a precedent. What potentialities did he see in the form that prompted him to turn to it after composing (we may suppose) several scripted dialogues? Here, we may usefully draw a comparison with the *Laches*, one of the most elaborately orchestrated of the scripted dialogues, which has often been seen as forming a pair with the *Charmides*. As *Charmides* tackles *sôphrosunê*, so *Laches* tackles courage, after an extended preface; each has one interlocutor who does not think in Socratic terms (Charmides, Laches), each has a more problematic interlocutor whose formulations seem to ape Socratic philosophizing, while leading only to impasse (Critias, Nicias). Each too is evidently preoccupied with the relation between *logos* and *ergon*, thought and behaviour – indeed, in the *Laches* the topic is explicitly thematized (*Lach*. 188c–e). The *Laches* can enact courageous behaviour by its representation of Laches' willingness to support Socrates in pursuing the argument despite his inexperience in philosophy (194a–b). But for illustrating *sôphrosunê* in action, particularly restraint where sexual desire is the issue, the narrated dialogue will plainly have given Plato greater scope. He must

---

[11] Kahn 1996: 18–23, whose translations of the Aeschines material I am borrowing. Aeschines' priority is guesswork. In its favour is the simple observation that writing an erotic dialogue in which Charmides figures as the object of Socrates' attention is a much less obvious thing to do than to compose an *Alcibiades* with that kind of focus, especially given the popularity of Alcibiades as a subject for *Sôkratikoi logoi* (Socratic conversations) in the Socratic circle. In the same direction is the consideration that the *Charmides* gains in intelligibility if we are able to see the representation of Socrates' relationship with Charmides as a sort of muted echo of his love for Alcibiades as explored by Aeschines. And when Plato exploited the comic potentialities of the overpopulated bench in the palaestra as he does in the *Charmides*, could any other writer subsequently launch a dialogue with reference to such a bench without fear of evoking the comparison?

surely also have relished the potentiality for comedy, a feature of *Lysis* and *Euthydemus*, too, as well as *Symposium* and *Protagoras*. Above all, perhaps, it enabled him to make Socrates himself both the self-conscious subject of the opening scene and the ironic lens through which others are presented as well as himself (the same is true *mutatis mutandis* of much of the *Protagoras*). The embarrassments and evasiveness of Charmides and Critias to which Socrates is made to draw attention could scarcely have been conveyed without deploying the devices of narrative.

In the *Lysis* and *Euthydemus*, these sorts of potentialities of the narrative form are further developed: once Plato had got into this vein, he was going to see how much more he could work it.[12] As already noted, the *Lysis* doubles the number of Socratic interlocutors in the reported dialogue, and in the opening scene (*Lys.* 203a–207b) Plato orchestrates a complicated sequence of conversations and associated physical manoeuvres designed to introduce and illustrate distinctions between *erôs* and *philia* which will get explicitly or implicitly explored in the philosophical conversation that follows. The *Euthydemus* works with the same number of Socratic interlocutors in the narrated dialogue as the *Lysis* but sets it within a frame dialogue between Socrates and Crito which first introduces it (*Euthd.* 271a–272d) and then rounds it off with concluding reflections apparently designed to make a contemporary reference to Plato's rival Isocrates (304b–307c). Notoriously, however, the frame dialogue does not merely bookend the reported conversation. At a crucial point in Socrates' account of what the boy Cleinias said in his conversation with him, it is interrupted by the frame dialogue when Crito questions whether Cleinias really did say what Socrates claims he did. Socrates then withdraws the claim, at the start of a stretch of scripted dialogue between him and Crito about knowledge, the good, and the expertise constituted by kingship that occupies more than two Stephanus pages (290e–293b), before the narrated conversation is once again resumed. The intervention highlights the way the *Euthydemus* is at this juncture playing with ideas about the relation between mathematics and dialectic that would be more at home in a different kind of dialogue (such as the *Republic*).[13] The intervention is thus a mechanism whereby the dialogue draws attention to its own fictionality and to the unreliability of the fiction that it is. Here is Plato at his most postmodern.

---

[12] Here, I am assuming a relative chronology of composition (albeit commonly enough accepted) on a combination of literary and philosophical grounds which in a fuller treatment would obviously require defence.

[13] For the controversial suggestion that the *Republic* is already written and assumed to be accessible to Plato's readers by the time the *Euthydemus* is composed, see, for example, Burnyeat 2002: 64 n. 46; McCabe 2015: 272–3 (cf. 237 and n. 49).

With the phenomenon of self-advertising fictiveness having made its appearance, we are ready to approach my second category of narrated dialogue: those where someone other than Socrates is narrator. A look at Critias' performance in the preface to the *Timaeus* will afford a good way into this kind of dialogue, even though it is narrative *within* a dialogue that as a whole is scripted. The key features for us to notice are these: first, Critias' narrative concerns an event (the war between ancestral Athens and Atlantis) supposed to have taken place in a remote past; second, it is an event Socrates has never heard of (*Ti.* 21a) – there is of course no previous mention of it in surviving Greek literature or in references to that literature, and Socrates is here no doubt reflecting a general ignorance; third, Critias has himself heard the story as the last in a chain of informants; fourth, though Solon's testimony is produced as warrant of its truth in entirety, his informant is an old Egyptian priest – and only if you believed every word Herodotus wrote about Egypt on that kind of basis would you be reassured of the veracity and accuracy of what is related. This cluster of features is presumably what is meant to mark Critias' narrative as purely fictive.

Two of the three dialogues that fall into our second category – *Symposium* and *Parmenides* – together with the *Theaetetus*, which initially shapes up as though it is going to be a third, have features that bear similarities with Critias' narrative. Remoteness in time is one. The frame dialogue in the *Theaetetus* is set very precisely in the year of Theaetetus' death from his wounds in battle, some time after the philosophical conversation Eucleides purports to report (although there is uncertainty over the identity and date of the battle in question). The conversation recorded in the *Parmenides* allegedly took place when Socrates was very young (in fact it is very doubtful that Parmenides would still have been alive at that point). But since among those listening to the narration are Plato's brothers Glaucon and Adeimantus, we must imagine its retelling happening towards the end of the fifth century. The opening lines of the *Symposium* emphasize that the gathering at Glaucon's house was not that recent. Chains of informants are also in evidence. In both the *Symposium* and the *Parmenides*, details of the event reported in the dialogue are transmitted via such a chain, in what has often been seen as a 'Chinese box' effect.[14] Plato goes out of his way to emphasize that the speaker who actually

---

[14] Cf. Halperin 1992. For the *Parmenides*, no subsequent account has surpassed in interest Proclus' interpretation of the nested conversations: as an allegory of the structure of the intelligible universe, and of the different modes of apprehension that correspond to its different levels. He presents it in outline at *in Parm.* 625.37–630.14. Cf. further Morrow and Dillon 1987.

delivers the account is at several removes from its ultimate source, even though in the *Symposium* Apollodorus says he checked part of the story with Socrates himself (as does Eucleides in the *Theaetetus*), and in the *Parmenides* Antiphon – the intermediate narrator – is said to have practised his narrative to perfection and to have an excellent memory of it, despite (a warning note) his subsequent loss of interest in philosophy.

Do these forms of distancing constitute coded indicators of fictiveness, as was argued above for Critias' narrative in the *Timaeus*? All Plato's dialogues are fictions and would have been recognized as such by his first readers. So, why for just some dialogues in particular should he resort to special literary devices to draw particular attention to their fictive status? For Critias' narrative it is not hard to see what the answer must be: Critias is making the strong claim that the story he is about to tell is real history, albeit until now a family secret. He is in effect *denying* that his fictive narrative is a fiction. So Plato needs to invest the denial with signs of inauthenticity that the reader can decode and register as such.

I suggest that something similar is going on in the prefaces to the *Symposium*, *Parmenides*, and *Theaetetus*, in all of which speakers other than Socrates are made to assert and try to prove the veracity or reliability of their narratives. The forms of distancing Plato employs – distance in time, distance from narrative source – all function as health warnings. Perhaps it is only in the *Parmenides* that the health warning is as stark as that attached to Critias' introduction of his narrative. Perhaps in the other two cases, instead of saying: 'This did not happen', the message is: 'It *might* have happened this way – but I would not vouch for it.' But why should it be just in this trio of dialogues that Plato employs devices for claiming veracity and reliability which simultaneously undermine that very claim?

One answer might be that these are dialogues in which philosophical enterprises are developed that are distinctive of what we take to be Plato's own thought – going far beyond what Socrates himself is likely to have taught, even if they might be regarded as extrapolations from Socratic preoccupations. In the case of the *Symposium*, this is marked as explicitly as one ever gets in a Platonic dialogue by the introduction of Diotima as the figure who instructs Socrates in mysteries of which she says she is doubtful that he is capable. The *Theaetetus* presents a Socrates who has migrated from ethics to epistemology much more decisively than in the *Meno*; and it flags intertextuality with the *Parmenides*, where Parmenides, not Socrates, is the main speaker, and where the topic is what we have to think of as the Platonic theory of Forms, perhaps already by then being hotly debated as such in the Academy. Use of the form of the dialogue narrated by a speaker other than Socrates, in a reported conversation exhibiting one or more of the marks of distancing I have identified, constitutes the code by which Plato indicates that he is here taking the liberty to create his own transformation of the sorts of conversations in which Socrates may be represented as having participated.

The *Phaedo* is rather different. Although in the first lines of the dialogue Echecrates stresses the remoteness of Phlius in the Peloponnese (where he is settled) from Athens and the unavailability there of proper information about Socrates' death, there are two strong dissimilarities from the three dialogues we have so far been considering, as from Critias' narrative in the *Timaeus*. Socrates' death is represented as recent; and the focus from the outset is on Phaedo's own presence in the prison on the day he died, with Phaedo implying that he takes pleasure in recounting his total recall of things to do with Socrates. However, in the course of his listing those who were there with Socrates at the end, he is made to note that Plato was not present. In his brief statement to this effect, a significance has always been perceived way beyond its laconic matter-of-fact appearance.[15] Whatever one makes of this feature of the *Phaedo*,[16] for our purposes the obvious thing is to note that, if Plato wanted to present Socrates in conversation on the day of his death, and above all to show how he died, he had no option but to have a speaker other than Socrates narrate the proceedings. A narrated dialogue of that type simply chose itself.[17]

A final word on the *Republic*, where once again Socrates himself is narrator throughout. Book 1, particularly in the opening pages and in his presentation of Thrasymachus, exhibits some of the characteristics we noted earlier that are distinctive of dialogues narrated by Socrates himself. In subsequent books, these are much less frequently in evidence. They might have worked just as well had they been put into the scripted mode. There may well be another reason as has often been suggested, however,

---

[15] In a sense, the *Phaedo* is presented as a dialogue composed by Phaedo, a writer of *Sôkratikoi logoi* himself, and not by Plato, just as the *Theaetetus* presents itself as the work of another author of Socratic dialogues, Eucleides – a fictive Phaedo and a fictive Eucleides, of course. For an interesting discussion of this dimension of the *Phaedo*, see Boys-Stones 2004.

[16] Perhaps one is got to wonder: but did it really happen just that way – and did Socrates really say all that?

[17] The main discourse of the *Phaedo*, like the *Protagoras* and the *Symposium*, is encased in a short exchange between the narrator and another figure that serves as frame dialogue. In both the first two cases, the frame dialogue is used to introduce an erotic dimension otherwise absent from the conversation (not so, of course, in *Symposium*), highlighted in the *Phaedo* by its brief resumption (initiated by Echecrates, Phaedo's interlocutor) before the climax: Phaedo is soon telling him how Socrates stroked the hair on the back of his neck – though the meta-dialogical philosophical point is to introduce the topic of misology (*Phd.* 88c–91b).

why Plato wanted not to abandon the narrated mode of dialogue here. As Harold Tarrant, for example, puts the point in discussing the passage on the *lexis* (style) appropriate for storytelling in Book 3 of the dialogue (*Rep.* 3.392c–398b):[18]

> When we examine the argument of *Republic* III, we understand how Plato could, at this period, have qualms about publishing dialogues in dramatic form. The emphasis falls on the acknowledged need for each person to play a single role only within the *Republic*'s society. No individual could successfully adopt different mimetic roles just as no individual can successfully adopt real roles (395b).

After arguing against the view that Plato would have considered that such a consideration need not apply to his own writing of dramatic dialogues, Tarrant asks: 'How is it, then, that *Theaetetus* could revert to dramatic form on the grounds that it is less tedious?' His suggestion is that there Plato presented a record of 'the whole conversation *as if* it had been reported non-mimetically by the philosopher, purging the words of all speakers of all emotive elements that the reader or listener ought not to imitate'.[19] That way the 'voice of reason' could be made to dominate throughout while avoiding the tedium that dogs much narration when arguments, not scenes of human drama, are being reported.

Such a solution to the authorial puzzle is certainly congruent also with the colourlessness that is often remarked and regretted in the late scripted sextet of Platonic dialogues. Perhaps, however, it will not quite work for the *Phaedrus*, a dialogue which also reverts to the scripted mode and is usually considered to be positioned chronologically on the threshold of lateness. Here, Socrates describes Phaedrus as just having delivered a speech which he clearly considers morally unacceptable (allegedly composed by Lysias) in a 'Bacchic frenzy' – his own response to it, too, he says (*Phdr.* 234d). Phaedrus rightly thinks he is being teased. As often in a Platonic dialogue, pinning anything down here is not easy.

---

[18] Tarrant 2013: 309.   [19] Tarrant 2013: 311.

CHAPTER 3

Against System
The Historical Plato in the Mid-Victorian Era

Introduction

Like most commentators in Victorian times and ever since, Monique Canto-Sperber, in her long essay on the rediscovery of Plato in the Victorian era ('Le redécouverte de Platon à l'époque victorienne (1835–63)' in *Éthiques grecques*), presents the two key figures in the Victorian Plato revival[1] – George Grote and Benjamin Jowett – in contrasting terms, as presiding over successive phases of Plato's rehabilitation differing radically in the picture of his thought that they presented. The contrasts are certainly there to be drawn, and they will force themselves on our attention at various points in this chapter. But my main object here is to bring out something not so often emphasized: what Grote and Jowett had in common. Hence the title I give to my essay: 'against system'. Both men were fiercely opposed to the idea that Plato's dialogues present the reader with a system. To think that there is in Plato a system is in their view to misunderstand him completely. For that reason alone, they would have thought much subsequent Plato scholarship – not least in our time – to be as misguided as the interpretations of their own period (or a little before it) from which they were dissociating themselves.

It may be useful at the outset if I indicate the chapter's overall structure. In the first section, I begin my discussion by recalling some highlights in the recent scholarship on the Victorian reception of Plato, and by agreeing with Canto-Sperber on the rise in Grote's stock and the decline in Jowett's. The next section returns to the texts – Grote's *Plato and the Other Companions of Socrates* (1865) and Jowett's *The Dialogues of Plato* (1871) – and points out some fundamental common ground between them: the atomism inherent in the hermeneutic approach to Plato they both shared, before commenting on the sense of its limitations expressed by the

---

[1] She says of the publication of Grote's *Plato* (in 1865) and Jowett's *Dialogues* (in 1871) that from that moment the whole of Europe came to recognize the excellence of English Plato scholarship ('L'Europe entière reconnaît dès ce moment-là l'excellence du *Platonic scholarship* anglais': Canto-Sperber 2001: 361).

American Plato scholar Paul Shorey, and his evident preference for John Stuart Mill as interpreter of Plato. With the following section, I turn to consider the importance of the quest for the historical Plato for both Grote and Jowett, and what each thought it meant to give him his place in the history of philosophy.

Finally, I come in the last section to what Jowett called the 'modern applications' of Plato in their work. For as John Glucker wrote in a paper published in 1987, 'our protagonists ... are not some obscure antiquarians languishing in the twilight of their garrets in the company of their ancient folios and writing *sibi et doctis*, but people who stood at the centre of crucial developments in literature, philosophy, education – and ... near enough to the arena of politics'.[2]

Some Recent Scholarship

Monique Canto-Sperber begins her study by noting familiarity on the part of the French philosophical public with the names of the British Platonists Benjamin Jowett (1817–93), Lewis Campbell (1830–1908), and Ernest Barker (1874–1960), before getting down to business and arguing for the equal importance of what she speaks of as the *first* Platonic revival in Victorian England.[3] She means the revival spearheaded by the 'Philosophical Radicals', and particularly the innovative scholarly work of George Grote (1794–1871) and John Stuart Mill (1806–73). Explaining the nature, context, development, and political thrust (Canto-Sperber is particularly interesting on divergences between Grote and Mill over what to make of Plato as political thinker)[4] of the radicals' engagement with Plato is the main task she undertakes in her attempt to bring out its crucial importance for the restoration of his fortunes in Britain. In a brief conclusion, she returns to Jowett and reflects on his impact and legacy in the light of her findings. At the end of the nineteenth century, she suggests, his Plato seemed to prevail over the Plato of Mill or of Grote. But at the end of the twentieth, work on Plato produced in Britain looked closer, in general style and dominant interests, to the writings of the Philosophical Radicals than to those of Jowett's pupils and heirs.[5]

It is not so very long since interest in Victorian Hellenism was virtually non-existent. Then, just over forty years ago, two pioneering studies

---

[2] Glucker 1987: 151. His text reads 'writings', not 'writing'; but it is hard to resist the thought that the noun is a typographical slip displacing the verbal form.
[3] Canto-Sperber 2001: 355.   [4] Canto-Sperber 2001: 403–24.   [5] Canto-Sperber 2001: 425.

appeared almost simultaneously: Richard Jenkyns's *The Victorians and Ancient Greece* (1980) and Frank Turner's *The Greek Heritage in Victorian Britain* (1981), whose chapter on 'The Victorian Platonic Revival' remains a key resource for anyone interested in the topic. Since then, the Victorian reception of ancient Greece in every conceivable aspect has become a considerable scholarly industry; and one product of that has been a sequence of important books and essays devoted to the Platonic revival. It is probably fair to say that the Philosophical Radicals have excited more interest and sympathy than any of the other Victorian writers from scholars working on the material, with the Grote scholar Kyriakos Demetriou a particularly frequent commentator on different aspects of the radicals' Plato.[6] With one or two honourable exceptions – I would mention Jonathan Barnes's 1981 article (prompted by his reading of Jenkyns and Turner), 'Greek philosophy and the Victorians', and Myles Burnyeat's study 'The past in the present: Plato as educator of nineteenth-century Britain'[7] – discussion of Jowett has been more cursory and less well-informed and appreciative.[8]

As Canto-Sperber suggests, and as John Glucker commented in his 1987 paper,[9] much late twentieth-century discussion of Plato in the English-speaking world had more affinities with Grote and Mill – without, I might add, any of their crusading political agenda. F. E. Sparshott, introducing the volume on 'Philosophy and the Classics' in Mill's *Collected Works* in 1978, considered that 'the Platonism of Grote and Mill is substantially that still imparted to most Anglophone undergraduates'.[10] Fashions in translation have changed, too. As reviewers commented admiringly when Jowett's *Dialogues of Plato* first appeared, he succeeded in making his rendering of the Greek simple and natural English,[11] capturing 'the whole' and 'the spirit' before all else – even if that was at the cost not infrequently of accuracy.[12] By the later decades of the next century, the pendulum had swung nearer the opposite extreme: accuracy, clumsy if necessary, invariably trumped elegance or flow. In the early twenty-first century, we are seeing yet another change, perhaps more in the Jowett spirit, with translators like Tom Griffith (for Cambridge University Press), Adam Beresford (Penguin), and Robin Waterfield (in the Oxford World's Classics series) setting a premium on lively idiomatic conversational English.

---

[6] See Demetriou 1999, 2011. [7] See Stopper 1981; Burnyeat 1998.
[8] Thus both Turner and Glucker, for example, are distinctly better on Grote than on Jowett.
[9] Glucker 1987: 186. [10] Mill 1978: xxxix. [11] Monro 1871: 494. [12] Grant 1871: 309.

Atomist Hermeneutics

For Paul Shorey, the dominant figure in American Plato scholarship in the first third of the twentieth century, it was not Grote nor Jowett, but John Stuart Mill who was 'perhaps the greatest of nineteenth-century Platonists', even if he does not cry 'Plato, Plato' insistently.[13] Why Shorey thought so highly of Mill as a Platonist is something I shall return to at the end of this section. What made him less enthusiastic about Grote or Jowett is my immediate concern. The answer comes in a remark Shorey makes near the beginning of his short book *The Unity of Plato's Thought* (1903). In commenting on the challenge the expositor of Plato faces in finding the right systematic form for their exposition, he acknowledges that there is no entirely satisfactory way of doing it. 'The atomism of Grote, Jowett, Bonitz, and Horn', however, 'that treats each dialogue as an isolated unit, is the renunciation of all method.'[14]

Readers of Grote's *History of Greece* who have not looked at his *Plato* might be surprised at the suggestion that Grote was a hermeneutic atomist in his approach to Plato. There we are told, in the famous chapter 67 (in Book VIII, first published in 1850):

> He was a great and systematic theorist, whose opinions on ethics, politics, cognition, religion, etc., were all wrought into harmony by his own mind, and stamped with that peculiarity which is the mark of an original intellect. So splendid an effort of speculative genius is among the marvels of the Grecian world.[15]

By 1865, when his *Plato* was published, Grote had come to exactly the opposite conclusion, by virtue of his own intensive study of the whole corpus of dialogues and his no less intensive engagement with German Plato scholarship. Ever since Schleiermacher (in the first decade of the century), scholars in Germany had proliferated schemes designed to explain how Plato's thought possessed a unity which is gradually disclosed, or alternatively how it develops as an organic growth through different phases, with disclosure or development articulated in the order in which (it was supposed) the dialogues must have been composed. Chapter V of Grote's *Plato* is devoted to an extended critique of that enterprise. An

---

[13] Shorey 1938: 231 (cf. also 232). This posthumously published book – *Platonism Ancient and Modern* – presents to a reading public the Sather Classical Lectures delivered in 1928–9, when Shorey was seventy-one.
[14] Shorey 1903: 8.   [15] Grote 1850: VIII.536.

eloquent passage at the beginning of VI ('Platonic compositions generally') carries the header 'no common characteristic'. It begins:

> It is in truth scarcely possible to resolve all the diverse manifestations of the Platonic mind into one higher unity; or to predicate, about Plato as an intellectual person, anything which shall be applicable at once to the Protagoras, Gorgias, Parmenidês, Phaedrus, Symposion, Philêbus, Phaedon, Republic, Timaeus, and Leges. Plato was sceptic, dogmatist, religious mystic and inquisitor, mathematician, philosopher, poet (erotic as well as satirical), rhetor, artist – all in one: or at least, all in succession, throughout the fifty years of his philosophical life.[16]

And this is how Grote rounds off the paragraph:

> On the whole – and to use a comparison of Plato himself – the Platonic sum total somewhat resembles those fanciful combinations of animals imagined in the Hellenic mythology – an aggregate of distinct and disparate individualities, which look like one because they are packed in the same external wrapper.[17]

Grote would go on to emphasize and itemize the difficulties of harmonizing different specific theses of what he classified as dogmatic Dialogues of Exposition (II.392–3, 472, 549–51, 619–20) as much as the impossibility of finding common ground between (for example) the expository *Republic* and the sceptical Dialogues of Search (III.164–5). Near the end of chapter VI (I.278), he does allow that there are a few themes ubiquitous in all the dialogues: the relation of the universal to its particulars, the contrast of the constant and essential with the variable and accidental. And principles of classification, if a main focus only in the *Sophist* and *Statesman*, are often applied elsewhere. But he comes back at once (I.279) to his intention of exhibiting in the dialogues no one positive doctrinal system, nor any determinable scheme of philosophical development. They exist for us 'as distinct imaginary conversations, composed by the same author at unknown times and under unknown specialties of circumstance'.

Jowett was broadly in agreement with Grote's main point.[18] This is how he expresses himself on the subject in the brief Preface to the first edition of

---

[16] Grote 1865: 1.214–15.   [17] Grote 1865: 1.215.

[18] There appear to be only two recorded meetings between the two men. The first is recorded by Harriet Grote in her life of her husband as follows (Grote 1873: 260): 'In September [1862] a few guests came to Barrow Green; among the number were Professor Jowett, Mr. Robert Lowe, and Dr. William Smith. Excellent "scholar talk" went on (especially about Plato, with Mr. Jowett); and the Historian appeared to enjoy the double pleasure of walking and discussing various subjects of interest with these learned friends.' The following May, during a rare visit by the Grotes to Oxford, Jowett entertained them to breakfast in Balliol, 'where we had a select company of Oxford men of

The Dialogues of Plato (1871; reprinted in both the much expanded second edition of 1875, and in the more lightly revised third and final edition of 1892). Jowett writes:

> I have also derived much assistance from the great work of Mr. Grote, which contains excellent analyses of the dialogues, and is rich in original thoughts and observations. I agree with him in rejecting as futile the attempt of Schleiermacher and others to arrange the Dialogues of Plato into a harmonious whole. Any such arrangement appears to me not only to be unsupported by evidence, but to involve an anachronism in the history of philosophy. There is a common spirit in the writings of Plato, but not a unity of design in the whole, nor perhaps a perfect unity in any single Dialogue. The hypothesis of a general plan which is worked out in the successive Dialogues is an after-thought of the critics who have attributed a system to writings belonging to an age when system had not as yet taken possession of philosophy.[19]

That said, Jowett remarks that he approaches Plato from a point of view – idealism – opposed to utilitarianism (Grote is not named at this point, but the reader can be in no doubt that Jowett has him in mind). He explains himself:

> He is the poet or maker of ideas, satisfying the wants of his own age, providing the instruments of thought for future generations. He is no dreamer, but a great philosophical genius struggling with the unequal conditions of light and knowledge under which he is living.[20]

Jowett returns to this evaluation in the final remarks on Plato he was to make in *Dialogues*, retained unchanged in all three editions, at the end of his Introduction to the *Laws*. They constitute his farewell to the dialogues as a whole:

> That which is the most familiar process of our own minds to him appeared the crowning achievement of the dialectical art. For by his conquests in the world of mind not only are our thoughts widened, but he has furnished us with the instruments and levers of thought. We seem to have seen him as he is, a great original genius struggling with unequal conditions of knowledge, not prepared with a system or evolving in a series of dialogues ideas which he had long conceived, but inconsistent, contradicting, enquiring as he goes along, following the argument from one point of view only, and therefore coming at opposite conclusions, hovering round the light, but always

---

various grades': Grote 1873: 267. At Mrs Grote's wish, Jowett was to act as one of the pallbearers at Grote's funeral in 1871.

[19] Jowett 1871: I.viii-ix. [20] Jowett 1871: I.ix.

moving in the same element of ideal truth. We have seen him also in his decline, when the wings of his imagination begin to droop, but his experience of life remains, and he turns away from the contemplation of the eternal to take a last sad look at human affairs.[21]

Paul Shorey was never going to find the atomistic hermeneutics of Grote and Jowett acceptable, nor the Plato they are thereby primed to discover: 'inconsistent, contradictory, enquiring as he goes along'. There are, he conceded, 'obvious and inevitable variations in Plato's moods, and minor beliefs from youth to old age'. 'Nor', he adds, 'in the study of such development would I reject the aid of a sober and critical method of style statistics', pioneered in Britain by Jowett's pupil, friend, and eventually biographer Lewis Campbell in his great edition of the *Sophist* and *Statesman* (1867). But his thesis is 'simply that Plato on the whole belongs rather to the type of thinkers whose philosophy is fixed in early maturity ... rather than to the class of those who receive a new revelation in every decade'.[22] All the same, one might find surprising that high estimate of John Stuart Mill as 'perhaps the greatest of nineteenth-century Platonists'.[23] For when Mill came to review Grote's *Plato* (in the April 1866 number of the *Edinburgh Review*), he made it clear that he was thoroughly persuaded of the main elements of the book's approach to Plato, including its identification of 'two complete Platos in Plato – the Sokratist and the Dogmatist – of whom the former is by far the more valuable to mankind, but the latter has obtained from them much the greater honour'.[24] That was very far from Shorey's view of the matter – yet for all that, he said of Mill's review (writing at the end of the 1920s) that it 'remains to this day the best available general introduction to the study of Plato';[25] and he ends *The Unity of Plato's Thought* quoting Mill approvingly on how often Plato's 'mind and purpose' are misapprehended.[26]

---

[21] Jowett 1871: IV.173*.   [22] Shorey 1903: 88.   [23] Shorey 1938: 231.

[24] Mill 1978: 415. But Mill immediately nuances this apparently uncompromising Grotean assessment of the two Platos, in a passage one might mistake for a slice of Jowett: 'There is, indeed, ample justification for the homage which all cultivated ages have rendered to Plato simply as a moralist – as one of the most powerful masters of virtue who have appeared among mankind. Amid all his changes, there is one thing to which he is ever constant – the transcendent worth of virtue and wisdom (which he invariably identifies), and the infinitely superior eligibility of the just life, even if calumniated and persecuted, over the unjust, however honoured by men, and by whatever power and grandeur surrounded. And what he thus feels, no one ever had a power superior to his of making felt by his readers. It is this element which completes in him the character of the Great Teacher. Others can instruct, but Plato is of those who form great men, by the combination of moral enthusiasm and logical discipline.'

[25] Shorey 1938: 232.   [26] Shorey 1903: 88.

What did Shorey find so appealing about Mill, and in that book review in particular? He clearly held him in high regard as a 'typical Platonist in his combination of severe logic with a passion for reforming the world'.[27] He finds a Platonic strain in the essays on religion and the treatise on representative government. The tract *The Subjection of Women* 'adopts Plato's argument that you might as well exclude all red-headed men from politics as all women'. *Utilitarianism* 'finds the ultimate ethical sanction in the direct adoption of the argument of the *Republic* (582Aff.) that the *virtuous philosopher* has experienced both the higher and the lower pleasures while the hedonist knows only the lower'.[28] Shorey might have mentioned Mill's conviction (inherited from his father) that Bentham's 'practice of never reasoning about wholes till they have been resolved into their parts' had (unbeknownst to him) been anticipated by Plato, 'in the process to which he too declared that he owed everything'.[29] What Shorey does goes on to recall is Mill's being set to read the *Theaetetus* at the age of eight,[30] and his rereading the whole of Plato in Greek in preparation for reviewing Grote ('and Mill's affirmation that he had read a book means more than a similar statement from Coleridge or Landor').[31] As for the review itself, Shorey seems to have thought that Mill gives the reader a uniquely balanced overall view of Plato.

Mill's treatment is recommended as the 'stabilizer' that will be required by someone who has picked up 'single illuminating sentences' about Plato in Emerson, helpful ideas about 'Plato's relation to the politics and social life of his time' from Emile Faguet, and insight into his 'literary style and artistic genius' from Walter Pater, or again has met 'the many eloquent and random observations on Plato diffused through Ruskin's writings'.[32] Shorey does not comment on how Grote fares at Mill's hands. But in truth, this is Grote's Plato urbanely crystallized and de-Benthamized. Mill has rather more sympathy with Plato the 'Dogmatist' than did Grote, and in fact he is at pains to bring out how *un*dogmatic the 'Dogmatist' is, even on Grote's own finding, except in the sphere of ethics and politics.[33] In ethics, 'failures in logic' do not prevent Plato from making one of the greatest steps 'ever made in moral culture – the cultivation of

---

[27] Shorey 1938: 232. He continues: 'That he did not add to these qualities the unction of the mystic Plato and the genius of Plato the poet and artist, is no abatement of his claim to the title of Platonist.'
[28] Shorey 1938: 231. [29] Mill 1969: 86, 88. Cf. Mill 1981: 25.
[30] Shorey had misremembered: Mill says that it was in 1813, that is, when he was seven (Mill 1981: 9). His reading then of the 'first six dialogues (in the common arrangement) of Plato' is the subject of an ingenious and pertinacious study by Myles Burnyeat (Burnyeat 2001).
[31] Shorey 1938: 232. [32] Shorey 1938: 232–3. [33] Mill 1978: 430–1.

a disinterested preference of duty for its own sake, as a higher state than that of sacrificing selfish preferences to a more distant self-interest':[34] this very unGrotean reading of the *Gorgias* plainly represents it as an advance on the *Protagoras*, 'one of the best parts of the Platonic writings' for Grote as indeed for Mill.[35] In politics, Mill hails in Plato 'the vigorous assertion of a truth, of transcendent importance and universal application – that the work of government is a Skilled Employment',[36] adopting an outlook that, as Frank Turner observed, took him a long way from Grote's own.[37]

'His Place in the History of Philosophy'

Grote and Jowett shared the view that the right way to approach Plato was through scrupulous historical scholarship. It is application of this methodological principle that is what yields the atomist hermeneutics illustrated in the previous section. If the dialogues present themselves to sober historical scholarship as nothing other than 'distinct imaginary conversations, composed by the same author at unknown times and under unknown specialties of circumstance',[38] then we must interpret them accordingly, not as the building blocks of a fully conceived or still evolving system.[39] For both Grote and Jowett, reading the text properly, as it is and not as we might like it to be, was the basic responsibility of the Plato scholar – just as for Jowett it had been in his commentaries on St Paul (published in 1855), and as for Grote in the *History of Greece* scrutinizing and evaluating the source material critically was the fundamental requirement of a Greek historian. This shared conviction is presumably what led both scholars to devote the lion's share of their discussions of the dialogues to detailed analytic summaries as accurate as they could make them, sometimes at very great length (Alexander Grant, in the most searching of the early reviews of the *Dialogues of Plato*, considered that a misjudgement on Jowett's part).[40] By the same token, the text had to be liberated from the systematizing metaphysical interpretations with which it had been overlaid in intervening centuries, and from the hermeneutic strategies devised more recently by the German commentators, for which (as Grote put it) there could be neither proof nor disproof.[41] 'In interpreting Plato', said Campbell

---

[34] Mill 1978: 416.   [35] Grote 1865: 11.45; Mill 1978: 418.
[36] Mill 1978: 436. I discuss this passage (along with Jowett's treatment of the 'ideal statesman' in the Introduction to the *Gorgias* in his second edition) in Schofield 2006: 138–44.
[37] Turner 1981: 401–3. Grote thoroughly disapproved of the direction Mill's thinking about politics was taking him in his later writings: see, for example, Clarke 1962: 177.
[38] Grote 1865: 1.279.   [39] Jowett 1871: IV.173*.   [40] Grant 1871: 318–19.
[41] Grote 1865: 1.187. There is a good treatment of Grote's interpretative assumptions in Demetriou 1998: 36–45.

of Jowett, 'as before in interpreting St Paul, he sought to get behind the accretions of after ages, such as the Neo-Platonism of the fifth and fifteenth centuries, and to bring out the original meaning of the author.'[42]

Needless to say, agreement on methodology did not mean unanimity over the concrete results achieved through its application. For example, Jowett thought Grote quite mistaken 'in admitting as genuine all the writings commonly attributed to Plato in antiquity';[43] and he argued particularly vigorously that all the Platonic *Epistles* were forgeries, at ever greater length in successive editions (the sustained case he makes in the third edition remains good value today).[44] Nor did historiography mean the same thing for Jowett as for Grote. What Grote practised, as M. L. Clarke, his mid-twentieth-century biographer put it, was in effect 'Benthamite historiography', as articulated by Grote's original intellectual mentor, James Mill. Clarke summarizes Mill's view of the historian's task as twofold: 'he has a strict regard for evidence, and he combines this with a readiness to pass judgment' – moral, political, philosophical, as might meet the case – on what it tells him.[45] 'Nothing was more important to the Philosophical Radical', said Momigliano, 'than the careful examination of evidence. His voice became particularly solemn when he spoke of the "law respecting sufficiency of evidence".'[46] As for the assessment which the historian has an 'obligation' to make (according to Grote, articulating what Mill had called 'philosophical history'), he will need in thinking about any particular society such as the ancient Greeks to take into account comparative material on other societies. Otherwise he will not 'convey the rank they occupy in the scale of human improvement', for example in 'providing securities for good government', and in the Greek case particularly by virtue of 'the intellectual philosophy of this illustrious people'.[47] Grote's Benthamite historiography is recognizably an Enlightenment project.

Where the text of Plato was concerned, discharging the obligation of judgement meant treating it from the vantage point 'of the Experience philosophy', in John Stuart Mill's words at the end of his review of Grote's *Plato*. As Mill went on to add, 'readers will esteem the discussions more or less highly, according to their estimation of that philosophy'.[48] That is indeed more or less what happened, as when Jowett hints at his own reaction in the Preface to his translation, when he says of Plato that 'he is

---

[42] Abbott and Campbell 1897: 1.261.   [43] Jowett 1871: 1.ix–x.   [44] Jowett 1892: 1.xxvi–xxix.
[45] Clarke 1962: 106.   [46] Momigliano 1994: 21.
[47] Grote 1826: 280–1; see the discussion in Vaio 1996.   [48] Mill 1978: 440.

not to be measured by the standard of utilitarianism or any other modern philosophical system'[49] (in other contexts he was more outspoken: to Florence Nightingale in April 1874 he describes Grote's *Plato* as 'utterly mistaken & misguided').[50] But while sympathy or otherwise with utilitarianism or with the subjectivism of the 'Experience philosophy' certainly played its part in helping to determine the way Grote was received, critics from the Jowett stable also felt that for all his merits as an analyst, his reading of the evidence itself missed rather too much of what was there in Plato.[51] Thus Edward Caird commented that 'the variety, the humour, the poetry of the Dialogues, the fresh play of changing situation and character, disappear, and are intended to disappear, in a dry analysis, which brings into clear light the different points of the argument, but leaves all else in shadow'.[52] And Lewis Campbell, in a particularly thoughtful assessment, was not alone in finding Grote's exclusive distinction between Dialogues of Search and Dialogues of Exposition much too inflexible.[53]

By contrast, Jowett's historiography was (in a broad sense) Hegelian. Jowett had visited Germany in 1844 and again in 1845; as well as acquiring many works of Kant, Schleiermacher, Fichte, and other German philosophers and theologians for his library, he came to own six volumes of Hegel in editions published in the 1840s. With Frederick Temple, Balliol colleague and future archbishop of Canterbury, he had embarked on a translation of (it seems likely) the *Logic*, broken off in 1849 but never completed, and he was certainly full of Hegel in his teaching and his talking and thinking at that time.[54] But although, as he puts it in the Introduction to the *Sophist* in the *Dialogues*, 'we acknowledge his originality, and some of us delight to wander in the mazes of thought which he has opened to us', he confesses that 'when we are asked to believe the Hegelian to be the sole or universal logic, we naturally reply that there are other ways in which our ideas may be connected'. Indeed: 'The spirit of Hegelian criticism should be applied to his own system, and the terms being, not being, existence,

---

[49] Jowett 1871: 1.ix.   [50] Jowett 1987: 255.
[51] See the useful collection of reviews of Grote's *Plato* and *Aristotle* assembled in Demetriou 2004.
[52] Caird 1865: 351. Contrast the impact made by Jowett's *Dialogues* (Abbott and Campbell 1897: 11.6–7): 'as a literary work, a classic rendering of a Greek classic, its merit was at once recognized, for Jowett's style was irresistible; but as a work of philosophy and scholarship it was less appreciated'. However, there were those 'who left Plato unread' but 'lingered with delight over Jowett's essays'.
[53] Campbell 1866: 114–29.
[54] Abbott and Campbell 1897: 1.89–97, 129; Faber 1957: 177–83; Hinchcliff 1987: 79–83. Yet as these writers point out, he was already critical of Hegel: witness a letter of his written to Arthur Stanley in 1846 that they all quote, which begins a comment on the subject with the words: 'Hegel is untrue'. In the period 1854–60, however, he 'still encouraged the ablest of his pupils in the study of Hegel' (Abbot and Campbell 1897: 1.261).

essence, notion, and the like challenged and defined.' And Jowett later gets autobiographical:

> These are some of the doubts and suspicions which arise in the mind of a student of Hegel, when, after living for a time within the charmed circle, he removes to a little distance and looks back upon what he has learnt from the vantage point of history and experience. The enthusiasm of his youth has passed away, the authority of the master no longer retains a hold on him.[55]

Distancing himself from Hegelianism was something Jowett did not infrequently. For example, in a letter of 1873 to Florence Nightingale (there are several in the same vein), he reports that he has persuaded 'the Revd Hegel Green' – the middle name of his Hegelian former pupil T. H. Green was not 'Hegel', nor was he an ordained clergyman – 'to give up lecturing for a year and take to writing – whereby the minds of our undergraduates will be greatly clarified'.[56] He thought Green (and his fellow Hegelian Caird) did not pay enough regard to 'common sense and experience' (though in his view Hegel himself did have a lot of 'common sense').[57] In the sermon he preached in 1882 on Green's premature death, he 'gently censured' him 'for not having treated with proper reverence the great Englishman, John Locke'.[58] Jowett for his part was 'an incorrigible eclectic', in the judgement of Peter Hinchcliff, even if (in the words of H. W. C. Davis, the historian of Balliol) 'eclecticism was the last result at which he aimed'.[59] As a teacher, his style was critical: 'not infectious with his own ideas, but concerned to check "false tendencies" in his pupils, and to stimulate them in those directions where they might be most effective'.[60] 'I never found', said W. L. Newman, 'that he made any effort to enforce on me any

---

[55] Jowett 1875: IV.413–14, 422. But thanking Lord Arthur Russell for the gift to his college of a bust of Kant in a letter dated 19 July 1885 (Hegel had arrived from the same source six months earlier), he wrote (Abbott and Campbell 1897: II.250): 'Though not a Hegelian I think that I have gained more from Hegel than from any other philosopher.'

[56] Jowett 1987: 235.

[57] Jowett 1987: 241, 52. Elsewhere he writes to Nightingale (1987: 290): 'A curious sort of Neoplatonism or Neohegelianism is beginning to overspread both Britain & America – of which the two leading representatives have been Prof. Caird of Glasgow and Prof. Green of Oxford, both men of great force of character. Their teaching has been, unconsciously to themselves, a self-contradictory eclecticism which they privately expound, but do not defend against attacks. It is too metaphysical & political & too little eternal & religious. They want to rescue the world from materialism & Darwinism & Utilitarianism. And they are right in their spirit, but not in their method, which is naught.' On Green and the influence of his teaching in Oxford, see further Richter 1956: 444–5, 456–61, 468–70.

[58] Jowett 1899: 216 (quoted by Hinchcliff 1987: 166).   [59] See Hinchcliff 1987: 77.

[60] Caird 1897–8: 42. This could be an uncomfortable experience. Lewis Campbell (Abbott and Campbell 1897: I.203) told of how: 'His long silences were felt as an awkward bar to conversation

particular set of views'.[61] Caird said of him that 'his treatment of great questions never took the form of an attempt to think them out conscientiously, but of a series of glances at truth from various points of view ... even sometimes ... somewhat inconsistent with each other'. In other writers, what he prized most was 'what is best in his own work, inspired gleams of insight, the vivid and epigrammatic expression of particular aspects of truth, and he prized them still more if they were lighted up with a touch of humour'.[62]

In his conception of historical method, however, Jowett *was* Hegelian – in a sense not unlike that in which we are most of us Hegelian today.[63] He supposes that there is development in the range and articulation of human knowledge and self-understanding over time; and that a proper sense of history will require the ability both to appreciate the constraints governing the different ways in which philosophy is conceived and practised at different stages of that evolution, and also to see how what at an early stage is inchoate would or could develop into something more full-fledged at a later. Jowett intimates something of this in a sentence from his general Preface already quoted above (p. 57), together with the remarks with which he continues the line of thought. He says of Plato:

> He is no dreamer, but a great philosophical genius struggling with unequal conditions of light and knowledge under which he is living. He may be illustrated by the writings of the moderns, but he must be interpreted by his own, and by his place in the history of philosophy. We are not concerned to determine the residuum of truth which remains for us. His truth may not be our truth, and nevertheless may have an extraordinary value and interest for us.[64]

An example may serve to bring out what Jowett means. Commenting on the concept of dialectic introduced in the *Republic*, he imagines us asking

---

by those who did not understand that he himself was hardly aware of them, as the intervals were filled with active thought. ... To interrupt the silent process by starting a fresh topic was often to provoke a snub.' On Jowett's critical bent, see further Abbott and Campbell 1897: II.408: 'In philosophy he was more critical than speculative, more intuitive than systematic'. But Abbott goes on to add (II.409): 'Yet his criticism was also a philosophy.'

[61] Abbott and Campbell 1897: i.257.

[62] Caird 1897–8: 44–5. This makes Jowett sound a little like Jowett's Plato: see Jowett 1871: IV.173* (quoted above, pp. 57–8).

[63] It could be argued that quite a lot of contemporary Anglo-American technical analysis of Plato and Aristotle still operates *de facto* with a 'Benthamite' conception of historiography that resembles Grote's.

[64] Jowett 1871: I.ix. The most thoroughgoing exercise in historicist interpretation of an ancient philosophical text in this Hegelian spirit attempted in Victorian Britain was the edition of Aristotle's *Ethics* by Jowett's former pupil Alexander Grant, first published in two volumes in 1857 and 1858 (a third had been meant to follow; Grant did not present the whole of the *Ethics* until the second edition of 1866). Its character and importance are well brought out by the discussion in Turner 1981: 340–52.

'whether the science which Plato only half reveals to us is more akin to logic or to metaphysics'. He replies with 'the answer that they are not as yet distinguished in his mind': philosophy had not developed that far – Plato is where he is 'in the history of philosophy', and we should not be so anxious to find 'our truth' in him that we make him more determinate than he is.[65] Nonetheless: 'The germ of both of them [sc. logic and metaphysics] is contained in the Platonic dialectic' – in other words, something of 'extraordinary value and interest for us' will or could grow from Plato's conception.[66] He provides *us*, therefore, with an 'instrument of thought'[67] – something we can use to do philosophy ourselves.

In sum, the historian's first obligation is to get Plato right (here he and Grote would have had no quarrel with each other). But it is not his job to pass judgement upon him in Grote's Benthamite mode and simply take from him 'our' truth (whatever that might happen to be), rejecting everything else. Instead, the historian will be aware that thought and the capacity for thinking thoughts of a specific kind are things that develop and evolve over historical time. And so the good historian of philosophy will be alert to the value and interest of what later generations, and of course his own, would or could *make* out of Plato: using him as an 'instrument of thought'. And Jowett declares that he himself will do so by representing Plato 'as the father of idealism'.[68]

What exactly is meant here by 'idealism'?[69] The next sentence in the Preface seems designed to clarify the claim: Plato 'is the poet or maker of ideas'. And a passage at the beginning of the Introduction to the *Republic* is particularly helpful in illustrating the point – the first of its two sentences belongs to material added in the second edition:

> He is the father of idealism in philosophy, in politics, in literature. And many of the latest conceptions of modern thinkers and statesmen, such as the unity of knowledge, the reign of law, and the equality of the sexes, have been anticipated in a dream by him.[70]

These remarks may be compared with another passage from the same Introduction, this time from the final page:

> Human life and conduct are affected by ideals in the same way that they are affected by the examples of eminent men. . . . Most men live in a corner and

---

[65] For the third and final edition of *Dialogues*, Jowett composed a new section of the *Meno* Introduction attacking the 'modern view' (he seems to have Henry Jackson in his sights: cf. Jowett 1892: I.xxix–xxxvii) which gives to the 'doctrine of ideas' what he thought 'an imaginary clearness and definiteness' (Jowett 1892: II.13–19).
[66] Jowett 1875: III.182.   [67] Jowett 1871: I.ix.   [68] Jowett 1871: I.ix.
[69] This question is well discussed in Burnyeat 1998: 365–7.   [70] Jowett 1875: III.1–2.

see but a little way beyond their home or place of occupation; they 'do not live up their eyes to the hills'; they are not awake when the dawn appears. But in Plato, as from some 'tower of speculation', we look into the distance and behold the future of the world and of philosophy. The ideal of the State and of the life of the philosopher; the ideal of an education continuing through life and extending equally to both sexes; the ideal of the unity and correlation of knowledge; the faith in good and immortality – are the vacant forms of light on which Plato is seeking to fasten the eye of mankind.[71]

So idealism, as Jowett deploys the notion, supplies a perspective on Plato which focuses on ideas in the dialogues that illuminate what human beings could think or achieve if they keep their eyes fixed on the forms of life or knowledge represented in those ideas. That, it would appear, is why a utilitarian vantage point could in Jowett's eyes never do justice to Plato. As he puts it at the end of his Introduction to the *Theaetetus*, to the 'Epicurean or Utilitarian philosopher' 'obligation, duty, conscience' are only names. What Mill called the 'Experience philosophy', which is ultimately interested simply in 'our natural perceptions of pleasure and pain', is 'fatal to the pursuit of ideals, moral, political, or religious' and 'deprives us of the means and instruments of higher thought, of any adequate conception of the mind, of conscience, of moral obligation'.[72]

It has sometimes been supposed, however, that what Jowett primarily meant in talking of Plato as 'father of idealism' is that he was a precursor of Hegelian idealism. John Glucker observed in his 1987 article that 'Jowett was more than sympathetic' to idealism, mainly in the Hegelian form; and he suggested that Plato's dialectic he could accept 'only as a stepping-stone to a more systematic Idealism'.[73] In a later paper, Glucker argues more strenuously for the notion that Jowett's Plato is a 'Hegelian Plato'.[74] He first points out that already in the first edition of Jowett's Introduction to the *Sophist*, he wrote that 'the kindred spirit of Hegel seemed to find in the Sophist the crown and summit of the Platonic philosophy – here was the place at which Plato most nearly approached to the Hegelian identity of Being and not-Being'.[75] Glucker then quotes a substantial passage from the extended version in the second edition (reproduced with cosmetic alterations in the third) beginning: 'In Plato we find, as we might expect, the germs of many thoughts which have been further developed by the genius of Spinoza and Hegel.'[76] Jowett subsequently goes on to point out differences between Plato and Hegel (as Glucker noted). But the sketch he then provides of Hegelianism – 'of all

---

[71] Jowett 1875: III.192. [72] Jowett 1875: IV.284. [73] Glucker 1987: 180, 196.
[74] Glucker 1996: 392–4. [75] Jowett 1871: II.445. [76] Jowett 1875: IV.403.

philosophies ... the most obscure'[77] – includes as its first item: 'It is an ideal philosophy which, in popular phraseology, maintains not matter but mind to be the truth of things, and this not by a mere crude substitution of one word for another, but by showing either of them to be the complement of the other.'[78]

That is Glucker's core evidence for taking Hegelian idealism to be what was above all in Jowett's mind when he speaks in the general Preface of Plato as 'father of idealism'. It might have been reinforced by reference to a further passage – not exactly Hegelian, but perhaps pointing in a Hegelian direction – which Jowett included in the Introduction to the *Meno* in the third edition. Having referred to 'the spirit of idealism' as what we find in Plato (rather than articulated doctrine),[79] he goes on a little later to explain the kind of coherence he thinks there is in the variety of formulations in the text: 'It is the spirit, not the letter, in which they agree – the spirit which places the divine above the human, the spiritual above the material, the one above the many, the mind before the body.'[80] On this basis, we may certainly conclude that Hegelianism is a *version* of what Jowett counted as 'ideal philosophy'. But Glucker takes no account of the reservations about Hegel's thought expressed by Jowett later in the Introduction to the *Sophist*;[81] and he leaves out of the reckoning the many other passages in his Introductions (a few quoted above)[82] that indicate the importance he evidently attached to the way ideals are glimpsed in Plato's writing on all manner of topics with no obvious Hegelian subtext. Decisive against the Glucker interpretation is that repetition of the expression 'father of idealism' at the beginning of the Introduction to the *Republic* (always for Jowett the supreme Platonic masterpiece).[83] The sentence in which it appears was (as noted above, p. 55) introduced in the second edition, and was presumably intended to clarify what had been meant by the use of the same phrase in the general Preface: 'He is the father of idealism in philosophy, in politics, in literature.' And the following sentence (repeated from the first edition) talks as we have seen of 'the unity of knowledge, the reign of law, and the equality of the sexes'.[84]

---

[77] Jowett 1875: IV.404. [78] Jowett 1875: IV.405. [79] Jowett 1892: II.14. [80] Jowett 1892: II.19.
[81] Quoted above, pp. 62–3. [82] See pp. 57, 65–6.
[83] 'Certainly the greatest' of his works (Jowett 1871: II.1, repeated in subsequent editions). For Mill, it was one of 'the four greatest masterpieces of Plato's genius', along with *Protagoras*, *Phaedrus*, and *Gorgias* (Mill 1978: 407). Even Grote, who so much preferred the 'Dialogues of Search' and regretted the way the *Republic*'s Socrates had abandoned the role of 'leader of the opposition' and 'passed over to the ministerial benches', nonetheless described it as 'that splendid monument of Plato's genius', 'undoubtedly the grandest of all his compositions; including in itself all his different points of excellence' (Grote 1865: III.165, 122).
[84] Jowett 1875: III.1. Interestingly, as in the first edition of the Preface, 'idealism' here has lower-case initial letter, as indeed quite generally, so far as I have discovered, throughout Jowett's Introductions in all three editions – with just one exception. As Glucker points out, the word *is* given an initial

'Modern Applications'

Grote was a banker, Mill a civil servant; they were notably active in various spheres of public and literary life, and key figures in the foundation and subsequent development of the University of London – and both served, albeit not simultaneously and not very influentially, as Members of Parliament for a while.[85] Only Jowett was a university teacher: the greatest single force in establishing the *Republic* as the central text in the Oxford curriculum,[86] and exceptional in his ability to catch the ear of government from time to time when it came to reforming university governance, introducing new entry standards for the Home and Indian Civil Service, or promoting schools reform.[87] The publications in which the major reviews of Grote's *Plato* and Jowett's *Dialogues* appeared are themselves indicative of the intellectual world in which their books were to take their place. These were not professional philosophical or classical journals: in mid-Victorian Britain, there were none.[88] The periodicals which commissioned the reviews, many of them effectively long, learned articles in their own right, often by the best British scholars, were journals such as the *Edinburgh Review*, the *Quarterly Review*, the *Westminster Review*, the *Fortnightly Review*, *Macmillan's Magazine*, *Fraser's Magazine*, *Blackwood's Magazine*, whose appeal was to a serious reading public wanting knowledge and analysis of new books and contemporary political and cultural developments. These were the readers whose minds Grote and Mill and Jowett hoped to interest, instruct, and prompt to fresh questioning and

---

capital 'I' in the Preface in the second and third editions. Why so? At this point in the Preface, Jowett is contrasting 'idealism' or 'Idealism' with 'utilitarianism or any other modern system'; and one might take Glucker to have a point when he asks whether 'Idealism' (with initial capital) is not just as much a 'modern system' as utilitarianism or any contemporary rival (Glucker 1996: 392). My conjecture is that Jowett wanted to find some way of indicating that 'idealism' here was precisely *not* intended here to signify a 'system' such as utilitarianism was (and is), and that he thought use of the capital would flag that up. My evidence is the use to which he puts 'Idealism' (with initial capital) on the one other occasion I have found him writing the word that way in *Dialogues*. This is towards the end of the discussion of the theory of ideas (initial lower case is his standard usage here, too) in the new material he wrote for the Introduction to the *Meno* in the third edition. He says by way of conclusion (Jowett 1892: 11.19): 'So various, and if regarded on the surface only, inconsistent, are the statements of Plato respecting the doctrine of ideas. If we attempted to harmonise or combine them, we should make out of them, not a system, but the caricature of a system. They are the ever-varying expression of Plato's Idealism.' Plato's 'Idealism' is *not* a system: strange as it may seem, Jowett deploys the initial capital 'I' precisely when he is wanting to convey that point.

[85] See (for example) Clarke 1962, Mill 1981.
[86] See (for example) Glucker 1987: 176–7, with qualifications in Stopper 1981: 268–9, 278–80.
[87] See (for example) Hinchcliff 1987: 26–44, 95–106; Jowett 1987: x–xxxii.
[88] But at Cambridge in 1868 the *Journal of Philology* was founded (or re-established), although book reviewing was no part of its remit.

aspiration – from the universities, from the professions, or however their lives might be occupied. As D. B. Monro put it in his review of *Dialogues* – but the same might have been said of Grote or Mill *mutatis mutandis* – it was 'the noble task of Mr. Jowett's life, like Socrates, "to bring philosophy into the market-place", to awaken the spirit of research in active and growing minds, and to gain for knowledge and the faith in knowledge their true place in human affairs'.[89]

If authors and readers alike lived in a world remote from our contemporary Plato scholarship, so the notion of scholarship itself as Grote, Mill, and Jowett conceived it differed strikingly from any ideal of pure research (what Jowett spoke of dismissively in his time as 'useless learning').[90] Here, we may reflect on the conception of 'philosophical history' we have been exploring, whether in its Benthamite or its Hegelian version. Philosophical history is very far from being a Rankean enterprise exclusively preoccupied with value-free empirical investigation. The philosophical historian of either kind is under the 'obligation' – to use Grote's expression – not simply to scrutinize the evidence with critical rigour, but just as importantly to exercise judgement: the Benthamite historian to assess how far the dialectical method of the Platonic dialogues and their treatment of knowledge, truth, and the good represent genuine advances 'in the scale of human improvement'; the Hegelian historian to discern those ideas in Plato which provide the germs from which fully fledged moral, political, and philosophical ideals would or could grow. To remain neutral on such questions would constitute a dereliction of the philosophical historian's duty.

At one point in his correspondence with Florence Nightingale, Jowett wrote as follows (early January, in what his editors conjecture was 1874), referring to the draft of what must be the second edition version of his Introduction to the *Republic*:

> Will you give me some criticisms on the 'Republic'? I shall be at work on that next Term. It is, of course, the greatest of Plato's works, & affords the greatest opportunity for modern applications of all sorts. You may show all your political feelings in commenting on the Republic. Have I not attacked Mr. Gladstone in several places?[91]

---

[89] Monro 1871: 493.   [90] Faber 1957: 43.
[91] Jowett 1987: 250. No doubt he is referring particularly to the passage in the Introduction on the 'corruptions of these philosophical statesmen', albeit itemized in entirely generic terms (Jowett 1875: III.173–4). In his correspondence, he frequently gave vent to his dissatisfaction with Gladstone, for example in a letter of 17 October 1876 (Abbott and Campbell 1899: 80): 'Never was there such a power of self-delusion in any man as in Gladstone. He impersonates in his own genius all the passing movements of the people.'

For a philosophical historian of either stripe, those applications or the possibilities of making them were intrinsic to their very idea of what historical understanding has to consist in. Unless you have worked out how far Plato represents a real improvement in human understanding of truth or of how to live, or what compelling ideal forms of life or knowledge or reality he has glimpsed, if not yet articulated as they would or could be in future eras, then you have not got a proper historical grasp of his thought – precisely because you have not seen the point to which it has taken the human mind, or to which it is or could be going to take it. And if you have not communicated that with conviction to your reader, you have not done your job as a writer.

The 'modern applications' that Grote, Mill, and Jowett indicated in their presentations of Plato were not presented as immediate political imperatives. They were conceived rather as challenges to the reader to think differently – whether for example about the importance of population control,[92] a particular preoccupation of the Philosophical Radicals;[93] or Mill's favourite theme of the need for 'skilled agency' in government;[94] or – something in which Jowett considered Plato 'far in advance of modern philosophers and theologians', but where his thought 'may not be wholly incapable of application to our own times' – his teaching that 'education is to be continued throughout life' and 'extending equally to both sexes'.[95] Perhaps we can still learn a thing or two from reading the Victorians.

---

[92] Grote 1865: III.226–34; cf. Jowett 1875: III.160–9. Both have exceedingly thoughtful discussions of the issue: 'this most difficult of social problems', in Jowett's words. Both find Plato's approach to it morally objectionable, with Grote endeavouring more dispassionately to make his treatment historically intelligible, whereas Jowett is revolted by Plato's regarding the human being 'with the eye of a dog- or bird-fancier' but concedes that, although 'children can only be brought up in families', Plato is not wrong 'in asserting that family attachments may interfere with higher aims'.

[93] Mill 1981: 107–8.   [94] Mill 1978: 436; cf. Mill 1981: 265.

[95] Jowett 1875: III.183–4, 192. While neither Grote nor Jowett was the champion of sexual equality that Mill was to become, both did take practical initiatives regarding university education for women: Grote in trying (unsuccessfully) to persuade the Senate of the University of London to render 'female students admissible to the degrees and honours' of the University (Clarke 1962: 165–6), Jowett in getting his college to contribute towards the funding of a new institution in Bristol that would educate adults as well as adolescents, and women as well as men: it eventually became the University of Bristol (Abbott and Campbell 1897: II.57–8; Jowett 1987: xxvii).

PART II

Argument and Dialogue Architecture

CHAPTER 4

Callicles' Return
Gorgias *509–22 Reconsidered*

Introduction

The *Gorgias* has unsurprisingly been attracting considerable philosophical attention in recent times. No one who has got into Plato ever forgets the perennially intriguing figure of Callicles presented there, perhaps the most eloquent and passionate of all Socrates' discussion partners in the dialogues, invested – some readers have felt – with an unusual personal emotion. And the confrontation Plato stages in the dialogue between Callicles and Socrates and its many theoretical dimensions has stimulated much fine philosophical scholarship of late.

Discussion, however, has largely been confined to Callicles' initial presentation of his position (482–6), to Socrates' ensuing critique (487–500), and to his subsequent attempt to substitute his own view of the good life as governed by order and restraint (*sôphrosunê*) (501–9). These are the stretches of argumentation which (for example) Charles Kahn and John Cooper in two significant studies make their focus.[1] And one might sometimes get the impression that, although the dialogue has almost another twenty pages to run, it will present no further philosophical conversation of much import between Callicles and Socrates.

Indeed, one of the latest contributions to study of the *Gorgias* says just that:[2]

> At 505d Callicles announces that he will no longer cooperate with Socrates. He tells him to either stop or carry on the discussion with someone else. Since no one present is willing to take over from Callicles, Socrates performs the remarkable feat of going it alone for almost another twenty pages. For the largest part of the remainder of the dialogue he asks and answers his own questions – a peculiar picture, unparalleled in Plato's writings.

There have naturally been plenty of exceptions to the general neglect of the argumentation of 509–13 in particular. Both Rachana Kamtekar and James

[1] Kahn 1983; Cooper 1999. [2] Dimas 2015: 84.

Doyle, in articles to which I shall recur, have written interestingly on that material.³ But these are not pages of the dialogue on which scholars generally dwell most – despite the importance of the material, which is what in this chapter I shall be trying to bring out. I offer a fairly detailed commentary on the progress of the discussion in these pages between Socrates and Callicles, with briefer comments on its further development from 513 to 522. Readers will find a résumé of its general upshot in my short concluding section.

The truth is that – contrary to what Panos Dimas suggests in the passage just quoted – Callicles resumes his role as Socrates' answerer at 509c.⁴ Nor does he subsequently again relinquish it in the passage launched by the combination of Socrates' question there and his reply, which is an extended one (509–22). The words that prompt him to re-enter the conversation are those Socrates speaks in a return to what has become its central topic of debate and will remain so to the very end of the dialogue: the question of what is the greatest evil that can befall someone – committing injustice, or being its victim? That finished up as the main and final focus of Socrates' preceding conversation with Polus (from 469b onwards). Socrates' increasingly provocative stance on the issue was what precipitated Callicles' initial intervention at 481b. And in summing up the morals he thinks should be learned from the dialogue's discussions as a whole, Socrates begins (527b):⁵

> Among so many arguments, while the others are proved wrong, this argument alone stands its ground – that we should more beware of acting unjustly than of being treated unjustly, and that more than anything, what a man should practice, both in private life and public life, is not seeming to be good, but being good.⁶

So with Callicles' re-engagement in argument at 509c, Plato not only announces a new phase in the treatment of the issues being discussed. It is also his way of engineering a move away from preoccupation with Callicles' own distinctive position on the good life, and with Socrates' attempts first to refute it and then to build an alternative conception of his own, back to what will end up being represented as the core argument of the entire dialogue in that passage on the last page of the retailing of the myth. In short, this is a marked as a moment of extraordinary significance in what is

---

³ Kamtekar 2005; Doyle 2006; see also, for example, Ober 1998: 207–9.
⁴ Socrates' virtuoso solo double act in fact lasts from just 506c to 507c: one Stephanus page only.
⁵ Sedley 2009: 53–4 points out that the morals Socrates draws here all in fact relate in the first instance to the arguments of the Polus section.
⁶ Translations of passages in the *Gorgias* used are those by Tom Griffith in Schofield and Griffith 2010 (with occasional minor variations).

by any measure one of Plato's most important works – and as it happens, longest, too (only *Republic* and *Laws* are longer). It is strange that it has not attracted greater attention.

Re-engaging Callicles

What most immediately pulls Callicles back into argumentative engagement is a question about security: Which is the most important form of security a person needs to be able to provide for himself (and his friends and family)? Socrates sums up a key observation he has just made on the issue in the preceding context as follows (509c):

> The credit of being able to help against each evil, and the disgrace of being unable, depends in each case on its magnitude.

And he then addresses Callicles:

> Is that wide of the mark, Callicles, or is that how it is?

Callicles breaks his prolonged silence and responds:

> No, it's not wide of the mark.

To understand why it should be at just this point that Callicles is drawn back into the discussion once more, we need to do a little retracing of Socrates' steps. Almost a page before, Socrates has concluded the line of reasoning launched by his solo double act with the words (508c):

> These things being so, let us ask ourselves what exactly your complaint is against me. Is it fair comment or not, when you say the result [i.e. of Socrates' position that committing injustice is a greater evil than being treated unjustly] is that I am incapable of helping either myself or any of my friends, or family either, or of rescuing them from the greatest dangers?

In other words, Socrates is signalling that he is now returning to the basic disagreement between him and Callicles. He goes on to insist famously that while he is not claiming to know the truth of the conclusion he asserts, the reasoning he had developed in the Polus conversation for the thesis that treating someone else unjustly is both worse and more disgraceful for the perpetrator than for the person being treated unjustly is 'held in place and secured by arguments made of iron and adamant' (508e–509a). Then he draws an inference, concluding with the summing up observation quoted above (509b–c):

> I take the view that this is how things are. If injustice *is* the greatest of evils for the person acting unjustly, and greater still than this greatest, if such

a thing were possible, is for the person acting unjustly not to pay the just penalty, what then is the 'help' of which it really is true to say that if a person can't provide it for himself he will become a laughing-stock? Isn't it that help which will avert the greatest harm from us? It necessarily follows that this is the help it is most disgraceful not to be able to give, whether to oneself or to one's friends or family. Second would be help against the second greatest evil, third help against the third, and so on. The credit of being able to help against each evil, and the disgrace of being unable, depends in each case on its magnitude.

I have two proposals to offer regarding the argumentative sequence I have set out here. First, what renews Callicles' interest in rejoining the conversation is precisely Socrates' return to what he correctly describes as Callicles' chief complaint against him: of being powerless in the face of injustice. Second, what elicits his agreement with Socrates is naturally not the thesis that committing injustice is worse than being its victim, but simply the observation Socrates makes in summing up the train of thought he is now presenting: 'The credit of being able to help against each evil, and the disgrace of being unable, depends in each case on its magnitude.'

What should lend persuasiveness to my first claim is the way Callicles formulated his ideas when he burst in upon Socrates' discussion with Polus in the first place. He formulated his theory of natural justice at the outset in terms of what is naturally most shameful or disgraceful (483a), turning the terminology Socrates had resorted to in the Polus argument on its head, and rejecting as contemptible the slavish person 'for whom death is preferable to life – who when he is treated unjustly and downtrodden is incapable of helping himself or anyone he cares for' (483b). It was Callicles, too, who in that same context introduced the talk Socrates recycles here of what makes someone a 'laughing-stock' (484d–485c), which morphed into the charge that Socrates' philosophizing would land him with the disgrace of being quite unable to help and save himself or anyone else from 'the greatest dangers' – such as being hauled before the court and ending up by being put to death (486a–b). So when Socrates at 508c explicitly recurs to these complaints, no wonder if his appetite for argument is freshly piqued.

Now for my second claim: When it is first introduced, the proposal that not being able to provide the help needed to avert the greatest harm from us represents the height of what is disgraceful or shameful is presented as contingent upon a condition. The suggestion is that we should adopt it *if* we accept the Socratic view that 'injustice is the greatest of evils for the person acting unjustly, and greater still than this greatest, if such a thing were possible, is for the person acting unjustly not to pay the just penalty'.

But 'if' does not equate to 'if and only if'; and as the passage goes on, Socrates enunciates the proposal in terms progressively less specific, almost as an abstract calculus, until in his final formulation it takes the entirely general assertoric form of the proposition that the greater the magnitude of the evil against which help is needed, the greater the disgrace of not being able to supply it. And most immediately, of course, that is the formulation of which Socrates asks: 'Is that wide of the mark?' With such a formulation, he offers Callicles something to which his interlocutor can assent, without necessarily implying acceptance of Socrates' identification of *what* the evil of greatest magnitude should be taken to be. Indeed, it could only be the general abstract formulation of the proposition that would have any chance – at this stage of the dialectic of the dialogue – of constituting any common ground between him and Socrates, and of drawing him into anything other than violent disagreement once more.

Power and Assimilation

What now follows is an exploration by Socrates – in which Callicles is kept actively engaged – of the kind of resources (the 'help') people need if they are to protect themselves from harm. It will crucially involve introducing considerations of power, and the development of what I shall be calling the *assimilation* thesis. In this section of the chapter, I present a commentary on the way Socrates first gets Callicles' assent to proposals put to him about power and assimilation and then seeks to get his agreement to what will be represented as a consequence he will find disconcerting.

Here, then, is how Socrates begins to pursue the question of what help or resources are relevant for the relevant self-protection (509c–d):

SOCRATES: Of the two, then – acting unjustly and being treated unjustly – we are saying that acting unjustly is a greater evil, and being treated unjustly is a lesser. What form of self-help, then, could a person equip himself with so as to have both these forms of protection – against acting unjustly and against being treated unjustly? Is it power or will he needs? Let me put it like this: will he avoid being treated unjustly if he *wants* not to be treated unjustly, or if he equips himself with some power (*dunamis*) of not being treated unjustly?
CALLICLES: Clearly the second – if he equips himself with some power.

'We are saying that acting unjustly is a greater evil, and being treated unjustly is a lesser.' In Socrates' previous speech, it was '*I* take the view that this is how things are.' And that was in a context in which his personal stance in philosophy was what was being stressed (*egô* and its related adjective occur emphatically no fewer than twelve times in the preceding sixteen lines of text: 508d–509a). Presumably the 'we' (but this is an unemphatic 'we') indicates that Socrates is proceeding here as though Callicles' agreement to what he had said there was not merely to the general proposition about the need for help against harm, but to identification of committing injustice as what constitutes the greatest harm.

However, what he then goes on to put to Callicles is a question about the kind of self-help needed to stave off both acting unjustly and being treated unjustly: Is it power or will? And interestingly – at this point, we begin to sense the development of a Socratic tactic for keeping Callicles not merely talking, but genuinely engaged – the version of the question for which he specifically invites a response from him relates to being treated unjustly. That is to say, he takes first the case that in Callicles' scheme of things it does indeed represent a very great danger, although a lesser one than committing injustice as Socrates himself sees it. So, of course, Callicles has no difficulty in continuing to cooperate, and to answer that the resource one needs is power.

Socrates can accordingly continue the questioning (509d–e):

> And what about acting unjustly? Is it just a question of not wanting to act unjustly? Will that be enough – he won't act unjustly – or is there a need in this case too to equip himself with some power and expertise (*tekhnê*), because if he doesn't learn them and put them into practice, he will act unjustly? That's the question I need you to answer, Callicles. Do you think the agreement Polus and I were driven to earlier in the discussion was correct, when we agreed that no-one acts unjustly on purpose, but that all those who act unjustly do so unwillingly?

Callicles' response to this question demonstrates that he is after all very far from having come round to Socrates' thinking about the evil of committing injustice. He indicates that he is prepared to say 'Yes', but only to assist completion of the argument, not because that is what he really thinks (510a):

> It may as well be, Socrates, if you like. Just so you can finish the argument.

Socrates is prepared to accept the answer as agreement enough. He continues (510a):

> It looks, then, as if here too we do need to equip ourselves with some power and some expertise – to stop us acting unjustly.

Callicles assents – 'We certainly do.' – but presumably once more to enable completion of the argument, rather than out of conviction.

With the next shift in the questioning, however, Socrates moves the discussion right back towards prime Calliclean territory – and Callicles is delighted (510a–b):

SOCRATES: In which case, what *is* the expertise that equips people with the power of not being treated unjustly at all – or as little as possible? See if you think as I do. This is what I think it is: I think a person needs to be either ruler himself – or even tyrant – in his city, or else a close associate (*hetairos*) of the existing regime.
CALLICLES: Do you see, Socrates, how ready I am to give praise when you get something right? I think what you've just said puts it quite admirably.

By now we may not be surprised that in raising this question about the requisite power to provide needed resource against harm, Socrates first takes the case – being untreated unjustly – for which Callicles may be expected to be truly keen to find an answer. What, however, might come as a shock is the suggested answer that Socrates has volunteered, and not least the insertion in it of the elaboration 'or even tyrant'. The idea that tyrants are those who have great power was earlier the line Polus took – quite mistakenly, as Socrates argued (e.g. 466a–e). And a little further on in this exchange with Callicles, he indicates once again that he for his part distances himself from that notion: 'as you and your lot would argue it' (510e).

But Socrates' stance is perhaps more complex than one might on that basis infer. The issue most immediately at stake in that part of the Polus conversation was whether a tyrant who puts someone to death demonstrates in doing so the power to do what he really wants – to achieve something good – rather than what he merely pleases. That was what Socrates contested. Yet if a tyrant (or anybody else) had the power to *protect himself* or others from being subject to injustice, the same line of argument could not easily be used to deny that that was at least a power of some significance. Nor would Socrates have similar motivation to argue that it was not. He had agreed earlier in the conversation with Polus (469c) that he himself would not want to be treated unjustly (but would rather that than act unjustly). And at the latest stage of that discussion, where he was arguing paradoxically for not bringing enemies to justice, he had inserted the rider 'provided we are not ourselves being unjustly treated by our enemy' (480e). In truth there is nothing that is intrinsically 'tyrannical' in the power to protect against injustice, even if it was thought characteristic of tyrants to surround themselves with bodyguards (*Rep.* 8.566b).

Nonetheless, in reintroducing the tyrant into the conversation, Socrates is undoubtedly shifting discussion into territory that Callicles might be expected to find more appealing than much other Socratic talk. No wonder that Callicles makes in response his most enthusiastic answer in the entire dialogue. Why the resort to this argumentative expedient? Precisely because Socrates needs to find a premise Callicles is truly happy to embrace, consistently with the fundamental beliefs about power he articulated in his long speech (especially at 483a–484c), which can then be exploited to drive him at last into something like genuine confession of the inadequacy of his entire stance.

Socrates starts the process of trying to achieve just that by developing next at some length what we may think of as the highly significant *assimilation* thesis, first in general terms (510b–d):

SOCRATES: Very well. Then see if you think I'm right about something else as well. I think one person is most a friend to another when it's a case, as wise men of old say, of 'like to like'. Don't you think so too?
CALLICLES: I do.
SOCRATES: So where a tyrant is a savage and uncivilised ruler, if there were someone in the city much better than him, would the tyrant presumably fear him, and be incapable of ever becoming friends wholeheartedly with him?
CALLICLES: That is so.
SOCRATES: And even if there were someone much inferior, this person couldn't be his friend either. The tyrant would despise him. He'd never be able to take him seriously as a friend.
CALLICLES: That's true as well.
SOCRATES: The only friend left worth speaking of, then, for a person like this, is someone of the same character as himself, someone who condemns and approves the same things – but is prepared to be ruled and submit to the ruler. This person will have great power in this city, this person no-one will treat unjustly without regretting it. Isn't that how it is?
CALLICLES: Yes.

Then Socrates applies the thesis to the likes of Callicles himself (510d–e):

SOCRATES: In which case, suppose one of the young men in this city were to wonder: 'In what way could I have great power and make sure nobody treats me unjustly?' There is a way for him, it seems, which is to accustom himself, from an early age, to have the same likes and dislikes as the despot, and take appropriate steps to become as like him as possible. Isn't that how it is?
CALLICLES: Yes.
SOCRATES: So for this person, the goal of not being treated unjustly and having great power in the city – as you and your lot would argue it – will surely have been accomplished.
CALLICLES: Indeed it will.

The intention to exhibit the *ad hominem* attractions of this scenario for his interlocutor could not be underlined more clearly.

The assimilation thesis is eventually going to prove crucial for the attempt to undermine Callicles' conviction that friendship with the tyrant or other ruler will afford a person with the power to protect himself against unjust treatment. And that (not the commission of injustice, which is what of course concerns Socrates himself more) has remained the focus throughout the present stretch of argument. It is therefore important that Callicles is represented as entertaining no qualms whatever about the thesis. One might wonder whether he might have objected that only the appearance of assimilation is needed for such friendship. That is a possibility Socrates will envisage being raised as an objection later on in this section of the dialogue (513b) and will be discussed at the appropriate point below (p. 88). One might also wonder whether it is being too easily taken for granted that the security friendship is assumed to bring can be treated as unqualified? What if the ruler or tyrant ultimately turns on his friend (before the friend turns on the tyrant)? Socrates will indeed exploit something akin to that possibility in due course (515e–516e). However, perhaps Plato calculates that it will seldom be a possibility sufficient to deter those hungry for power from cultivating friendship with the ruler, even if – as would be likely enough – such eventualities occur to them. The security of the friendship is simply the hypothesis they will act upon, to protect themselves from injustice as best they can at the hands of others.

So it is understandable if Callicles is represented as content with the reasoning he is presented with. But by now we might almost have forgotten that the question of the help needed to secure ourselves against great evils was originally raised by Socrates in the context of reiteration of his own claim that the greatest of all evils is *committing* injustice. Now he returns to that topic of acting unjustly (510e–511c):

SOCRATES: And not acting unjustly as well? Far from it, if he's going to be like the ruler, assuming an unjust one, and exercise great power alongside him. No, I think it'll be just the opposite. He will so equip himself as to be able to do as much injustice as possible, and not pay the penalty for it when he does act unjustly. Yes?
CALLICLES: It looks that way.
SOCRATES: So the greatest evil will be his, maimed in soul and in a bad way as he is, through his imitation of the despot and the power it gives him.
CALLICLES: I don't know how you keep twisting the argument, Socrates – turning it upside down. Don't you realise that this person who does imitate the tyrant

will, if he feels like it, put the person who doesn't imitate him to death, and confiscate his possessions?

SOCRATES: Yes, I do realise that, my worthy Callicles. I'm not deaf. I've heard it enough times today from you and Polus – and from pretty well everybody else in the city. Now it's time for you to listen to me. Yes, he will put him to death, if he feels like it, but it will be someone bad putting a fine, upstanding individual to death.

CALLICLES: Isn't that what's so upsetting about it?

SOCRATES: Not if you look at it sensibly, as the argument shows. Do you think a person needs to equip himself for this: to stay alive as long as possible, practising those skills which always preserve us from danger – like the rhetoric which you instruct me to practise because it keeps us safe in the law courts?

CALLICLES: Yes, very sound advice too, for goodness' sake.

This is another rich and richly indicative passage.

First of all, we should notice that Socrates now makes clear – if that was not already clear – the distance between his own position and the idea of friendship with a tyrant as supplying the power we need to stave off the greatest evils. As James Doyle points out, his initial suggestion in this argumentative sequence effectively implies that 'if you are bent on avoiding suffering injustice, you must ally yourself with evil' – or at least it does if your conception of power is a tyrannical one.[7] Callicles' response – 'It looks that way (φαίνεται)' – sounds as though we are meant to think this turn in the conversation takes him somewhat by surprise. The impression is reinforced by his next reply: the accusation that Socrates is 'twisting the argument'.

What prompts that further reply is Socrates' use next of the most forceful vocabulary at his disposal. The assertion that if someone equips himself with the ability to commit as much injustice as possible, and to get away with it, then 'the greatest evil will be his, maimed in soul and in a bad way as he is', is strong meat. In expressing himself in such terms, Socrates reverts not only to the position he had eventually argued in the conversation with Polus (to Callicles' violent indignation), but to language reminiscent of the Polus episode too: for example, his talk there of a soul that is 'rotten' (479b), or again 'festering and incurable' (480b).

When Callicles then accuses Socrates of 'twisting the argument' and 'turning it upside down', his further comment indicates – in the vein Polus had worked before him (470c–471e) – that he has no problem with the thought that the tyrant's imitator and friend will be prepared to commit

---

[7] Doyle 2006: 98.

murderous injustice against someone who is not such an imitator and friend, and (presumably) that he will prosper that way. He for his part makes clear his continuing disbelief that any sane person could rate committing injustice a worse evil than being put to death and having one's property sequestered.

Perhaps the most interesting element in the exchange is Socrates' subsequent observation: 'Yes, he will put him to death, if he feels like it, but *it will be someone bad putting a fine, upstanding individual to death*', and the way Callicles replies: 'Isn't that what's so upsetting about it?' His talk of someone 'bad' (*ponêros*) putting to death a 'fine, upstanding individual' (*kalos kagathos*) interestingly combines his own characteristic vocabulary with language Callicles is himself happy to use. 'Bad' (*ponêros*) once more calls the Polus conversation to mind. Socrates had there (477b–e; cf. 470e) identified injustice as what above all makes for 'badness of soul' (*psukhês ponêria*). It is presumably on that identification that he relies in calling 'bad' the person who equips himself with the ability to commit as much injustice as possible. *Kalos kagathos*, on the other hand, is an expression Callicles uses (not in general Socrates himself in this dialogue) in talking of the aristocratic ideal to which he aspires (484d), and indeed as something for which Socratic philosophy cannot equip a person.

So at this point, Socrates is switching into a form of words that Callicles might well find resonating with his own scheme of values. Terry Irwin[8] appositely draws attention to a passage, again in the Polus conversation (470e), where Socrates contrasts someone who is *kalos kagathos*, and as such happy, with the 'unjust and bad (*ponêros*)' person, whom he calls 'wretched'. Socrates would presumably there intend *kalos kagathos* to imply a Socratic ideal of virtue,[9] whether or not he means it to convey its usual aristocratic connotations.[10] But Polus can take it simply in that latter sense. He has just introduced a mention of Archelaus, ruler of Macedon. And when he responds to Socrates' contrasts, it quickly becomes clear that an aristocratic *kalos kagathos* is very far from what he takes Archelaus, the duplicitous and ruthless son of a slave, to be (471a–c).

What should we make of Callicles' reaction: 'Isn't that what's so upsetting about it?'? Dodds comments: 'We need not (with Ast and Stallbaum) construe this as malicious mockery; Callicles feels genuine *eunoia* [good will] (487a3) towards Socrates and the Socratic man, however mistaken he

---

[8] Irwin 1979: 230.   [9] So Dodds 1959: 242–3, in an excellent note.
[10] Dodds (1959: 242–3) says that 'Socrates deliberately excludes the social meaning here' (and at 515a, also cited). But how would Polus be meant to know or accept that? I find Socrates' dialectical tactics in these contexts rather more ambiguous than does Dodds.

thinks them.'¹¹ I think it more likely that what disturbs Callicles is the thought that an aristocratic *kalos kagathos* might be the victim of the injustice of the tyrant or his friend.¹² In his responses to Socrates' probing, he had earlier taken the view that the 'better' are the 'more powerful' (488b–489d, with further subsequent clarifications). But when Socrates introduces the idea of two sorts of rhetoric – one designed simply to flatter people and indulge their desires, the other to make them better citizens – Callicles has no difficulty in accepting it and suggests Themistocles, Pericles, and others as practitioners of the second type (502d–503d). Clearly this is a different way of thinking about 'better' than one which predicates it only of the powerful.

Moreover, earlier in this very sequence of argument he has had no qualms about agreeing to consider the case Socrates puts to him of someone 'much better' than a 'savage and uncivilised ruler', and therefore no realistic candidate for his friendship (510b–c). The earlier equivalence between 'better' and 'more powerful' begins to show its colours, as something extorted from Callicles under dialectical pressure, but not fully representing the rather contradictory set of values he actually seems to hold. There is much of the traditional civic-minded aristocrat about him. So he can perhaps see as real possibility the prospect that such an admirable person might be victimized by a despot, or by the friend of a despot. And he owns that this is indeed an upsetting thought. I would suppose that he does make the remark in a sarcastic spirit (*contra* Dodds): 'Of course, Socrates. The point all along has been that we "fine, upstanding individuals" do need to be in a position to wield power ourselves if we are to defend ourselves against being unjustly treated.'

So Socrates' comment in response to the charge that he is 'twisting' the argument does not begin to shift Callicles from his position. The turn it took was meant to start focusing on the 'bad' person who commits injustice. What concerns Callicles, however, remains the harm sustained by the person unjustly treated. And right to the end of the dialogue, he will continue to prove impervious to Socrates' suggestion that he should take the 'sensible' view: by which, I take it, is meant the view that being treated unjustly is not nearly such a bad thing as committing injustice, as indicated by what 'the argument shows' (the argument developed at 474c–475e, in the Polus conversation, already referred to just previously at 508c–509a). But by adopting what I have supposed

---

¹¹ Dodds 1959: 346. His construal of Callicles' comment here perhaps better fits the similar but not quite identical exchange at 521b–c.
¹² So Irwin 1979: 230–1.

to be Callicles-speak at this point ('fine, upstanding individual' – further telling use of related Calliclean talk of the real 'man' will shortly be made: 512d–e), Socrates succeeds once again in keeping him engaged in the conversation.

Security

In one sense, Socrates has so far achieved very little in the dialectic since Callicles decided to rejoin the conversation. On the central issue of what the greatest harm is that a person can suffer, they remain as far apart as ever they were. On the other hand, the introduction of the issue of how one should avoid getting into the shameful position of being unable to secure oneself against harm has certainly succeeded in tempting Callicles back into re-engagement with Socrates. He is particularly pleased with the return to a preoccupation with power. And there is one key proposition he is prepared to accept: the assimilation thesis. But once the conversation shifted to the issue of committing injustice, any hope of further convergence of view disappeared.

Callicles' latest response – avowing some distress at the prospect of some 'fine, upstanding individual' being unjustly put to death – gives Socrates an opening for taking discussion back to the issue of self-protection, which is where his questioning has so far been most productive. He says (511b–c):

SOCRATES: Not if you look at it sensibly, as the argument shows. Do you think a person needs to equip himself for this: to stay alive as long as possible, practising those skills which always preserve us from danger – like the rhetoric which you instruct me to practise because it keeps us safe in the law courts?
CALLICLES: Yes, very sound advice too, for goodness' sake.

Socrates' initial remark ('as the argument shows') refers back to the Polus section of the dialogue, on whether acting unjustly or being treated unjustly is worse (474c–475e) and recalled by him just before Callicles reenters the discussion (508c–509a) as 'arguments made of iron and adamant'. But he now changes tack: to consider the general question of techniques needed to ensure self-preservation. When Callicles is challenged outright as to whether what he attaches importance to is the acquisition and practice of life-preserving skills, such as the rhetoric of the law courts that he encouraged Socrates to take seriously in his great speech (485e–486d), he gives a robust positive answer. That triggers the following brief exchange (511c):

SOCRATES: Is it really, sir? And what about knowing how to swim? Are you equally impressed by that as a branch of knowledge?
CALLICLES: Oh, for heaven's sake! Of course not.

At this point, Socrates adopts a further change of tack: not in subject matter, as in the extracts of text just quoted, but in mode of argument. He reacts to Callicles' enthusiasm for rhetoric by launching into an extended torrent of rhetoric himself. He starts by comparing in familiar style the view we take of generally recognized life-saving skills, such as those commanded by helmsmen, the makers of siege engines, and doctors. These are all very well in their way, although if the helmsman gets you safely to port that will not be of much significance, if the life you then go on to lead is not worth living. Experts such as these are aware of the limited scope of their skills, and for that reason give themselves no great airs. Here is what Socrates ends up saying about the makers of siege engines (512c–d):

> When you call him a maker of engines, it's by way of disparagement. You wouldn't be prepared to give your daughter to his son in marriage, nor would *you* take his daughter for your son. And yet, given your reasons for praising your own accomplishments, what justification do you have for looking down on the maker of engines and the other people I mentioned just now? I know you would say you are a better man, and of better family. Yet if better is not what I say it is, but virtue and human excellence come down to just this – preserving oneself and one's possessions, whatever kind of person one may in fact be – then it becomes absurd, your finding fault with the maker of engines and the doctor and all the other arts and sciences (*tekhnai*) which have been developed with a view to keeping us safe.

And he now invites Callicles to consider a different point of view, appealing to that conception of the real 'man' Callicles himself had etched in his portrait of the ideal of the 'fine, upstanding' individual (512d–513a; cf. 483b, 484d):

> Would you deign to consider whether the noble and the good may not be something other than keeping safe and being kept safe? Maybe this is something – living for a particular length of time – which the real man should forget about, and maybe he should not be too devoted to life, but trusting to god in these matters, and believing the old wives' tale that nobody can escape his destiny, should on that basis decide how he can best live whatever time is given him to live – and whether it is by assimilating himself so far as possible to the political system in force where he is living?

It is the final question appended to this longish sentence that crystallizes the challenge to Callicles that Socrates is throwing down. Is the prospect of security through assimilation to the ruling power really what is consistent with his talk of the real 'man', and with a conception of the best way to live that measures up to that? It is the sort of question that might already have been prompted by Callicles' passionate opening speech (482c–486d), in which he advocates successively shattering and overriding law and convention, but then working within them, in each case as what someone who wants a realistic strategy for protecting himself against injustice will do.[13]

Assimilation with the *Dêmos*

But Socrates has not yet dropped his bombshell. That is delivered in the next sequence of remarks that he makes. Here, Socrates points out that assimilation to the Athenian *dêmos* is what Callicles must embrace if, committed to the assimilation thesis as he has expressed himself, he is to cultivate the prevailing local power (513a):[14]

> But in that case you should now be making yourself as much like the Athenian *dêmos* as you can, if you are going to endear yourself to it and have great power in the city. See if that is in your best interests and mine. Heavens, we don't want what they say happens to those who draw down the moon – the women of Thessaly – to happen to us. We don't want our choice of this degree of power in the city to cost us the things that are dearest to us.

This is a personal address to Callicles in which Socrates includes himself too, I suppose attempting a human gesture of friendship towards and solidarity with him. Presumably he does so as someone who himself sets great store by independence from the way the mass of people behave and think: an address quite different in style from the impersonal generalities about the real 'man' in the immediately preceding passage. The unspoken thought behind it is an assumption on Socrates' part, that when Callicles earlier subscribed to the assimilation thesis, it never occurred to him that the ruling power there discussed in general terms might in practice have to count as the *dêmos*, in the case relevant to his own situation.

He now tries to pre-empt any attempt that Callicles might now make to argue that he could obtain the power he wants without assimilation to the *dêmos* as the city's ruler (513a–c):

> But if you think that anyone in the world is going to pass on to you some expertise of the kind which will make it so that you have great power in this city – whether for better or for worse – without assimilating yourself to its political system, then in my view, Callicles, you are making a big mistake.

---

[13] See Woolf 2000.
[14] I make a stronger break than do Dodds or the OCT between the clause beginning here ('But in that case') and the question that closes the previous extract. Socrates now switches from considering an issue articulated in general terms, initially by use of impersonal verbs before introducing third person locutions, to addressing Callicles directly in the second person, and soon including himself in the considerations he puts to him.

It's not just a question of mimicking these people. You have to be like them in your very nature, if you are to make any real progress towards friendship with the Athenian *dêmos*[15] – or in heaven's name with the son of Pyrilampes, come to that. That's why it's the person who will make you most like these people – that's the person who will make you into a politician and rhetorician in the way you want to be a politician. All groups of people take pleasure in speeches that conform to their own ethos, and are offended by an ethos that isn't theirs.

Why will only real assimilation to the *dêmos*, not the pretence or aping of it, produce the political relationship with them that Callicles or any aspiring Athenian politician desires?[16] It is easy enough to conceive of a general argument which would deliver this conclusion: for example, that those who pretend assimilation to a tyrant must already like him have an overpowering appetite for power, leading them to make the pretence – which shows that it is no mere pretence.

Socrates offers a general consideration of a different but similar kind, with its focus on rhetoric making it particularly relevant to politics in Athens. In effect, he is suggesting that what counts there is the pleasure people take in the political oratory they hear (one of the dialogue's major themes, of course), and that crucial to that is the ethos or – as Dodds explains it – the 'spirit'[17] which informs the rhetoric. Ethos or spirit is evidently taken to be something that cannot easily be simulated and then sustained, whether in politics or indeed in love (as the emphatic reference to the son of Pyrilampes, recapitulating Socrates' initial salvo on the subject of Callicles' affections (481d), is designed to remind us). The implication is that, given an Athenian political context, assimilation to the ruler or 'the existing regime' (510a) must mean becoming like 'the weak and the many' that Callicles despises (483b), the more convincingly and authentically so if one has accustomed oneself 'from an early age to have the same likes and dislikes' (510d) – but at the cost of 'the things that are dearest to us' (513a).[18]

---

[15] Kamtekar 2005 constitutes a sustained examination of what for a politician functioning like Callicles in the Athenian democracy friendship with the *dêmos* should be taken to consist in. What should be noted, however, is that in the present context the idea of friendship with the *dêmos* is introduced without further elaboration simply as an instance of the general notion of friendship with a ruler or despot: where it is represented as involving accustoming oneself 'from an early age, to have the same likes and dislikes as the despot, and take appropriate steps to resemble him as closely as possible' (510d).
[16] Kamtekar 2005: 330–4 supplies an interesting discussion of this question.   [17] Dodds 1959: 351.
[18] As Irwin 1979: 232–3 points out, the interpretation of the dynamics of democratic politics that Socrates suggests here is further developed in the *Republic*, in which the *dêmos*, not the politician, is in the driving seat: see in particular *Rep.* 6.493a–c.

Socrates now seeks a response from Callicles (513c–d):

SOCRATES: Or do you disagree, dear friend? Do we have any answer to this, Callicles?
CALLICLES: In a way I can't put my finger on, that is well said, I think, Socrates. But I still feel what most people feel: I'm not being entirely persuaded by you.[19]
SOCRATES: That's because you have the love of the *dêmos* in your soul, Callicles. That's what I'm up against. But if we examine these same questions often enough, and in a better way, you will be persuaded.

Callicles is not made to say what in Socrates' long speech he finds attractive, nor why he is not entirely persuaded. But it is probably safe to suppose that he is not impervious to the suggestion that a real 'man' will have higher aspirations than simply staying alive. After all, the ideal he articulated in his advocacy of 'natural' justice was of the right of those possessing superior intelligence and courage to exercise mastery over the weak (483a–485a). What is disconcerting him, and leaving him not yet convinced, must surely be meant to be Socrates' 'bombshell': the concluding argument that for an Athenian politician the *dêmos* is the ruler to whom he has to assimilate himself. This is of course the first time that the generalities of the assimilation thesis – where the ruler or the 'existing regime', when discussed in more specific terms, has so far been imagined as a tyrant or despot – have been applied specifically to Athens and to the pursuit of power in the Athenian democracy. While it is one thing to uphold the assimilation thesis with enthusiasm, as specifying a key general condition for acquiring power and so security, it is quite another to think through and accept the implications of its application to politics in Athens. Socrates catches Callicles unawares, unprepared for the idea that the successful Athenian politician must have assimilated himself to the *dêmos*.

That is certainly the interpretation that Plato has Socrates put on his response: 'That's because you have the love of the demos in your soul, Callicles.'[20] In other words, the diagnosis is not in the first instance of any more purely intellectual slowness. Blindness to what is in front of his nose

---

[19] 'I'm not being entirely persuaded by you': so most translators. But Schofield and Griffith 2010: 97 have 'I simply don't believe you'. Either rendering of the Platonic Greek might be possible. But 'not entirely' appears to be correct in most contexts, and the usual rendering fits better with Callicles' first statement.

[20] This *erôs* for the *dêmos* has little affinity with the tyrannical *erôs* driving every kind of lawless desire that governs the behaviour of the tyrannical kind of individual described in Book 9 of the *Republic* (9.572d–575a). Of course, by the time Socrates has pressed Callicles on the psychology of the naturally superior man presented in his initial outburst at 482c–486d, that turns out (491e–494c) to be not far removed from the *Republic*'s *erôs turannos*. But what emerges in the later stretch of

must be put down to something else. *Erôs* has to be the explanation. Presumably the suggestion is that Callicles is so infatuated that he cannot see that, for all his talk of the real 'man', he is already assimilated to the ethos of the *dêmos*, to its likes and dislikes.[21] And with it, Plato connects with a theme in Athenian political discourse given most memorable articulation in surviving Greek literature in Aristophanes' *Knights*. There, as Victoria Wohl explores in an exemplary study, Cleon (in the guise of a Paphlagonian slave) presents himself as lover (*erastês*) of the *dêmos*, personified as his master Demos (*Knights* 732): 'Pericles' noble "love of the polis" becomes, in Cleon's debased enactment, political prostitution.'[22]

We now start to appreciate Plato's rationale in launching Socrates' entire conversation with Callicles with a passage on their parallel twin love affairs. For himself, he said, it is with Alcibiades[23] and philosophy,[24] for Callicles the *dêmos* and the son of Pyrilampes. Here are the relevant comments he made on Callicles' behaviour and mental state (481d–482a):

> I notice that, clever as you are, it's the same every time. Whatever your darlings say, however they say things are, you have no power to oppose them, but keep changing your ground this way and that. In the assembly, if you say something and the Athenian *demos* disagrees, you change your ground and say what it wishes; and with the son of Pyrilampes, that beautiful young man, the same kind of thing happens to you. You are incapable of resisting the proposals and arguments of your darlings, with the result that, if anyone were ever to express surprise at the absurdity of what they are getting you to say on any particular occasion, you would probably say – if you wanted to tell the truth – that unless someone makes your darling give up this way of talking, then you won't ever stop saying these things either.

---

dialogue that concerns us is the gulf between Callicles' professed ideals and ambitions and the reality of the *erôs* for the *dêmos* that actually drives him.

[21] Ober 1998: 208 rightly says: 'This is a pregnant moment, and perhaps the most optimistic in the dialogue.' Much more doubtful is his further comment: 'Callicles has, at least momentarily, come to realize that he is infected with a certain "illness" and the source of his illness is "the many" – the very demos he has been taught to try to imitate, even to the point of losing his individual identity and voice.' As I read the exchange, and particularly Callicles' confession that in a way he cannot quite put his finger on, he finds what Socrates has argued 'well said, I think', he is represented as being very far from precise in any application he might make of it to self-understanding.

[22] Wohl 2002: 75. Readers of her chapter '*Pornos* of the people' (Wohl 2002: 73–123) will find multiple anticipations of the *Gorgias*' treatment of democratic rhetoric in the material on Cleon from Aristophanes and Thucydides that she discusses.

[23] Whom Socrates, in the first of the *Alcibiades* dialogues attributed to Plato, fears will be corrupted by becoming an *erastês* of the *dêmos*: see *Alc. i* 132a, with discussion in Wohl 2002: 124–70.

[24] For reflections prompted by the *Gorgias* on what Plato might there (and subsequently in the *Republic*) take the role of *erôs* in developing philosophical understanding to be, see Woolf 2000: 24–40.

Callicles' Choice

So, once again, there is argumentative success and failure: Socrates has retained Callicles' participation in discussion. But Callicles has not been persuaded away from the stances he has adopted throughout. Socrates sees no way of moving him on except by 'more and better arguments' about these same questions – which (he says) *will* persuade him (513c–d). The reader might find such Socratic confidence in the power of reasoning over-optimistic. Logic does not often cut much ice with the infatuated. However, as we shall be seeing shortly, in this instance it does obtain some degree of further success by the end of the long concluding stretch of the conversation now continued by Socrates and Callicles (513d–522d). To anticipate: the considerations Socrates will here put to Callicles do in the event succeed in getting him to see and understand his *erôs* for the *dêmos* for the humiliating servility it really adds up to – but he will fail to talk him out of the commitments and behaviour that have been given momentum by that *erôs*.[25]

Socrates' talk of 'more and better arguments' is the cue for a first instalment of further reasoning. In what follows, Socrates approaches the same issues from a different angle, which is indicated in his opening sally (513d):

> Anyway, remember how we said the activities that are directed to looking after each of these things – body and soul – were two in number. We said that one of them approaches its object with a view to pleasure, the other with a view to what is best, not indulging it but battling with it. Weren't those the definitions we laid down earlier?

Callicles had agreed previously to this distinction, albeit only to 'get your argument here completed, and do Gorgias here a favour' (501b–c); he now confirms that that was so. There follows an attempt to get him to reflect upon what is his conception of *political* activity, and whether he is equipped to engage in it, initially by the usual Socratic method of analogy with other activities of public significance, such as a public building project. Despite some reluctance to volunteer a view on Callicles' part,

---

[25] I hope this distinction helps to meet a pertinent question put by the reviewer for *Philosophie antique*: whether that *erôs* for the *dêmos* 'renders fruitless every attempt Socrates makes to persuade Callicles of the incoherence of his position' ('rend vaine toute tentative de Socrate pour persuader Calliclès de l'incohérence de sa position'). See further p. 93 below, and my remarks in the final section, 'Conclusion'.

he eventually reiterates his earlier opinion that there have been politicians in Athens who were good citizens and 'made the citizens better rather than worse': Pericles, Cimon, Miltiades, and Themistocles – for whom he shows sustained admiration (515c–d; cf. 503b–c, 517a–b).

This is the proposition Socrates now attacks, in an extraordinary passage mingling philosophical considerations put to Callicles with extended rhetorical denunciation (acknowledged as 'real demagoguery' by Socrates himself: 519d) of the statesmen he has singled out for their achievement of good for the city. They did *not* succeed in making the citizens better; and in the end, the people turned upon each and every one of them. Those who say they made the city great do not realize that 'the city is now a swollen, festering sore because of those figures of the past' (518e–519a). In fact, they were no better than Sophists, who similarly claim to be teachers of human goodness, but then incongruously and illogically accuse their pupils of injustice and ingratitude when they do not pay their fees or otherwise express their appreciation of their teachers. Callicles agrees that he has nothing but contempt for such illogicality on the part of such practitioners; and he agrees that the sign of a truly good practitioner is that the person who is well treated by him wants to do good in return (519e–521a).

So Socrates is now ready to put the crucial question to him: what is the right way to care for the city? Is it 'battling with the Athenians to make them as good as possible'? Or it becoming their 'servant' and trying to please them? He invites Callicles to speak 'well and nobly'. What is the response?

CALLICLES: I say the one that involves becoming their servant.
SOCRATES: Nobly spoken! So you invite me to become a sycophant – a flatterer!

And Callicles – through gritted teeth – agrees (521a–b).

Socrates has still not achieved the persuasion he hoped 'more and better arguments' would have achieved. Nonetheless he has made progress. He has not attempted to orient the reasoning to get more decisive recognition from Callicles that the assimilation thesis applies to the situation of a power-hungry politician in Athens as much as it does under tyranny – although Callicles' final response suggests that he does now recognize just that. What the argument has instead taken as its basis is indeed something 'better': an articulation of a more elevated conception of politics, contrasted with the politics of gratification. Callicles is represented as exhibiting not a little attraction to this conception; and Socrates' use of the vocabulary of nobility in that final exchange is presumably an attempt to indicate that this notion of politics is the conception that marries more readily with the vision of a true man articulated in his original statement of his ideals. When in response Callicles explicitly couches his reply in terms of the thoroughly demeaning alternative: 'becoming their servant', this represents all but explicit acknowledgement that the *dêmos*, not the real 'man', will be master. He must now be aware that there is something incoherent and conflicted at the core of his whole outlook, as Socrates had predicted at the start of their encounter (482b).

The conversation continues (521b–d):

CALLICLES: Otherwise...
SOCRATES: Don't tell me what you've told me over and over again – that anybody who wants to will put me to death. I don't want to have to say again that it will be a question of an evil man putting to death a good man. And don't say he will confiscate whatever I possess. That will save me saying: 'Well, when he's confiscated it he won't have any good use for it. Just as he confiscated it from me unjustly, so, once he has taken it, he will use it unjustly. And if unjustly, then disgracefully. And if disgracefully, then badly.'
CALLICLES: You really do seem confident, Socrates, that none of these things will happen to you. As if living a quiet life means you couldn't be dragged off to court, probably by someone utterly worthless and contemptible.
SOCRATES: Then I really am an idiot, Callicles, if I don't realise that in this city anything can happen to anybody. One thing I do know, and that is that if I go to court, to face one of these dangers you are talking about, the one bringing me there will be an evil man – no decent person would take somebody who was not acting unjustly to court – and it would be no great surprise if I were put to death. Do you want me to tell you why that is what I expect?

And with that, Socrates introduces his famous comparison with what would happen to a doctor prosecuted by a chef before a jury of children.

For his part, Callicles wavers not a moment from his conviction that having no power to protect oneself from injustice is the worst thing that could happen to someone (522d). And when Socrates indicates that he will tell a myth to spell out the consequences of acting unjustly that will be visited upon perpetrators after death, he makes it clear that as far as he is concerned the conversation, one-sided as he now represents it, is – finally – over (522e):

CALLICLES: Well, you've worked your way through the rest of the discussion, so you'd better work your way through this too.

Conclusion

'Socrates and Callicles cannot in the end make dialectical contact', says James Doyle, articulating a not uncommon assessment.[26] I hope this chapter will have done something to show that the situation is not in fact what that verdict might suggest. On the reading of the last section of conversation between the two protagonists offered here, these pages of the *Gorgias* emerge as something else. They are an attempt by Plato to show just why and how Socrates might successfully engage intellectually with an intelligent young politician hoping to rise within the Athenian democracy, such as Callicles is portrayed as being. All communication between them had broken down at 506c (effectively a page earlier, at 505c). But at 509c, Callicles re-enters the conversation when Socrates returns to the question of how we best protect ourselves against the greatest evils. That is territory he is willing to explore jointly with Socrates – or, in other words, to allow Socrates to question him about. On some things, they find a measure of agreement, on others not. At more than one point, Socrates abandons dialectic for rhetoric, in his efforts to persuade Callicles to look at things differently from the way he is predisposed to do. In general, however, there is no radical failure of mutual comprehension.

At one juncture, it is true, where Socrates spells out what he takes to be the implications of the assimilation thesis in the context of the Athenian democracy for a politician wanting to cultivate the friendship of the ruling power, Callicles is in effect made to confess that he neither fully understands nor is altogether persuaded by Socrates' line of thought (513c). *Erôs* for the *dêmos* is Socrates' immediate diagnosis: Callicles is blinded by the way the likes and dislikes of the *dêmos*, reinforced by his rhetorical training, have already shaped his soul. His affections have clouded his ability to grasp reality. Yet after several more pages of Socratic talk in more than one mode, he does take the point he could not quite grasp there: he bites the bullet and gives it as his view that good politics and good citizenship have to be a matter of flattering and gratifying the city's ruling power (521a–b).

So there is no ultimate failure of intellectual communication between them, at least in any basic sense. Plato does not represent the intelligent Athenian democratic politician as 'unable to take part in the same discussion'[27] with Socrates. What prompts Callicles to tell Socrates to finish things off himself, when after all Socrates is not actually inviting him to engage in further conversation, is something else. Callicles is now

[26] Doyle 2006: 96–7. [27] Doyle 2006: 97.

absolutely clear that, despite their best efforts, he and Socrates will never find enough agreement on what they value most to make further conversation worthwhile. That is a matter of what Plato wants us to understand as different fundamental commitments, not of mutual incomprehension, nor even of incompatible intellectual styles.

CHAPTER 5

Likeness and Likenesses in the Parmenides

That doesn't make any sense. But Parmenides, the way above all it clearly looks to *me* is like this: these Forms stand like models (*paradeigmata*) in nature, and the other things are similar to them and are likenesses; and this participation for the other things in the Forms turns out to be nothing other than being modelled upon them.

(*Parmenides* 132c12–d4)

Introduction

Ever since Gregory Vlastos's epoch-making article of 1954, Plato's *Parmenides* has meant – for most scholars and philosophers – just one thing: the Third Man regress argument (TMA). This was the effect chiefly, as I judge, of three distinct but intimately connected features of the article.[1]

First was its attempt to spell out the logical structure of the argument with much greater precision and explicitness than had ever been done before, or than was then customary in the analysis of Platonic arguments. The attempt was not wholly successful from a technical point of view, which is what led Geach, Sellars, Strang, Cohen, and others to contribute to a large and at its best distinguished literature on the TMA. But the quality of Vlastos's concentrated attention on the logic of this one short argument clearly did succeed in persuading his readers that Plato had produced a powerful and elegant instrument of criticism – couched in the form of an infinite regress, 'the prize product of Greek logical virtuosity' – which merited the most careful and ingenious study by contemporary logicians and logically sophisticated philosophers.

Second, in uncovering the principles which govern the regress – the One over Many principle and the Self-Predication and Non-Identity assumptions – Vlastos exposed the metaphysical foundations of one of

[1] Vlastos 1954.

the most celebrated of all philosophical theories with exemplary simplicity and economy, and then diagnosed an intriguing contradiction between them.² The TMA proved to be as fascinating a piece of metaphysics as of logic.

Finally, and perhaps most memorably of all, Vlastos presented the Plato who created the TMA as a figure of heroic proportions. In his well-known phrase, the *Parmenides* constituted 'a record of honest perplexity'. On his view, the text has to be read as not just the exploration of a philosophical problem, but (in Charles Kahn's terminology) the transparent disclosure of a quandary in the author's own mind.³ A great theory-builder confesses that he has discovered a flaw in his theoretical beliefs which he can neither pinpoint exactly nor decisively rebut – for the principles which generate the regress were not, on Vlastos's account, apparent to Plato himself. 'It is rare enough', said Vlastos, 'to find a philosopher employing his best resources to construct an argument which, were it valid, would have destroyed the logical foundations of his life's work.' Even more unusual and surprising is Plato's way of dealing with the difficulty. According to Vlastos's assessment, he makes no attempt to dispose of it, as he could easily have done by drawing distinctions as obvious to him as to us, but prefers to put on record his more deep-seated disquiet: 'the philosopher ris[es] far above the limitations of his philosophy'.

Every great achievement is won at the expense of something. As I reflect upon the view of the *Parmenides* to be offered in the present chapter, I am struck by its emphasis on something almost wholly absent in Vlastos's article and in much of the work it inspired, not just on the Third Man regress but on Platonic argument more generally – for in some quarters the study of Plato became for a good long time the study of his arguments. What governs the line of thought developed here is reflection on the *Parmenides* as a Platonic *dialogue*. I have in mind a whole range of considerations. A Platonic dialogue is a text, often steeped in intertextual resonances, particularly echoes or pre-echoes of other Platonic dialogues on which it may be commenting retrospectively or prospectively. A Platonic dialogue is the dramatic representation of a conversation between interlocutors, none of whom can be assumed to be merely spokesman for Plato's

---

² It was, of course, from the subsequent controversy that designation of 'the first step of the Argument' (Vlastos's (A1)) as *the* or *a* One over Many principle emerged. Vlastos's proposal of a direct contradiction between the Self-Predication and Non-Identity assumptions was heavily criticized, some finding no actual incompatibilities in the three assumptions at all, Vlastos himself eventually claiming that they constitute an inconsistent triad (see Vlastos 1969).

³ For the term of art 'transparency', see Kahn 1988a: 46; the idea recurs in Kahn 1988b: 82.

own views, any more than in any other form of drama. In such a text, unresolved disagreements or puzzles cannot necessarily be assumed to reflect unresolved tensions in Plato's own mind. A Platonic dialogue says as much in the structure of its conversations and in the themes it pursues through a variety of transformations as in its discrete individual arguments. A Platonic dialogue is a game played between Plato and the reader designed to baffle as much as to elicit interpretation, and thereby to provoke us to philosophy on our own account.

These observations about the Platonic dialogue are by now commonplace. I mention them principally to indicate the methodological assumptions which lie behind the reading of the *Parmenides* to be offered here. Its focus is – once again – the Third Man argument. However, I shall be preoccupied not with the initial version of the TMA presented at 132a–b, which has always had the lion's share of scholarly attention, but with the second version at 132c–133a. Is this regress a transparent disclosure of *aporia*? We cannot presume so.[4] To work out what Plato is doing in having Parmenides construct the argument, we need to see it in its context within the dialogue – which means not just its place in the critique of the Forms, but its relationship to a number of other passages in both parts of the *Parmenides*.[5] My contention will be that these contexts supply the reader with materials for resisting the regress. I put this down to Plato's perspicacity, not mine.

The section of the dialogue from 130 to 134 is commonly represented simply as a sequence of devastating or apparently devastating critical arguments against the theory of Forms. Proclus sees it as a carefully organized piece of philosophical midwifery in which Parmenides gradually coaxes Socrates into progressively less deficient apprehension of the nature of Forms and of their relations to particulars.[6] I shall follow him at least to the extent of taking Socrates' proposal of the original–copy model of participation to be intended as a significant achievement prompted by reflection on the inadequacies of the previous attempts in the dialogue to

---

[4] It is, accordingly, the third component of Vlastos's account of the *Parmenides* which I shall, in effect, be attacking. As Max Cresswell put it in a comment on the first draft of this chapter: 'If I understand you right you say that the dialogue doesn't read like a record of "honest perplexity". I'd go further and say that "honest perplexity" is *never* an attribute of Plato's writing. I think he's a very sneaky writer, and often subordinates substance to effect.'

[5] Thus, the chapter can be read as applying to a passage in the first part of the *Parmenides* the approach to reading the second part advocated in Owen's seminal paper: Owen 1986: 85–103.

[6] Proclus' richly rewarding account of the dialogue has now been made accessible as never before in the translation of Morrow and Dillon 1987, from which I quote below.

formulate the theory.[7] The next section of the chapter will present the case for this interpretation.

A reader might accept that the movement of the text does, indeed, prompt a sense of the original–copy model as a 'significant achievement'. But can it survive the regress argument levelled against the model? Subsequent sections of the chapter attempt an answer to this question. First, there is a discussion of this regress in which it is argued – against a common interpretation – that what it generates is an infinity of Forms of Likeness. The following section notes the pervasively thematic role assigned to the concept of likeness throughout the dialogue and suggests that its treatment in Part II in particular indicates a way in which the Platonist can save his Platonism from the regress. There is then a final reflection on the idea of a Platonism without a paradigmatic Form of Likeness.

The Original–Copy Model of Participation in Its Context

Parmenides' examination of the participation relation posited by the theory of Forms occupies the stretch of text from 130c to 133a. For our purposes, it is best regarded as divided into the following subsections:

(A1) The dilemma of whole and part, including Socrates' attempt to defuse it (131a–e).
(A2) The first version of the Third Man argument (132a–b)
(B) Socrates' suggestion that Forms are thoughts, and its immediate refutation (132b–c)
(C) Socrates' proposal that Forms are models or originals and particulars likenesses of them, together with Parmenides' attempt to refute it by the second version of the Third Man (132c–133a)

There is nothing particularly controversial in splitting the material up in this kind of way, but my rationale for it is more distinctive. It relates to Socrates' role in the conversation. In general, he is a docile interlocutor, but on just three occasions he volunteers suggestions. In each case, the immediate aim is to evade difficulties (or rather, as I shall argue, one and the same difficulty) raised by Parmenides. Despite this reactive function, each of the

---

[7] Here, there is an analogy with, for example, the successive attempts to account for false belief at *Theaetetus* 189–200, and with the demands that that passage makes on the philosophical resources of the reader, well brought out by Burnyeat 1990. I am much indebted to the idea that Burnyeat elaborates of the resistance of a Platonic text to interpretation (as opposed to creative philosophical engagement).

proposals constitutes a positive hypothesis about Forms and their relations to particulars: the day analogy (A1: 131b3–6); the idea that Forms are thoughts (B: 132b3–6); and the original–copy model of participation (C: 132c12–d4). Moreover, the three hypotheses exhibit a progression in both style and substance. First a tentative comparison, then a general idea, finally a fully fledged theory of participation, confidently advanced. At one extreme, the day analogy attempts to save an immanentist conception of participation in Forms, which makes them properties of particulars. At the other, the original–copy model makes Forms transcendent blueprints on which particulars are somehow dependent. I note in passing that it is only Parmenides with his formula of a 'one over many' – first introduced in his sail analogy of 131b7–9 and then reinstated in the first version of the Third Man (A2: note especially 132a11–b1) – who is clearly construing Forms as individuals comparable with particulars, or ὁμοταγεῖς, 'of like order', 'of the same category', as Proclus puts it (in Prm. 891.36; cf. 886.15–887.3).

This map of 130e–133b requires explication and defence. So the rest of this section offers as economical a sketch of the way that the conversation develops between Parmenides and Socrates as will serve to recommend the thesis that the original–copy model introduced in (C) is to be read as a definite achievement on the part of the dialogue.

The whole–part dilemma with which the section begins has sometimes been taken to be the outcome of a crude materialist interpretation of the Forms,[8] perhaps adopted for *ad hominem* purposes against Eudoxus' immanentist version of the theory.[9] Neither component of this interpretation is convincing. Eudoxus' ideas may be in the offing,[10] but the reason why Parmenides begins his critique of the concept of participation in Forms by attacking the assumption that they are immanent in particulars lies closer to hand. The theory, as just presented in the text, distinguishes between F-ness itself and the F-ness we have (130b1–4) – what the *Phaedo* calls F-ness in us (*Phd.* 102d–103b). Parmenides is presumably made to assume the point of this distinction to be that F-ness in us or the F-ness we have simply *is* F-ness itself *as participated in*.[11] To put the same point another way, the whole–part dilemma of 131a–e reasonably supposes that

---

[8] So e.g. Cornford 1939: 85.   [9] So e.g. Cherniss 1944: app. VII, esp. 536.
[10] The possibility is left open in the properly sceptical discussion of the issue by Dancy 1991: 20–3; cf. 35–8.
[11] This corresponds to a common but controversial reading of the account of the relation of Forms to particulars in the *Phaedo*: both in the passage where Socrates mentions 'presence or sharing (*koinônia*)' of the Forms as possible specifications of the relation (100d3–8) and in his subsequent talk of 'the F-ness in us' (102d7; cf. 102e6, 103b5). See Fine 1986: 73–9. I am much indebted to this article.

Forms when participated in are (by 130b1–4) properties that we have immanent in us (131a8, b1–2, b5–6, c6–7).[12] Once that supposition is made, it becomes the obvious and pressing question to ask whether a participated Form is not, one way or another, pluralized by the particulars which all have it immanent in them. What is more, this is precisely the kind of question that one would expect to trouble an Eleatic monist: there is no reason to think that Parmenides is now subscribing – even *argumenti causa* – to materialism.

The first of Socrates' three proposals about Forms and particulars comes early on in (A1), at 131b3–6. Parmenides has put the dilemma: if x participates in a Form F-ness, is the whole of F-ness in x or only a part of it? He has argued that, on the whole option, the Form as a whole will be in each of its participants, and so will fail to be a unity. All of it will be in participant x, but all of it will also be in participant y – but, since x is separate from y, the Form too will be separate from itself. Socrates' reply offers the analogy of a day: a unity (not, I think, a whole) which is in many separate places *without* being separate from itself, that is, without forfeiting its unity.

Scholars have found the analogy obscure: day*time* or day*light*? They have also divided on its merits. Some have thought it a hopeless evasion of Parmenides' line of argument, exposed as such by the rival sail analogy which Parmenides at once substitutes for it (131b7–9). Others have seen it as a promising move, which does something to free our minds from the rigidity of Parmenides' whole–part alternatives. Suppose that what Socrates had in mind was day*time*. Then the point is that it is one and the same daytime (e.g. twelve noon) simultaneously in Cape Town and Budapest; and we reject as inappropriate the question: do both Cape Town and Budapest have the whole of it separate from itself? So construed, the day analogy neatly sidesteps Parmenides' line of reasoning by calling its whole–part framework into question.[13] But Plato cannot or does not work it out further, perhaps because it only promises escape from the dilemma by leaving obscure whether the assumption of immanentism is really maintained. So in the end immanentism is represented as successfully impaled on the dilemma's horns.

Sidestepping is also the strategy which appears to inform the second suggestion that Socrates volunteers, at the beginning of (B). The conclusion of the first version of the Third Man is the proposition (132b1–2):

> No longer, then, will each of your Forms be one, but they will each be infinite in number.

---

[12] See Fine 1986: 79–87.   [13] So Allen 1983: 147.

Perhaps prompted by the reference to the soul surveying Largeness and other large things at 132a6–7, Socrates responds (132b3–6):

> But Parmenides . . . perhaps thought is what each of these Forms is, and it is not appropriate for it to come in any other place than in souls. In this way each would remain one, and would no longer be subject to the consequences which were just now being spelled out.

Parmenides proceeds to criticize this proposal, with arguments generally regarded as varied in their success (132b7–c11).

Is Socrates' suggestion intended as a *rejoinder* to the Third Man argument? So it has sometimes been taken, as by Proclus long ago (*in Prm.* 891.33–40) and in R. E. Allen's commentary.[14] On this reading, Socrates has to be seen as attacking the assumption of the Third Man that Forms and particulars can be ranked together, that is, as belonging to one and the same group of *F* items. His point will be that if Forms are thoughts, the assumption becomes untenable.

This interpretation is unattractive. It is unclear why the TMA's assumption *must* fall just because Forms are thoughts. We would need a supplementary line of argument: if the Form *F*-ness is a thought, either it cannot itself be *F* or it must be *F* in such a different sense from that in which other things are *F* that it and they could not be *F* in virtue of the same explanans. There is no sign of such a train of thought in the offing. Instead, Socrates elaborates the proposal with considerations about *where* Forms are to be found – which seems irrelevant to the issue the Allen interpretation wants him to be concerned with.

In fact, the proposal does not relate to the Third Man argument at all, even though it is occasioned by the bringing of the Third Man to a conclusion. As Cornford evidently saw, it looks back to the whole–part dilemma of (A1).[15] Socrates tries to tell us as much by referring to the consequences 'which were just now being spelled out' (132b6) – not the ones Parmenides is presently pressing. In other words, the suggestion that Forms are thoughts aims to save the unity of the Form not from the infinite reduplication of the TMA, but from the division from itself or into parts argued in the whole–part dilemma. Given that this is its purpose, Socrates' insistence that thoughts are nowhere except in souls is entirely appropriate. The dilemma had taken it that Forms when participated in will be *in* particulars whether as wholes or as parts. So Socrates looks as though he

---

[14] Allen 1983: 147.
[15] Cornford 1939: 90–1. This, too, is an idea espoused by Proclus, *in Prm.* 891.40–892.2.

might be able to escape it by proving that they are not in particulars, only in souls. For if they are not in particulars, it follows that they will not be in them either as wholes or as parts, and hence that their unity will not be threatened by the different kinds of division which the whole–part options entail. Once again, Socrates attempts to sidestep Parmenides' dilemma, though coming closer to a direct challenge to its assumptions.

Parmenides has two lines of reply. The first (132b7–c8) is to argue that a thought must have an object, which is going to turn out to be precisely the Form as originally conceived, a one over many. Here, he echoes the formulation in the Third Man argument. This might be construed as indicating that, after all, Socrates *was* meaning to react directly to the Third Man. I take it that Parmenides' point is, rather, the following: Socrates' suggestion that a Form is a thought must be regarded as no more than a diversion; once it is analysed, we are left with that very conception of a Form which invited the Third Man argument in the first place. In other words, Socrates needs to address the regress, not to change the subject back to the 'in' that prompted the whole–part dilemma.

Parmenides' second complaint is that Socrates' proposal leaves the notion of participation in the Form problematical. Particulars will have to *consist* of thoughts (presumably as immanent properties), but then either all particulars will think or there will be thoughts that do not think. This way of putting the complaint (132c9–11) has not found much favour with the commentators, but the complaint itself seems highly plausible. It is, of course, the question which occasions Socrates' third and final attempt at the beginning of (C) to volunteer a contribution of his own to the discussion (132c12–d4). The original–copy model of the relation between Forms and particulars is explicitly presented to him as an account of the nature of the participation relation, that is, of the topic initially considered in (A1). Why should Socrates think of it as an improvement on any such account offered so far? Because – I submit – once again it undermines the whole–part dilemma by revoking the assumption on which it is based, while avoiding the difficulties which the suggestion made in (B) encountered.

If what it is for x to participate in F-*ness* is for it to be *modelled upon* F-*ness*, there is no reason to think that F-*ness* will thereby belong to x or be a property of x. It is not, in general, the case that models are properties of their copies, nor originals of their derivatives. Moreover, if the Forms stand *in nature*, as the original–copy proposal has it, they cannot be immanent in particulars. So, on this new picture of participation, the whole–part dilemma just does not arise, originating as it does from the immanentist conception of participation. Socrates does not say outright that the new picture is non-immanent. Plato presumably thought the point too obvious to spell out.

With the original–copy model, we have at last arrived – for the first time in the course of Parmenides' critique – at a properly articulated thesis about Forms volunteered by Socrates. It is presented as Socrates' own preferred opinion, not as merely a possibility which has just occurred to him, as in the first two cases in which he ventures suggestions. I quote Proclus' eloquent observations on this point (*in Prm.* 906.37–907.22):

> He has placed so much confidence in this argument, that, whereas he had formerly sworn that it was no easy thing to define the nature of this participation and how the Forms come to be in sensibles [cf. 131e6–7], now he says that 'it appears to him very likely' that this is the method of participation, and by his use of the phrases 'very likely' and 'plainly appears' (*kataphainesthai*) rather than simply 'appears' (*phainesthai*), he shows that he is especially confident about this theory. He has arrived at this position both through his own intellectual acuity, and through Parmenides' faculty for bringing to fruition his spontaneous notions about divine things. This makes it plain that the method of these discussions is midwifely, not contentious; for otherwise Parmenides would not have caused his interlocutor to make progress and to grow always more perfect in his concepts. For the end result of 'midwifery' is the eliciting of the thought hidden within the interlocutor, but of a verbal contest victory over the opponent and the reduction of him to complete perplexity. If, then, Socrates rises to new heights on the head of each problem raised, and perfects and articulates his ideas about the primal Forms, it must be said that he is having his ideas brought to birth by Parmenides rather than being overthrown, and that this action is performed for his improvement rather than his defeat.[16]

The Second Regress

This account of the status and point of the original–copy proposal at 132c–d would not command much credence if there were reason to think that the regress argument Parmenides goes on to deploy against it was regarded by Plato as unanswerable, either absolutely or at any rate given the logical resources he currently had at his disposal. Vlastos, of course, argued that Plato did lack the requisite resources: he could not identify the implicit assumptions of Self-Predication and Non-Identity which drive the Third

---

[16] In its general approach, my reading of the development of the argumentation of 130e–132c has similarities with that advanced by Turnbull 1989.

Man – hence his 'honest perplexity'. There has been general agreement ever since then, however, that the two assumptions are entirely obvious; that they are all but spelled out by Plato himself; and that he could not have constructed the regress in the first place if he had been unaware of them. So far as I am aware, no subsequent scholar addressing the argument has accepted Vlastos's claim that, at the time he wrote the *Parmenides*, Plato *could* not have seen ways of offering legitimate resistance to the TMA. I shall argue that there is in fact reason to believe that in the second part of the dialogue he supplies the materials for resistance. I shall argue that he has given such prominence in the first part to the notion of likeness (on which the second regress turns) as to nudge us into noticing their availability for the purpose.

I have been speaking of '*the* TMA'. But the second regress, the version of the argument specifically directed against the original–copy model of participation, is, as we shall now see, significantly different from the first, which has been the main focus of analysis from Vlastos on. To begin the demonstration of this thesis I set out a translation of the passage (132d1–133a7):

(1) These Forms stand like models in nature, and the other things are similar to them and are likenesses; and this participation for the other things in the Forms turns out to be nothing other than being modelled upon them.

(2) If, then, he said, something is similar to the Form, can that Form fail to be like what is modelled upon it, to the extent that it is made a likeness of it? Is there any device by which what is like something can be like something not like it?
   No.

(3) Surely there is great necessity that of two like things the one should participate in one and the same Form[17] as the other?
   It is necessary.

(4) But given that there is something such that by participating in it like things are like, will not that be the Form itself?
   Absolutely.

(5) Then it is not possible for anything to be like the Form, nor the Form like anything else. Otherwise, always alongside the Form another Form will be appearing, and if *that* is like something, another one again; and it will never fail to be the case that there is always a fresh Form turning up, if the Form turns out to be like what participates in it.
   What you say is true.

---

[17] I retain the MSS reading εἴδους, excised in the OCT and Budé edition. The issue is discussed below pp. 107–110.

(6) Then it is not by likeness that the other things participate in the Forms, but we must seek for something else by which they participate. It appears so.[18]

A first and crucial problem in the interpretation of the second TMA is the issue of the identity of the regress of Forms that it claims to generate. Apply the general Socratic thesis about Forms as models enunciated in (1) to the case of Beauty. Is Parmenides arguing that, by repetition of the assumptions he specifies, a potentially infinite set of Forms of *Beauty* is generated (the standard view)? Or is it his argument that there will always be a fresh Form of *Likeness* turning up (my own position)? On the standard interpretation, the second TMA is essentially a form of the first TMA. On the alternative view, it constitutes a marked shift in the focus of Parmenides' attack, away from the primary hypothesis of the theory of Forms (target of the TMA) back to the explanatory apparatus introduced to account for the relation between Forms once hypothesized and the items which participate in them (as in (A1) and (B)). It turns out to be a close relative of Bradley's regress, according to which there must always be a further relation to relate any relation to its terms. This feature of the alternative reading is itself an argument in its favour: *ceteris paribus*, one would expect something novel in the second TMA; and concentration on the likeness relation seems a more appropriately pointed response to the main thrust of Socrates' proposal of the original–copy conception of participation.

The standard view is shared by scholars who otherwise agree on very little, such as G. E. L. Owen in a celebrated article on the *Timaeus* and Harold Cherniss in his riposte.[19] As Owen expresses it: 'Parmenides has no trouble in proving that, if participation in some character *A* is to be construed as resemblance to some *paradeigma* [model] in respect of *A*, then, since resemblance is symmetrical, both *paradeigma* and *homoiôma* [likeness] must exhibit *A* and hence *ex hypothesi* resemble a further *paradeigma* in that respect. And so on, in regress.'[20] Cherniss would question only the prefatory claim that this is a successful proof: he accepts that it is what Parmenides means to prove. Thus, to take again the case of Beauty, on this

---

[18] M. M. McCabe pointed out to me that ἀεί (132e7) is apparently illogical. 'Always ... another Form will be appearing' would be fine if we were to take it as implicitly general: another Form will appear, and then another, and so on. But the next clause – 'and if *that* is like something, another one again' – undercuts a generalizing interpretation. I wonder whether ἀεί might govern the whole sequence 'alongside the Form ... another one again', and I have placed 'always' accordingly in the translation. But perhaps Parmenides starts off in generalizing vein, and then, with 'and if *that* ... ', changes tack to specify the steps of the regress in a recursive formulation. Excision of ἀεί would remove the difficulty, but it is probably best to acknowledge a harmless illogicality.

[19] Owen 1953; Cherniss 1957. [20] Owen 1953: 82.

reading step (5) of the argument will begin by referring back to (2), and will be saying that we had better *not* say, as (2) did, that beautiful things are like Beauty and Beauty like beautiful things. For if we do, then by virtue of the considerations adduced under (3) and (4), we shall have to posit another Form of Beauty besides the original Beauty – a third man. As Owen's account brings out clearly enough, the standard interpretation requires us to take (3) and (4) as providing that things that are like each other *in respect of A* (in the present case, *beauty*) must participate in the Form *A-ness* (in the present case, *Beauty*). Once this requirement of the interpretation is accepted, then a regress of Forms of Beauty does indeed follow, given an appropriate version of the Non-Identity assumption. That is, the Form of Beauty in which the original Form of Beauty and beautiful things participate in virtue of their likeness in respect of beauty must be another Form of Beauty than the original; self-participation in excluded as playing no part in the interpretation's explanation of the likeness.

The chief obstacle in the way of this standard interpretation is step (4) of the passage. It presents at least three serious difficulties. First, it appears to be redundant. What Parmenides needs to generate a regress of Forms of Beauty is a version of the One over Many principle which can then be applied to a plurality consisting of beautiful items including the Form or Forms of Beauty. But such a principle is precisely supplied or implied by (3). (4) adds nothing required to secure the conclusion.

One way of avoiding this embarrassment was tentatively proposed by Henry Jackson in 1882.[21] He suggested deleting the word εἴδους at 132e1, so that (3) would run 'participate in one and the same [something]'. The emendation has been extraordinarily popular. It was adopted by Burnet in the Oxford Classical Text and Diès in the Budé edition but has since been jettisoned in the Hackett one-volume translation of Plato – so may well be heading for a less popular future.[22] The advantage of Jackson's proposal is that Parmenides is then to be seen as in effect moving to the One over Many principle in two stages: (3) makes it more explicit than it would be with the manuscript reading that any two like things must be like in respect of something common to them – presumably a common character; (4) then states that participation in a common character requires postulation of a Form corresponding to that character, replicating the similar move at 132a2–4 in the first version of the Third Man argument.

---

[21] Jackson 1882: 291 n. 1.
[22] The Hackett translation (1997) reproduces that first published by Gill and Ryan 1996 (Gill argues at pp. 44–5 for retention of εἴδους, citing the present essay in support).

With the standard interpretation, the attractions of excising εἴδους appear to have obscured the attendant implausibility of the excision. What (3) so emended retains firmly entrenched in the proposition it enunciates is the expression μετέχειν, 'participate' (132e1). Jackson's proposal requires 'participate' to function as a metaphysically unloaded word signifying 'have in common'. But only half-a-dozen lines above (in (1)), 'participation' is treated as the familiar technical term used by Socrates to characterize the relation of particulars to Forms (132d3: 'this participation' – i.e. the participation first introduced into the discussion back at 129a and under debate since 130e). And, of course, the whole point of Socrates' intervention in (1) is to advance a thesis about how participation, so conceived, should be understood. At the end of the regress, Parmenides' conclusion (6) is that they will have to find some other account of what participation (μεταλαμβάνειν) in Forms is, given the difficulties that the argument has brought to light in Socrates' suggestion. In short, there is an obvious sense in which participation as a relation in which *F* items stand to a Form *F-ness* is *the* topic of the second TMA. In these circumstances, it is simply improbable that Parmenides should use the word 'participate' on just one occasion (in (3)) with the reduced metaphysical commitments envisaged in Jackson's proposal – without warning, and without any flagging of the exceptional switch in usage involved, even if in less technical contexts Plato might do something similar with apparent nonchalance.[23]

A second problem for the standard view is the interpretation it must give to the expression 'the Form itself' in (4) (132c4). What is the force of 'itself'? Presumably the point is to stress that, where two or more items are like in respect of *F*, it is participation in the very Form of *F-ness* which explains the likeness – that is, just such a Form as (1) envisages in its proposal about participation. But if that is the rationale of 'itself', the choice of the word is at best infelicitous. As becomes clear at once in (5), if it is not already apparent from (2), the items to which Parmenides will initially be applying the principle formulated in (4) are the *F*s (in virtue of their likeness to *F-ness*) *and F-ness* (in virtue of its likeness to the *F*s). The implication of 'itself' in 'the Form itself' will then be that what explains the likeness *F-ness* has to the *F*s is participation in *itself*. Yet, of course, (5) assumes

---

[23] A similar criticism applies yet more strongly to those who want to avoid substantial metaphysical commitments in (3) but to retain εἴδους as meaning here not 'Form' but nothing more than 'thing' or 'character': e.g. Cherniss 1957: 253 n. 114. In a context such as *Parmenides* 129–35, where εἴδη as Forms are the principal topic, and where every other instance of εἶδος means 'Form', Cherniss's proposal is simply bizarre.

Non-Identity, and (like the first TMA, 132a10–b1), makes the explanans '*another* Form', 'a *fresh* Form', and so on.

But the principal objection to the treatment of (4) in the standard interpretation is its basic supposition that by 'the Form itself' Parmenides means not the Form Likeness, but the form F-ness corresponding to the feature F in respect of which like things are like. When in (4) Parmenides asks whether the 'something such that by participating in it like things are like' is not 'the Form itself', he seems to be echoing Socrates' own formulations from earlier in the discussion. Socrates' very first introduction of the Forms in the dialogue consists in the hypothesis of Forms of Likeness and Unlikeness (128e6–129a2), followed by remarks about participation in them which culminate in the general formula (129a4–5) 'the things which participate in Likeness become like in this way [*sc.* by participation in it] and to the extent that they participate in it'. Similarly, Parmenides launches his critique of the idea of participation with the summary statement (130e5–131a2): 'In your view, as you say, there are certain Forms, such that by participation in them these things carry names derived from theirs, e.g. things become like by participation in Likeness, large by participation in Largeness, just and beautiful by participation in Justice and Beauty.' Given this background, it seems unlikely that 'the Form itself' is to be understood otherwise than as 'the Form Likeness', itself picking up 'likeness' in the first part of the sentence. There is a heavy burden of proof on proponents of any other interpretation to show how the reader can be supposed to cancel the expectations built up by earlier statements about what makes like things like, especially as these statements do not just occur in passing remarks, but are prominently placed at key junctures in the exposition of Socrates' theory.

The standard view, then, has great difficulties – in my judgement fatal – in offering an adequate account of (4). The only real remedy at its disposal would be wholescale excision of 132e3–5, that is, the lines translated in (4). It would have to be supposed that these lines were inserted by an intelligent but misguided reader of (3), puzzled by the reference intended in 'participation in one and the same Form' at 132d9–e1. Lines 132e3–5 might have been added to make it clear that the Form in question (or if εἴδους at 132e1 is deleted, the thing participated in) has to be the Form of Likeness. If so, the insertion will have been misconceived, according to the standard view.

Any such excision, however, would plainly be an expedient of desperation. It is not a subsequent reader but Plato himself who writes (4) into his argument, to make it crystal clear that 'the one and the same Form' referred to in (3) is precisely 'the Form itself' of Likeness. Having introduced the

Form of Likeness – he must have thought as explicitly as was needed – Plato then has Parmenides develop the regress in (5). It begins with the sentence (132e6–7) 'Then it is not possible for anything to be like the Form, nor the Form like anything else.' 'The Form' is now naturally taken as 'the Form Likeness', introduced at the end of (4). Parmenides' point will be this: we have so far, up to the end of (4), got perfectly good reason to introduce (a) some likes (namely, particular *F*s and corresponding original Form *F*-ness), and (b) the Form Likeness, but we must not let (a) and (b) resemble each other. Why not? The answer is given in the rest of (5), 132e7–133a3: if we do, there will be a regress of Forms of Likeness. To explain resemblances of (a) likes and (b) Likeness, we will need another Form of Likeness. And so on *ad infinitum*.[24]

Of course, it is not open to Socrates to avoid the regress by agreeing that (as Parmenides suggests at 132e6–7) (a) likes and (b) Likeness do *not* resemble each other. From the thesis he advanced in (1), it straightforwardly follows that the participation relation in which (a) likes stand to (b) Likeness *is* (133a5, in (6)), or more accurately (132d1–6, in (1)) entails resemblance. (a) and (b) *have* to resemble each other, given the original–copy thesis of (1) together with the point about the symmetry of resemblance made in (2). Thus the regress may be presented as turning on the following premises (where NI is the assumption of Non-Identity):

(I) Like things are like in virtue of being modelled on an original, Likeness.
(II) Copies and original are like each other.
(NI) Nothing can be like by being modelled upon itself.

These three premises suffice to generate the conclusion:

(III) Likeness and other like things are like in virtue of being modelled on their original, Likeness$_2$.

And so by further application of (II) and (NI) *ad infinitum*. The comparison with the first TMA is instructive. (I) could be read as a specific application of the One over Many principle; (II) has the same function in this argument as the nonetheless distinct principle of Self-Predication

---

[24] The only other proponent of this non-standard view of the second TMA I had identified at the time of writing, in admittedly patchy forays into modern scholarly writing on the *Parmenides*, was Allen 1983: 159–60. But although he made some of the main points in favour of it, he thought that the argument is designed to be ambiguous, and to permit *both* readings. The non-standard view as argued here has subsequently met with some favour from scholars, notably by M. L. Gill in Gill and Ryan 1996: 42–5.

performs in the first TMA – and is absolutely explicit: interestingly so, given Vlastos's conviction that the Self-Predication principle was unapparent to Plato.

There are in theory a huge number of different ways in which a reader sympathetic to the thesis about Forms proposed in (1) might attempt to resist Parmenides' regress. The challenge is to identify possibilities which might plausibly be taken to have been favoured by Plato himself.

One suggestion might be that the argument is invalid, that is, that the conclusion does not follow from the premises. There is little future in this idea. Analyses of the Third Man argument have by now been produced (for instance, by Cohen) which show it to be capable of perfectly valid and indeed elegant formal expression.[25] Sometimes, of course, the notion of validity is used rather loosely. Someone might complain that the argument is invalid because it exploits the symmetrical relation likeness, whereas Socrates' original–copy proposal posits an asymmetrical relation between Forms and particulars. To this, the appropriate reply is that, even if the original–copy relation does not *reduce* to the symmetrical likeness relation, does it not *entail* it? If it does (as (II) asserts), then, for all that the objector has shown, the argument is not only valid but reveals very effectively an unacceptable consequence of the original–copy model. If it does not, then what is wrong with the argument is not invalidity but the falsehood of (II).

The thesis that (II) is false – or should be regarded as false by a Platonist – is maintained in a novel way in one of the more interesting contributions to the Third Man debate as it developed. Edward N. Lee argued that Plato's own presentation of the theory of Forms in both the *Phaedo* and the *Timaeus* shows that he would reject the idea that a symmetrical relation of similarity obtains between the Forms and the sensibles they explain. In different publications, he offered different defences of this proposal. In the first instance, Lee maintained that, according to the *Timaeus*, sensible *F*s are treated as mirror images of the Form *F*-ness, reflected in the 'receptacle', not as substantial copies which have being in their own right. He then argued: 'The image is not something which is "like" the original. It is not, for it is not a "something" (not an "it") at all.'[26] This line of argument clearly will not work. My image in the mirror is like me, even if it is not a thing.

At the second attempt, Lee pointed particularly to the equals passage at *Phaedo* 73–4 and noted its implication that particulars are always striving to be such as the Form is, but never achieve that. For Plato, he inferred, the

---

[25] See Cohen 1971. [26] Lee 1966: 363.

image–original relationship characteristic of particulars in their relation to Forms is one of dynamic frustration, not static achievement.[27] From this he concluded (as T. W. Bestor, following his account, put it): '*M can easily be striving to liken itself to N* ("copy") *without ever necessarily managing to possess some characteristics which N possesses* ("be like").'[28] This will not work either. Whatever may be the case with the *Phaedo*, both in Socrates' original–copy proposal at 132c–d and in the *Timaeus* it is assumed that sensibles *have* achieved a degree of likeness to the Form – as the aorist tense *eikasthênai* ('having been modelled' at *Prm.* 132d4) and the very expressions *homoiôma*, *aphomoiôma* ('likeness', *Prm.* 132d3, *Ti.* 51a2) and *mimêma* ('imitation', *Ti.* 48c, 50c, 51b) prove, firmly indicating realisation as they do. Nor in the *Timaeus* is this merely an assumption. *Ti.* 52a5 actually asserts it: 'Second is what has the same name [i.e. as the Form] *and is like it*, sensible, created, etc.'

The more traditional way of denying the second premise, going back to Proclus, *in Prm.* 912.19–38, is to say that likeness is not always a symmetrical relation. In other words, it is not always the case that, if *x* is like *y*, then *y* is also like *x*. It is then argued that while particulars as copies certainly stand in a relation of likeness to Forms as originals, this form of likeness relation is asymmetrical. Different explanations have been given of how we should conceive of this supposedly asymmetrical relation. W. J. Prior holds that 'like' here means 'deficiently like'.[29] But while a Platonist will certainly maintain that sensibles are like Forms but deficiently so, it need not be the word 'like' which expresses the thesis. There is no reason why 'like' should not import a symmetrical relation, leaving 'deficiently' to do all the work of indicating the asymmetry in question. Indeed, this seems the more plausible account of the matter, given that Plato never elsewhere recognizes an asymmetrical sense of 'like' and notably fails to do so in the second part of the *Parmenides*, which otherwise explores all sorts of contrarieties in relative terms.

So a Platonist should accept (II), and its implication that between sensibles as copies and Forms as originals, the symmetrical relation of likeness will obtain. What will need to be questioned is (I), the application of the original–copy model of participation to the case of likes.

Likeness in Parts I and II

At this juncture readers can either keep their eyes and mind fastened on the passage in front of them, or they can let them wander. Letting them wander might be thought irresponsible, particularly if one recalls Parmenides'

---

[27] Lee 1973.   [28] Bestor 1980: 65.   [29] Prior 1985: 73.

strictures on the drifting minds of undiscriminating mortals in fragment 6 of his poem. But in the methodological prescriptions which follow the critique of the Forms, 'wandering' is one of the descriptions applied to the exercise that Parmenides and Zeno paradoxically (in view of fr. 6) recommend (136e2; cf. 135e2). They do so, presumably, in consideration of the benefits to be had from leaving a subject and then returning to it or to a related topic with fresh eyes from a different point of view. In any event, once it strikes readers that in (1), and in the ideas about likes canvassed in (3) and (4) of the text of the regress, they meet a recurrence of one of the pervasive themes of the *Parmenides*, it seems irresponsible *not* to pause and explore its fortunes both earlier and later in the dialogue.

It can hardly be an accident that Plato makes the second regress turn precisely on the concept which formed first the subject of the only Zenonian paradox specifically reported and discussed in the dialogue (127d–e), and then the example with which Socrates introduced the theory of Forms (129a–b) and Parmenides recapitulated it (130b). It is as though Parmenides is now in the second regress made to say: 'Platonism propounds a thesis about likeness which (as it claims) shows Zeno's paradox about like and unlike to be trivial. If that thesis is conjoined with the original–copy model of participation, however, it wrecks the Platonism of which both are elements.'

But Part II of the dialogue has yet more to say about likeness. This should come as no surprise when we note that it is one of three concepts (with one and many) which Parmenides at the outset takes as subjects of relatively fully stated examples of the principles of the hypothetical method that he urges Socrates to practise (136a–c). In the actual demonstration of the method which occupies Part II, consequences relating to likeness and unlikeness are drawn in each of the eight deductions relating to *the one*, sometimes perfunctorily, but mostly at greater or lesser length.

In the first deduction, the relevant stretch of argument goes as follows (139e7–140a5):

> Nor yet will it [i.e. *the one*] be like or unlike anything, neither itself nor another thing.
> Why?
> Because what is qualified (*peponthos*) in the same way is like.
> Yes.
> But sameness was seen to be apart from unity in nature.
> It was.
> Again, if *the one* is qualified in any way apart from being one, it would be qualified in more ways than one, and this is impossible.

Yes.

In no way, then, can *the one* be qualified in the same way as another thing nor itself.

It appears not.

Not even, then, can it be like another or itself.

It seems not.

Much might be said about the way in which this argument and its component moves are supposed to work. But there is only one point on which we need to focus.

This is Parmenides' proposition 'What is qualified in the same way is like', which like previous commentators I take as articulating an analysis of *like*. For 'what is qualified in the same way', it would be tempting to substitute (as less ungainly) 'what has the same attribute or predicate', since that is the notion of being qualified which Plato has in mind. There is an advantage, however, in rendering Plato's verb with an English verb. In this way, we avoid any impression that an *ontology* of attributes or predicates is being explicitly or even tacitly introduced here. To put it in Quinean language, Plato thereby avoids inclusion of attributes within the range of individual variables, and so is able to resist any ontological commitments regarding their metaphysical status. The same treatment of *like* as *being qualified in the same way* recurs in the second, third, and seventh deductions (147c–148d, 158e–159a, 165c).

Fundamental to this treatment is the use of the verbal forms *peponthei* or *peponthos*. The corresponding noun *pathos* is employed in passages dealing with *like* and *unlike*, but always as a shorthand for something more fully expressed by a verbal phrase. For instance (148b1–2): 'But being the same as the other things is the opposite attribute or predicate (*pathos*) to being different from the other things.' Or again at 158e2–159a4:

> Inasmuch as all things are unlimited in their own nature, in this respect they will be qualified in the same way.
>
> Very much so.
>
> Yet inasmuch as they all participate in limit, in this respect too they will all be qualified in the same way.
>
> Yes.
>
> But inasmuch as they are qualified so as to be both limited and unlimited, in being qualified by these attributes or predicates (*pathē*), they are qualified by opposite attributes or predicates.
>
> Yes.
>
> But opposites are maximally unlike.
>
> So?

Then in respect of *each* attribute or predicate, they would be like both themselves and each other, but in respect of *both*, they would be maximally opposite and unlike in both relations.
The conclusion is unavoidable.

It is surely significant that on the first three occasions that the second part of the dialogue asks us to think about likeness and unlikeness, it offers us a treatment or analysis of the predicates *like* and *unlike* which completely dispenses with any reference to the metaphysics of Forms and participation, or indeed to ontology of any sort – even to the point of avoiding the abstract nouns likeness and unlikeness. What Plato is showing us is that we can handle claims that something is like or unlike perfectly adequately by taking them simply as assertions to the effect that something is qualified in the same or a different way. In case we had failed to take the point, he reverts in the fourth deduction to the old analysis in terms of the metaphysics of Forms, so ponderously as to underline in red the contrast between the two sorts of account (159e2–160a3):

> Nor yet are the others, then, like or unlike – neither themselves to *the one*, nor is there likeness and unlikeness among them.[30] For if they themselves were like or unlike or had likeness and unlikeness among themselves, the others would surely have two Forms opposite to each other in themselves.
> It appears so.
> But it proved impossible for things which don't participate even in one thing to participate in two.
> Impossible.
> Then the others are neither like nor unlike nor both. For if they were like *or* unlike, they would participate in *one* thing – one or other of the Forms; if both, then in *two* things – the opposite Forms. But these options appeared to be impossible.
> True.

We should note that *like* and *unlike* are among a very small number of predicates given detailed treatment in this short deduction, so that our elbows get nudged even more firmly than appears from the quotation.

It is time to return to the second regress argument at 132d–133a. Recall premise (I):

(I) Like things are like in virtue of being modelled on an original, Likeness.

---

[30] The 'neither . . . nor' alternative is not entirely perspicuous. I take it that as 'neither . . . ' focuses on likeness and unlikeness of the others to *the one*, 'nor . . . ' applies to themselves. I would therefore incline to amend the MSS ἐν αὐτοῖς (159e3) to ἐν ἑαυτοῖς, as at 159e4, and meaning 'among or between themselves' as there (but ἐν ἑαυτοῖς at 159e5–6 has to be 'in themselves').

I submit that readers of part II of the dialogue will see reason to reject this premise. They have come to appreciate that to understand talk about items being like each other is merely to grasp that they are qualified in the same way, that is, have the same predicate true of them. To put it differently, what readers have effectively recognized is that *like* is a second-order predicate: 'is like' means 'share the same first-order predicate', not 'participates in the Form Likeness'.

Thus Part II of the *Parmenides* supplies materials for resisting the regress; and the presentation of likeness as a theme which we are invited to pursue through both parts alerts us to the fact *that* they are available and are pertinent to the business of evaluating Parmenides' critique of Socrates.

A Final Reflection

It might be granted that Part II of the dialogue gives one reason to reject (I) and so to resist the second version of the TMA. But would someone who took this line still be a Platonist? Is a Platonism without a Form of Likeness – introduced as a focal example in Socrates' original presentation of the theory at 129a–e – really Platonism? There would be little point in trying to save the theory by effectively abandoning it.

The response that one makes to this line of questioning depends, *inter alia*, on whether one supposes that, at the time of writing the *Parmenides* and subsequently, Plato believed that any viable metaphysics would have to be monolithic in its logical structure. Against such a supposition is, for example, the way that he takes pains in later dialogues to differentiate the roles of classes of Forms or concepts which he treats as functionally distinct, in the famous programmatic passages at *Theaetetus* 197d, *Sophist* 253–4, *Philebus* 16–18 for instance. In passages of the *Timaeus* pertinent to our present concerns, the Form of Animal is presented as a *paradeigma* (model), and as such the original of which the sensible *kosmos* is a likeness (*Ti.* 30c–31b). But there is nothing for, and much against, any idea that Being, Same, and Different, although undoubtedly talked of in terms appropriate only to Forms, are similarly to be understood as paradigms conceived in terms of the original–copy model of participation (*Ti.* 35a–b).

So the problem of evaluating the notion of a Platonism without a paradigmatic Form Likeness is part of the more general problem of what happens to Forms or their successor concepts in Plato's later dialogues. If it is conceded that his approach to metaphysics in this period becomes less uniform and more experimental, less like the hedgehog and more like the fox in strategy, then it may be that there is room for the possibility that, for instance, Man, Fire, Water (*Prm.* 130c) end up being conceived as paradigmatic Forms, whereas transcendentals such as like, unlike, same, different, being, one, many (the preoccupation of Part II of the *Parmenides*) are on one ground or another conceived in different terms, whether or not they count as Forms on some other criterion. This might be a Platonism quite different in its focus and explanatory ambitions from that familiar in the middle-period dialogues. It is not prima facie impossible that it could accommodate the conceptual explorations of the transcendentals conducted in the *Sophist* and the second part of the *Parmenides* within the substantive paradigmatist framework outlined in the *Timaeus*, provided that there is no attempt to give the *same* kind of account of, for example, *like* and *animal*.

CHAPTER 6

The Elusiveness of Cratylus in the Cratylus

An Unresolved Quandary

Not far off 150 years ago, Benjamin Jowett began the introduction to his translation of Plato's *Cratylus* with these words:[1]

> The *Cratylus* has always been a source of perplexity to the student of Plato. While in fancy and humour, and perfection of style and metaphysical originality, this dialogue may be ranked with the best of the Platonic writings, there has been an uncertainty about the motive of the piece, which interpreters have hitherto not succeeded in dispelling.

In short, the *Cratylus* was for the Master of Balliol a paradigmatic old chestnut.

Have things changed since he was writing? Certainly the dialogue has been the beneficiary of some superb philosophical scholarship in recent years, with the highlights three major book-length studies of the highest quality from Rachel Barney (2001), David Sedley (2003), and Francesco Ademollo (2011). All these authors in their very different ways are trying to crack one particular version of Jowett's puzzle: is Plato in the *Cratylus* a naturalist (of some sort) or a conventionalist (of some sort) about what makes words the right words for the things they signify? But they give very different answers to the question.

Barney's Plato is a pessimistic naturalist: if a word is to be right for what it is designed to signify, then ideally it should reflect or imitate the nature of that thing – yet in principle no imitation, as he has Socrates argue, can ever be correct 'except in a very limited degree', and an approximation would be 'of no particular use'.[2] Sedley, by contrast, presents us with a more bullish Plato, who sees in the practice of etymology a means of revealing the 'genuine illumination' about things that was cast by early Greek intellectuals in their coinage of the vocabulary of the language. While his Plato will firmly

---

[1] Jowett 1875: 11.163.   [2] Barney 2001: 141.

reject etymology as a route to secure knowledge, it can 'offer us a whole range of decodings which any Platonically attuned reader will recognise as philosophically correct'.[3] Ademollo for his part is prepared to allow that Socrates remains for most of the dialogue (if not all: his stance on that is not sufficiently clear)[4] a naturalist of a kind. But on his account, Plato as author steers the reader from the outset into seeing that words could in principle as in practice only ever count as right for their job by virtue of convention.

One presupposition shared by most participants in this long-running debate, to which Barney, Sedley, and Ademollo are just the latest major contributors, is that Plato himself does adopt a stance of his own in the dialogue, which he communicates to the reader either through the proposals or arguments that he attributes to Socrates (as Barney and Sedley assume) or through the evident weaknesses in the naturalist positions propounded by Socrates and subsequently by Cratylus when he is subjected to Socrates' questioning (as Ademollo thinks). A main challenge for interpreters is then to try and work out exactly what that Platonic stance should be taken to consist in. Their radically divergent attempts to do so may suggest, however, not only how difficult such an interpretative project is, but perhaps also that there is something questionable about the presupposition that underpins it. I agree with Rachel Barney against some of those who have stressed the 'open-ended non-authoritarian character' of the Platonic dialogue that 'the mere fact of being written in dialogue form does not preclude the *Cratylus* from expressing positive arguments for philosophical doctrines – arguments and doctrines which we may legitimately (if not automatically or with certainty) ascribe to Plato himself'.[5] Nonetheless I think it is worth attempting an approach to the dialogue which does not assume that its chief purpose is to communicate its author's own views.

The Puzzling Role of Cratylus

My starting point and indeed my focus in this chapter will be something that earns less comment in those distinguished studies. It is Plato's own starting point. After Cratylus has acquiesced in Hermogenes' suggestion that Socrates join their discussion, Hermogenes makes a report of the position Cratylus has been taking (383a–b):

> This fellow Cratylus, Socrates, says that for each of the things there are there is a correctness of name that is naturally constituted; and that a name is not

---

[3] Sedley 2003: 153, 98.   [4] See Schofield 2013b: 490–1.   [5] Barney 2001: 18.

> whatever some people who have agreed with each other to call a thing call it, applying to it a bit of their own speech.⁶ Instead there is a kind of naturally inherent correctness to the names, the same for all, Greeks and foreigners alike.

He then describes his unsuccessful attempt to get Cratylus to say what he means. He tries him with some proper names. In response Cratylus says his own name truly is 'Cratylus' and Socrates' 'Socrates', but that 'Hermogenes' is not his interlocutor's name – even if that is what people call him. But beyond that Cratylus only toys with him (384a):

> He makes nothing clear and is teasingly coy with me, making out that he does have a meaning in his own mind, claiming to know something which if he were willing to speak clearly he would make me too agree and take the same line as he does himself.

Hermogenes asks Socrates' help: if Socrates can somehow make out what Cratylus' oracular utterance means, he would be pleased to hear it; although he would prefer to know the opinion Socrates himself has on the subject.

Socrates duly takes up the invitation. And for more than forty pages of text, he conducts a conversation just with Hermogenes, which effectively constitutes an elaborately theorized and then comprehensively illustrated account of what he takes Cratylus to have in mind (the attribution of the account of the theory itself to Cratylus becomes explicit as Socrates concludes his exposition: 390d–e). Only in the dialogue's last thirteen pages does Cratylus re-enter the conversation, now as a thoroughly equable and cooperative discussant, to endorse Socrates' whole treatment of the topic, but also to advance some more extreme claims of his own about names, which are then subjected to devastating criticism. So Cratylus' reluctance to say straight out what he means is highlighted on the dialogue's first page and not redeemed until its finale, when he seems to behave quite differently: at once a curious transformation, and a curiously structured piece of writing. Why did Plato write the dialogue that way? Could an answer to that question help us to answer Jowett's puzzle about its motivation? That is the approach to the old problem that I want to explore in this chapter.

An Answer: First Attempt

The most economically speculative answer to the question might run as follows. Plato writes the dialogue because he wants to examine the

---

⁶ Ademollo 2011: 24–5 proposes that *phônê* here should be translated 'voice' rather than 'speech' or 'language'. But Plato needs a reference to some particular language in order to set up the contrast with a correctness that is 'the same for all, Greeks and foreigners alike'.

prospects for a naturalist theory of names developed in distinctively Platonist style – to see just how far he can make it work, and where overambitious claims for its potency would have to be withdrawn. He attributes the basic idea for the theory to Cratylus at the start of the dialogue because he is well aware that Socrates had never proposed any such idea; and it was also useful to be able in its last few pages to represent Cratylus as the over-claiming opponent needed if Socrates is to direct a critique against any inflated ambitions that might be entertained for that theory. But the main ingredients in the theory he constructs are indeed Platonist, notably the treatment of name-making as a *tekhnê* conforming to Socratic ideals of craftsmanship, including appeal to a version of the theory of Forms reminiscent of Book 10 of the *Republic*, and a vastly extended and systematic exercise in the kind of etymologizing Plato engages in *en passant* in many other dialogues, which he here represents not as application of any Socratic method, but as a temporary and perhaps disavowable inspiration that has taken hold of Socrates following conversation with the soothsayer Euthyphro. It is accordingly Socrates who is made to work the theory out, in unchallenging conversation with a compliant member of his intimate circle, Hermogenes. The historical Hermogenes, younger brother of the wealthy Callias (familiar from the *Protagoras*) was present at Socrates' death (*Phd.* 59b), and someone upon whom Xenophon relied for his account of the trial that preceded it (*Apol.* 2–10, *Mem.* 4.8.4–10). His fictional counterpart figures in the *Cratylus* initially as a proponent of an alternative conventionalist view of names. But his main role in the dialogue, sustained over the greater part of its length, is to act as Socrates' collaborative but basically passive interlocutor. There is nothing in either the dialogue or the historical record (such as it is) to indicate that he was an independent intellectual force to be reckoned with.

This rationale for the curious construction of the *Cratylus*, in particular of its restriction of Cratylus' role to initial statement of the basic idea it explores and then to target of its closing critique, can accommodate a variety of interpretations of the philosophical attitude to the naturalist theory that Plato might have been wanting to communicate in the dialogue. It is compatible with either Barney's or Sedley's reading, although perhaps less readily with Ademollo's, for whom a distinction between Socratic and Cratylan versions of naturalism is not easy to draw. Whatever the attractions of such a rationale, however, it suffers from one obvious deficiency. It treats Cratylus as no more than a useful counter on the board of the game of intellectual chess Plato has decided to play in the *Cratylus*. Yet Cratylus is evidently no mere counter. On the dialogue's opening page, Plato puts art and energy into investing Cratylus with colourful oddity.

An Answer: Second Attempt

One thought might be that Plato wants the dialogue to sum up his own personal engagement with Cratylus and his thinking. For Plato's Cratylus had a historical counterpart, who not only espoused a version of Heracliteanism (and Heracliteanism becomes an increasingly important preoccupation of the dialogue as it progresses), but according to Aristotle was on that account a significant figure in Plato's own philosophical development. As such, Cratylus seems to occupy a quite special place among the cast of Socrates' interlocutors with whom Plato populates his dialogues.

Aristotle's key pronouncement on the matter is articulated in the following well-known passage from Book A of the *Metaphysics* (6.987a32–b10):

> In his youth he [Plato] had become familiar first of all with Cratylus and with Heraclitean views to the effect that all perceptible things are always in flux, and there is no knowledge that relates to them. This is a position he later subscribed to in these terms. Socrates, on the other hand, engaged in discussion of ethics, and had nothing to say about the general system of nature. But he was intent on finding out what was universal in this field, and was the first to fix his thinking on definitions. Plato followed him in this, and subscribed to the position that definition relates to something else, and not to the perceptibles – on the kind of grounds indicated: he thought it impossible for there to be a common definition of any of the perceptibles, since they were always changing. Plato, then, called these kinds of realities 'ideas', and claimed that the perceptibles were something in addition to them, and were all spoken of in terms of them – what he said was that, by virtue of participation, the many shared their names with the forms.

In other words, whatever encounters the historical Socrates might or might not have had with the historical Cratylus, that Cratylus according to Aristotle played a major role in Plato's own intellectual formation.

Scholars have often questioned the reliability of Aristotle's testimony. But its basic historicity has been well defended by Sedley, whose arguments and conclusions are with some qualifications endorsed by Ademollo.[7] The sceptics suggest that with his penchant for constructing philosophical genealogies, Aristotle has simply extrapolated an explanation of how Plato came to hold his own theory of knowledge from the ending of the *Cratylus* itself.[8] There, Socrates argues that there can be no knowledge of things in the sort of Heraclitean flux Cratylus sees as the comprehensive truth about the nature of reality: if there were knowledge, it would have to take as its objects entities exempt from such flux like the beautiful itself, which is always such as it is (439b–440e).

There is more reason to reject than to embrace the sceptical take on Aristotle's report. It is certainly plausible that he used these last pages of the dialogue to interpret his biographical information, and to make sense of the way Plato came to use the Heracliteanism he heard from Cratylus. But he knew more about Cratylus than the *Cratylus* discloses, for example that Cratylus ended up thinking that one should say nothing – and that he simply 'used to move his finger', presumably when he did want to communicate. And he reports a no doubt related complaint that Cratylus levelled against Heraclitus: you cannot step into the same river even once (*Metaph.* Γ.4.1010a10–15). Moreover (to repeat a point made earlier in this book), the biographical claim is not required for his main purpose – to explain Plato's motivation for positing Forms; and his highlighting it at the beginning of the passage suggests someone who thinks he has real news to impart.[9]

The closest correspondence between the Cratyluses of Aristotle and of the *Cratylus* is in that commitment of both to a theory of Heraclitean flux. In the *Cratylus*, that theory is construed as a general truth about the whole of reality, whereas Aristotle restricts its scope to the domain of the perceptible. However, there may not be much significance in the difference. The *Theaetetus*, too, presents the theory in similarly universal terms but

---

[7] See Sedley 2003; 16–21, Ademollo 2011: 14–18. Sedley 2003: 17 n. 37 thinks the balance of the evidence suggests that Plato had actually been Cratylus' pupil, but Ademollo 2011: 318 takes the view that 'Cratylus probably had *no* pupils at all', principally on account of the way he is characterized on the first page of the dialogue, together with the claim made in this regard about Heracliteans in general at *Tht.* 180b–c: see further pp. 126–7 below. When Cratylus re-enters the discussion late in the *Cratylus*, Socrates is made to assume that he does take pupils; and Cratylus in reply does not rule out the possibility of taking on Socrates as such (428b–c). But as I shall be arguing below, Cratylus undergoes ahistorical transformation in this final part of the dialogue.

[8] Diogenes Laertius clearly engages in such extrapolation, making Plato attach himself both to Cratylus and to Hermogenes, taken to be an Eleatic (D.L. 3.6).

[9] Chapter 1 above, p. 34. We should note also that from the Socratic Aeschines of Sphettus Aristotle takes another piece of information he retails about Cratylus: the way he waved his hands and hissed while he spoke (*Rhet.* 3.16, 1417b1–3).

develops it within an argumentative context that is largely restricted to discussion of perception and what is perceptible. Otherwise, the most striking affinity Aristotle's Cratylus has with Plato's is his interest in language and in the way it relates to the world. Aristotle's report that he ended up just moving his finger – pointing at things, presumably – has often been persuasively construed as due to his final conclusion about flux: as Socrates argues in the *Theaetetus*, if everything is always changing in every dimension, then it is impossible to apply an expression in referring to or describing it more or less correctly than its negative counterpart. If that interpretation is on the right lines, then just as in the *Cratylus*, Aristotle's Cratylus will have been a thinker whose interest in language is intimately connected with his ideas about the nature of the reality to which language is taken to apply. And it might be possible to go further (with Sedley, followed by Ademollo) and see the ending of the *Cratylus*, where Socrates presses upon Cratylus the question of 'whether it is possible to speak of a thing correctly if it is always slipping away' (439d), as deliberately foreshadowing the sceptical stance on language that Aristotle's Cratylus eventually found himself having to adopt.[10]

So to this extent, there is a pretty good doctrinal fit between Aristotle's Cratylus and the Cratylus of the dialogue. There is reason to expect that that would have been so. When in the dialogues Plato brings on stage thinkers of some stature for Socrates to engage with, he may not always treat them with the respect they might have thought they deserved. But where we have independent evidence about them (often we do not: on whether the historical Thrasymachus held that justice is the advantage of the stronger we are in the dark), he turns out to be reasonably scrupulous in ensuring that the words he puts in their mouths accord with what they are elsewhere recorded as having said or thought. Thus the Zeno of the *Parmenides* is recognizably Zenonian, and its Parmenides understandably finds metaphysical pluralism problematic, although here Plato is of course freely extrapolating to what such a brand of philosophical monist he takes him to be might have said (we shall return to consider extrapolation and the freedom with which Plato engages in it below, pp. 129–33). When Plato's Gorgias makes persuasion and its power his central preoccupation and agrees with Socrates that it produces conviction but does not teach, we recognize the author of the *Encomium of Helen*, and the claim there that speech in a public forum 'delights and persuades on account of the art (*tekhnē*) with which it is written, not because it is spoken with truth' (*Helen*

---

[10] Sedley 2003: 18–19; Ademollo 2011: 17–18.

13). The *Theaetetus* goes out of its way to construct a defence of Protagoras, in which Socrates develops on his behalf an explanation of how it is possible without inconsistency to hold both that man is the measure of all things (which is cited as the opening of his book *Truth*) and that some people are wiser and better able to teach than others. Here, we are reliant on Plato himself for the information about what Protagoras thought. But this way of proceeding would make no sense if the representation of his views were in any obvious way unfaithful to them.

According to Aristotle, it was the historical Cratylus' Heracliteanism that made such a significant impact on Plato. But although Heracliteanism plays an explicit and significant role in the *Cratylus*, most notably as the representation of reality many of its etymologies communicate, it is of course not the dialogue's main focus. So if one reason that might have prompted Plato to write it was a fascination with Cratylus' philosophical thinking, there seems little case for supposing that it was that encounter with his Heracliteanism that primarily motivated composition of the *Cratylus*. If it was some idea of the historical Cratylus that played a major part in prompting it, that idea must obviously have been one concerned with the nature of language. Aristotle's evidence that Cratylus did make at least one statement on the subject has been mentioned. So there is at least some reason to think that the stance ascribed to him on the opening page of the dialogue might represent a position the historical Cratylus took, at any rate at one time in his philosophizing on the subject – although not his final view (if we may believe Aristotle) that 'one should say nothing'.

The basic proposal attributed to Cratylus in the dialogue is the thesis that 'for each of the things there are there is a correctness of names that is naturally constituted' (383a), subsequently summarized by Socrates as the view that 'the names belong to the things by nature' (390d–e). We have no other evidence that Cratylus held such a view. But it seems highly likely that he was a proponent of the natural correctness of names in some shape or form, even if the wording given at 383a might be suspected of being Plato's own articulation, designed to enable precision in the theory Socrates will go on to elaborate. Otherwise, it would be hard to see why Plato would or indeed could have selected him as the advocate of the naturalist position he wanted to examine. Moreover, if he was a Heraclitean, some kind of naturalist stance on names would be what one would expect, once debates about what is natural and what is conventional had got under way, as they did above all in the age of the Sophists – the time, evidently, when Cratylus was active. For Heraclitus saw names and especially similarities between them as providing us – if we are intellectually alert – with a window on reality. It suffices simply to mention some well-known fragments: 'The name of the bow is life; its work is death' (Fr. 48, with its play on *bios* and – when differently accented – *biós*); 'One thing alone is the wise: it is not willing and is willing to be called by the name of Zeus (*zênos*)' (Fr. 32); 'Greater deaths (*moroi*) gain greater portions (*moirai*)' (Fr. 25); 'If it were not Dionysus for whom they march in procession and chant the hymn to the phallus (*aidoia*), their action would be most shameless (*anaidestata*). But Hades (*aidês*) and Dionysus are the same, him for whom they rave and celebrate Lenaia.' (Fr. 15).[11]

So this dialogue on what makes names correct probably does start off with a Cratylus close to the Cratylus of history, a figure at one time of some philosophical importance for Plato. But as I shall now argue, from that observation fuel for further interpretation seems to run out. Our second attempt at understanding the structure of the *Cratylus* – as a working out of Plato's personal engagement with Cratylus – takes us some distance, but not far enough. It is time to consider the way Plato presents him as he re-enters the conversation in the dialogue's final phase.

The Two Cratyluses of the Dialogue

Given Cratylus' silence throughout most of the dialogue, it is hard to know how many of the other propositions about names he is eventually represented as being prepared to assert are any more than extrapolations on Plato's own part. Sometimes he is credited as a likely source even for elements in Socrates' theory – such as at least some of the etymologies, or the idea of an etymological programme – that are not ascribed to him.[12] I agree with Ademollo that what influence he had on the material in that part of the dialogue or its shaping is 'impossible to evaluate'.[13] But aside from the dangers of equating what may very well be Platonic extrapolations with proposals actually made by Cratylus, there is a further reason for caution over what we ascribe to him. Plato's fullest engagement with Heracliteanism comes, of course, in the *Theaetetus*, where there is a particularly indicative passage on the intellectual modus operandi

---

[11] The discussion of Fr. 48 in Kirk 1954: 116–22 is still worth consulting; see also Kahn 1979: 201–2.
[12] See e.g. Barney 2001: 52–5; Sedley 2003: 76, 104.
[13] Ademollo 2011: 190. Socrates makes an interesting remark to Cratylus at 428b: 'But if *you* are in a position to say something finer than these things [*sc.* Socrates' own exposition of a linguistic naturalism], I would not be surprised. For you seem to me to have both looked into such matters yourself and to have learned from others.' On the face of it, this looks like first an implicit assertion of his own originality on Plato's part, and then an indication that he knows quite a bit about Cratylus' own ventures in etymologizing.

adopted by Heracliteans presumably of Socrates' time, in this evidently aping what they plausibly enough took to be Heraclitus' own oral as well as written style. When Theodorus suggests that they respond to questions by firing 'some little enigmatic phrase from his [Heraclitus's] quiver' and never give a proper account of anything, Socrates replies that he supposes they keep proper explanations for pupils whom they want to assimilate to themselves. Theodorus remarks in turn that 'there are no pupils and teachers among these people'. Theodorus goes on: 'As I was just going to say, you will never get these men to give an account of themselves, willingly or unwillingly. What we must do is to take their doctrine out of their hands and consider it for ourselves, as we should a problem in geometry' (*Tht.* 180a–c).

Considering Cratylus' doctrine for themselves, after listening to a succinct account of unsuccessful attempts to elicit anything clear from him, is precisely what Socrates gets Hermogenes to help him do, for the next forty pages or more of text – without in the course of it attempting to consult Cratylus himself. It does not seem much of an interpretative leap to see Plato as meaning his readers to take him to be presenting Cratylus from the outset as a typical Heraclitean: conforming to the stereotype Theodorus draws in the *Theaetetus*, in as much as he contents himself with making a pregnant and enigmatic pronouncement of which he then refuses to give a clear account,[14] and adopting an 'ostentatious mysteriousness'.[15] Intensification of that mysteriousness must be what Plato intends to convey by making Hermogenes refer to the frustrating discussion he is represented as having attempted to conduct with Cratylus in a conversation that we do not hear, but that is supposed to have preceded the start of the dialogue itself.

However, there is an apparent obstacle to this seemingly attractive line of interpretation. For Cratylus is made to adopt a quite different demeanour when he rejoins the philosophical conversation at 427e, and particularly once Socrates starts quizzing him on what commitment to the basic naturalist thesis on names entails. Now Cratylus conducts himself as a mostly reasonable and altogether cooperative respondent, who is made

---

[14] So when Sedley says (2003: 51): 'No one is likely to doubt that Cratylus, for all his reticence about explaining it, has a worked out theory of names', I find myself disagreeing. Perhaps the confidence he is represented as having (383b) in the correctness of the names 'Cratylus' and 'Socrates', and in regarding 'Hermogenes', however, as not Hermogenes' name, indicates that he – like the author of the Derveni papyrus – thought etymologizing could reveal the nature signified by a real name. But to hold such a view is a long way from having worked out anything we might want to call a theory. See Ademollo 2011: 319 for judicious comments on this issue.
[15] Ademollo 2011: 27.

to signal respect for Socrates at the outset, albeit qualified by the implication that Socrates merely divines what he himself knows by dint of long study (428b–c). He takes some extreme positions: (1) All names that count as real names are well made, with no possibility of faulty or less than optimal construction, nor of incorrect application – or indeed of false speaking of any kind (428e–433c). (2) Getting someone to understand the names of things is the only and best way of teaching the reality of things (435d–436a). (3) All things without exception are in flux: a thesis whose truth he not unreasonably takes to be implied by the combination of (2) and the general outcome of the etymological analysis conducted in the long central section of the dialogue: 436e–437a, 440d–e. He is quite stubborn in his defence of (1) and (2), and with (1) in particular resists the obviously powerful logic of Socrates' refutations. But he never ducks answering Socrates' questions, and he certainly does not snarl or sulk or sweat or throw tantrums like a Callicles or Thrasymachus. In fact, Plato gives him no distinctive colouring of any sort. His style of answering certainly bears no resemblance to that memorably ascribed to Heracliteans in the *Theaetetus*.

What the objection indicates, I suggest, is that the dialogue presents the reader with a further kind of two Cratylus problem beyond the one notoriously articulated by Socrates in the course of his critique of (1) (432b–c).[16] The Cratylus portrayed at the outset and the Cratylus we meet with from 427e onwards seem quite different performers, so far as intellectual style is concerned. The fact that proposition (3) above is explicitly presented as a Heraclitean thesis does nothing to disturb that conclusion. In fact, the way Cratylus is represented as subscribing to the truth of (3) reinforces it. At the end of the dialogue, Socrates advises Cratylus to think carefully about the matter. Cratylus responds as follows (440d–e):

> But let me assure you, Socrates, that even right now my view of the matter is not unconsidered, but as I consider it and struggle with the issues [literally: am having trouble] it seems to me that things are much more the way Heraclitus says.

Sedley (following Kirk's 1951 article) suggests that the considering and the 'having trouble' (*pragmata ekhein*, under-translated by him as 'turn over in the mind') refers to the thinking Cratylus has been doing just in the course

---

[16] Might the choice of Cratylus as example in the problem Socrates is raising at 432b–c be a steer to the reader that he might actually be speaking with an imitation, not the real Cratylus? The same postmodern meta-textual thought occurred independently to me and to David Sedley.

of the dialogue, not in past reflection, as indicated by the present tenses of the relevant Greek verbs.[17] That seems to me implausible: Cratylus is surely wanting to impress upon Socrates that he has thought long and hard about the topic.[18] Nonetheless, Sedley rightly points out that when just before at 440c Socrates refers to 'the Heracliteans', he does not seem to be including Cratylus in their number. And Cratylus is plainly not in this closing passage of the dialogue being presented as a declared Heraclitean dogmatist. In fact, his style of talk here much more resembles Socrates' than the 'prophetic' mode of utterance reported at the outset by Hermogenes (384a).

The mysterious Cratylus to whom we are indirectly introduced by Hermogenes at the beginning of the *Cratylus* is turning out to be less of a mystery than the figure that re-enters the conversation in its final section. The dialogue's initial Cratylus was a typically cryptic Heraclitean. But the philosophical identity of Socrates' partner in the last thirteen pages of the discussion is proving more of a puzzle.

The Second Cratylus Reviewed

At this point, it seems sensible to reflect on the overall philosophical shape of the clutch of positions sustained by this second Cratylus in that final stretch of dialogue (428e–440e). It might be described as a comprehensive linguistic naturalism pushed to radical extremes, with semantic, epistemological, and ontological components, articulated in theses (1), (2), and (3), respectively, and in an order of exposition that reflects logical sequence. Any name to count as a name, and therefore to satisfy the requirements of natural appropriateness, must be entirely successful in uniquely capturing the nature of the referent to which it is applied, inevitably therefore correctly and truly. Getting people to understand names so conceived is the ideal and indeed the only way of teaching them the nature of that referent: the only route to knowledge of it. Examination of names so understood (in line with the etymological analysis of 391b–421c) reveals the universal truth about things: reality consists in flux – everything real is in motion if it is real.

---

[17] Sedley 2003: 18 n. 40; cf. Ademollo 2011: 487. For argument to the contrary, see Allan 1954: 279–80.
[18] I agree with Sedley that in the discussion of (2) Cratylus has been making it clear that he is persuaded that the Heraclitean ontology is true: see 436b–c, 436e–437a. But there does not seem to be any sign there or later that thinking about the issue is something he is in the immediate present having any trouble with.

Did any one Greek philosopher advocate such a theory, with all its three components? Not so far as we know. Socrates in the *Euthydemus*, in associating use of the argument that it is impossible to contradict what anyone else has said with Protagoras and his followers, and even earlier thinkers, takes this to be tantamount to claiming that there is no such thing as false speaking (*Euthd.* 286b–c); Aristotle associates the same line of thought with Antisthenes, who likewise couples denial of the possibility of contradiction with the impossibility of false speaking (*Metaph.* Δ.29.1024b32–4). In the *Sophist*, the impossibility of speaking falsely is associated ultimately with Parmenides' prohibition of saying what is not and is treated as the basis of sophistry (*Soph.* 236d–237b). Next, for the idea that understanding names is the path to knowledge the best parallel is again Antisthenes, although this must effectively have been a position taken by others also – Prodicus is the obvious example. Epictetus (*Diss.* 1.17.10) credits Antisthenes with the dictum: 'The principle/starting point (*arkhê*) for education is the study of names.' Finally, the doctrine of universal flux is of course identified above all with Heraclitus and the Heracliteans, Cratylus included, although at the start of his discussion of it in the *Theaetetus* Socrates is made to characterize it as a feature of the general stance of all previous thinkers other than Parmenides, naming Protagoras and Empedocles as well as Heraclitus, and enlisting Epicharmus and Homer from among the poets too (*Tht.* 152d–e).

Thus, the individual elements of the theory all have identifiable antecedents. But the package as a whole is most plausibly viewed as Plato's original construction. Perhaps we should interpret it as an ingenious tour de force, in which he was attempting to show – just as with the etymologies in their very different mode – how a great deal of previous philosophy and (no less importantly) current sophistry can be fitted together to form a synthesis: in this case (whatever may be intended with the etymologies), an utterly wrong-headed synthesis. As such, it might be regarded as an exercise (presumably earlier in date) comparable with the comprehensive map of philosophical positions in ontology constructed with similar critical intent in the *Sophist* (242b–249d). The mainspring for the synthesis here is the naturalist theory of names. So Plato makes Cratylus the speaker from whom Socrates gradually teases it out over the course of the final discussion. But he is now only tangentially connected with what I am supposing was the more authentically cryptic Cratylus presented at the beginning of the dialogue. This new Cratylus is more of a symbolic indication of where that original Cratylus' initial idea might lead someone if it was pressed to the limit.

I suspect that Plato was particularly wanting his readers to see both how readily and how unSocratically the views of his rival Antisthenes (who evidently saw himself, not Plato, as Socrates' true heir) belong within such a context. It was an old suggestion that 'Cratylus' stood as proxy for a contemporary whom Plato did not wish to name or engage with directly. Antisthenes was often a preferred candidate, and indeed his claims were revived in Guthrie's *History* (1978).[19] Hypotheses like that have, however, fallen out of general favour, partly because any such identifications are bound to be insecure, and partly because the working assumption prevalent in most English-speaking Plato scholarship at the present and for a good time past has been that analysing the arguments on the page, or latterly also making sense of the dynamics of the philosophical drama as it is presented to the reader, is what the job of the philosophical interpreter should consist in, not speculating about the provenance of the material. Nonetheless, it has become progressively clear, particularly in scholarship of the present millennium, how important reflection on the Greek philosophical tradition was for Plato, and particularly in his later period: in the present context I need only refer to M. M. McCabe's *Plato and His Predecessors* (2000).[20] And with Sedley's pioneering work (2003), and more recently with Ademollo's rich treatment of the etymologies (2011), it is now more evident than ever that in the *Cratylus* such reflection constitutes a centrally important dimension of the dialogue.

However, whereas in the section comprising the etymologies Socrates makes it clear enough that he is drawing on a great deal of historical material from Homer to Anaxagoras, such hints are scarcer in the closing conversation with Cratylus, which is couched in entirely abstract terms, with even the mentions at the end of Heraclitus and Heracliteanism (440c–e) simply a conveniently economical way of indicating the flux doctrine. That does not mean that there are no other philosophical presences making themselves felt in what Cratylus is made to maintain. It is rather that where such presences are contemporary, Plato mostly resorts to tactics other than the veiled or less veiled references that in the etymology section he used with the earlier thinkers.[21] The best parallel is with the *Theaetetus* (whose affinities with the *Cratylus* are well known).[22] When Plato wants there to engineer discussion of Heracliteanism (which as noted above he wants conceived broadly, as a metaphysical tendency with which many previous

---

[19] Guthrie 1978: 2–4.   [20] However, see also Adomenas 2006.
[21] For just one particularly notable example, see the treatment of *dikaiosunê* at 412c–413d, with the discussion in Sedley 2003: 114–19.
[22] I am grateful to David Sedley for the suggestion.

thinkers can be associated), he makes Socrates introduce it as the secret doctrine Protagoras taught his pupils (*Tht.* 152c). The tactic here is not dissimilar. He makes Cratylus the proxy for the proponents of views in recent and current philosophy that he wants to associate with the naturalist theory of names: Cratylus' own secret doctrine, one might say.[23] At just one point this is more or less explicit. At 429c–d (in the discussion of (1)), Socrates suggests that Cratylus' view that 'Hermogenes' is not Hermogenes' name implies that if one says of him 'This is Hermogenes', that is not even a false statement. And he puts it to him that this adds up to the thesis of the impossibility of falsehood which quite a lot of thinkers have subscribed to, 'both now and in the past'.

The evidence that Antisthenes was among those thinkers has already been cited (*Metaph.* Δ.29.1024b32-4). It was connected with his key doctrine that nothing can be spoken of except by its own proprietary *logos*, 'one on one', which is very close to the view of the relation between a name and the thing for which it is the name that Cratylus is represented as contending for in this stretch of the *Cratylus* (429e–430a), and which is then spelled out by Socrates with an analogy with portraits which is pressed to show the untenability of the view – whether as applied to names or to *logoi* (430a–431c). Treatment of names was itself clearly a matter to which Antisthenes attached huge importance. Diogenes Laertius' catalogue of his writings records a work entitled 'On education, or names', in five books (6.17). His pronouncement on the subject retailed by Epictetus (*Diss.* 1.17.10) has similarly already been cited: 'The principle/starting point (*arkhê*) for education is the study of names.' It is striking that one of only two emphatic claims Cratylus is made to make without any feeds from Socrates in the final section of the dialogue is his response to the question what power or function (*dunamis*) names have.[24] He says (435d): 'Teaching, Socrates, in my own opinion – and it's altogether straightforward: anyone who knows the names knows the things too.' And in an exchange or two later, responding to Socrates' query as to whether there is any better or indeed other form of teaching than this, he declares (436a): 'That is what *I* think – that there is none other at all: this is both the only

---

[23] Making Cratylus a proxy figure is a device, of course, not nearly as transparent to the reader as is explicit talk of a secret doctrine. If, as most scholars think, the *Cratylus* precedes the *Theaetetus* in date of composition, it may be that Plato decided he needed a more indicative way of intimating that Protagoras was meant to function in part as a proxy for other thinkers than the use of Cratylus as a proxy that I am maintaining.

[24] The other is his argument that consistency in what names reveal should be regarded as a very important proof that the original name giver had true knowledge of the things he was naming (436b–c).

one and the best.' I think it hard to resist the thought that Antisthenes at this point becomes the most important figure in the amalgam that I am arguing Cratylus has become in these closing pages of the dialogue, at any rate until Socrates raises the issue of the validity of Heracliteanism at the very end.

The critique Socrates is made to launch against the positions Cratylus upholds in them is generally recognized to be the most argumentatively strenuous section of the entire dialogue, with sustained onslaught on (1) constituting the most brilliantly resourceful passage in the range of dialectical stratagems it deploys, the discussion of (2) including *inter alia* an attack on the first explicit appearance in philosophy of something beginning to approach a coherence theory of truth, and the treatment of (3) the hardest to interpret in its extreme concision and compression. The arguments developed here are undoubtedly what have in recent times most excited those philosophical readers who have approached the *Cratylus* with a mindset shaped primarily by engagement with dialogues such as the *Theaetetus* and *Sophist*, as perhaps most notably Bernard Williams in his influential paper 'Cratylus' theory of names and its refutation' (1982). M. M. McCabe, in 'Putting the *Cratylus* in its place' (1986), effectively took three paradoxical contentions she saw as salient in the position attacked in the final section to be what shape the entire structure and thrust of the dialogue. '"Hermogenes" is not Hermogenes' name', 'Falsehood is impossible', 'Coming to know is impossible' are the trio she had in mind: all of them striking strong resonances with one or other of the *Euthydemus*, *Theaetetus*, or *Sophist*.

One thing these responses to the *Cratylus* get us to remember is just how intensely Plato became preoccupied especially in those other three dialogues with the cluster of issues in semantics, epistemology, and ontology that are pursued in its closing pages. For example, where their treatment of the problem of falsehood is concerned, Sedley speaks of 'the long road' that is widely held to have 'started in Socrates' encounter with the sophists in the *Euthydemus*, continued in the *Cratylus* and *Theaetetus*, and ended triumphantly in the *Sophist*, with some further related thoughts in the *Philebus*'.[25] And it has always been recognized that the question of whether knowledge could take things in radical universal flux as its object that is raised at the very end of the *Cratylus* prompts a hint of the *coup de grâce* delivered to Heracliteanism at the end of the first part of the *Theaetetus* (*Tht.* 182c–183b). The closing discussion with Cratylus, and the debate over

---

[25] Sedley 2003: 132.

the distinctive theses he is made to propound there ((1), (2), and (3)), enable Plato, therefore, to work at paradoxical philosophical stances with which he is evidently obsessed, ingeniously brought together on this one occasion within the framework of a consolidated – if perverse – total theory. It is hard to think of his discussion here just as conclusion or coda to examination of the viability of the naturalist conception of names. This final stage of the dialogue is surely not merely its last chapter, but its *telos*.

Conclusion

I have been arguing that the figure of Cratylus is both one of the puzzles of the *Cratylus* and a key to interpreting what Plato was about in the dialogue. The opening page sets out to make Cratylus a man of mystery. He is then all but forgotten through the bulk of the dialogue, where Socrates is made first to develop in characteristic Socratic style an economically argued Platonic theory of how there has to be a natural correctness for names, and what in general terms its basis must consist in; and then to produce in a dazzling and protracted display of ingenuity a comprehensive account of the way etymological analysis and subsequently phonemic dismemberment of the vocabulary of Greek can exhibit its natural correctness – or at least disclose the views about reality held by those who coined it. After such a performance Plato needs to produce something that will move the reader sharply to a different intellectual plane and enable the dialogue to reach a yet more impressive conclusion, satisfying in dramatic and philosophical terms alike.

His *coup de théâtre* is achieved by bringing Cratylus back on stage, not to issue dogmatic pronouncements, but surprisingly enough to converse with a Socrates who is now by contrast once more the argumentative critic par excellence. Cratylus for his part has been transformed into a rather artificial interlocutor, humanly much less interesting than in Hermogenes' initial descriptions. Rather quiet theatre, one might think, compared with the drama of many other Platonic dialogues. But Plato surely expects us to find ourselves intellectually transported (in the company of Williams and McCabe) to a new and deeper level of philosophical engagement by the paradoxicality of that cluster of extreme claims about matters fundamental to all philosophy (claims familiar to readers of the later dialogues, which are now made by Cratylus, and here developed from his basic idea of the natural basis of naming); and by the power and ingenuity of the Socratic elenchus to which they are subjected. We sense that Plato is in these final pages using 'Cratylus' to work through some of the deepest and most insistent concerns in his mature philosophizing.

If that is indeed his ultimate focus, then the need to reach a decision between a naturalist or a conventionalist view of language (a focus of our first shot at an answer to Jowett's perplexity) has become by the end somewhat secondary, as has any interest Plato had in constructing a testament to the significance of the personal encounter with the Cratylus he had met in his youth (the tack followed in our second shot). What most matters in the dialogue's last chapter is the project of teasing out an entire complex of interconnected logical, epistemological, and metaphysical positions that might be taken to be implicit in linguistic naturalism, if interpreted in radically simplistic terms, and of getting us to see the absurdities they generate. To reach that end point must have been one of the major objectives Plato had in composing the *Cratylus*. His construction of the strange role of Cratylus within its idiosyncratic structure and trajectory was the way he decided to achieve it. His strategy here may therefore be seen as a foretaste of the later dialogues' technique, brilliantly exhibited by M. M. McCabe in *Plato and His Predecessors*, of associating metaphysical positions that he will reject – as in the end beyond the reach of rational dialogue – with shadowy versions of great figures of the philosophical past: Parmenides, Heraclitus, Protagoras.

PART III

Myth and Allegory in the Republic

CHAPTER 7

The Noble Lie

The Politics of Lying

Socrates' introduction of the *Republic*'s notorious 'noble lie' comes near the end of Book 3 (414b–c). 'We want one single, grand lie', he says, 'which will be believed by everybody – including the rulers, ideally, but failing that the rest of the city.' G. R. F. Ferrari has a good note on the issue:[1] 'The lie is grand or noble (*gennaios*) by virtue of its civic purpose, but the Greek word can also be used colloquially, giving the meaning "a true-blue lie", i.e. a massive no-doubt-about-it lie (compare the term "grand larceny").' This is not the only point on which there might be argument about the translation. Some prefer to 'lie' the more neutral 'falsehood' (which need not imply deliberate deception), others 'fiction' (perhaps trying to prescind from a focus on questions of truth and falsehood altogether). Cornford had 'bold flight of invention'.[2] I think 'lie' is exactly right. But the argument for that will emerge later.

The noble lie is to serve as charter myth for Plato's good city: a myth of national or civic identity – or rather, two related myths, one grounding that identity in the natural brotherhood of the entire indigenous population (they are all autochthonous, literally born from the earth), the other making the city's differentiated class structure a matter of divine dispensation (the god who moulds them puts different metals in different souls). If people can be made to believe it, they will be strongly motivated to care for the city and for each other. The *Republic*'s explicit reliance on such a mechanism to secure assent and commitment to the political arrangements it proposes still has the capacity to shock and offend. It makes the noble lie a natural focus for many of the major questions the dialogue provokes.

First and most obviously, the use of the noble lie is what more than anything may prompt the charge that the *Republic*'s preoccupation with

---

[1] Ferrari and Griffith 2000: 107 n. 63.   [2] Cornford 1941: 106.

political unity is a recipe for 'the collectivist, the tribal, the totalitarian theory of morality', to quote Popper's formulation – inasmuch as it licenses wholesale deception of individual citizens as the means to secure the good of 'the state' (as Popper conceptualized Plato's city).[3] Such deception is quite incompatible with the assumption of modern liberal political philosophy since Locke that the only valid way of legitimating the political order is by appeal to reason: to *rational* considerations that have the power to motivate acceptance of a political authority by those who are to be subject to it. It is similarly and connectedly in conflict with the fundamental moral requirement, often associated above all with Kantian ethics, that people be treated as ends, not means. The noble lie seems an affront to human dignity, and something that undermines the human capacity for self-determination in particular.

Our own time is seeing both an explosion in knowledge and the media by which it is communicated, and unprecedented levels of concern about standards of probity in public life, and about lying and the manipulation and suppression of information in particular. We now have the nasty phenomenon of 'fake news', often rendered the more vicious by use of social media. Not that it would be reasonable to expect these ugly processes to stop. As John Dunn wrote back in 1979 (commenting on realization that moral and practical insight is not the preserve of any elite):[4]

> If this realization dictates a hugely more democratic conception of political rights and capabilities than Plato favoured, it neither dictates nor indeed permits that ruthlessly evasive and disingenuous egalitarianism which pervades the ideologies of the modern world, capitalist and socialist alike, and pretends that the problems of power have been solved or would be solved if the power of human beings was rendered equal. And since the structural inequality of power in the societies of the modern world, however drastically reorganized these might be, is so intractably vast and since such power cannot be rendered safe, insulated from the capacity to harm, it is clear enough that one of the most widely deplored characteristics of the Platonic Republic, the noble lie, has at least as guaranteed a place in any possible structures for our world as it had in that of Plato.

Plato is in fact nowhere more our contemporary than in making similar preoccupations – knowledge, virtue, truth, deception – central to his own vision of what matters in politics.

Nor is that just a contemporary perspective. In having Socrates sanction lying as a basic ingredient in political discourse, Plato must have known he

---

[3] Popper 1945: 107.   [4] Dunn 1979: 116.

was breaching the norms of the democratic political ideology of his own time and place. It is true that Odysseus the trickster is held up as a figure commanding admiration from the readers of the *Odyssey*. That was a reflection of the archaic worldview symbolized by Hesiod when he made Zeus first marry Metis ('Resource') and then, when she is pregnant with Athena, turn her own powers against her, 'deceiving her wits by trickery with wily words' and swallowing her whole (*Theogony* 886–91). *Mêtis* involves 'flair, wisdom, forethought, subtlety of mind, deception, resourcefulness, vigilance, opportunism ... and experience'. It has to do with 'the future seen from the point of view of its uncertainties' and is at a premium in 'transient, shifting, disconcerting and ambiguous' situations. As Marcel Detienne and Jean-Pierre Vernant have shown, *mêtis* encapsulates a cluster of attributes and values that remained prized (although not characteristically by the philosophers) throughout Greek literature and thought, down to Oppian's *Treatise on Fishing* in the second century AD and beyond.[5]

Odysseus was not always presented as he had been in the *Odyssey*. More pertinent for our purposes is Sophocles' *Philoctetes* of 409 BC, a profound meditation – played out in the theatre before the Athenian *dêmos* – on the moral corrosiveness and dubious political advantage of Odysseus' attempt to get the youthful Neoptolemos to hoodwink Philoctetes into what was to be an enforced return to the Greek camp at Troy. The Athenians generally thought of lying and deceit as the way not they but the Spartans conducted political life, as is testified above all by Pericles' antitheses on the subject in the funeral speech attributed to him by Thucydides (2.39.1). A democratic political culture, by contrast, required a general commitment on the part of speakers in the assembly to tell the truth. As Demosthenes put it on one occasion (19.184):

> There is no greater injustice anyone could commit against you than to speak falsehoods. For where the political system depends on speeches, how can political life be conducted securely if these are not true?

Hence, the Athenians' intense resentment against speakers they suspected of manipulating them: the demagogues who figure so prominently in Aristophanic comedy and Thucydidean history. Hence too Diodotus' reflections during the debate on Mytilene of 427 BC (again as reconstructed by Thucydides) about the spiralling debasement of democracy and

---

[5] Détienne and Vernant 1978 (quotations at 3–4, 107).

democratic rhetoric produced by widespread contravention of the norm of veracity (3.43.2–4):

> It has become the rule also to treat good advice honestly given as being no less under suspicion than bad, so that a person who has something good to say must tell lies in order to be believed, just as someone who gives terrible advice must win over the people by deception. Because of these suspicions, ours is the only city that nobody can possibly benefit openly, without thoroughgoing deception, since if anyone does good openly to the city, his reward will be the suspicion that he had something secretly to gain from it.

What Diodotus sees as the ultimate degradation of political culture – an outcome where 'a person who has something good to say must tell lies in order to be believed' – is apparently embraced by the Platonic Socrates as no more troubling than the white lies someone tells a child when getting it to take some medicine.[6]

'One *single*, grand lie' might suggest a possible line of defence on Plato's behalf. Did he perhaps think that relations among citizens in general and between rulers and ruled in particular should exhibit openness and candour, but that there had to be just one exception: the myth that spelled out the basis on which that relationship was founded? No, that is not what Plato thought. The noble lie might with luck be the one thing needed to induce in the citizens an overriding concern for the good of the city. But lying and falsehood are seen as pervasive necessities in the politics and culture of the good city, and in this regard there is an asymmetry between rulers and ruled. One particularly chilling remark on the subject occurs in Socrates' discussion in Book 5 of the mechanisms that will be needed to sustain belief in the eugenic system for controlling breeding. 'It will be a necessity', he says (459c), 'for the rulers to use many drugs.' He then explains what he has in mind (459c–d): 'It looks as though the rulers are going to have to use a great deal of falsehood and deception for the benefit of those they are ruling.' So in this instance, the ruled (here not the economic class, but the young soldiers who are to support the rulers) will be told that the mating arrangements are simply the outcome of a lottery. The ruled, by contrast, should have nothing to do with lying. For an ordinary citizen to lie to the rulers is worse than for a patient or someone in training to lie to their doctor or trainer about their physical condition, or for a sailor not to tell the navigator the truth about the state of the ship and

---

[6] For an excellent treatment of the material surveyed in this paragraph (and of a great range of similar evidence), see Hesk 2000.

those sailing it. If a ruler catches any of the artisans lying like this, 'he will punish him for introducing a practice which is as subversive and destructive in a city as it is in a ship' (3.389 b–d).[7]

Socrates' insistence on the need for lying to sustain the political order is all of a piece with his general treatment of culture and society more broadly. The cave analogy of Book 7 – the most striking and memorable image in the entire dialogue – represents uneducated humanity as imprisoned by illusions, feeding uncritically on third-hand images of reality (7.514a–515c, 516c–d, 517d–e). When Socrates subsequently argues that philosophers must be compelled to return to the cave to exercise their function as rulers, the implication is presumably that most of those they are to govern, although citizens of an ideal city, have very little ability to resist deception or to respond to anything better than images of truth (cf. 520b–c). That implication is not contradicted by the radical programme of censorship of the poets that he works through in Books 2 and 3, in the context of his treatment of the upbringing of the 'guardians' or 'guards'.[8]

Of course, there is an important sense in which the reason why Homer and Hesiod are attacked, and great tracts of their poetry ruled unfit for consumption, is that they tell falsehoods. Sometimes, Socrates seems to mean by this that gods or heroes are represented as doing things which they did *not* do: for example, it simply is not the case (according to Socrates) that Kronos took revenge on his father Ouranos by castrating him (2.377e–378a) or that Achilles dragged Hector round the tomb of Patroclus and slaughtered prisoners taken alive on his funeral pyre (3.391b). But the reason why Socrates disputes what we might call the factual truth of these accounts is that they are at odds with the conceptions of god and of moral virtue that should inform the education of the guards. His real objection is that such stories are 'not admirable' (2.377d–e) and 'impious' (3.391b).

---

[7] In the prelude introducing legislation to govern sale and exchange of goods, the *Laws* construes adulteration of coinage as a form of lying and deceit and treats someone who does it as in effect guilty of swearing a false oath. It pronounces that anyone who commits this sort of crime will be 'most hateful to the gods' (cf. *Rep.* 2.382a) as well as liable to a flogging (*Laws* 11.916d–918a).

[8] From now on I shall say 'guards'. Probably the principal associations of this word are nowadays on both sides of the Atlantic those conveyed, e.g., by 'security guards' (who protect a company's property and employees from external dangers). This function closely parallels the prime function of Plato's *phulakes*, at least as originally articulated in the guard-dog comparison (see, e.g., 2.375a–d), although 'prison guard' is the association that may be conjured up by Socrates' remark that locating the guards in their own garrison will best enable them to 'control [lit. 'hold down'] those within, if any of them refuse to obey the laws' (3.415d–e).

In fact, in the passage in which he first introduces the notion of lies as useful drugs, he concedes that with stories such as those told by Homer and Hesiod, we do not *know* where the truth lies so far as events long ago are concerned. In these circumstances, the right thing is to 'make falsehood as much like the truth as possible' (2.382b–c): that is, to tell a story that encapsulates *moral* truth even if – inevitably – it is fanciful if conceived as fact. Education *has* to begin with stories like this – 'broadly speaking false, though there is some truth in them' (2.377a). In other words, the culture is and must be saturated with myths that are literally false, and deceptive if believed to be factually true. But the deception is legitimate if, like the noble lie and the stories Socrates *wants* the young to hear, they are morally admirable fictions that drug people into sound convictions and lead them to virtue (2.377b–c, 378e–379a). What is wrong with Homer and Hesiod is not in the end that they lied, but that there was nothing morally admirable in most of the lies they told (2.377e).[9]

The Morality of Lying

So far we have been looking at ways in which the noble lie, and the whole conception of a well-ordered society it represents, conflicts with the outlook of ancient Athenian ideology and modern liberal ethical and political thought alike – even if ideological mechanisms of this sort may be a political necessity. It could also be argued that some deep-seated tensions in the project of the *Republic* itself rise to the surface at this point. The Platonic Socrates is quite explicit that his proposals for a role for the philosopher in government will be perceived as generally paradoxical (5.473c–e) and nothing 'fine' or 'good' so far as the philosophers for their part are concerned (7.540b; cf. 1.347c–d, 7.520d, 521a). The need to employ lies and deceit to maintain the social and political fabric is presumably itself one of the reasons why Plato has him attribute that view to them. Popper thought such lying and deceit by philosopher rulers actually incompatible with the *Republic*'s own definition of genuine philosophers as those who love truth and the contemplation of truth.[10] Getting to grips with this issue will take a little time.

In a key passage of Book 2 Socrates finds it helpful in his discussion of whether the gods lie or dissemble to distinguish between lies in the soul and

---

[9] For fuller treatment of the topic covered in this paragraph, see, e.g., Ferrari 1989: 108–19; cf. also Burnyeat 1999b.
[10] Popper 1945: 138.

lies in speech – between the true or real lie and a spoken imitation or image of it, something that is 'not quite an unadulterated lie' (2.382b–c). He goes on at once to observe that the true lie is hated not only by gods but by humans, whereas lying in speech has uses (for humans, not gods) that don't merit hatred (2.382c–e). What does he mean by the 'lie in the soul'? Nothing very exalted, he assures us. 'All I am saying is that to lie, and to be deceived, and to be ignorant about reality in one's soul, to hold and possess the lie there, is the last thing anyone would want.' And this – the true lie – is then defined as 'the ignorance in the soul of the person who has been deceived' (2.382b).[11]

Socrates' distinction is a simple one. It turns on the implicit thought that lying is such a profoundly disturbing thing that we ought to try to identify what it is that is so disturbing about it and let that control our use of the expression 'lie'. What is disturbing about lying is not in the end saying something false out loud in words to someone else, nor deliberately trying to mislead them, but *saying something false in your own mind to yourself*, particularly something false about 'the most important things' (2.382a). So we should adjust our use of the language of truth and falsehood accordingly. Saying something false to another with intent to deceive is certainly a lie (the 'lie in words'), but the outcome lying in speech tries to achieve – belief in a falsehood – is what the real evil of lying consists in: the true lie (the 'lie in the soul'), therefore. It is still appropriate (Socrates seems to think) to speak then of a *lie*, not just the internal enunciation of a falsehood, because that falsehood expresses the state of mind of someone who is *deceived* into believing what they say to themselves. To put it differently, deception is an ambiguous notion. It can mean being deceived by oneself or by another (real deception), or it can mean trying to deceive someone else – which if deceivers are not themselves deceived is 'not unadulterated' deception, but a mere image of the real thing (the fact that you are saying something false makes it sound as though you are deceived, even though you are not).

The Stoics seem to have built on this distinction in developing their own absolutist solution to the problem of reconciling philosophical love of truth and the expediency of lying for political and other prudential reasons. According to them, the wise person – that is, the person who is perfectly rational – will sometimes say things that are false (*deliberately* say such things, as the standard examples they recycled make clear). But there will

---

[11] For a fuller treatment of this passage (and of others related to it), see the extended analysis of Harte 2013.

be no intent to deceive, even if the speaker knows very well that the outcome will be deception. And the wise will say what is false 'without assent'. So they will not count as lying, 'because they do not have their judgment assenting to what is false'. This is as much as to say that the wise are not in the grip of what the *Republic* describes as the true lie, the lie in the soul. The difference is that the Stoics stick to common usage in reserving the word 'lie' exclusively for speech acts.

Of course, the upshot is an innovative conception of lying in speech: someone counts as lying only if they are *themselves* deceived in some way (although presumably not the same way as the person to whom their falsehood is uttered is deceived) – above all, no doubt, regarding what is good and bad. The root cause of such deception of soul would be a morally bad disposition, as emerges in the Stoics' treatment of examples of falsehoods that may legitimately be told. Doctors who tell their patient or generals who tell their troops something false do not lie provided their intention is not bad. Just so, the Stoics' wise person says false things from a morally good disposition. The implication of their radical conception of lying is the counterintuitive proposition that the Platonic Socrates' useful medicinal lies are not lies at all.[12]

Just because the lie in words (to revert now to Socrates' own categories) is a lie only in words, not in the speaker's soul also, and therefore 'not quite an unadulterated lie', it obviously does not follow that there is any blanket justification for telling such lies. To say that they are 'not quite unadulterated' suggests a shade of grey a lot closer to black than white. And it is not hard to think of reasons why Socrates might want to encourage general aversion to them: not least because a successful lie in words will often be responsible for deception – a 'true lie' – in the *hearer*'s soul (although like the Stoics he might have wished to insist that principally and ultimately it is everyone's *own* responsibility whether they give their assent to a falsehood). Exceptions would always need a special defence, such as the argument that the telling of the right kind of myths to children induces not deception but *truth* in their souls in regard to 'the most important things' (2.382a).

Nonetheless we should not be surprised that the *Republic* allows for such exceptions. It was Augustine, not Plato, who was the first notable champion of what we might call the absolutist position on the morality

---

[12] The relevant texts are Plutarch, *On Stoic Contradictions* 1055f–1056a, 1057a–b; Sextus Empiricus, *Adversus Mathematicos* 7.42–5; Stobaeus, *Eclogae* 2.III.10–17; and Quintilian, *Institutio* 12.1.38. For discussion, see Bobzien 1998: 271–4.

of lying: holding that all lying is wrong, and forbidden by God as sinful. Indeed, Augustine represents a watershed between antiquity and modernity in the history of the moral philosophy of lying. The massive influence of his view on the matter was such that much subsequent discussion has felt obliged at least to grapple with the absolutist position, even though few have embraced it like Kant without qualification.[13] The questionability of the absolutist stance is brilliantly exhibited in the chapter entitled 'Sincerity: Lying and Other Styles of Deceit' in Bernard Williams's last book, *Truth and Truthfulness*.[14] But in treatments of lying by Greek and Roman authors before Augustine, there is not much to suggest that it even occurred to people that absolutism was a serious option. It is the Stoics who stand out as exceptions to the general rule, but exceptions only of the highly qualified kind we have just glanced at. The *Republic*, however, unquestionably envisages justifications for lying.

In the passage at the end of Book 2 we have been considering, Socrates lists a few types of occasion on which lying may be 'useful, so as not to be deserving of hatred' (2.382c). Stories about events long ago – the myths he subjects to censorship – constitute one category of useful lie. The other cases he mentions form a pair: lying to enemies and lying to one's so-called friends, if in derangement they are attempting to do something bad. These two sorts of useful lie are no less important for him. Their articulation as such may not be due originally to Plato. Conceivably the category of the useful lie is one he took over from Socrates himself, or perhaps it was becoming common coin in ethical discussion. In Xenophon's *Memorabilia*, *his* Socrates engages in rather more extended and pointed discussion of the topic of whether it is just to lie to one's friends as well as one's enemies, with permissible examples including lying to a depressed and indeed suicidal friend, lying to children to induce them to take medicine when they need it, and lying by a general to encourage his downhearted troops (*Mem.* 4.2.14–18). Xenophon may be drawing on Plato in this (the *Memorabilia*, like most of Xenophon's 'Socratic' writings, is usually thought to date to late in his life, and after the *Republic*). But already the last of these examples is mentioned as a commonplace in a speech to the Athenian assembly by Andocides delivered in 391 BC: 3.34). Interestingly, Socrates in the *Republic* starts by characterizing useful lies in general as 'taking the form of a drug [*pharmakon*]', as though the

---

[13] See, for example, Bok 1978: 34–49. Although in the end absolutist, Augustine's treatment of the topic (primarily in *De mendacio* [late 390s AD] and *Contra mendacium* [422 AD]) is highly nuanced and extremely subtle: for an analysis, see Kirwan 1989: 196–204, and more recently Atkins 2018.
[14] Williams 2002: 84–122.

medicinal lie is the core case: the point here being that just as only doctors – the experts – should administer drugs, so in the public sphere it is appropriate for the rulers alone to lie, for the benefit of the city, whether as regards enemies or citizens (3.389b–c).

The example of the deranged or depressed friend who needs to be lied to for their own good takes us right back to the beginning of the dialogue. In the initial conversation between Cephalus and Socrates, the idea begins to emerge that justice might be a matter of telling the truth and repaying one's obligations. Socrates raises the case of the deranged friend by way of objection. Suppose such a person had lent you weapons when of sound mind and now asks for their return; then it *would not* be the act of someone behaving justly to comply with the request, or to tell the whole truth. So 'this isn't the definition of justice, speaking the truth and giving back what one takes' (1.331a–d). The issue of truth telling and indeed of its ambiguity is thereby marked out as something we may expect to figure on the agenda of the dialogue as a whole. Socrates' position – that there will always be cases where truth telling *would not* be just – is later reinforced by epistemological and metaphysical considerations advanced at the end of Book 5. There, he argues quite generally that *any* particular exemplification of beauty or justice or largeness or heaviness and so on may turn out to be an exemplification also of precisely the opposite: ugliness, injustice, smallness, lightness. So it would be a mistake to suggest that they could constitute part of the essence of beauty or justice and so on and qualify as objects of knowledge rather than opinion (5.479a–480a). An absolutist position on truth telling proves therefore to be incompatible with Platonism. In Platonism, the realm of the absolute is the Forms, not the world of human experience and activity.

In his account at the beginning of the next book of the dispositions that must become second nature to the philosopher as one devoted to knowledge, Socrates early on lists 'aversion to falsehood' (6.485c), which he explains as 'not willingly accepting falsehood in any form – hating it, but loving truth'. In the conversational exchange that then ensues, it is argued that this requirement simply follows from the philosopher's love of wisdom. Someone who genuinely loves learning things 'must make every possible effort, right from earliest childhood, to reach out for truth of every kind' (6.485d). Adam in his great commentary on the Greek text of the *Republic* thought 'truth' here meant 'metaphysical truth' – of which someone whose soul harboured a lie about 'the most important things' would be ignorant.[15] I am not sure Plato meant to be so restrictive. 'All truth' or 'truth of every kind' sounds as though

---

[15] Adam 1963 [1902], II.4.

it might include truth in speech as well as truth in the soul.[16] Adam was right, however, in the main thing he wanted to deny. Plato cannot be tacitly withdrawing the claim that, in their capacity as rulers, philosophers will necessarily resort to deception in order to maintain the social and political fabric of the city. What does follow (on the more inclusive view of what 'truth of every kind' encompasses) is that even as they tell politically expedient lies, philosopher rulers will hate doing it. There really is a tension at this point between their aspirations as philosophers and the constraints under which they must operate as rulers. A little later Socrates asks (6.486a): 'Do you think, then, that the mind which can take a large view, and contemplate the whole of time and the whole of reality, is likely to regard human life as of any importance?' Everything to do with ruling – as preoccupied exclusively with the affairs of humans – must for a philosopher be irksome triviality, and that presumably includes the need to tell lies.

The influential political philosopher Hannah Arendt wrote in 1967 as follows:[17]

> I hope no one will tell me any more that Plato was the inventor of the 'noble lie'. This belief rested on a misreading of a crucial passage (414c) in the *Republic*, where Plato speaks of one of his myths – a 'Phoenician tale' – as a *pseudos*. Since the same Greek word signifies 'fiction', 'error', and 'lie' according to context – if Plato wants to distinguish between error and lie, the Greek language forces him to speak of 'involuntary' and 'voluntary' *pseudos* – the text can be rendered with Cornford as 'bold flight of invention' or be read with Eric Voegelin . . . as satirical in intention; under no circumstances can it be understood as a recommendation of lying as we understand it.

It will by now be evident that Arendt was simply wrong about the interpretation of *pseudos*. The noble lie is specifically introduced as one of the 'falsehoods that get created as needed which we were talking about a little while back' (3.414b). Socrates is referring to the useful medicinal lies first exemplified in Book 1 by the case of the deranged friend's dagger and then categorized near the end of Book 2. The noble lie, like the entire discussion of acceptable and unacceptable narratives in Books 2 and 3, is

---

[16] Does 7.535d–e suggest otherwise? According to Socrates, a 'crippled' soul hates telling or hearing a deliberate lie, and gets terribly cross about it, but puts up with the 'unwilling lie', wallowing in ignorance and experiencing no distress when its ignorance is revealed for what it is. This is someone who has an inverted and perverted sense of the relative importance of falsehood in words and falsehood (albeit unwitting) in the soul. It would be wrong to infer that lies in words are *not* to be viewed with distaste. But they are a minor matter compared with 'true' lies.
[17] Arendt 1968: 292 n. 5.

conceptualized in terms of the polarity of lying and truth telling and resonates as such with discussions of political expediency in many other Athenian texts of the late fifth and fourth centuries, as well as with Plato's own metaphysical preoccupation with truth. Carl Page rightly comments on 'how deeply woven into the fabric of the entire conversation' is his treatment of lying.[18] Nietzsche was a surer guide than Arendt when he congratulated Plato on 'a real lie, a genuine, resolute, "honest" lie' (*Genealogy of Morals* 3.19).

Caring for the City

The first part of the myth of the noble lie concludes with its moral. The earth – their mother – releases her sons, 'and now it is their duty to deliberate on behalf of the country they are in and defend it – just as they would their mother or nurse – and to regard the rest of the citizens as their brothers, born from the earth' (3.414e). When the whole narrative is over, and Glaucon and Socrates have finished their brief discussion of it, Socrates says (3.415d–e):

> Our job now is to arm our earthborn, and lead them forth, with the rulers at their head. Let them go and look for the best place in the city to put their camp, a place from which they may best control those within, if any of them refuse to obey the laws, or repel those without, if any enemy comes down on them 'like a wolf on the fold'.

All the citizens are 'earthborn', but these passages make it crystal clear that Socrates is focusing principally on the rulers (deliberation being their job) and the military (defence being theirs), just as he does in addressing the story to them in the first instance before the rest of the city, and endeavouring to persuade *them* to believe it. To understand why the noble lie is written this way we need to attend to the broader context.[19]

After nearly forty pages' discussion of the military class and its selection and education, Socrates asks almost casually which of them are to rule and which to be ruled (3.412b; not for him debate about whether monarchy, democracy, or some form of oligarchy or aristocracy is the right system, just the *assumption* that rulers will be drawn from the guards – who are now (414b) divided into guards proper and 'auxiliaries' or 'supporters'). In answering his own question, he specifies three principal qualifications those selected as rulers will need to possess. They are to be wise (*phronimoi*,

---

[18] Page 1991: 2.   [19] For a similar approach to the one adopted here, see Hahm 1969.

Aristotle's word for *practical* understanding), able, and above all people who care for the city (412c). In the immediate sequel, Socrates focuses exclusively on acquisition of the third and (as he represents it) most important of these attributes; the others are apparently reserved for later, when the rulers have been identified as philosophers. In launching his treatment of the third desideratum, his first move is to suggest that someone is most likely to care for something if he loves it (*philein*). And then he makes the following intriguing remark (412d):

> And he would be most likely to love a thing when he believed that what is in its interest is the same as what is in his own, and when he supposed that if it did well, he would do well too, and if it didn't, neither would he.

This formulation of perceived coincidence of interest as a key condition needing to be satisfied if a person is to love something might have led one to expect some argument next on why it *will* be in the interests of wise and capable guards to promote the interests of the city. That never happens. Why not?

It is not that the *Republic* is not concerned with that kind of issue. After all, Book 2 begins with Glaucon's articulation of the idea that a social contract prohibiting mutual wrong, and more generally institution of the rule of law, will be perceived as in the interests of the individual, assuming standard conditions of general 'weakness when it comes to wronging others' (2.358e–359b), or mutually assured destructive capability, as they used to say during the Cold War. A train of thought in Book 1 may give us a clue as to why we get nothing like that here. There, Socrates argues against Thrasymachus at some length that no art or skill (medicine and seamanship are the favourite examples) is practised as such to secure what is best for the practitioner, but only for what is under its control and in its care. So if people are to be prepared to undertake political rule (conceived as a form of expertise), there has to be 'payment' to induce them to do it – money, or prestige, or else some penalty for not ruling.

Now the good, the sort of people who would make suitable rulers, are not interested in money or prestige. So in their case a penalty will be required, to compel them to take it on. The main element in that, and the main reason why they will agree to exercise rule, is the prospect of being ruled by someone worse if they refuse to do it themselves. They undertake rule, therefore, not as something good, which will be a good experience for them, but as something unavoidable (1.346d–347d).[20] From this piece of

---

[20] I am grateful to Melissa Lane for emphasizing to me the importance of this passage in Book 1 for interpretation of the political philosophy of the *Republic*.

reasoning, there emerges an example where – to revert to the thesis in Book 3 that concerns us – the interest of the city is indeed perceived to coincide with that of the person we would wish to be its ruler. It is in the interests of the city that such a person exercise rule, because that is its best chance of being well governed. And it is also in the interests of that kind of person, because otherwise they risk being ruled over by someone worse than themselves.

But this is hardly a recipe for securing rulers who will *love* their city. Coincidence of perceived interest may be a *necessary* condition of such an outcome, but if the ruler perceives what is in his interest not as something positively good but as merely unavoidable (as is reiterated later in the dialogue, too, most explicitly at 7.540a–b; cf. 520d), it will not be *sufficient* to motivate love. Indeed, when Glaucon says (2.358c) that on the contractarian view of justice, people practice it *unwillingly*, as something unavoidable, not something good (exactly echoing Socrates' words at 1.347c–d), his formulation simply expresses what is implicit in Socrates' assessment of the attitude to ruling that the good person will form in the light of calculation of self-interest, not just in Book 1, but in the central books of the dialogue, too.[21]

It is therefore understandable that having introduced perceived coincidence of interest between city and ruler as a necessary condition of the ruler's loving the city in our Book 3 passage, Socrates says no more at this point to explain *why* rulers will believe that their interests coincide with those of the city. It is not that he could not give an answer. It is rather a problem about the kind of answer that might be forthcoming if he remained within the conceptual framework of rational egoism, within which the *Republic* invariably discusses questions of interest. An answer of that sort could not supply him with an adequate account of the motivation to care for the city that he is looking for here. So having stipulated that rulers will love the city only if they think its interests coincide with their own, Socrates moves on at once to conclude that the right members of the military class to select as potential rulers (or guards proper) are people who (1) throughout their lives are utterly determined to do what they think to be in the city's interests and refuse to act in any way whatsoever which they think would be against its interests and (2) throughout their lives guard unswervingly the conviction that it is their duty to do what at any time they judge best for the city (3.412d–e; cf. 413c). A whole page is then given over to the tests and trials they must be put through from earliest

[21] See further Sedley 2007.

childhood to ensure that they do not involuntarily lose this true conviction (involuntarily, because it is only false beliefs that people give up voluntarily). Three areas of risk are identified, and three kinds of test proposed accordingly. They might be prone to forget their conviction or be persuaded out of it; pain or grief might cause them to abandon it; or they might be seduced out of it by pleasure or terrified out of it by danger. The person who under constant testing emerges unsullied should be appointed ruler and guard of the city (3.412e–414a).

So far there is nothing on *how* guards who come successfully through this process *acquired* their motivation and the conviction that underpins it in the first place. Enter the noble lie. In his closing comments on the myth, Socrates indicates that a main purpose in inculcating it in the minds of the citizens is precisely to bring them 'to care more about the city and one another' (3.415d). This is the nearest he gets to an explicit statement on how guards develop commitment to the city: they will need to be persuaded by the noble lie or something like it. It is of course a paradox that the one specific mechanism he proposes for generating a motivation that is supposed to be rooted in unshakable true conviction is a lie – something explicitly labelled a 'device' (3.414b). Yet once we set the noble lie in the context of education of the young (which I assume is the main context appropriate for it – more on this later), the paradoxicality is mitigated, and indeed a thoroughly sensible rationale begins to emerge.

Socrates does not explain in so many words why children have to be started off on stories whose truth is encased in falsehood, but various things he says in the first page or two of his critique of Homer and Hesiod make the rationale for this and the criteria he expects such stories to meet fairly clear. For example, he thinks the minds of children highly malleable (2.377b) and unsophisticated (they cannot judge what to take literally or otherwise, 378d), but at the same time the opinions they take on board at this early age tend to be difficult to wash out and unchangeable (378d–e). This is doubtless why fictive stories about a paradigmatic but inaccessible past rather than abstract arguments are the things to teach them – and it is extraordinarily important that from the outset these be 'as beautiful as possible', to lead them toward virtue (378e).

Here, considerations of the good of the city must be paramount. If we want the people who are to protect our city to regard it as a crime to fall out with each other at the drop of a hat, stories about battles between giants and the many and varied enmities of gods and heroes towards family and kin must be off the agenda. If we want to convince them that no citizen has ever quarrelled with another citizen – that such a thing is an impiety – then that is what old people must tell children from the word go, and poets must be made to compose stories to that effect for them as they grow older (378b–d). This is a job for poets, not philosophers – presumably because it is the poet, not the philosopher, who is skilled in exploiting cultural tradition to produce images and narratives with the requisite resonance and power and who is experienced in moulding people's souls by such means (378e–379a). Hence, when Plato tries his own hand at myth in the noble lie, he adapts well-known stories: the myth of Cadmus and the earthborn warriors sown from dragons' teeth, and Hesiod's myth of metals.[22]

A Question of Identity

The noble lie tells the guards (rulers and auxiliaries) and the rest of the citizens something quite different from all the other stories expurgated and wished for in Books 2 and 3. It instructs them about *themselves* – in fact, it tells them who they are. The territory their city occupies is literally mother to them all, and so the rulers in particular are to conceive their obligations as those of sons who must deliberate about the welfare of the mother who has nurtured them, and the military their obligations as those of sons who must defend her, regarding all the other citizens as brothers (3.414e). The implication is that they are *not* to identify themselves primarily as individuals, with interests defined in terms of rational egoism, but as parts or members of a whole, understood on the model of a family – something immediately intelligible to children, of course.[23]

The second part of the myth – Plato's adaptation of Hesiod – complicates the picture. While all the citizens are brothers, god has used 'gold' in creating those fit to be rulers, 'silver' for the auxiliaries, 'iron' and 'bronze' for the farmers and artisans: not human, perishable gold (and so on), as we hear a little later, but pure divine gold, in their souls (3.415a, 416e–417a). The focus of the narrative, however, is on the imperative god issues to the rulers. The first and most important instruction they are given as guards relates to the adulteration of these metals in the souls of the offspring produced in each of the classes. Precisely because all citizens are members of the same family and have the same genetic material, it will sometimes happen that gold parents will produce children with an admixture of iron or bronze: these

---

[22] There is a good deal more to say about the mythical discourse of the noble lie as such than I have room for here. For some further remarks on the subject, see Schofield 2009; for a radically different approach, the wide-ranging study by Rowett 2016.
[23] On this topic and its ramifications, see now Sheffield 2021.

have to be expelled into the ranks of artisans or farmers. Conversely, when farmers or artisans produce children with admixtures of gold or silver, they are to be promoted to guards or auxiliaries. The entire myth concludes dramatically, with ominous mention of an oracle predicting the destruction of the city should iron or bronze guards take charge (3.415a–c). Caring for the city will therefore require the guards to take pains not least – perhaps above all – to ensure that that never happens.

The story of the metals also says something further about the citizens' identity or, rather, identities. Of course, it is a way of expressing the fundamental argument for the specialization of functions according to natural aptitude that Socrates has already articulated (2.369b–370c), and particularly of insisting on the consequential need for mobility between classes where appropriate (that will be reiterated in non-mythical terms a little later: 4.423c–d; cf. 4.434a–b, 5.468a). But the noble lie insinuates the thought that these political arrangements are not due at all to the fiat of human decision, but *simply* reflect the way people indeed are (that they are that way is in itself no falsehood, on Socrates' premises, and given his eugenic programme). And it conveys the warning that resisting or neglecting the implications of that will be politically disastrous – because people cannot be what they really are not.

The metaphor of filial obligation, to sum up, is what the noble lie makes underpin the overriding commitment to the good of the city required of its rulers, supported by its military. There is no non-metaphorical piece of political theory developed elsewhere in Books 2 to 4 into which it can be translated (contrast the story of the metals). And crucial to it is an existential dimension untranslatable into theory. In effect, it says to the rulers: '*This* – the city – is *your* mother, *you* must deliberate on her behalf and defend her.' We have to wait until Book 5 for a non-mythical articulation of the relationship between city and citizens that could transform the metaphor into something more literal (though still an imaginative projection). The radical eugenic breeding provisions Socrates there proposes require a reconceptualizing of the family. All the young are to think of *anyone* else who was evidently conceived during the same mating festival as brother or sister, and parents are to treat *all* such children as their sons and daughters (5.461d–e). In fact, every time one guard meets another, they will *assume* it is a brother or sister or mother or father, or the child or parent of one (5.463c). In such a city, more than in any other, the binding unity that Socrates calls the 'footprint' of the good will be apparent. Everyone will use 'I' and 'my' simultaneously. All will rejoice and grieve over exactly the same events (all saying with reference to the same thing 'I'm really upset by that', etc.). They will behave like the parts of one body, which are all affected by pain or pleasure in any one of them (e.g. the finger), so that we say, 'The *person* feels pain *in* the finger' (5.462a–d, 463e–464b).

What this passage in Book 5 brings home is something of essential importance for an understanding of the noble lie. Plato evidently sees no way of developing the motivation to care for the city *independent* of the creation of what one might call a holistic political ideology. The metaphor of filial obligation or recompense is his favourite way of articulating such an ideology. Something like it recurs in the famous discussion in Book 7 of the return of philosophers from contemplation of eternal truth to the cave of human existence. At the end of the cave analogy, Socrates says that 'the best natures' must not be allowed to avoid descending from their philosophical studies back into the cave – to fulfil their duty to take their turn as rulers over the other citizens. Glaucon objects (7.519d): 'What? Are we going to do them an injustice, and make them live a worse life when a better is possible for them?' On the second point, Socrates issues a reminder that their concern as legislators is the good of the whole city, not of any particular class within it. His reply on the first point does not (as some commentators would have preferred) invoke the metaphysics of the Forms but turns on considerations of reciprocal obligation. Significantly, he moves into direct speech to address his argument direct to the philosophers. He appeals to the understanding *they* need to have of *their* existential situation.

Other cities, Socrates has remarked, do nothing to nurture the political potential of their philosophers. 'But we have produced *you* as leaders and kings', he begins, 'and have educated you accordingly, so that you can share in both the philosophical and the political life.'[24] When his fairly lengthy speech to them is complete, he asks Glaucon: 'Then do you fancy those we have nurtured will disobey us after hearing this, and refuse to take their turn in sharing in the exertions of the city?' 'Impossible', says Glaucon, now convinced: 'It is a just instruction, and they are just.' It is striking how he couches his verdict in terms of justice. The verdict is prepared for by reflection not on justice as it comes to be conceived in the main argument

---

[24] Whether their counterparts in the cities of contemporary Greece would be regarded by Socrates as having any political obligations reciprocating for their education and upbringing is a moot point. If one supposed it legitimate to extend the argument made by the laws of Athens in the *Crito* to other cities generally, an affirmative answer might be inferred. But the *Republic* takes the view that in most actual or conceivable *politeiai*, education and upbringing are so deficient that keeping one's hands free from impiety and injustice may often be the most one can reasonably expect of a philosopher (cf. 6.496a–e, 9.592a–b).

of the *Republic*, but on justice as Simonides thought of it – paying back what you owe to somebody (1.331d-e).[25] Not that the dialogue in the end sees any necessary incompatibility between these two conceptions of justice. The first thing we are told about the characteristic behaviour of the just person defined at the end of Book 4 is that he is someone who repays his debts (442e–443a). Such a person counts behaviour in the political as in other spheres 'just' when it preserves and promotes psychic harmony (443c–e, presumably a necessary, not a sufficient condition).[26]

There is a notable anticipation in the earlier *Crito* of the pattern of argument I am detecting in these passages of the *Republic*. In that dialogue, the issue for Socrates' friend Crito is why the philosopher will not effect an escape from the prison to which he is confined, awaiting execution of the sentence of death passed on him by the Athenian court. The main body of the explanation Socrates offers him is contained in an extended piece of political rhetoric put in the mouths of the personified laws of Athens and addressed in the second person direct to Socrates himself and to his existential situation (compare the *Republic* contexts we have been considering). The laws appeal for the most part to Simonidean justice, and in the first instance to considerations with which we are now familiar. The laws and the city produced Socrates – it was under their auspices that his parents married and brought him to birth. They too are similarly responsible for his upbringing or nurturing and his education. So if the laws and the city now decide that Socrates must perish, the reciprocity of obligation dictates not that he should do what he can to destroy the laws and the city (which is what ignoring their jurisdiction would amount to), but that he should obey the decision out of filial respect (*Crito* 50d–51c).

The issues at stake in all three of these texts – the *Crito* passage, the treatment of the return to the cave in Book 7 of the *Republic*, and the noble lie – are closely comparable: how to *persuade* the individual to do something required by the good of the city. In each case, the considerations put forward in favour are drawn not from the deeper resources of Socratic or Platonic philosophy but from more popular discourse. In the *Crito* and the return to the cave passage, the argument is presented as a piece of political rhetoric addressed in the second person to the philosopher, while in the noble lie Socrates has recourse in myth to another popular form, and again in its second part adopts a more urgent mode of expression by addressing

---

[25] For this reading of Socrates' argument as an appeal to justice as reciprocity, see, e.g., Gill 1996: 287–307; Nightingale 2004: 131–7.
[26] Here I glide past issues much debated in modern scholarship. See, e.g., Annas 1978; Dahl 1991; Burnyeat 2013.

the citizens in the second person. The second person is for the Platonic Socrates peculiarly appropriate to communication between members of a family about their obligations and commitments. 'I was always concerned with you', he tells the Athenians at his trial (*Ap.* 31b), 'approaching each one of you like a father or an elder brother to persuade you to care for virtue.' When there is a need to move people to make particular commitments to a particular community, the arguments Plato produces for elevating the good of the city above that of the individual have nothing metaphysical about them.

Believing the Lie

'You seem reluctant to tell your story', says Glaucon (3.414c), having heard Socrates' prefatory remarks about it. 'It's a very reasonable reluctance', replies Socrates, 'as you'll find when I tell it.' Socrates in fact hedges his narrative around with a good deal of commentary. Three elements in the commentary – obviously interconnected – stand out. First, the noble lie is presented with a show of considerable reluctance. Socrates claims to be at a loss to know how to present it, and indeed to pluck up the nerve to do so. Second, there is an implication that the Lie is somehow outrageous. After hearing the first Cadmeian part of it, Glaucon indicates that he now realizes why Socrates was ashamed to tell the Lie, and Socrates himself may be suggesting that his story sounds archaic – not the sort of thing that happens or could happen in the contemporary world. Little wonder. Apart from any other problem there may be with it, he envisages its recipients having to be persuaded that 'the entire upbringing and education we gave them, their whole experience of it happening to them, was after all merely a dream, something they imagined, and that in reality they spent that time being formed and raised deep within the earth – themselves, their weapons, and the rest of the equipment which was made for them' (3.414d–e).

Unsurprisingly (and finally), the interlocutors express little confidence that the rulers of the city could be made to believe such a myth.[27] Socrates confesses that a great deal of persuasion would be needed. And when he asks Glaucon whether he can think of any device whereby the rulers *could* be persuaded of the story, Glaucon says: 'No way' (3.415c). What he does concede – and I take the concession to be of the utmost importance – is that with their sons and in subsequent generations there would be more chance, presumably because the first rulers would tell it of themselves to

---

[27] Especially on the problem of securing belief, see Wardy 2013.

their children at a stage in their development when they are impressionable and uncritical. Socrates replies (415d): 'Even that' (I interpret, having children believe the Lie) 'would help to make the rulers' (I suppose, the first rulers) 'care more for the city and each other.'

Let us take a step backwards and reflect briefly on the complexities of what is going on in this extraordinary section of text. One thing at least must now be abundantly clear. The noble lie is very far from being simply a brazen piece of propaganda designed primarily to control the mass of the population of the ideal city (as usual, it is not the population at large that is uppermost in Plato's mind).[28] It is aimed at the rulers in the first instance (3.414d), and its main purpose is to get them to be public-spirited. It is a lie because it attempts to persuade citizens of false things about their origin and upbringing, but noble because it communicates in symbolic form truths about the good city, its foundation in human nature, and the behaviour it requires. And it is the subject of authorial commentary shot through with sophisticated intellectual embarrassment, and not with the Machiavellian blandness associated with the amoral manipulation of information typical of our own time or with its analogue in Diodotus' Athens. In short, it is a decidedly unstraightforward piece of writing.

The focus of the embarrassment is somewhat elusive. Perhaps it is Plato's way of signalling a mainly literary discomfort. Socrates and his interlocutors are imagining themselves as legislating for a city they are *founding* in some sense or other (cf. 7.519c), as new Greek cities had often in recent history been founded all over the Mediterranean and on the coast of the Black Sea. Yet if a city is to have a charter myth, its origins need to be represented as more than human and as rooted in a remote past. The credibility of the myth will depend on creating in the telling a psychological distance that ensures no conflict between present experience and the very different original condition being imagined. There is therefore a problem in trying to conceptualize what it would be like for citizens of a newly created community to believe a myth that will imply that it came into being very differently. Plato faces the problem head on. He has Socrates seize the bull by the horns and tell the citizens of his good city their charter myth without making the least attempt to generate the requisite psychological distance. The myth of the earthborn is about *them*, and they must be got to

---

[28] This was the interpretation of R. H. S. Crossman, in Crossman 1937: 130. A different view is in Dunn 1979: 116 n. 68.

think that what they all know perfectly well about their real upbringing is a dream – impossibly, one might suppose, though in our own time conversion to belief in alternative realities is not unknown.

Plato *need* not have written the noble lie passage this way. He could from the outset have made it something the original citizens tell the *children* about the remote origins of the city (the scenario presumably envisaged by Glaucon when he pronounces his verdict, as likewise by Socrates when he speaks of it as something that will turn into a tradition or *phêmê*: 415d). That way the problem of non-existent psychological distance would never have arisen in the first place. The very fact that this alternative was so obviously available to Plato suggests that the embarrassment he injects into the dialogue at this point has dimensions other than the one we have singled out so far. Socrates started by describing the myth – evidently with reference to the Cadmeian section – as having something Phoenician about it (hardly just because Cadmus came from that part of the world)[29] and as being the kind of thing usually said (and believed) about the past, not the present. This may suggest a 'modern' and Greek disdain for such crudities, comparable with that implicit in Phaedrus' incredulity that Socrates might really believe the story of Boreas' abduction of Orithuia (*Phdr.* 228b–e).

Socrates remarks that the thing the story tells of – generation of human beings from the earth – 'has happened in many places, as the poets say and have succeeded in convincing people' (3.414c). This may be a sly reference to the Athenians' own myth of autochthony.[30] They claimed to be the *only* Greek people that had literally sprung from the soil they lived off: 'Alone of the Greeks', said Isocrates in a work of 380 BC (*Paneg.* 24, in words that parallel Socrates' at *Rep.* 3.414e), 'we can call her [Attica] not only native land but mother and nurse.' Plato himself had exploited the Athenian claim – investing it with strongly democratic and egalitarian commitments quite contrary to those of the myth of the metals here – in his pastiche of Pericles' funeral speech in the *Menexenus* (*Menex.* 237b–239a). No doubt he envisages for the *Republic* a readership of urbane sceptics, to whom some sort of apology is needed for advocating the use of such material. To a degree, Socrates had prepared the way, with his general theory of the use of false stories in bringing children up. But this is the first actual example he presents of a myth whose employment he is recommending, not criticizing (other than the flat retelling as narrative, not dramatic representation, of the beginning of Book 1 of the *Iliad* earlier in

---

[29] Cornford 1941: 106 has 'Eastern tale', which I think gives the appropriate 'orientalizing' flavour.
[30] For which see Loraux 1993: 37–71.

Book 3 (393c–394b)). This, we might conjecture, accounts for some at least of the parade of nervousness at this juncture.

In Book 2 of Plato's *Laws*, there occurs the following exchange (2.663e–664a):

CLEINIAS: Truth is a fine thing, Visitor, and it has staying power. Yet it appears to be something not easy to persuade people about.
VISITOR: I'll allow you that. Yet it proved easy to persuade people of the Sidonian [i.e. Phoenician] story, incredible though it was, and thousands of others.
CLEINIAS: What do you have in mind?
VISITOR: The story of the teeth that were sown, and of how armed men grew from them. Here in fact is a notable example for a lawgiver, of how someone who tries can persuade the souls of the young of anything, so that the only question he has to consider in inventing such stories is what would do most good to the city, if it were believed. Then he must discover every possible device to ensure that the whole community speaks with one and the same voice about these subjects, constantly and throughout their lives, in their songs, their stories, and their speeches.

Like so many passages in the *Laws*, this one constitutes among other things a commentary on the *Republic*. It serves to reinforce a reading of the noble lie that relates it above all to the educational programme of Books 2 and 3, and in particular to the question of motivating people to care for the city from their earliest years. Given Socrates' theory of the efficacy of myths in moulding children's souls, it is highly plausible that the children of the rulers and of the other citizens could be persuaded of its charter myth – just as the Athenian visitor envisages. The hypothesis that Plato thinks they could is supported by – and helps in its turn to explain – the way Socrates argues in the Book 7 passage on the return of the philosophers to the cave. With a further look at that passage my argument will conclude.

Socrates there appeals to the philosophers' recognition that they are obliged to repay the city for the upbringing and nurture they have received (7.520a–d). One might worry (scholars have worried a great deal) that this is an argument pitched at too superficial a level to be appropriate to thinkers who have been deeply immersed in study of the Form of the Good and all that that entails.[31] But let us suppose that philosophers had indeed been persuaded in childhood of the myths of the noble lie. And let us further suppose that they have never lost either the conviction thereby instilled in them that above all they must care for the city as a matter of reciprocal obligation or (yet more important) the motivation to do so that

---

[31] For an excellent review of some major issues of interpretation, see Brown 2000; also Sedley 2007.

the conviction supports. What will have changed for them now that they have achieved philosophical understanding? First, they will no longer believe the myths as myths. They will have the sort of grasp of the rationale for the good city that is articulated in the philosophical argument of the *Republic* (cf. 6.497c–d). Second, they will have become only too aware that in the pursuit of knowledge of eternal truth they have discovered something incomparably more important than the city, and something also far more desirable as a good. They will consequently need to be *compelled* to take their turn at ruling. But patriotic conviction – 'hard to wash out' and tested in every kind of trial – will remain writ deep in their souls, something Socrates stresses once again after he has introduced the topic of an education fit for philosopher rulers, even as he allows that the discussion back in Book 3 glided past and veiled the difficulty that would be presented by that loftier perspective (6.503a).[32]

On this supposition, it should follow that, however clear and universal the philosophical vision they enjoy outside the cave, and however small human life appears from that perspective, or again however preoccupied they might be with the health and happiness of their own souls, nonetheless the philosophers' conviction of their political duty and the sense of their own identity that goes with it are so deeply entrenched that its unphilosophical and pre-dialectical dictates will in the end trump all other considerations and serve as the instrument of 'compulsion'. The problem of adjusting perspective on re-entry to the cave is alluded to and may mean that they need *reminding* of it – hence the argument about reciprocation Socrates imagines himself and the other interlocutors putting to them. But any lapse in recollection of what they have all along been committed to could be no more than temporary. And a reminder of their obligation, together with a statement of the contribution they are uniquely capable of making thanks to their philosophical grasp of truth, is all that will be necessary for them to recover themselves. In short, what Plato makes Socrates say, philosophically undemanding as it may be, turns out to be the appropriate thing to say, precisely because of the depth of the conviction and motivation it appeals to.

---

[32] Adam has a good note on this point: see Adam 1963 [1902]: II:46.

CHAPTER 8

The Cave

A Diagnosis and a Remedy

Of all Plato's memorable images, the Cave is the most compelling, and perhaps indeed 'the most famous metaphor in the history of philosophy'.[1] Yet it is a headache for philosophical scholarship. A determinate interpretation has eluded commentators – not for want of their trying. The Cave was notoriously the one topic on which R. C. Cross and A. D. Woozley, in their textbook guide to the *Republic* of 1964, found themselves in disagreement.[2] In *An Introduction to Plato's Republic* (1981), Julia Annas concluded flatly that 'the imagery, memorable though it is, has no consistent overall interpretation'.[3] In the subsequent fifty years, studies of the Cave from one perspective or another have proliferated. But I have no sense of incipient or imminent consensus.

In fact, I agree with Julia Annas: it is impossible to give one single consistent account of everything Socrates says in developing the Cave analogy. So what I propose in this chapter is not another treatment of the Cave that will attempt to square the circle. Instead, I offer an exercise in what might be called metaspeleology: a diagnosis of the crux of the difficulty that generates interpretative impasse, and an associated remedy for interpretative angst. The diagnosis is a simple one. The Cave communicates not one philosophical vision but two – both of great interest, but different. One is developed in the Cave as initially narrated. The narrative tells its own compelling story, dropping plenty of hints – varying in directness or mysteriousness – on how it is to be read. The other vision is articulated mostly in the philosophical commentary on the Cave Plato's Socrates supplies when he tells Glaucon how to decode it.[4]

---

[1] So Blackburn 2006: 101. [2] See Cross and Woozley 1964: 227–8. [3] See Annas 1981: 256.
[4] For the crucial observation, see Burnyeat 1999b: 243: 'It is only in retrospect that we learn that the Cave has to do with mathematics as well as cultural values (532b–c).' I am not however persuaded by his suggestions for harmonizing the two projects, and in particular for seeing progress in mathematics as the way the prisoners in the cave achieve 'a better understanding of justice than they had before' (Burnyeat 2000: 45). The proposal does not seem to me to take the full measure of the incommensurability between Plato's two projects in the Cave.

The remedy? We get that from seeing that what the commentary proposes is a *re*reading of the narrative offering no more than an *alternative* construction of its meaning, not the single compulsory version. Consistency of interpretation as between original narrative and subsequent commentary is not mandatory. A little more precisely, we should take the commentary as enunciating *inter alia* a set of instructions not on what the narrative means as originally articulated, but on how it is to be *re*read as an allegory of the trainee philosopher's education. Those instructions for rereading are what link the Cave with the Sun and Line analogies. Moreover, the parallel signalled between Cave and Line may be seen as limited to one rather general point that need not require interpretative contortions on the part of the reader.

The contortions are usually occasioned in large part by the need interpreters have felt to find a way of explaining the original intellectual condition of the prisoners in terms of the Line analogy as a form of *eikasia* (imagination, conjecture), with the state of mind they achieve upon release from their chains accordingly equated with *pistis* (conviction; not so tricky to achieve in principle, despite Socrates' emphasis on puzzlement rather than conviction: 7.515d). The two segments of the bottom half of the line, sometimes labelled L1 and L2, are thus correlated with two stages in a similar – but highly contentious – division of the prisoners' progress into four, namely with those represented as occurring inside the cave itself (conventionally labelled C1 and C2). On my proposals, any such move would be a mistake.[5] When Socrates bids us connect the Cave with the Line (7.517a–b), all he explicitly enjoins is that we marry the upward journey and the viewing of what is above (as in the Cave narrative) with the ascent of the soul to the realm of the intelligible (in the Line). In other words, he says only: connect ascent with ascent, and contemplation of what is higher with contemplation of what is higher.

While interpreters have strained too hard to map Cave onto Line in all its detail, the repurposing of the Cave allegory from its first telling to subsequent explanation has been neglected. The Cave as narrated begins as a moral and political allegory of the condition of ordinary people in the city – in the first instance, the democratic city – and of their need for redemption from it.[6] The

---

[5] I am inclined in any case to suspect the passages which schematize a quartet of cognitive states of different relative clarity (6.511d–e, 7.533e–534b) of being late additions to the text, whether made by Plato or someone else intervening at an early point in its transmission, but not altogether well fitted to their immediate contexts in any case. I entertain a parallel suspicion with regard to the closely related clause at *Ti.* 29c3.

[6] It ends with a celebrated account of the philosophers' return to exercise rule in the cave, now understood as the ideal city in which they have been nurtured and educated (7.519d–521b). This might be considered as introducing yet a third function to which Plato puts the Cave allegory, and one which presupposes incorporation of features drawn *both* from the narrative as first developed *and*

Cave as reinterpreted in philosophical commentary is an image of the reorientation of the soul which can be achieved by the practice of mathematics, as prescribed in the educational curriculum of the ideal city devised for the ruling intellectual elite. Morals and politics versus mathematics; ordinary people versus the ruling elite; the democratic versus the ideal city: these three key polarities strike and puzzle all readers of the Cave. My argument is that they become altogether less puzzling once we notice that one set of elements functions primarily within the Cave as first narrated, the other in the Cave mostly as presented in Socrates' philosophical commentary, which dwells on elements in it that were not given particular prominence in the original telling.[7]

The body of the chapter has a tripartite structure. First comes a relatively brief section on the Cave's place in the developing argument of the *Republic*, and on the interpretation of the image Socrates supplies in order to explain the way it contributes to that argument. Second is a rather longer section on the Cave as actually narrated. Finally, I offer some brief concluding reflections: on why Plato may have decided to combine two such very different projects, and on how his instructions for rereading nonetheless leave them different. My aim is to liberate readers of Plato from the tyranny of thinking they have to find significance simultaneously ethical and mathematical in every detail of the Cave narrative, harnessed to just one overarching interpretation.

The Cave in the Argument of the *Republic*

From (roughly) the middle of Book 6 (502c) to the end of Book 7, the *Republic* discusses the studies which the philosophers who are to rule the ideal city must pursue if they are to be equipped for the task. The image of the Sun (6.507a–509c) introduces the ultimate and most important *subject* of study, the Form of the Good, in its relation to knowledge and reality quite generally; the Line (6.509d–511e) then develops that topic further. The Cave (7.514a–521b) launches a related but different project: explaining the *education* that will be needed if a person is to be in a position to gain an understanding of true reality and above all the Good. Education (*paideia*) is announced as its topic at the outset (7.514a); and when Socrates attempts an interim summary of its moral at 518b–d, he talks again of education – as

---

from the subsequent philosophical reinterpretation. I shall have little however to say about this section of the passage in the present chapter.

[7] This is especially true of the way Socrates works out the relationship with the Sun analogy, in particular (7.517b–c; cf. 516b–c).

rightly conceived, not as the ability to put sight into blind eyes that some claim to possess. Once the Cave has illuminated the general nature of that education, the next item on the agenda will be to identify the studies it will need to consist in if it is to achieve what it promises (7.521c–d; cf. 518d).

About education the Cave has a simple message.[8] Education is conversion: a conversion of the whole soul from concern with what is in process of becoming – the sensible world – to a focus on intelligible reality, and ultimately the Good (7.518c–d). This is what Socrates means to tell us when he imagines prisoners turning around from darkness (in the cave below) to illumination (in the sunlit world above). The ascent to reality that is constituted by conversion is what he goes on to call 'true philosophy' (7.521c). In the immediate sequel to the Cave, he goes on to explain something which the narrative itself has done nothing whatever even to intimate. He identifies the intellectual practice that will enable someone with a natural gift for philosophy to undergo this conversion. It is to be mathematics – arithmetic and plane geometry pretty much as currently practised, the new science of solid geometry, and a reformed astronomy and musical theory which will treat the study of the heavens and harmonic ratios just as geometers treat the triangles they draw on their whiteboards, in other words as approximations to purely intelligible motions and ratios (7.522b–531d).

The telling of the story of the Cave at the point in the *Republic* at which it is told is made to become relevant only because it dramatizes the power of mathematics to effect that reorientation of our minds which is to be discursively explicated in the pages that follow for each of the mathematical sciences in turn. In a notorious anacoluthic sentence near the end of the whole discussion in Book 7, Socrates says (532b–c):

> The release from the chains, the turning round away from the shadows to the images [i.e. the images which cast many of the shadows the prisoners take to constitute reality] and the firelight, the upward journey from the underground cave into the sun, and in the world above the inability yet to look in the direction of the animals and plants and the light of the sun, but instead at their divine reflections in water[9] and shadows of real things (rather than shadows of images cast by a light which is itself a shadow in comparison with the sun) – all the practice of the sciences we have just described [i.e. the

---

[8] Or more exactly, the message as it is represented in Socrates' commentary on the Cave is a simple one. As we shall see, the commentary omits much that the actual narrative suggests, in this as in other respects.

[9] 'Divine' is predicated of mere appearances, doubtless to emphasize that *everything* in the upper world is changeless intelligible reality.

mathematical sciences] has this power of leading the best element in the soul up to the contemplation of the best among the things.[10]

Or to adapt a more careful formulation adumbrated by Socrates himself a little earlier (7.518c–d), mathematics is the technique needed to orientate the *soul*'s own intrinsic capacity for truth in the right direction. To be sure, the anacoluthic sentence suggests a rather more complex point than that. It implies that the power of mathematics is despite that limited: it is associated with an *in*ability to look at reality other than through images (cf. 7.533b–c).[11] This nuance will prepare us for the reintroduction of dialectic as the capacity we need to take us all the way to understanding first principles and grasping the account of what each thing is, above all the Good itself (7.532d–e, 534b–d; cf. 6.511b–c). But initial orientation towards what is real and intelligible is represented as a job for mathematics, not dialectic.

The decision to stake so much on mathematics might seem to be a mistake – on Plato's own premises. Isn't Socrates failing to attend to something he has himself stressed at some length in Book 6? Isn't he forgetting that what is likely to divert a mind naturally equipped for philosophy from pursuit of the truth is moral corruption – the pleasures of the flesh and the varieties of ambition: in short, the entire false value system fostered by democracy and its creature sophistry? People who have fallen victim to all that are in need of urgent *moral* reclamation before there is any chance of interesting them in the intellectual problems that fascinate mathematicians. Mathematics may be necessary but can hardly be sufficient for conversion.

In fact, the point is not lost on Socrates. The passage on the need for a technique to engineer conversion is followed at once by a discussion of the problem of the person whose intellectual faculties are keen enough, but who is 'compelled to pay service to vice' (7.519a). The solution is expressed in counterfactual terms. If the soul of someone like that had been hammered into shape from childhood, it would have had struck from it the leaden weights of becoming which otherwise grow into it through gluttony

---

[10] In Burnyeat 1987: 227 n. 37, Myles Burnyeat rightly insisted that mathematics is here made responsible for achieving everything in the Cave narration that Socrates lists – including the initial release from chains. Plato presumably wants primarily to convey the commensurately general message that it is mathematics that enables us to look up to intelligible reality (albeit through images or appearances of one sort or another), instead of down to the realm of the sensible (cf. 7.529a–c).

[11] It may also hint at mathematical significance in the difference marked in the narrative between (a) looking at images in the cave and (b) looking at reflections in the world outside. Perhaps (a) relates to the way mathematicians use visible diagrams (cf. 6.510d–511a), (b) to the way their apprehension of intelligible reality has a dreamlike obliqueness about it (7.533b–c): see Burnyeat 1987: 227–9.

(presumably Socrates wants to exploit the thought that such people get overweight), and turns the soul's vision downwards.

Those whom Socrates envisages as suitable potential rulers of the ideal city *are* persons who have been hammered into shape before they begin an education in mathematics. He makes it clear – in passages just before the Sun, Line, and Cave analogies are developed and just after – that they will have been tried and tested by methods described in Book 3 to ensure that they have acquired the unshakeable moral character that education in music and gymnastics was designed to produce (6.503a–e, 7.521d–522b; cf. 3.412d–414a). In the second of the passages, in particular, he is also insistent that music and gymnastics cannot themselves constitute the art or science that will 'act as a magnet to the soul, drawing it away from the world of becoming towards the world of what is' (7.521d): physical education because in its concern for the body it presides over what comes to be and perishes, music because it trains by good habits, not on a basis of knowledge. They may not drag the soul down with leaden weights, but they do not have the power to turn it upwards.

So while the Cave itself does not address the question of the moral preparedness of the elite who are to be given the education that will prompt their intellectual conversion, the wider argument to which it contributes certainly does. To be suitable material for intellectual conversion from concern with the sensible world to a new focus on intelligible reality, a person needs not just the native equipment Socrates has detailed – a bent for learning, a good memory, a courageous disposition, largeness of spirit (6.490c, 494b) – but a properly and securely developed moral character, 'inculcated by custom and practice', as he puts it in his commentary on the Cave (7.518e). That development is the subject of the discussion of music and physical training that occupies much of Books 2 and 3. And it is emphatically training and development, not moral reclamation or *moral* conversion.

There is a great deal in Plato's narrative of the Cave that this brief sketch of its contribution to the argument of Books 6 and 7 has omitted. That is partly because brevity is what I have been aiming at. But it is mostly because much of the narrative is evidently preoccupied with different concerns that have no obvious or direct connection with mathematics and its role in the education of the rulers of the ideal city. To these concerns we must now turn.

The Cave as Narrative

The story the Cave actually tells or intimates is in many ways ill fitted to function as the allegory of philosophical education that its role in the developing argument of the *Republic* requires it to be. More precisely, what the Cave tells us about the world *outside* the cave, and about what dawning realization of its nature and structure is like, fits the requirements of the allegory well enough (complementing what we have already learned from the Sun and the Line).[12] But with the world *within* the cave, it is another matter. In the first place, what the cave represents is at the outset not the sensible world in general (as the philosophical commentary will urge us to assume: 7.517b), but the city: the city as it is, above all the democratic city, not the ideal city – although it will apparently transmute into that when the issue of the philosophers' obligation to descend again to it is broached.[13] Conversion is certainly the crux of the narrative, and that certainly means intellectual conversion. But it involves primarily the shock of disillusionment about the moral values current in the world of the city as it is, and pre-eminently of its conceptions of justice, not a better grasp of the realities studied by mathematics.

In the first instance, in fact, it is a conversion from a state of almost total illusion and delusion about the world of the democratic city to a faltering grip on the 'realities' of *that* world – not enlightenment about true intelligible reality, although of course that is the ultimate destination of the intellectual journey the prisoners are to undertake. Conversion is not here a metaphor for the shift in intellectual focus from the sensible to the intelligible which Socrates' commentary on the Cave represents it as constituting. *That* shift is marked in the narrative by emergence from the cave into the sunlit world outside. Conversion is something that happens *within* the cave, when someone who could to begin with see only shadows is compelled to turn around, and to look with great difficulty and uncertain success at the objects – more real than the shadows, but still only themselves images – that cast them.

---

[12] Here as elsewhere I write 'Cave' ('Sun', 'Line') when referring to the entire analogy or image, 'cave' ('sun', 'line') when referring to the cave as it figures as an element in the narrative at various points.

[13] The narrative seems to want to have it both ways at this point. For example, Socrates denies philosophers the option of refusing to 'come back down again to the prisoners we were talking about, or share in their hardships and rewards – whether of the more trivial or the weightier kind' (7.519d). This presupposes that they started life in the world of the city as it is described in the opening stretches of the Cave (514a–516e; the echo of 'rewards' [*tīmai*], 516c, is especially notable). But a few lines later on, he is explicit that the philosophers have been brought up and educated in a very different environment: the ideal city (520a–c).

It will help to see the force of these points if we look at the narrative in more detail. When we do so, we find a lot of mystery, no doubt much of it deliberate on Plato's part.[14] What exactly is it that the shadows on the wall of the cave and the statuary throwing the images represent? What precisely is symbolized by the prisoners' inability to see anything except the shadows, and by their belief that reality is constituted by the shadows? Why are they represented as imprisoned in the first place? A lot is destined to remain fairly obscure. None of the questions I have just posed is answered by Socrates' philosophical commentary on the Cave – again, no doubt deliberately. Interpreters scrabble over the clues Plato seems to be letting slip at various points. But consensus notoriously remains elusive.

The passage that gives most away is perhaps this (7.517d–e):[15]

> And here's another question. Do you think it's at all surprising if a person who turns to things human from contemplation of the divine cuts a sorry figure, and is made to look a complete fool – if before he can see properly or can get acclimatized to the darkness around him, he is compelled to compete, in the law courts or anywhere else, over the shadows of justice or the images which cast those shadows, or to get into argumentative conflict about whatever assumptions regarding these things are made by those who have never seen justice itself?

The scenario Socrates portrays is of course dense with allusion to his own plight before the court at his trial for impiety and moral corruption. That theme is one to which Plato often returns. And the mention here of 'the law courts or anywhere else' is echoed almost exactly in a much-expanded version of this analysis of the philosopher's plight in the 'digression' of the *Theaetetus* (174c), where it picks up a reference to 'the law court or the council chamber or any other public gathering of the city as a body' (173c). The evocation of forensic and deliberative rhetoric conveyed by 'compete' and 'conflict' over shadows and images of justice inescapably brings democratic Athens to mind – not only the trial of Socrates, but such episodes as the debate over policy towards Mytilene between Cleon and Diodotus (as represented in Book 3 of Thucydides' *History* (3.37–48)).

In this *Republic* passage, as in the *Theaetetus* digression, Plato is working with a simple polarity between things human and things divine as focus of cognitive interest, with justice itself – the Form of Justice – the prime example of an object of contemplation, and images and shadows of justice

---

[14] Contrast the painstaking and indeed rather schoolish explanations of the different elements of the Sun and Line analogies Socrates supplies as he develops them.
[15] Translations are mostly based on Tom Griffith's version in Ferrari and Griffith 2000.

treated (apparently indifferently) as what the unenlightened argue about and jostle over. These are presumably human conceptions of what is just or unjust, uninformed (as Socrates says) by understanding of what justice really is, as his reference to people's 'assumptions' makes fairly plain. Democratic politics is also suggested by an earlier passage in which Socrates describes the kind of intellectual activity characteristic of the prisoners in the case (7.516c–d):

> Back in the cave they [i.e. those who have escaped from it] might have had rewards and praise and prizes for the person who was quickest at identifying the passing shapes, who had the best memory for the ones which usually came earlier or later or simultaneously, and who as a result was most capable at predicting what was going to come next. Do you think someone who had escaped from the cave would feel any desire for these prizes? Would he envy those who won esteem and exercised power among the prisoners? Or would he feel as Achilles does in Homer? Would he much prefer 'to labour as a common serf, serving another man with nothing to his name', putting up with anything to avoid holding those opinions and living that life?

Some readers think Plato must here be writing about the populace as they watch the passing show of politics (like a theatre audience, as Cleon complains in the Mytilenean debate: *History* 3.38). But prizes go to the politicians, not ordinary members of the *dêmos*. Perhaps everybody in the assembly does engage in a sort of guessing, spotting, and remembering game, but politicians are distinguished by being the ones best at it, by that's being recognized to be their strength, and by their exercising power in consequence.[16] I am put in mind of a different passage of Thucydides: the eulogy of Themistocles for his supreme ability to form judgements instantly with minimal deliberation, his no less impressive success at guessing for the most part the future turn of events, and his capacity to interpret what is on the city's hands at the moment (*History* 1.138). I take it that that is the sort of intellectual performance Socrates has in view in the extract I have just quoted. Themistocles is the kind of person who has 'what passes for wisdom there [i.e. in the cave]' (516c), and on that account wins esteem and comes to wield significant power in the city.

One further passage confirms the view of the Cave that has been emerging so far from our examination of the narrative. When Socrates imagines himself persuading those who have become true philosophers

---

[16] This point is well made by Wilberding 2004: 121–8. But to my mind his further suggestion that the puppeteers are 'the multitude' is misconceived.

that they must come back down among the prisoners, this is how he concludes his address to them (7.520c–d):

> So you must go down, each of you in turn, to join the others in their dwelling-place. You must get used to looking at things covered in darkness. When you do get used to it, you will see a thousand times better than the people there do. You will be able to identify each of the images there, and recognize what it is an image of, because you have seen the truth about what is beautiful and just and good. In this way the city – ours and yours – will enjoy government that is really awake, rather than the kind of dream in which most cities live nowadays, governed by people fighting one another over shadows and engaging in factional conflict over ruling, as if it were some great good.

Once again the focus is on values – the good, the beautiful, the just – and on the difference between the truth about them (seen outside the cave) and images (what philosophers will be able to recognize inside it once their eyes have got used to the darkness). Once again, the suggestion is that in the ordinary pattern of things the city which the cave represents will be the city as it is, riven by faction (that would fit oligarchies as much as democracies) and 'fighting over shadows', unless it is reformed by philosophy.

What sort of conversion is possible within such a world? That question takes us back to the intensely mysterious opening passage of Book 7. It and its details have been the subject of minute scrutiny and speculation in buckets. I am not going to try to recapitulate all of that. I shall focus on just one cluster of elements in the narrative. What are the shadows the prisoners are looking at?[17] What are the images that cast them? What is symbolized by their turning from the one to the other? Why does the reorientation leave them so confused? What did their imprisonment consist in? If we can get no reasonably clear idea what answers to give to these questions, we are left simply baffled by the Cave's narrative. And given that the clues to Plato's meaning we have been identifying and following so far have yielded a reasonably coherent and intelligible interpretation, our best hope of understanding what the opening passage means by conversion is likely to rest in the assumption that it, too, is telling us something about the values of the city as it is.

Readers who share that general assumption may well have their own favourite conjectures as to how my list of questions is to be answered. In

---

[17] But I shall offer no discussion of the remarkable information that the prisoners have never seen anything of *themselves or each other* than the shadows cast by the fire on the wall of the cave in front of them (7.515a). For a fascinating exploration of what might be being suggested, see Brunschwig 2003: 145–77.

what follows, I offer a hypothesis of my own which does not exactly duplicate any other I have come across. But I should stress that its status within my overall argument is merely exemplary: to indicate the *sort* of story that needs to be told to give substance to details the narrative clearly means to invest with symbolic significance. And it is a non-exclusive hypothesis: I do not want to deny that there may also be validity in other answers to the questions. Indeed, I take it Plato's writing is of set purpose multiply suggestive.

Here is the hypothesis: most people in the city as it is hold values – above all about justice – that are mere reflections of something else. What is that something else? Later in the text Socrates will refer to them compendiously as images (*eidôla*, 520c; *agalmata*, 517d). But when he first introduces them he refers to 'all sorts of vessels and implements ... and statues of men and other animals, artefacts made of stone and wood and all kinds of materials' (514c–515a). The intent must surely be to emphasize the immense variety and comprehensive range of the craftsmanship and artifice that is represented in these images. If we transpose that idea to the realm of human values, we get the thought that the values most people hold are reflections of the all-embracing *culture* they inhabit – which is itself a hugely complex human artefact. When Socrates goes on to explain that the prisoners think they are naming what they see (515b), he is in effect also making the point that – confined as they are to looking at shadows – they are completely *unaware* that what they treat as reality is nothing other than a reflection of human cultural artifice, and that their words really refer to something they have no awareness of.[18] Let me offer an illustration for the point.[19] Suppose some of the prisoners hold that justice is telling the truth and repaying your debts. Socrates will be saying: that opinion is something *they* take to be the truth about justice – what justice really is. But it is in fact nothing more than the shadow in their minds left by the culture in which they have been raised. That culture exercises universal control over their minds. And because they have no cognitive resources that might enable them to extricate themselves from its control, they are actually its prisoners.

Conversion will require a complete reversal of outlook, sparked by the acutely painful and reluctant realization that what they had been taking to be reality is *not* reality. Suppose that is achieved (*how* I shall discuss shortly). What the prisoners then need to come to appreciate is that that

---

[18] For text, translation, and discussion of 515b4–5, see Harte 2007.
[19] In using this example (and in subsequent reflections on it), I am indebted to the stimulus of Smith 1997.

something has *more* reality than what they had taken reality to be. Socrates represents the process as extremely difficult and confusing (515d):

> When someone is released and compelled suddenly to stand up and turn his neck round and walk and look towards the light, and finds all these things painful to do, and because of the flickerings of the fire can't see those things distinctly whose shadows he was seeing before, what do you suppose he'd say if he was told that what he used to see before was just nonsense, whereas now he is seeing better, since he is closer to what is, and turned towards things that have more reality? Suppose further that each of the passing objects was pointed out to him, and he was asked what it is, and compelled to answer. Don't you think he'd be puzzled? Wouldn't he think the things he saw before to be more true than what was being pointed out to him now?

Within the terms of the Cave's own narrative, Socrates' final suggestions here are perhaps not hard to account for.

In their original condition, it was well-nigh inevitable that the prisoners would take the shadows to be reality. In fact, they had every reason to take them to be living creatures. All of the shadowy figures moved, and some of the figures (humans and animals, presumably) uttered sounds, as it must have appeared to the prisoners. There was nothing in their cognitive lives to make them doubt that these appearances constituted reality. In confronting the objects they are now being shown, they experience understandable difficulties. The main problem is fully described here by Socrates. The released prisoners have to look in the direction of the *fire*, and that makes it hard for them to see the objects in front of it clearly at all: it dazzles and it flickers. They find it hard to accept that what is now being presented to them has more truth or reality than the shadows they used to observe.

There is something distinctly familiar about this new condition of theirs. The puzzlement (*aporein*) which Socrates attributes to them has obvious affinities with the sense of helplessness induced in interlocutors in early Platonic dialogues by his own characteristic form of questioning. Indeed, if we ask what technique could bring someone to turn around, as the prisoners are made to do, from illusions about reality to a degree of realization that they are illusions (coupled with a consequential disabling numbness of mind), then the questioning practised in Socratic elenchus is surely the obvious candidate. The light it casts initially brings confusion and dismay, and an inability to see the way forward. Socrates' interlocutors typically start with the confident or complacent assumption that X is F (courage is standing in line and not running away, *sôphrosunê* is doing things with due order, justice is telling the truth and paying your debts), and are brought to see that *that* is not the reality – because sometimes X is *not-F* instead. They do not thereby get much understanding of what the status of their initial convictions is, nor of how to make headway beyond them. Characteristically, they make fresh attempts to articulate their ideas, but the eventual effect of the illumination they have gained is more like the paralysis car headlights induce in rabbits and stoats that get caught in their glare, or as Meno complained like the numbness the sting of the stingray fish produces (*Meno* 80a–b).

The ex-prisoners' problems continue even when particular objects are pointed out to them. Comparison with the passage already quoted on the return of the philosophers to the cave suggests why. Once the philosophers' eyes adjust to the darkness, they will see 'a thousand times better than the people there do': philosophers would be able to 'identify each of the images there, and recognize what it is an image of', because they have 'seen the truth about what is beautiful and just and good' (7.520c). We infer that the released prisoners who have *not* yet emerged from the cave would be just puzzled by these images. Perhaps they could not even become aware that lifeless images are what these things are – given that they have never encountered any of the originals. Certainly any identifications they might make would have to be based on experience in unpropitious cognitive conditions – and experience that they do not yet have much of. No wonder if the shadows they once looked at still – to begin with – seem to them truer realities.

But *we* – the dialogue's readers – know that the objects they now see are artefacts manipulated by handlers. On the interpretation I am proposing, Plato thereby intimates to us something the ex-prisoners themselves do not grasp: that the values that were reflected in the judgements they formed in their original state are no more than *nomoi*, conventions, human cultural artefacts. Let me recur once more to the example of justice conceived as truth telling and debt repayment. Because this conception is widely believed, but because telling the truth or repaying your debts turns out – on the examination Socrates gives that proposal in Book 1 of the *Republic* – to be just sometimes, but sometimes unjust (1.331c–332a), the principle qualifies as one of those many cultural norms (*nomima*) about what is beautiful and the rest which people in general accept, but which in Book 5's formulation 'roll about between not being and pure being' (5.479d). Thus we find the materials for the idea that a failed candidate for the truth about justice may actually be a culturally acceptable norm available – and so available for allegorization in the Cave – elsewhere in the dialogue.[20]

---

[20] Socrates does not think such *nomima* have no validity at all. In Book 4, he allows that the person whose soul is just will go in for what he nonetheless describes as 'the usual rubbish' (*ta phortika*, 442e–443a). He will not embezzle gold or silver deposited with him for safekeeping. He will not have anything to do with temple robbery, theft, or betraying people. He will stick by his oaths and other

Conversion to a perspective from which illusions about, for example, justice can be seen as such does not however mean that the converts themselves will perceive them as the shadows of cultural norms that they are. (It is one thing to grasp that X is *not-F* as well as F, and that *being F* is therefore not the reality of what X is, another to appreciate that the idea that X is F is merely a *nomos*.) Still less does conversion presuppose or constitute a grasp of the intelligible reality of justice itself (of what X really is). To revert to the Cave narrative, the prisoners are released from their chains and forced to turn around *before* they make their journey out of the cave up into the world outside. Even if they are at any rate now pointed in the right direction, the journey they still have to make is portrayed as a pretty long haul, and it is particularly emphasized that they will have to be dragged forcibly and painfully over a steep and rough path to get outside. In other words, conversion was one thing, ascent is quite another. Nor does the narrative indicate that there is much relationship between the two. In particular, there is no suggestion that what will help to drag the released prisoners out of the cave into the sunlight bears any relationship to further reflection on the nature of the objects of whose existence they became aware when first forced to turn their necks around.[21]

We are now in a position to return to the simple and basic question: what was it that shackled the prisoners in the first place – that *made* them prisoners? The answer I have already suggested is: culture itself. Culture – the culture of the city as it is, and especially the democratic city – is what imprisons them.[22] It imprisons them because they are quite unaware that their beliefs about justice and other values are not straightforwardly true, but the reflexes of something else; and because left to their own devices they are quite unable to achieve awareness of that. On my reading, the prisoners' shackles are inseparable from the manipulation of images and other artefacts which brings about the shadow-play on the wall of the cave and so effects the only cognitive input they ever receive. Only something like Socratic questioning has the power to unsettle their beliefs in such a way as

---

agreements. The artefacts that constitute the furniture of the cave are fairly solid stuff – within that limited framework (it is from higher perspectives that they are 'rubbish').

[21] There is nothing here resembling the use of visible forms to think about the intelligible which is ascribed in the Line to geometers (6.510d–e).

[22] I need hardly add that my argument here – as in this section of the paper generally – owes much to Myles Burnyeat's illuminating observations on the Cave: Burnyeat 1999b: 238–43.

to release them from their intellectual shackles, albeit at the cost of leaving them thoroughly puzzled about what is real and what is not.[23]

Plato's Alternative Caves

The Cave therefore is a picture which incorporates alternative instructions – one set explicit, the other largely implicit – on how it is to be read. Unsurprisingly, they generate rather different philosophical models of intellectual imprisonment and liberation. The official instructions advise us to imagine a Cave whose contribution to the argument of the central books of the *Republic* is clear and determinate. From the end of Book 5 to the end of Book 6, Plato has been making us think about the philosopher – latterly about the intelligible reality for which philosophy has a consuming passion, and about its dependence on the Form of the Good. Glaucon had coped well enough with the image of the Sun; had wanted to know more; had listened to Socrates developing the image of the Line by way of response; and despite something of a struggle had finally got an adequate grip – so Socrates assures him – on what it is saying. By the end of Book 7, he will be in no doubt what the Cave contributes to this ongoing discussion of philosophy and the philosopher. It is supposed to symbolize the conversion from preoccupation with the sensible world to understanding of intelligible reality that mathematics will enable someone to make – if they have the right natural aptitude for philosophy, and if as a potential ruler they have thoroughly assimilated the training in moral virtue which will be provided in the ideal city.

But the Cave is a piece of writing that ambushes the reader. What it actually portrays in its narrative at the beginning of Book 7 is something quite different: another sort of conversion altogether, from being wholly captive to reflexes of cultural norms of justice and the good construed as the real truth (as people typically are captive in the city as it is), to a numbed and faltering appreciation that the truth lies elsewhere. This form of conversion is something which *anybody* might experience if

---

[23] It is worth noting that Plato gives us no reason to think that he conceives of the ruling elite of the ideal city as having been imprisoned by the culture *they* absorbed through poetry, music, and gymnastics – which includes myths, notably the myth of the Noble Lie – controlled and controlling though it is. The higher education they are to get through the practice of mathematics and dialectic seems to leave that culture intact, although they presumably acquire a new understanding of its proper basis. Cf. Wilson 1976: 126–7.

subjected to Socratic questioning – although there would then have to be a long and difficult *further* process of intellectual struggle if such a person were to achieve an adequate grasp of the real nature of justice and other values. In short, Plato brings the argument back to *us* – the ordinary person in the world as it is – and to something like the everyday preoccupations with justice and injustice which launched the dialogue back in Book 1. It announces an image which will illuminate *our* nature when it comes to education and being uneducated (7.514a). And though we might have been expecting more on philosophers and *their* education, for a while at least Socrates is going to talk about *us*. His prisoners are strange prisoners, says Glaucon. 'Like us', says Socrates (515a).[24]

This is a brilliant stroke on Plato's part. The Cave narrative gives us something less intellectually strenuous and more immediately accessible (despite its manifold mysteriousness) than the Sun, and above all than the Line: what is more, something no reader can ever forget. And in turning attention in the first instance to us, it manages to suggest that reflection on the requirements of philosophical education needs to be set in the broader context of self-examination about the human condition, and about its imprisonment by the cultural limitations imposed by human society as it actually is. The price Plato plays is a degree of confusion. The conversion he specifically has in mind for philosophers (e.g. 7.521c, 524e–525a) is something they would need to undergo even if they had escaped or avoided that sort of imprisonment, and enjoyed the benefit of moral acclimatization and training in an ideal city.[25] In the terms first elaborated in the narrative, it is not really conversion but *ascent*; and it is liberation – if liberation it is – not from cultural assumptions, but from reliance on the senses, and their focus on the realm of becoming, instead of the intellect, with its access to being.[26] Narrative and philosophical

---

[24] Does Socrates mean to suggest that even he was once the prisoner of the culture in which he was raised? Certainly his picture of the difficulties a philosopher will experience on descending once more to the cave from which he has escaped has – as we have observed – a strong autobiographical dimension.

[25] I say 'even if they had escaped or avoided' the kind of imprisonment imposed by living in the social and cultural environment of the city as it is. But of course Book 6 had argued that those with the natural potential for philosophy are – in all but exceptional cases – so corrupted by that sort of environment that they can never fulfil their potential (6.490e–497a). From its point of view, escape from politics in the cave of the democratic city to philosophical contemplation in the realm of the intelligible beyond it comes close to counterfactual fantasy.

[26] Yet it is important that the two conversions on my interpretation share a key fundamental feature. What liberates the prisoner of the culture of the democratic city is realization that X is $not\text{-}F$ as well as F. Similarly, it is famously appreciation that, e.g., the middle finger is both large and small that illustrates the way engagement with the predicates typically studied in mathematics turns the soul away from the sensible towards the intelligible (7.523b–525b).

commentary upon it work out ideas that are not merely different, but in terminology as well as in substance at odds with each other.

Nonetheless, Plato has Socrates give some directions which ought to have done much to minimize the confusion, had they been taken as they should be: as instructions on how to *reread* the Cave as an allegory of the philosopher's education. These directions are spelled out in the famous passage where we are told to fit the image of the Cave as a whole to what has been said before, that is, to the Sun and the Line (7.517a–c). That need not mean: in every detail.[27] The assumption that we are being told to bludgeon everything in the Cave to fit whatever parallels could be identified in Sun and Line has caused much of the interpretative damage. In fact, Socrates is extremely selective. The material in the narrative that we explored in the previous section is completely ignored. Socrates now urges us just to make some very general connections with elements in the two previous images.

He picks out two. First, we are to compare or assimilate the cave dwelling to the visible region illuminated by the power of the sun (from the Sun analogy). Socrates does not say it *is* the realm of the visible – with good reason, since in the original telling the cave in fact there represented the city (the city as it is). Second, his hope is that the upward journey and the view of things in the world above can represent the soul's journey up into the realm of the intelligible (as in the Line), though he expresses qualified confidence about claiming that that is what coming to understand the intelligible would be like. The story he has told, however, about gazing on the sun itself and figuring out that it is what sustains seasons and years and everything in the realm of the visible – and indeed is in a way the cause of all of them – does capture the way things appear to him. The Form of the Good is the last thing to be understood in the realm of the knowable, and we need to reason out the way that it is cause of all that is right and beautiful whether in the visible or the intelligible realm, if we are to act wisely in private or public business.

Reread the Cave like that, and you will not make it consistent, but you will not be left terminally disconcerted or deciding that it is all baffling conundrum. In fact you will be poised to extract what you are to be told you need for the main business in hand in this part of the *Republic*: the educational method by which someone can be put on the upward path *from* the realm of the sensible *to* the realm of the intelligible (7.521c–d; cf. 518c–d) – which proves to be mathematics.

---

[27] So Burnyeat 1987: 228 n. 38: 'The solution [to the intractable problem of trying to establish a one–one correspondence between the four stages of the Cave and the four sections of the Line] is to let Plato's stage-directions tell us what *kind* of relationship he means us to establish between his images.'

PART IV

*Projects, Paradoxes, and Literary Registers
in the* Laws

CHAPTER 9

Religion and Philosophy in the Laws

Not so long ago, it would have seemed extraordinary to devote a Plato conference to the *Laws*, probably still a strong contender for the prize of least-known and least-loved item in his oeuvre. But interest has been stirring; and during the last thirty years or so in particular, the dialogue has prompted some of the most interesting and valuable work currently being done on Plato. Everyone will have their own candidates here. There have been many valuable articles, some important collected volumes, new translations of the whole work or individual books, and some fine recent monographs, notably perhaps Lucia Prauscello's *Performing Citizenship in Plato's Laws*, Marcus Folch's *The City and the Stage*, and Myrthe Bartels's *Plato's Pragmatic Project*.[1] The importance of the seminal articles of André Laks, Christopher Bobonich, and Andrea Nightingale has not diminished, with Laks's magisterial chapter in the *Cambridge History of Greek and Roman Political Thought* summing up his work to that date (2000) on the dialogue, and Bobonich's major and highly influential study *Utopia Recast* doing the same for his (and much more besides).[2] Then one cannot fail to mention Klaus Schöpsdau's indispensable three-volume commentary or Trevor Saunders's *Plato's Penal Code* (not to mention any of the papers which continued to pour from his pen).[3]

It was a terrible sadness that at the conference for which the present essay was composed, we could not enjoy the opportunity of benefiting from Trevor Saunders's immense and seldom-rivalled knowledge of everything to do with the *Laws*, and from the insight and freshness of the perspectives he brought to its study. As I was working on the dialogue in preparation for this study, I came to realize all over again the merits of his wonderfully evangelical Penguin translation of the dialogue: it was a bit interventionist,

---

[1] Prauscello 2014; Folch 2015; Bartels 2017.
[2] Laks 1990, 1991; Bobonich 1991; Nightingale 1993; Laks 2000; Bobonich 2002.
[3] Schöpsdau 1994–2011; Saunders 1991.

in that Saunders was not afraid to inject interpretation into his rendering, but that gets one thinking in a way versions more neutral and literal in intention do not; and the whole presentation of his version – from the Cornfordian summaries and headings to the unPlatonic liveliness and crispness of his prose – made the work accessible as no other had ever previously done.[4]

Let me start for my own part by citing a remark I find particularly provocative, in an article published by Andrea Nightingale in 1993 which I much admire. Early on, it contains the following sentence: 'The *Laws* is, of course, a philosophical dialogue.' The next sentence begins with a 'But', but Nightingale's 'of course' has already in any case achieved what I suspect she wanted it to achieve: the raising of both eyebrows.[5] Is the *Laws* not more expository and dogmatic than dialogical? How much philosophy is there in it? How far does it even present itself as philosophical? Does Nightingale not herself go on to argue that the *Laws* is best understood as something rather different – a monological sacred text (her title was: 'Writing/reading a sacred text: a literary interpretation of Plato's *Laws*')?

The two issues 'how dialogical?', 'how philosophical?' are needless to say intimately related. Plato scholarship today is more than ever as preoccupied with questions about *how* he writes as with questions of *what* he has to say – including in that what remains compelling in the problematic or the argument or the vision developed in any of his writings. Indeed, we no longer find it helpful to characterize the 'how?' as a literary question categorially quite distinct from the 'what?' as a philosophical question. The *Laws* illustrates the point with particular clarity and force – perhaps unexpectedly so. In the main body of this chapter, I will be exploring the relation of 'how?' and 'what?' as it bears on the status and intention of the work as a whole. But one only has to consider the role of the so-called 'preludes' to laws to see the salience of the issue in the dialogue.

Law neat, says the Athenian Visitor (4.722e–723b), is dictatorial prescription: 'do this or that will be done to you'. Better for a legislator dealing with free men, not slaves, to proceed more gently, and preface law with a prelude. Preludes do not prescribe: they persuade – if successful, they put people in a favourable state of mind, more apt for learning, and so make them more amenable to accepting legal prescription. What the Athenian Visitor refers to as the 'doubleness' of legislation is applied not just in the detailed provisions of the code he will construct (at any rate from the penology of Book 9 onwards), but to the legislative project of the *Laws*

[4] Saunders 1970.   [5] Nightingale 1993: 281.

itself (722c–d; cf. 723d–e). The interlocutors have at this point only just started enunciating laws. 'What went before was all preludes to laws.' Political theory and reflection on discourse are here inextricably intertwined – and the reflection is at least embryonically self-reflexive, given that the discourse of the interlocutors themselves is treated by the Athenian Visitor (echoed by Cleinias) as 'preludic'. The idea of a prelude is a major ingredient in the political theory of the *Laws*, but any view of what that theory is and of how preludes contribute to it must address the issue of what their persuasiveness as discourse consists in – an issue which remains highly controversial.[6]

With these thoughts in mind, we may return to our original question: is the *Laws* a philosophical dialogue? Or rather we may go back to one of the glosses I offered on that question: how far does the *Laws* present itself as philosophical? This latter formulation will allow us to capitalize on our musings about theory and discourse and reflection on discourse and their interconnection. One thing we should expect – as practised readers of Plato, and as instructed, for example, by Proclus, Leo Strauss, and Myles Burnyeat – is that, if he is true to his usual form, the way he sets up the conversation between his interlocutors will have been precisely designed to key us in to its principal themes and even conceivably to the style of treatment of them we are to expect; and not merely to acclimatize us, but to entice us into engagement with the issues on our own account.[7]

I thereby disclose an assumption I make about the difficult issue of the intended readership of the *Laws*. I am supposing (and I will be producing some considerations to support the supposition as we go along) that the *Laws* was written for practised Platonic readers: not exclusively so, but most importantly for them. Indeed, I suspect that by the time he composed the dialogue Plato had long been incapable of *not* writing with that practised reader chiefly in mind.[8]

---

[6] The position advocated in Bobonich 1991 was disputed, e.g., by Stalley 1994 and by Laks 2000: 285–90. There is a balanced assessment by Annas 2010. I give a succinct statement of my own view in Schofield and Griffith 2016: 15–18 (cf. also Schofield 2006: 84–8).

[7] See, e.g., Proclus's commentary on Plato's *Parmenides* (there is a convenient translation by Morrow and Dillon 1987); Strauss 1975; Burnyeat 1997. My reading of the *Laws* owes a certain amount to Strauss's commentary and to his general view of philosophy's relation with religion (Athens vs. Jerusalem).

[8] For another treatment of the philosophical importance of dialogue in the *Laws*, and of the several different imagined groups identified within its pages as participating in such dialogue, see Bobonich 1996.

An Idiosyncratic Text

'If he is true to his usual form . . . ' But that is quite an 'if'. When we pick up the *Laws* and read in the beginning of Book 1 for a few pages, I fancy that our most immediate reaction may not to be to say to ourselves 'This isn't real philosophy', or 'Yes, this in its way *is* philosophy', but rather 'There is a lot that's odd about this'. Perhaps the sense of strangeness and idiosyncrasy gets erased or suppressed or displaced as the text becomes more familiar to us. Anyway, let me list some features of the dialogue as we first meet it (I mean: first revisit it) that mark it out as a pretty atypical Platonic production.

Physical Setting

The conversation takes place not in Athens (as in every other dialogue), but in Crete, not otherwise celebrated as a centre of intellectual life. The major reason for this choice will become clear quickly enough: although the first stretch of argument in the dialogue is a critique of Cretan and Spartan assumptions about the goals of political life,[9] and although there is much that is Athenian about its penal code, the vision the *Laws* promotes of a closed political and social order regulated at every point by public law is one whose inspiration is obviously Laconophile and Cretophile. The conversation takes place in the countryside and the summer heat (mention is made of the protective shade of the trees along the route) – rather as in the *Phaedrus:* something Cicero perhaps noticed when he exploited the *Phaedrus* in constructing the setting for his own *On Laws* (see especially 1.3, 2.6). It is hard to know what to make of the parallel with the *Phaedrus*, beyond noting that in the *Laws* there are elements of the 'meta-conversation', the discourse *about* discourse, written and oral, which is the dominant mode of the *Phaedrus*. Perhaps the *Laws* thereby puts us on notice to be alert to its own distinctive rhetoric and to its preoccupation with persuasive speech.

The Conversational Context

The context is unusually purposive. As always, the conversation whiles away time free from the occupations of life. But this conversation is imagined as conducted during the course of a journey undertaken for

---

[9] Or rather of one construction of Cretan and Spartan ideology. The Athenian goes on to challenge its credentials and to present an alternative construction: see Schofield 2021 (= Chapter 11 below).

unspecified religious purposes – an ascent to the cave of Zeus on Mount Ida, perhaps echoing the visits Homer says Minos made to converse with the god (624ab; cf. 625ab). There is accordingly an expectation that it might in some sense be a religious conversation. The expectation is confirmed by (1) the immediate focus, from the very first word of the dialogue: 'god' (*theos*), twice reiterated by Cleinias in his response to the Athenian Visitor's use of it, in a question about the divine origin of law, as well as by (2) the religious and indeed theocratic framework presupposed in the legislation which becomes the *Laws'* major undertaking. It is confirmed too by (3) the fact that when a theoretical foundation is developed for the ethical standpoint adopted in the legislative programme (first in Book 4 and then more argumentatively in Book 10), it is a theological foundation. One might be put in mind of the *Euthyphro*. An encounter at the court of the *arkhôn basileus*, where suits alleging impiety had to be filed, occasions the *Euthyphro*'s conversation between Socrates and Euthyphro on the nature of piety. But differently from the *Laws*, it is not conducted actually within a context of religious practice.

The Interlocutors

The interlocutors, again uniquely, do not include Socrates (even in dialogues where he is not the main speaker – like the *Timaeus*, or the *Sophist* and *Statesman*, for example – he makes some contribution, and in one way or another his presence is flagged up as important). Or perhaps the Athenian Visitor *is* Socrates: no doubt that is a possibility Plato wants us to wonder about (there is indeed a Socratic cast to the Athenian Visitor's fundamental ethical stance), although probably not for very long, and certainly without ever confirming or disconfirming the thought, unless leaving his personality entirely colourless is designed *inter alia* to do just that job. It is established early on in the dialogue that unlike the Athenian Visitor, Megillus the Spartan, and Cleinias the Cretan are unpractised in intellectual discussion (presumably reflecting a common Athenian view of Spartan and Cretan culture); and that all three of them are elderly, something unusual in a Platonic dialogue – most interlocutors other than Socrates himself are young or in vigorous middle age, and even when not so, the limitations imposed by age are generally not emphasized (with the treatment of Cephalus at the beginning of the *Republic* the most notable exception), and certainly not turned into an explicit theme – as is the case in the *Laws*.

These idiosyncrasies are individually arresting, and still more so collectively. The practised reader will take note of them and proceed warily. I shall dwell first on the last of the characteristics I have picked out: the age and inexperience of the Athenian Visitor's interlocutors.

Elderly Non-Swimmers

Although the Athenian Visitor slips in an allusion to the age of the interlocutors in only his third contribution to the conversation (625b), he makes nothing significant of the fact of their elderliness and seniority until a few more pages have elapsed. At 634c–635a, he raises the issue of criticism: is it appropriate for any of the three of them to criticize the laws of each other's cities? He puts a contrast between the old and the young:

- For the old it is quite appropriate to discuss the merits of laws privately and without taking offence at criticism. But they should definitely not do so in front of young people. The public position has to be one of unanimity: all laws must be said to be well framed, as a result of divine enactment.
- So far as the young are concerned, the Cretans and Spartans have the right approach. They forbid anyone young from enquiring which laws are well framed or not.

This is the first more or less explicit hint that religion will not just frame the political thinking of the *Laws* but will be manipulated in the service of politics. More to my immediate point, this is also our first warning that the political system to be advocated has a strong gerontocratic dimension, and with it the curtailment of freedom of enquiry (there is of course something reminiscent here of the discussion of the dangers of allowing young people to be exposed to dialectic in *Republic* 7.537e–539d). But the observation to which I want to draw most attention is that – as Plato takes pains to bring out – Megillus and Cleinias are not well placed to exercise the freedom that is allowed to them. Having grown up under such restrictive regimes, they do not know what is said elsewhere about Cretan or Spartan laws (cf. 634d). And they have no experience of institutions other than their own, with the consequence that (as Cleinias says) even if they encountered such institutions they would not immediately see what was right or wrong in them (639e–640a; cf. 639c–d). By contrast, the Athenian Visitor has a wide experience of a range of social and political institutions (639d; cf. 12.968b).

Elsewhere in the dialogue, the most memorable talk about the young is heavy with foreboding. I have discussed elsewhere the treatment in Book 3 of the young ruler given absolute powers, and we shall return to him later (691c–692c; cf. 4.709e–710a, 713c).[10] Another striking passage occurs in Book 10, where it is young people who are portrayed as vulnerable to relativist views about the gods and about moral values. This is the occasion for the Athenian Visitor to develop the one sustained sequence of general, abstract argument Plato gives us in the *Laws:* the theology which is to underpin Magnesia's laws against impiety. It is also one of the very few locations in the work where the vocabulary of dialogue and refutation familiar from other works of Plato is used. Strauss called it 'the most philosophic, the only philosophic part of the *Laws*'.[11] But it is almost as though the philosophy is there on sufferance. What prompts the passage is just the kind of talk and thought which, though permitted and doubtless common enough in Athens, would have been illegal under the provisions of the Cretan and Spartan constitutions referred to at 634d–e.

Against youthful error, the Athenian balances the scarcely admirable inexperience of Cleinias and Megillus in argument and their consequent intellectual helplessness (10.892d–893a; cf. 886b) – and again this is the point I want to emphasize. An analogy with travellers attempting to ford a river in flood says it all (in Saunders's version):

> Imagine the three of us had to cross a river in spate, and I were the younger and had plenty of experience of currents. Suppose I said, 'I ought to try first on my own account, and leave you two in safety while I see if the river is fordable for you two older men as well, or if not, just how bad it is. If it turns out to be fordable, I'll then call you across and put my experience at your disposal in helping you to cross; but if in the event it cannot be crossed by old men like yourselves, then the only risk has been mine.' Wouldn't that strike you as fair enough? The situation is the same now: the argument ahead runs too deep, and men as weak as you will probably get out of your depth. I want to prevent you novices in answering from being dazed and dizzied by a stream of questions, which would put you in an undignified and humiliating position you'd find most unpleasant.

As we recall from Book 12, the gerontocracy which is to review Magnesia's legal system will have had a more intellectually demanding moral and theological education than Cleinias and Megillus, inexperienced as they are either in alternative ways of thinking or in social and political practices in currency elsewhere. But the choice of the elderly non-swimmers Cleinias and Megillus as the interlocutors with whom the conversation of the *Laws* is conducted looks as though it has been made

---

[10] Schofield 1999b: 43–50.   [11] Strauss 1975: 129.

to symbolize a point about the character and status of that conversation: it will quite deliberately be intellectually limited and limiting.

We need to explore what the self-imposed limitation of the argument of the *Laws* consists in, and then why Plato decides to write the work this way. There is a great deal one might try to say on these questions. I shall confine myself to some brief comments about philosophy, and then some comments about religion (and very briefly indeed theology).

Philosophy within Limits

In the first sentence of the dialogue, the Athenian Visitor asks the other interlocutors 'the cause of the disposition of the laws' of Crete and Sparta (624a). Their replies prompt him to propose a conversation about *politeia* (political system) and *nomoi* (laws; 625a; cf. 641d, 3.678a). And at 3.702a–b, we reach what sounds like a definitive statement: 'The object of all that has been said is to discern how a city might best be managed and – on an individual basis – how a person might best conduct his own life.' This is precisely the sort of topic which elsewhere in Plato – as in Aristotle's *Ethics* and *Politics* – is thought to call for philosophical treatment. And much in the handling of the topic in the *Laws*, especially and no doubt symbolically in Book 1, reminds one of Socratic methodology. Recall that that book starts with something very like an elenchus of the Cretan and Spartan view that (as Cleinias and Megillus construe it) the principle governing the organization of a well-managed city is the need for it to be able to defeat other cities in war (626–34). Then follows an explicit discussion of the proper method (even Megillus endorses that: 638e–639a) for examining what is good and what is bad about a social institution; followed in turn by argument that understanding the institution of the symposium requires an understanding of music, and that in turn an understanding of education – so they must first *define* education: what is it? what function does it have (638–43)? All this – especially the symposium itself – will need extended discussion, as Cleinias agrees (645c). And much of what is said subsequently about *paideia* (education) in general and music in particular reworks ideas first developed in the *Republic*.

So I cannot agree with the claim that Book 10 is 'the only philosophic part of the *Laws*', nor with Nightingale's verdict from an entirely different perspective that 'the argumentation in the *Laws* is ... wholly unsocratic'.[12] True, it does not much resemble the dialectic of *Charmides* or *Protagoras* or

---

[12] Nightingale 1993: 295.

Book 1 of the *Republic*, but in some ways it is not that different from the way Plato makes Socrates argue in later books of the *Republic*. Moreover, Cleinias and even Megillus have an appetite, albeit untutored, for intellectual discussion quite unlike Cephalus' aversion. All the same, there is an important contrast to be drawn with the *Republic*. The situation is *not* that the way ideas are developed in the *Laws* is too unlike what counts as philosophy elsewhere in Plato to be reckoned philosophy itself. In fact, quite the contrary. As I have sought to remind us, Plato seems in Book 1 of the dialogue to go out of his way to mark the Athenian Visitor's procedure as philosophical (one reason why one might think he is Socrates incognito, in fact). The point is rather that issues are at crucial junctures not pushed back to first principles. Here, there is an important disanalogy with the *Republic*. Much of the argumentation of the *Republic* is conducted at the level of hypothesis, image, analogy; very little at the demanding level of the dialectic adumbrated in Books 6 and 7, the digressive 'longer way round', as it is sometimes expressed. Yet the *need* for a more searching enquiry is kept in view.[13] The *Laws* by contrast seldom offers any glimpse of a better way of handling the issues it deals with, or even of the need for such a thing. To put it another way, the idea of intellectual ascent so central to the philosophical method of the *Republic* is pretty much absent outside Book 10, where – tellingly, I submit – Cleinias makes several speeches supporting the need for a long excursus on theology like that on the symposium, even if it looks as though they are 'stepping outside legislation' (890–1: quotation from 891d).

In short, the problem is not that there is no philosophy in the *Laws*, but that the philosophy there is appears for the most part to have rather limited horizons. What above all else limits them is, I propose, religion: or more precisely, a propensity on the part of the Athenian Visitor, not resisted by the pious interlocutors for whom it is contrived, to invoke the divine at decisive moments in the discussion. I shall shortly be illustrating this phenomenon from a well-known passage in Book 4. But before looking at that text, let us note that Plato's decision (as we have reminded ourselves) to launch the *Laws* with the word *theos*, and to give the conversation of the dialogue a religious context, already indicates to the practised reader that religion will somehow or

---

[13] See above all Scott 2015: 9–101.

other dominate the work. I suggest that if as we read on we stay alert, its domination will register itself as (no doubt *inter alia*) limitation.

Religion as Limitation

The section of Book 4 I have in mind is 712b–715e, a passage in which the Athenian Visitor faces the question of what form of *politeia* should be given to the city that the interlocutors are founding in *logos*. It is framed by remarks that flag up their elderly status. Its opening at 712b has the Athenian Visitor make what is to follow an old person's version of a children's story. And as the section closes, at 715d he is complimented on the sharpness of his vision. He responds with the claim that he has the advantage over youth in matters such as they are discussing. The significance of the passage's frame must be being pointed up by a suggestion from Megillus near the beginning of the section (712c). He proposes that he should comment on the Spartan constitution before Cleinias comments on the Cretan because he is older than him. One has some temptation to agree with Strauss when he says of this passage: 'the difference between old age and wisdom disappears from sight altogether'.[14]

The answer the Athenian gives to his own question establishes Magnesia as in a sense a theocracy. The first part of the passage, 712b–713a, introduces that thesis. The Athenian begins by invoking the aid of god in tackling the ordering of *polis* and *nomoi*. Then follows properly puzzled discussion by Megillus and Cleinias of whether Sparta and Knossos can be adequately described using the usual categories for classifying constitutions – tyranny, democracy, aristocracy, monarchy. Finally, we get the Athenian's verdict. Such *politeiai* as tyranny and the rest are not real *politeiai* (political systems), but what he will later (8. 832b–c) designate *stasiôteiai* (forms of 'party rule', in Saunders's rendering) – because each is named after a mere faction that is the ruling power under that dispensation. The city the interlocutors are imagining that they are founding should rather be called after 'god who is the true ruler of those who have reason' (713a) – or as Saunders freely and boldly translates, 'god who really does rule over those who are rational enough to let him'. Cleinias asks 'What god?', which as we shall see is one of the more significant questions put by the Athenian

---

[14] Strauss 1975: 59. Dougal Blyth pointed out to me that there may be some spin here on the ancient suggestion that Lycurgus and the Spartans borrowed much in their laws from Crete: see Herodotus 1.65.4, [Plato] *Min*. 318c–d, Aristotle *Pol*. 2.10, 1271b24–30, with Perlman 1992: 193–205.

Visitor's interlocutors. And that prompts the Athenian to develop his train of thought.

The main argument runs from 713a to 715d. From a retelling of the myth of the age of Cronos, the Athenian derives what he represents as the truth that 'wherever cities have a mortal, not a god, for ruler, there is no respite for them from miseries and hardships' (713e). The right *politeia* will therefore be one in which reason – the immortal in us – is what we obey. And an ordering of the city in accordance with reason we can name 'law'. Then, the Athenian discusses and dismisses an alternative view of things: the idea that justice is the advantage of whichever faction in the city is strongest. He ends with a linguistic innovation. When law is at the mercy of the ruler, ruin for the city is not far off; 'rulers' ought to be and be called 'servants of the law'[15] – and then we shall see salvation and (to return to the point of departure) the blessings gods bestow on cities.

What I want to suggest is that this passage, which constitutes one of the pivotal moments in the whole work, is of fundamental importance for its entire legislative strategy. Plato chooses to offer us something which we can variously read either as negligible in intellectual content or else as extraordinarily condensed. In other words, he chooses what I am calling philosophical limitation. His key move was to have the Athenian tell a myth, and then to let the myth do most of what might otherwise have been the argumentative work. Thus, when it comes to extracting a moral from the story, it is taken for granted, not argued out, that true law looks to the common interest of the whole city. It is assumed, not argued, that true law so understood will be an ordering devised and discovered by reason; and it is implied, not argued, that to accord this role to reason is tantamount to introducing a theocracy.

The Practised Reader

How far does Plato himself flag up the intellectual limitations of his presentation of these core assumptions, or of their being no more than assumptions? I think the answer may turn on whether we assume a naive or a practised reader. A naive and religiously minded reader might respond rather as Cleinias does to the inferences about government which the

---

[15] An interestingly different recommendation from the *Republic*'s proposal that they be called 'saviours' and 'helpers' (*Rep.* 5.463a–b): although salvation is still the goal.

Athenian Visitor draws from his tale of the age of Cronos. When the Athenian says at the end of the long speech containing the tale (714b):

> So we must examine this *logos*, Cleinias, to see whether we shall go along with it – or what.

Cleinias answers:

> Then we have no option, I suppose, except to go along with it.

Saunders is not atypical in rendering Cleinias' reply in more enthusiastic terms:

> Of course we must go along with it.

In any event, Cleinias seems to see no room or no need to carry out the examination of the *logos* enjoined by the Athenian: no sense in that quarter of any limitation in the *logos*. Cleinias' response, however, is not to be read, I think, as the voice of traditional piety. The conception of the divine implicit in the Athenian Visitor's gloss on his age of Cronos narrative is anything but traditional. He gestures at a recasting of divinity in entirely abstract terms as rationality, retrospectively justifying the need for Cleinias' earlier question: 'What god?' For in the Cronos era, the myth tells us, we enjoyed a law-governed way of life, marked by peace, a sense of shame, and justice in abundance. Law (*nomos*) is then etymologized as the dispensation of reason (*nous*; cf. 12.957c, quoted below, p. 197), recalling – as Alice van Harten has pointed out – the *Cratylus*' derivation of Cronos from *koron nou* as 'undefiled purity of intellect' (*Crat.* 396b).[16] We should read Cleinias' answer, therefore, as reflecting assent to a conception of divinity and society that has at least in this register offered something that goes beyond traditional piety. There should be no paradox in accepting that the Athenian Visitor's line of thought is at one and the same time philosophically limited but more challenging when considered as a religious statement.

Those limitations are likely to register with practised readers, on the other hand, if they are alert to the passage's intertextual resonances with the *Republic* and the *Statesman*. I deal first with the *Republic*. Here, there are two quite separate things to notice, the first fairly straightforward.

It is after the long speech in our *Laws* passage containing the myth that the Athenian Visitor introduces the positivist view of law he wants to reject. That idea he relates immediately to the definition of justice as the

---

[16] Van Harten 2003: 132.

interest of the stronger propounded by Thrasymachus in *Republic* 1 (714b–c). The point he makes against a conception of law and justice expressed in these terms is simply that it turns the *politeia*, the political system or ordering, into nothing but a system for entrenching a faction in power. And he states that he makes the point because in the model city they imagine they have to construct things will be different: rulers will be subservient to the law, not masters of it (715b–d). What he offers is simply a contrast. There is no serious attempt here to engage argumentatively with the Thrasymachean position: a project reckoned important enough and difficult enough in the *Republic* to set the agenda for the main argument of the entire dialogue. The Athenian spells out the *Realpolitik* conception of law and justice merely to reinforce the attractions of the idea of a *politeia* in which law is framed in such a way as to promote the common advantage. What he says does nothing to reinforce the connection between rationality and law which readers of the *Laws* – not to mention the *Statesman*, to which I shall turn shortly – might want explicated.

The other echo of the *Republic* comes a bit earlier, in the Athenian Visitor's first words about the truth we can extract from the myth of the age of Cronos: 'wherever cities have a mortal, not a god, for ruler, there is no respite for them from miseries and hardships' (713e). Readers of the *Republic* will be reminded of the claim Socrates makes there about the conditions on which relief for cities from miseries may be secured. He famously stakes all on the installation of a philosopher ruler (*Rep.* 5.473c–e; cf. 6.501e). Our questions begin. Is the *Laws* deifying the philosopher ruler? Or abandoning the very idea of philosopher ruler in favour of the rule of law – understood as dispassionate rationality embodied in social and political institutions? Here, we should recall that the first thing said in the myth about Cronos is that the god knew no one human could cope with absolute power without being filled with arrogance and injustice (713c). So the second option seems more in the right area. And then the implication is that so far from being any kind of second best, the rationality of the law transcends the limitations of human nature. But at this point, practised readers will raise further questions, prompted now by recollections of the *Statesman*.

A similar story about the age of Cronos is told in a much fuller version in the myth of the *Statesman*, but with a rather different moral. The crucial feature in the *Statesman* version is a *contrast* drawn by the Eleatic Stranger between the age of Cronos and the present age. In the age of Cronos, the human race was governed and protected by the deity as sheep are tended by the shepherd. In the present era, *we* have to take on the responsibility and look after ourselves, in a community where there is no intrinsic difference in nature any more between ruler and ruled – all of us are human. To exercise rule adequately in these circumstances, we need a political knowledge rather differently conceived than as the skill of an overseer. And when the *Statesman* eventually debates the relationship between that knowledge and the rule of law, it treats law as a very inferior substitute, rigid and universal, incapable of responding to individual variation or to change as the practitioner of an expert statesman's precise knowledge is able to do. Law provides 'for the majority of people, for the majority of cases, and roughly, somehow, like this' (295a), in Christopher Rowe's brilliant rendering. Maybe in the absence of a knowledgeable statesman law is the best we can do. But considered on its own merits, reliance on law is far from being an optimally intelligent way to run our affairs, any more than would trying to pilot a ship simply by sticking unwaveringly to a rule book.

When we return to our *Laws* passage, we find the Athenian simply evading the problems the *Statesman* points up and eliding distinctions the *Statesman* is careful to establish. Government by humans following principles of rationality is in the *Laws* simply *assimilated* to the theocracy of a dispassionate divine dispensation; and that system of government is simply *assimilated* to the rule of law. Readers who remember their *Statesman* will surely protest: why have the strenuously articulated and carefully argued distinctions made by the Eleatic Stranger been collapsed in a single pregnant sentence of the *Laws*? And can the way the Athenian Visitor exploits the age of Cronos story, and the way he treats the rule of law, ultimately be reconciled at all with the line of argument from the *Statesman* that I have just sketched?

Working out an answer to the question would need an essay to itself. But before leaving the topic, I want briefly to offer a comment on the prospects for a developmental solution. Interpreters of Plato inclined to acknowledge elements of development in his writing and thinking might propose that there has been a shift in his ideas on the subject.[17] There are I think roughly speaking two directions for developmental solutions to take on the present issue. One line would be to suppose that the *Statesman* was written before this part of the *Laws*, and that Plato has now decided that he set his valuation of law too low in the earlier work. It is not merely at best a rough but inflexible substitute for the statesman's knowledge. If law is philosophically informed, it has the advantage over any human ruler, no matter how knowledgeable, that it is not susceptible to human passions

---

[17] Cf. e.g. Kahn 1995: 51–4.

and desires. Its rationality is in that sense of a higher order than his, just because it is an abstract principle, not one among a number of human capacities. 'Law', in Aristotle's pithy formulation, 'is reason without desire' (*Pol.* 3.16, 1287a32).

The other line would assume the opposite order of composition. On this view the *Laws*, which must on any reckoning have taken a long time to write, will have been begun a good while before the idea for the *Statesman* was conceived. Our passage in Book 4 will embody a rather sanguine but relatively untheorized conception of the rationality of law. We will then have to suppose that when Plato had had a fuller think about the issue, his opinion of the merits of law as the basic principle of government was revised a long way downwards. And this second opinion is to be seen as reflected not only in the *Statesman*, but in Book 9 of the *Laws* itself, which must accordingly on this hypothesis be put somewhat later in composition than Book 4. For in a famous passage explaining that human nature is not fitted to exercise absolute power in rule of the city without succumbing to the imperatives of private pleasure and private interest, the Athenian acknowledges that *were* someone to be able to act incorruptibly in knowledge of the common interest that *would* be better than the rule of law. Since such a thing happens so little anywhere, we have to choose law as our 'second-best' option. And the Athenian then describes law in the *Statesman*'s terms as looking to cover 'the majority of cases' (ὡς ἐπὶ τὸ πολύ; cf. *Plt.* 295a), not everything (*Laws* 9.875d).

The trouble with the first of these developmental approaches is that it cannot easily cope with the Book 9 passage, where the second scores strongly. The second, however, runs into difficulty with a subsequent passage in Book 12, where the Athenian Visitor's high valuation of the study of the laws as the most important of all disciplines for making the learner a better person is supported with the comment (*Laws* 12.957c): 'Were it not so, it would be in vain that law – our divine law, which evokes such wonder – bears a name akin to reason.' Which takes us right back to the intellectual ambience of the myth of the age of Cronos and the Athenian's gloss upon it (4.714a). So if the Book 9 passage represents Plato's latest considered view of law, the final part of Book 12, in the culminating section of the whole dialogue, looks as though it still reflects the perspective of the Cronos myth of Book 4.

A developmental solution to the apparent conflict between the *Laws*' treatment of law as a rational principle superior to human capacity to exercise rule and the *Statesman*'s view of it as a poor second best to knowledge might have worked. But we have to conclude that in fact it does not. The *Statesman's* position can also be found in the *Laws*; and there seems little prospect of distinguishing with any plausibility or security a *Statesman* stratum and a non-*Statesman* stratum reflecting different chronological stages of its composition. There is other evidence in the *Laws* that one might adduce to support this verdict, for example, its use, in parts of the text close to the age of Cronos passage, of the idea that the statesman looks to due measure and *kairos*, the right or appropriate moment, in seeking to perform his task (3.691c–d, 4.709b–c; cf.*Plt.* 283–4, 305c–d).[18]

It is better – I suggest – to recall that the passage in Book 9 characterizing law not as divine but as 'second-best' (9.875d) occurs in one of the dialogue's preludes or preambles to laws (in this case, as it happens, to the legal provisions recommended for dealing with those convicted of wounding). Of such preambles, André Laks has well said that they 'can also metamorphose into discussions of principles', and into 'meta-legislative reflection that calls into question the status of the legislative enterprise itself'.[19] This preamble presents us with a signal example of that metamorphosis. We are transported into the higher atmosphere of the *Sophist* and *Statesman*, paired dialogues palpably composed for a practised philosophical readership familiar and able to cope with abstract and highly sophisticated discussions of fundamental metaphysical and methodological questions: in short, for practised readers of Plato.[20] What he would have expected the more ordinary reader to make of such a radical change of tack is hard to guess, when the dialogue has expended so much energy on the legislative project and its divinely assured authority as the work of reason. It is tempting to harbour a suspicion that Plato deliberately tucked the passage away in the latter pages of the discussion of criminal offences against the person, prefaced to a section of that discussion (on wounding) with which it has no specific or intrinsic connection – in a place where few other than practised readers would be likely to encounter, let alone expect, such reflections.[21]

Religion and Theology

The starting point for the Athenian Visitor's whole consideration of the best *politeia* is, as we noticed, an invocation of god, followed by the telling of a myth about the relation of humans and the divine – the myth of the

---

[18] On *kairos* in the *Statesman*, see especially Lane 1995, 1998.   [19] Laks 2000: 266.
[20] I have discussed elsewhere the main difference I see in the approach to politics in the *Statesman* (top-down) from that distinctive of the *Republic* and *Laws* alike (bottom-up): Schofield 1999b: 37–42.
[21] Here we might recall Max Cresswell's remarks on Plato as a 'sneaky writer': Chapter 5 above, p. 98, n. 4.

age of Cronos. The moral he derives from the myth is a thesis about the supremacy of law couched in theocratic terms which simply shortcut whole swathes of argument in the *Republic* and hard-won distinctions drawn in the *Statesman*. This is religion being used to present the attractions of a particular conception of law and *politeia*, in a way which succeeds in avoiding further philosophical debate (although, as we have noted, debate is invited), but at the same time intimates to the practised reader the author's awareness that and how he is avoiding it.

If anyone were still in any doubt about the religious framework shaping the presentation of the political theory of the *Laws*, they need only read on to the section of the Athenian Visitor's argument in Book 4 that follows the Cronos passage. He assumes the arrival of the colonists who are to be the foundation citizens of their Cretan city and delivers to Cleinias and Megillus the address with which they would be greeted. It begins with an assertion of the need for all their conduct to be governed by consideration of divine justice – including a famous anti-Protagorean statement (4.716c): 'god is the measure of all things'. It continues with an account of duties to gods, *daimones*, heroes, and parents – and the tone of piety is sustained throughout the dialogue, not least in the penal legislation of Book 9. The language employed in this address is mainly the language of 'philosophical' religion and theology: an Orphic quotation launches the speech (715e–716a), and there is more than a hint of Pythagorean inspiration (notably at 717a–b).

In due course, the Athenian Visitor will give a reasoned justification of the religious assumptions which underpin his whole approach to the question of the best *politeia* and the construction of laws appropriate to it. For this, we have to wait until Book 10 and its ambitious philosophical argument against atheism and for a divine first cause, 'older than body' – the language of the proof is nicely congruent with the interlocutors' value system. It appears that the Athenian, hoping to take the elderly non-swimmers Cleinias and Megillus with him, does now move beyond what I have been describing as the limitation imposed by religion on the political theory of the dialogue to something generally recognized as philosophical reasoning. Here at least, there is a push back to first principles.

But it remains a question what status we should suppose we are to accord to the theology of Book 10. Is it 'Plato's theology' – that is, the theory about the divine that we can suppose represents Plato's own best view on the subject? Or is it rather what one might call his civic theology – that is, that theological system, no doubt as he would see it that true theological system, which gives the kind of foundation for the political theory of the dialogue that will justify its pervasively religious cast as well as the moral order it asserts? This is a large issue that deserves a full consideration that I do not begin to attempt here. Suffice to point out, however, that the second option is the more cautious interpretation. That is, it would approach the *Laws*' theology as to be understood in relation to its function in the dialogue, and to what I have been calling the limitation of religion. Nearly a century ago, Hackforth remarked:[22]

> We must remember that Plato is not concerned to give us the whole of his metaphysics, or even of his philosophy of religion, in the *Laws*; his object is to give us the necessary minimum of philosophical doctrine required for a sound basis of religion and morality; and from that point of view it was not necessary to go into the difficult question of the relation of *nous* to the Universe, or (what is the same thing) the relation of *nous* to *psuche* (soul), the principle of movement in the Universe. Indeed it would have been unreasonable to expect Cleinias and Megillus, or the citizen body to whom the 'preambles' to the laws are addressed, to follow him if he had.

Someone inclined to take this second 'civic theology' option might want to leave open the possibility that in other contexts Plato would have located the truest form of divinity elsewhere than in the first cause of motion. In fact, the Cronos passage in Book 4 already indicates that *nous*, as rational understanding, is more fundamental in his conception of the divine, as emerges more explicitly in the *Timaeus* and *Philebus*.[23] But how he might have wished to connect *nous* as divine with something metaphysically more fundamental still, such as – in the *Republic*'s scheme of things – the Form of the Good, or the *Parmenides*' One, was left for the ancient Platonist tradition to debate.

The Rationale of the Religious Strategy

It is one thing to make the diagnosis that religion limits the ambition and the openness of philosophical questioning in the *Laws*. It is another to try and account for Plato's decision to construct much of the political discourse of the dialogue within such a limiting religious framework. I have only a rather simple and obvious and unoriginal explanation to offer, paraphrasing the gist of Hackforth's remarks. I take it that Plato wanted two things above all of the discourse he was to develop in the *Laws*: first, that it should reflect and embody a sense of a transcendent moral framework for political and social existence; second, that it should be capable of

---

[22] Hackforth 1936: 6.   [23] See Hackforth 1936; Menn 1995.

being persuasive – because *inter alia* generally intelligible – to a population at large, not to just an intellectual elite. As he judged the matter, it was religious discourse, reformed and redirected as necessary, which could most palpably meet these two requirements.

Plato's Cretan city is to be a highly participatory political society, with women as well as men included in the participation, and without the sharp divisions between the governing elite and the rest of the citizens proposed in the *Republic*. In this life, education, and in the next, prospects for happiness are more generally distributed than in the *Republic*. The idea of punishment is conceived in terms of moral improvement rather than sheer retribution. And Plato's interest in a persuasive rather than a purely prescriptive public rhetoric may reflect at least some concern that, in the virtue which legislation is designed to promote, there needs to be the possibility of what could be described as true understanding, not just socially induced assent.[24] But the *Laws*, like the political world it imagines, is not the locus of a free enquiry, although Plato was perfectly well aware of what free enquiry is like, as he intimates to the practised reader. To my mind, the *Laws* constitutes a remarkable achievement not least for the way it works out from first word to last, and at several levels of discourse and meta-discourse, the consequences of constructing a political settlement conceived in terms of a controlling gerontocratic religious rhetoric – controlling, of course, in more senses than one. There is here a message for our times. But it warns as much as it beckons us.

---

[24] Here, I conflate considerations suggested by the work especially of Saunders 1991 and Bobonich 1991, 2002.

CHAPTER 10

The Laws' *Two Projects*

Aristotle's Puzzle

Plato's *Laws* has probably been the most unpopular of all his dialogues. 'Not only', says the Loeb editor in his introduction, 'does it lack the charm and vigour of the earlier dialogues, but it is marked also by much uncouthness of style, and by a tendency to pedantry, tautology and discursive garrulity which seems to point to the failing powers of the author.'[1] It represents itself as the record of a rambling conversation, 'framed apparently on no artistic plan', between three elderly men, who get immersed in masses of detail often of little general philosophical interest. Damning remarks of this and other kinds can be found without difficulty in modern literature about Plato.[2]

On a first inspection, Aristotle might appear to stand at the head of the queue of those thinkers who on reading the *Laws* have found little there to reward them. The last chapter of his *Nicomachean Ethics* is devoted to an explanation of why law is an essential instrument for shaping the characters and behaviour of citizens, and what sort of knowledge and experience someone needs to become a good legislator. His concluding paragraph begins with the notorious comment (*EN* 10.9, 1181b12–14): 'Our predecessors have left the topic of legislation unresearched, so it would probably be better to study it instead ourselves.'[3] Aristotle's remark here makes it sound as though he has temporarily forgotten even the existence of the *Laws*.

---

[1] Bury 1926: 1.vii.
[2] One further example may suffice. In his valedictory lecture as Laurence Professor at Cambridge, Myles Burnyeat concluded the paragraph he devoted to the *Laws* – commenting particularly on its pervasively repressive theocracy – with the observation (Burnyeat 1997: 9): 'It can hardly be an accident that the first word of this long and appalling work is *theos*, "God".'
[3] Perhaps he means: 'Better than going through their writings seeing if we can find useful observations on the subject'. If so, this contrasts strikingly with the procedure he says he will adopt with regard to the related and more fundamental study of *politeia*, 'constitution' or 'social and political system', where going through predecessors' writings with this intent is precisely what he prescribes for himself (1181b15–17) and does indeed execute in Book 2 of the *Politics*.

202

For besides its mass of legislative detail, the *Laws* contains powerful general reflection on law: for example, the need for law to be the locus of supreme authority in the political community (4.712a–715d), the importance of prefacing the prescriptions which constitute law proper with explanatory preludes designed to persuade (4.719e–723d), the extent to which law once established should subsequently be modified or regarded as modifiable (5.745e–746d, 6.772a–d), the relation between written and 'unwritten' law (7.793a–d), how the categories of the voluntary and the involuntary apply to acts of wrongdoing in which the law will need to take an interest (9.860a–864a). All that is left out of account by Aristotle's sweeping assertion.

In the *Politics*, there is one chapter of Book 2 specifically devoted to the *Laws*, as well as one or two other explicit references to the dialogue elsewhere in the treatise. This time, one wonders not whether Aristotle has forgotten the existence of the dialogue, but whether he has been reading the same dialogue as we have. 'All the discourses of Socrates', he says, 'have in them something extraordinary and clever and original and enquiring – but it's perhaps difficult to get everything right' (*Pol.* 2.6, 1265a10). On the surface, this sounds complimentary, and indeed a shrewdly appreciative assessment of works of Plato in which Socrates leads the conversation, whether one thinks of the early 'Socratic' dialogues or of the *Republic* itself. But the adjectives are not the ones that first spring to the lips of most readers of the *Laws*. Its main speaker is anyway not Socrates, but an 'Athenian Stranger' who does not even sound very like Socrates.

Should we infer that while Aristotle has decided to try to say something positive about the *Laws* at this point, he is so little focused on its overall intellectual project (as opposed to various particular topics in it that he has noted for criticism) that he has lost any sense of listening to the Stranger talking, or indeed of the dialogue as a dialogue at all? The only obvious alternative is to guess with Trevor Saunders that Aristotle here engages in 'ironic jesting'.[4] In which case he would presumably want us to read his string of epithets as meaning something like their exact opposite in their application to the *Laws*.

Aristotle's main interest in the *Laws* in the chapter he writes about it is not in its philosophy of law or the legal code it draws up, but in what it has to say on the subject of the *politeia*, the social and political system or constitution it envisages – understandably enough, given that this is the

---

[4] Saunders 1995: 128.

general subject of Book 2 of the *Politics*, and the main topic of the treatise as a whole. Here, he comments that the dialogue actually contains relatively little on the *politeia* but consists mostly of laws.[5] And that little, he says, is not really very different at the end of the day from the ideal articulated in the *Republic*, even though the original intention of the *Laws* was to institute a form of political system 'more common' to cities: presumably 'more capable of being shared in' by political communities generally, not just ones deliberately constructed as ideal, like the *Republic*'s Kallipolis, whose principal social and political arrangements he has just subjected to an extended and unremittingly harsh critique (*Pol.* 2.2–5). Thus, he comments (*Pol.* 2.6, 1265a4–8): 'Except for holding women and property communally, he makes everything the same in both systems: the same education, life to be free from menial tasks, the same provisions for common meals.' After these general remarks, Aristotle turns for the rest of the chapter to detailed criticism of political proposals unique to the *Laws*. As Richard Stalley puts it in his notes to Ernest Barker's English translation of the dialogue: 'His main concern is to point to what he sees as faulty in Plato's treatment rather than to engage in constructive discussion.'[6]

The paradox is that when we look elsewhere in the *Politics*, we find Aristotle making extensive, albeit mostly unacknowledged use of the *Laws*. In fact, Books 7 and 8 of the *Politics* read at times like nothing so much as Aristotle's own abbreviated version of the *Laws*' prescription for an ideal political community. Certainly, in these books there is force in Barker's verdict: 'If Aristotle wrote the *Politics*, and arranged the content under the categories and in the scheme of his own philosophy, Plato supplied a great part of the content.'[7] Whether this is because Books 7 and 8 constitute a stratum of the *Politics* earlier than Book 2, or because Aristotle does criticism and construction in entirely different modes, almost as if they had nothing to do with each other, is a question to which one might return on another occasion. For the moment, it will be instructive to focus on a point

---

[5] Aristotle is either exaggerating or adopting a much narrower definition of *politeia* (constitution strictly conceived as design of organs of government) than the more generous conception of social and political organization he often operates with, not least in Book 2 of the *Politics* itself.

[6] Barker 1995: 340.

[7] Barker 1918: 382. He gives a useful list of parallels between the *Politics* and the *Laws* at pp. 380–1, noting that those with Books 7 and 8 are 'too numerous to be mentioned' (here he selects just a few examples). One example he does not mention is the focus on music in Book 8: without the *Laws*' treatment of musical performance as the key shaping influence on character (especially as developed in *Laws* 2, to which particularly chapter 5 of *Politics* 8 is heavily indebted), Aristotle's decision to devote virtually an entire book of the *Politics* to music would be unintelligible.

I have reproduced above from the critical treatment of the dialogue in Book 2.

So far as I can see, scholars have not had much to say about Aristotle's suggestion at *Pol.* 2.6, 1265a3–4 that Plato's original intention in the *Laws* was to propose a 'more common' form of political system, from which he subsequently deviated. The same kind of issue recurs later in the chapter, where he writes as follows (1265b26–33):

> The tendency of the whole system is to be neither democracy nor oligarchy, but midway between them. People call it 'polity', because it consists of those who qualify as heavy-armed infantry [i.e. in the community's citizen army]. Now if he is framing this constitution for cities as the one which of all constitutions is most common [i.e. most capable of being generally shared], perhaps the proposal he has made is a good one; but not if he meant it as the best after the primary constitution [i.e. the ideal of the *Republic*] – for one might rather commend the Laconians' [i.e. the Spartan constitution], or some other with a more aristocratic leaning [e.g. perhaps Aristotle's own in Books 7 and 8].

Here, the idea that the political system to be worked out in the *Laws* is intended as 'most common' is put more hypothetically, and on a par with an alternative: that it is meant to be second-best after the city of the *Republic*. At first sight, this might seem to imply something inconsistent with the earlier statement that the political system advocated in the *Laws* is 'gradually brought back round to the other constitution' [i.e. to the system of the *Republic* Aristotle has just been discussing] from the 'more common' constitution he was *in fact* intending (1265a3–4). On further reflection, however, we can see that Aristotle is working with a perfectly coherent conception of the progress of the argument of the *Laws* and has exposed rather acutely something initially puzzling about Plato's whole project in the dialogue.

The *Laws*' Two Projects

There is no difficulty in identifying the parts of Plato's text where it looks as though he is attempting to construct a 'second-best' to the ideal city of the *Republic*, approximating to more and more of the institutions of Kallipolis as the discussion goes on. In the great introductory monologue (occupying the whole of Book 5) that prefaces the detailed exposition of his specific legislative proposals, the Athenian Stranger reaches a point (739a–e) where he judges it appropriate to acknowledge that 'reasoning and experience' indicate that the organization of a city (i.e. the sort of city under discussion) will turn out to be 'second' against the standard of the best. In consequence, the right plan is to describe political systems in order of excellence: first, second, third. A brief sketch of the 'first' then follows. It is clearly a version of the communist society of the guards expounded in (mostly) Book 5 of the *Republic*. The Stranger's verdict is that this is a system suitable for 'gods or children of gods'. So – given that what is now being looked for is something more practicable – the discussants will certainly need to keep a hold on the 'first' as paradigm but search now for the one that approximates to it as nearly as possible: the 'second'. Perhaps they will explore the 'third' later.

In the pages that follow (5.739e–745e), it becomes clear how the programme just articulated will be implemented. The abolition of private land ownership and housing proposed for the guards at the end of Book 3 of the *Republic* is revoked. Marriage as conventionally conceived and the nuclear family (similarly abolished in *Republic* 5) are restored. Finally, the use of money, forbidden the guards in *Republic* 3 (416e–417a), is permitted for one or two circumscribed non-mercantile purposes. Nonetheless, the ideals of community, equality, and friendship are still guiding principles. The *Laws* seeks to regulate the economic system in such a way as to minimise the differentials in wealth usually associated with the family, for instance by providing that all landholdings are equal in size and unalienable, as well as by debarring those who are to count as citizens from commercial activity, with no gold or silver permitted in the city at all. The economic class of the *Republic* is now excluded from citizenship altogether, in fact, and the communistic agenda of the *Republic* rewritten in the account of the 'first' *politeia* as a prescription which will apply to 'the whole city' so far as possible.[8] Nonetheless the 'second' city of the *Laws* is not itself communist. That is the most obvious way in which its political system is 'second', nor 'first' (cf. also 7.807b–c).[9]

Aristotle is right, however, that as the exposition of the institutions of the city further develops, it gradually gets to sound more and more like the *Republic*. As evidence, he mentions in the first instance the provisions for education, to which all of Book 7 is devoted. These do indeed flesh out in detail and at length the sketch in Books 2 and 3 of the *Republic*, with control of the use of poetry reaffirmed, and the role of suitable musical performance (already given extended treatment in Book 2) assigned particular emphasis, notably choral dancing and the singing of hymns in religious ritual. This is the general context in which leisure and its proper

---

[8] On this latter point, see Schofield 2006: 223 and n. 87.   [9] See further Schofield 2006: 231–4.

use are discussed (7.806d–807d; cf. 803c–804b) – another topic Aristotle mentions, and one which will become the guiding theme from *Politics* 7.14, 1330a14 to the rest of his treatise. Towards the end of the account of education, mathematics, too, is discussed. As in the *Republic*, advanced study is restricted to an elite, although the basics of arithmetic, geometry, and astronomy are to be taught to everyone, in the case of astronomy so that blasphemous opinions about the heavens are avoided (7.817e–822c).

The final item on Aristotle's list of parallels with the *Republic*, the institution of common meals, seems as if it is added just for good measure. The Athenian Stranger has already discussed the topic before he launches into education, in Book 6 (779e–783c), although (as Aristotle suggests) after other communistic institutions have been jettisoned in Book 5. One striking similarity with the *Republic* that Aristotle might have stressed is the insistence that the educational programme (like the common meals regime) will apply to females as well as males. In both these contexts, the Athenian conducts a vigorous assault on contemporary social and political arrangements that confine women to the home, not least as a waste of half the human resource available to a political community (7.805a–d).

So much, then, on how the project of discussing a second-best *politeia* gradually comes to resemble a detailed specification for the *Republic*'s ideal city, once communism is abandoned But Aristotle implies that the *Laws*' initial project, before discussion of any of the material we have just been considering, had a quite different objective: to institute a political system 'more common' than that of an ideal community – more capable of being generally adopted, more shareable. Here, he employs language he will use in the strategic opening chapter of Book 4 of the *Politics*, in categorizing the different intellectual enterprises that belong to the single science of politics. First mentioned is consideration of what would be the best system if there were no external obstacles to the realization of our hopes (or in Aristotle's words, our 'prayer'). This is the sort of theorizing he sees as undertaken in the treatment of the 'second' city in Books 5 to 8 of the *Laws* (where the impracticability of the 'first' city is a matter of what human nature will stand, not external circumstances). He then lists three other kinds of project. These are examination of what system fits particular circumstances (e.g. if the ratio of poor to wealthy citizens is high); what system is desirable given a certain basic premise (e.g. that political freedom is to be maximized, or that wealth is what must carry the greatest weight in constitutional provisions); and finally, 'the system that is most suited to all cities' – a question most writers on *politeia* ignore, Aristotle says, and in so doing 'miss out on what is useful' (*Pol.* 4.1, 1288b21–37).

This last sort of enterprise is the one he has in mind when he characterizes the original project of the *Laws* as aiming to institute a 'more common' system. He goes on to say this of his fourth and last category of project (*Pol.* 4.1, 1288b37–9): 'For it is important to consider not only the best, but also the possible, and likewise also the one that is easier and more common for all.' Once again, 'more common' must mean 'more capable of being adopted or shared in' by cities in general. What could have led Aristotle to read the *Laws* as embarked – initially, before the search for something that approximates the ideal begins in Book 5 – on that kind of more practical enquiry?

I suggest that the beginnings of an answer are to be found in the title Ernest Barker gave to Book 3 of the *Laws*: 'The Lessons of History'.[10] After the discussion of the fundamental aims of legislation in the opening books, the third book makes a fresh start (3.676a–b):

ATHENIAN: So much for that, then. But what are we to say of the origin of *politeia*? Wouldn't *this* be the easiest and finest vantage point for someone to observe it from?
CLEINIAS: What vantage point?
ATHENIAN: The one that has always to be adopted if we are to study the advance of cities to virtue or vice during the process of time.
CLEINIAS: What do you mean by that?
ATHENIAN: I suppose taking an indefinitely long duration of time and the changes that occur in such a period.

Cleinias still needs more explanation, until he appreciates that a survey of the growth and decline of regimes, and their improvement and deterioration, is what the Athenian has in mind.

In short, Plato proposes a historical survey, designed to discover basic principles of *politeia* construction which have to be observed if a political community is to achieve health and stability. The bulk of Book 3 is accordingly devoted to a history of Greece, from the flood – what the Greeks conceived of as Deucalion's flood – and a speculative account of the primitive isolated communities which will have formed subsequently to the inundation, through the period described by Homer, and on to more recent times, with a particular focus on the rise of Sparta. The book closes with parallel accounts of the histories of Persia and Athens. The narrative here starts in each case with a period (under Cyrus in the sixth century BC for Persia, and for Athens the time of the Persian invasion at the beginning

---

[10] Barker 1918: 307.

of the fifth) when each enjoyed a well-balanced constitution but culminates for both in terminal decline into opposite excesses: in Persia, tyranny; in Athens, the lawlessness of extreme freedom.

It is from Sparta and its success as a state in the classical period that the Athenian Stranger draws the chief moral for *politeia* design that Book 3 teaches. After a review of the different bases on which those who rule over others claim their authority (3.689e–690e), he propounds the view that a principal cause of internal faction and ultimate self-destruction for a city is the arrogance bred in someone whose rule is absolute. He observes that neglect of due measure in any area of life brings disaster of various sorts. There follows a striking passage (3.691c–d):

> What are we getting at? Just this: My dear friends, there does not exist a mortal soul whose nature will ever be able to cope with the greatest ruling position to be attained among humans, when young and unaccountable, without being filled in his thinking with that greatest of diseases, folly, and earning the hatred of his closest friends. And when this happens, it quickly ruins the soul and annihilates its entire power. To take precautions against this by discerning the due measure is the task of great lawgivers.

The Athenian then documents the way this feat was successfully achieved at Sparta, in Persia, and at Athens. At Sparta, Lycurgus' ingenious prescriptions for the division of powers between a dual kingship, a body of elders, and the annually elected ephors (five officials who exercised a degree of control over the kings as well as executive and judicial functions of their own) made of kingship a mixed constitution exhibiting measure, and thereby ensured both its stability and the stability of the political community in general (3.691d–692b). The contribution of the elders to the mixture is seen as wisdom ('power prudent with age'), whereas the ephors constituted a democratic element in the system ('a power which came very close to being held by lot'). Subsequently, these ingredients in a measured constitution will be specifically identified as the attributes of wisdom (*phronêsis*) and freedom (*eleutheria*), associated symbolically with monarchy and democracy, respectively. A third attribute alongside these is friendship (*philia*), which seems to be a way of articulating the harmony in society that is generated in a system which properly blends wisdom and freedom in the functions that are exercised by different agencies within it, although the Athenian couples it particularly with the equality that goes with political freedom in these circumstances (693b–694b; cf. 701d).

It was because Persia in its long past golden era under Cyrus embodied this trio of attributes in its political system, albeit quite differently from

Sparta, that it 'made progress'. The account of Athenian history is more nuanced. The Stranger refers only briefly and without naming him to the Athens of its great lawgiver, Solon. His narrative focuses on Athenian resistance to the Persian invasion in 490 and 480 BC, a century after Solon's reforms. He stresses the role of respect for law and fear of the enemy as the key to their maintaining the solidarity and friendship that enabled them to defeat superior Persian forces (3.698a–699d). The terse formula 'voluntary slavery to the laws' (700a) is the way the elements of freedom ('voluntary'), on the one side, and wisdom ('laws'), on the other, are now apparently being conceived as integrating to produce social cohesion.

Following this short summary of what were the main lessons Plato wanted his readers to draw from history, we are now in a position to return to Aristotle's discussion of the *Laws* in *Politics* 2.6, and to suggest why he may have thought the dialogue's initial constitutional project aimed to specify a political system 'more common' to cities. The historical reflections of Book 3 of the *Laws* are indeed devised with a view to prescribing for the sort of system capable of being generally adopted by political communities. What works – Plato is saying – is a constitution which by virtue of its measured balance of wise authority and popular freedom achieves social harmony. The evidence is supplied by Sparta, Persia, and Athens, at the times when these three major states were at their most successful (at any rate as judged in terms of their military achievements). Each had a political regime which embodied wisdom, freedom, and friendship in a balanced system.

Interestingly, the mode in which wisdom and freedom were mixed differed in each case. At Sparta, it was a matter of division of constitutional powers in such a way as to ensure that both a form of popular representation and the voice of wisdom and experience were given effect. In Persia, it was more a case of enlightened despotism, with the monarch encouraging free speech and the opportunity for anyone to contribute of their own wisdom in public discussion. At Athens, it was no more than voluntary obedience to the law, sustained by fear and shame, in straitened circumstances where any other way of behaving would obviously have been suicidal.[11] Presumably there would have been corresponding variation in the quality of social cohesion produced under the three systems – which

---

[11] On the fear that is represented as the Athenian's predominant motivation, see Rowe 2007: 85–91; Schofield 2013a: 293–6.

from the point of view of freedom we might characterize as representative democracy, direct democracy, and legal democracy.

Plato is obviously enjoying making both Sparta and especially his highly fictive Persia look more genuinely participatory than Athens. His Cyrus sounds very like Thucydides' Pericles (see the Funeral Speech, especially 2.37–40),[12] whereas his Athens more resembles the Sparta its deposed king Demaratus describes, when precisely at the time of the Persian expedition against Greece of 480 BC he says to Xerxes (Herodotus 7.164.4):

> When the Spartans fight individually, they are second to none, but when they fight in a body they are best of all. The reason is that though they are free, they are not completely so, because they have a master over them – the law – which they fear more than your subjects fear you.

Whatever the basis for the variations in the formula for the Stranger's mixture, it is plainly important for recommending his project for *politeia* design that there *be* such variations. The recipe for success – wisdom, freedom, friendship – will be the more persuasive the more flexibly it can be applied within political communities in widely differing sorts of historical circumstances.

Marrying the Two Projects

In the previous section, I have tried to work out why Aristotle might have found two quite distinct constitutional projects in the *Laws*: the original one, designed to identify a system generally applicable to cities (with no presumption that these will be 'ideal' from an ethical point of view), which then turns into something much more resembling the attempt to construct the best city previously undertaken in the *Republic*. Book 3 of the *Laws* does indeed fit Aristotle's notion of the original project. Books 5 to 8 – in the sections we have considered – do indeed 'keep a hold' on the 'first' city of the *Republic* as paradigm, and specify provisions for social organization and education that approximate it as closely as possible, once granted the jettisoning of communism as too great a strain on human nature.

The two theoretical enterprises clearly are different. The Book 3 project sees political system building as the attempt to strike a compromise which will recognize both political freedom for the citizens and the authority of wisdom in constitutional provisions. The Book 5 project is focused much

---

[12] But Plato did not believe in the wise Pericles portrayed by Thucydides: see *Gorgias* 515c–519b, with Schofield 2006: 67–74, 211–12.

more directly on community and on virtue and happiness (the chief topic of the long 'prelude' which launches the book (726a–734e)), and on the institutions needed to promote these within the basic framework of private property and the family. Of course, both projects share a general aim, of producing a system in which there is 'friendship' between the citizens. This was already explicit in the formulations of the non-ideal project I cited from the latter part of Book 3. But it is likewise explicitly articulated in the project of approximating the ideal initiated in Book 5. Not only is the Pythagorean maxim 'friends share what they have' the keynote of the ideal city which is conceived as the paradigm (739c), but a little later – à propos of the second-best system – the Athenian says: 'The premise on which our laws depend was the imperative to ensure that the citizens should be as happy as possible, and friends to each other in the highest degree' (743c). Yet the use of the superlative here is indicative. The non-ideal project looks for social and political cohesion, the project of approximating the ideal aims at *maximal* social cohesion.

The presence of the two projects within one and the same dialogue reflects a deeper tension. Is it the *Laws*' ambition to explain the kind of social and political system needed if we are to bring out the best in people and give them the best possible chance of achieving virtue and happiness? Or is the dialogue more interested in taking the citizenry of any political community more or less as the human beings they actually are, and putting in place laws and institutions which (in the terms of Book 3) constrain freedom with wisdom? The first objective seems to be strongly implied in the prefatory first book (e.g. 1.630d–632e, 644e–645b) and to be reaffirmed at the very end of the dialogue in Book 12 (12.863a). But the focus on the extensive legal code worked out in the later books, with its elaborate penology, suggests that for some of the dialogue Plato is devising a system to deal with people whose appetite for virtue is limited, and where constraint has to be the main order of the day.

There are a number of passages in which he has the Athenian comment on this last issue. They might be read as reflections on the problem of how the idealizing and more pragmatic[13] projects Aristotle diagnoses in the *Laws* are related in the mind of the author. Two are particularly worth a brief look, since they occur at strategic junctures in the argument of the dialogue

---

[13] The project designated 'pragmatic' here is not to be equated with that so described in Bartels 2017. Bartels sees the *Laws* as proceeding empirically and provisionally throughout, and without significant relationship with the idealizing mode of the *Republic*. In the usage of the present chapter, it is only those sections of the dialogue which propose legislation designed to legislate for men as they are, not as they might be if they became more virtuous, that further a pragmatic project.

as a whole. Both contrast the ambition to promote virtue with the human material the legislator will actually have to work with. The first comes in Book 4, at a point where the Athenian is beginning to explain his theory of the dual nature of legislation – its combination of persuasive preamble with coercive content. 'I would want people', he says (4.718c), 'to be as easy to persuade towards virtue as possible; and this is evidently what the legislator will try to achieve in all his legislation.' But the reality is that persuasion must count as a success if it accomplishes something much more limited: making people more amenable – 'a trifle easier to handle, and so that much easier to teach'. There is just not much supply of persons eager to be as good as possible as fast as possible (718d). It could not be more plainly stated that the *Laws* envisages itself as trying to cope with human beings as they actually are.

In Book 9, the Athenian makes a shift in direction and takes up the subject of crime, and the legislative provision for tackling it. This turn in the exposition makes renewed discussion of the human material the legislator must deal with particularly well motivated. The Athenian starts with the reflection that there is something shameful in proposing laws on crime, in a city 'which we are saying will be well managed, and where the provisions for promoting virtue are thoroughly sound' (9.853b). Even to think that there will be anyone in it as wholly depraved as in other cities – rendering necessary appropriate laws and forms of punishment – is shameful. But (853c–d, in Saunders's Penguin translation (adapted)):

> Unlike the ancient legislators, we are not framing laws for heroes and sons of gods. The lawgivers of that age, according to the story told nowadays, were descended from gods and legislated for people of similar stock. But we are human beings, legislating in the world today for the children of human beings, and we shall give no offence by our fear that one of our citizens will turn out to be, so to speak, a 'tough egg', whose character will be so 'hard-boiled' as to resist softening; powerful as our laws are, they may not be able to tame such people, just as heat has no effect on tough beans.

In the light of a passage such as this, it is now possible to see not only that the two projects identified by Aristotle are there in the text, but that Plato has a rationale for both and implies an indication of how they are connected. The fundamental enterprise of the dialogue is the idealizing project which he relates to the political philosophy of the *Republic* in Book 5: the attempt to approximate to the best ideal system so far as possible, in order to promote maximal happiness and friendship. Had Aristotle in *Politics* 2.6 started his account of how thinking about *politeia* is developed in Book 1 of the *Laws*, not with Book 3, he might have recognized that himself. The project introduced in Book 3, on the other hand, turns out to be *subordinate* to the idealizing project. On further reading and reflection, it will appear that the historical narrative of Book 3 is laying foundations for some principles that can be used to deal with ordinary human nature within the overall context of the idealizing project, and with its resistance to or lack of interest in the life of virtue with which the idealizing project is concerned. One of Plato's reasons for resorting to *history* at this point in the *Laws* is presumably to emphasize that thinking about *politeia* needs to deal with the contingent and the empirical as well as the ideal.[14]

The empirical as Plato understands it in the *Laws* is not exclusively or straightforwardly just a matter of how much or little ordinary humanity is disposed towards a life of virtue. He acknowledges its force in handling other – even if ultimately related – matters too. A notable example, which illustrates with great clarity the way the pragmatic project of Book 3 relates to the *Laws*' primary idealizing project, is supplied by his treatment of property. The idealizing project takes great pains to regulate the ownership of land, so as to ensure that (though communism is not enforced) there is as much equality in landholding, and in general in financial resources, as possible. Division between rich and poor remains for Plato as great a threat to a city as it did in the *Republic* (5.736c–738a, 739e–744a; cf. *Rep.* 4.421c–423a). But realism requires qualification of the ideal (744b–c):

> It would have been good if each person, on joining the colony, had all else equal as well [i.e. as well as the equal landholding now allocated to every householder]. Since this is not possible, and one person will come with more money, another with less, it is necessary for many reasons, and for the sake of equalizing opportunities in public life, to ensure that offices and taxes are distributed on the basis of what someone is worth. It is not just his personal virtues or his ancestors', nor his physical strength or good looks that should be taken into account, but use of wealth or poverty.

Equality of landholdings did mean equality. 'Equalizing' political opportunities means distributing them in *proportion* to *all* property. A complex connection with virtue is made, notably through assessing *use* of wealth (or its opposite). But it is easy to understand why Aristotle objects that the *politeia* of the *Laws* is a mixture of oligarchy and democracy, with a bias towards oligarchy (*Pol.* 2.6, 1266a5–28). For as he notes, proportionality supports a highly complicated system of election to the city's

---

[14] Samaras (2002: 219) proposes: 'In the *Laws*, this type of experience [i.e. historical] becomes the main informing principle of Plato's political philosophy.' See also Morrow (1960): part 1.

governing council, albeit involving limited use of the lot as well as arrangements designed (as Plato himself puts it) 'to confer high recognition on virtue, but less on those weaker in virtue and education' (*Laws* 6.757c). The objective as Plato sees it is accordingly *not* oligarchy. Because there is recognition of both virtue, doubtless taken to include wisdom, and the equality of the lot, which the Greeks associated with democratic freedom, the goal is something 'midway between a monarchical and a democratic constitution, as should always be the case with the constitution' (756e) – an explicit reference to the principles of political system building enunciated in Book 3.

I suspect it is no accident that the last of the historical embodiments of the balance between wisdom and freedom (or monarchy and democracy) the Stranger discusses in Book 3 is the voluntary slavery to the laws that characterizes Athens at the moment of the Persian invasion. The theme of voluntary slavery to law is to be sustained in the theory of law and the dual nature of legislation spelled out in Book 4, which will then constitute the overarching framework taken for granted in all the subsequent development of law in the dialogue. This theory might therefore be considered the guiding thread followed throughout the implementation of what I am calling Plato's subordinate project. According to Book 4 (which, after the historical Book 3, is devoted to placing the study of *politeia* on theological foundations), the final authority in a *politeia* that deserves that name is law, conceived of as public reason (4.713e–714a), an idea appropriated from this section of the *Laws* without acknowledgement by Aristotle (*Pol.* 3.16, 1287a28–32). Unless its authority is respected in a city, ruin lies round the corner. When the rulers are slaves of the law, on the other hand, and law is their master, 'I see salvation and all the good things gods bestow upon cities' (715d).

But the political freedom that citizens enjoy as citizens is the counterbalancing element Book 3 has discerned as essential to a healthy constitution. Freedom is enshrined within it not simply or primarily by provisions making the *politeia* a matter of government by participating citizens, chosen for the job according to the terms of a principled electoral process.[15] Freedom will be given due respect only if the lawgiver attempts to persuade the entire citizen population of the appropriateness of his legislation, so that they voluntarily accept its provisions. There is no denying that the great body of law developed in the later books of the *Laws*[16] is designed to exercise a high degree of control over the lives of the citizens. Nonetheless, the *voluntariness* of their submission to law is of

---

[15] On citizen government in the *Laws*, see Bobonich 2002: ch. 5.
[16] The subject of a masterly treatment in Saunders 1991.

paramount importance. This is the principal ingredient in the dialogue's conception of political freedom. The connection between freedom and voluntary compliance with law is all but explicit in Plato's development – in the final section of Book 4 – of the notion of a preamble or prelude to a law. In the famous analogy which he draws between the modus operandi of a slave doctor and the procedure of a freeborn doctor, dictating medical prescriptions without explanation or persuasion (as the slave doctor does), and without voluntary acceptance by the patient, is branded 'tyrannical' (721c; cf. 722e–723a). The freeborn doctor's method of explanation and persuasion, employed as it usually is in dealings with freeborn patients, shows him to be a better doctor (721e), and the lawgiver who does likewise in his preambles to laws reveals himself as someone who is not legislating so much as 'educating the citizens' (9.857e).[17]

Conclusion

I began this chapter with a brief reminder of the harsh criticism of the *Laws* familiar in modern comment on the dialogue, and of some of Aristotle's strictures too. I have been in effect attempting to respond to just two of the charges made against the dialogue: the Loeb editor's complaint that it follows no apparent plan, and Aristotle's that it seems to be attempting two quite different projects, which are not convincingly related to one another. The plan may not be articulated as such, but a detectable plan there certainly is.[18] It does indeed involve two distinct projects, which however are connected to each other in a way that Plato himself indicates at crucial junctures.

Book 1 introduces the main enterprise: constructing a social and political system that will best enable citizens to achieve virtue and happiness. This project is further advanced and described in Book 5, which launches the substantive business of the dialogue after the different kinds of further preparatory discussion undertaken in Books 2 to 4. Key here is the Athenian Stranger's introduction of the notion of the search for a second-best *politeia* that will approximate the ideal of the *Republic* and deliver on the promise of the enterprise articulated in Book 1. It will be implemented above all in the provisions for social organization and education developed in Books 5 to 7 (and where education is concerned – the overriding

---

[17] On the doctor analogy, see the classic study of Bobonich 1991; also Laks 1991, 2000: 285–90; and Schofield 2006: 84–8, 319–21.
[18] See also the sections 'The plan of the dialogue' and 'Synopsis' in Schofield and Griffith 2016: 8–12, 20–2.

preoccupation of the whole dialogue – anticipated in important ways in Book 2). It is reaffirmed at the end of Book 12, which returns to the theme of education. However, Plato recognizes that if the *politeia* is going to be realizable in communities consisting mostly of unregenerate humanity, another project – subordinate to the first – must be undertaken. Education for virtue and happiness is not enough. The coercion of law is also required. How to balance and relate these two requirements is the great challenge the *Laws* attempts to meet, with its distinctive theory of the 'double' nature of law: law is of its very nature coercive, but it must be made educative too.

Plato's subordinate project needs to encapsulate reflection on human nature as it is, not just as it could be.[19] Hence the historical narrative that constitutes the fresh start in Book 3, which develops ultimately into a theoretical proposal. Experience shows that successful states are those where through a balance between wisdom (a 'monarchical' principle) and freedom (a 'democratic' one), friendship or social cohesion is secured. This proposal is one conceived as having a general validity for the circumstances of all actual political communities. What follows in Book 4 is the beginning of Plato's attempt to theorize the monarchical and democratic principles further, as the doctrine of the rule of law on the one hand, and the idea of preludes or preambles to legislation on the other. Here, he is in effect working out the basic ingredients of the version of the general proposal that he will adopt for his own *politeia*.

The need for wisdom to govern will be recognized above all by assigning ultimate authority to the rule of law (although later books will embody wisdom and virtue also in particular bodies, such as the various boards and councils to be established in the city, and in the end most importantly in the Nocturnal Council described in Book 12 – which is to be charged with reviewing the city's laws and keeping them in a sound state of preservation: 12.960b–969d). The need for the free status of the citizens to be respected is to be met principally by providing that law is to have a dual nature: with a persuasive and educational as well as a coercive function. This subsidiary project is what is mostly being worked out in the later books of the dialogue (Books 9 to 12 especially), but as we have seen is already under way in the rules for property classes in Book 5 itself, and for appointment of officials and administrative and other bodies in Book 6.

---

[19] 'By so resolutely taking into account the human factor,' says Laks (2000: 275), 'the *Laws*, in its specific and still very Platonic way, opens the path to Aristotle. One might even go so far as to wonder whether there is already something truly Aristotelian in the *Laws*.'

The subsidiary project is indeed (as Aristotle puts it) 'more common', more capable of being widely shared in. Plato's ideas for a comprehensive legal code, worked out in detail, and for a variety of regulatory bodies ensuring that its provisions are respected, constitute a blueprint for an ordered citizen society that has quite general applicability, not confined to the particular ideal system envisaged in the *Laws*' construction of the city it is imagining. Insofar as law is educative, not merely coercive, however, it always has the potential to contribute to the higher goal of the dialogue's main project.

CHAPTER 11

Plato, Xenophon, and the Laws of Lycurgus

My focus in this chapter is on the opening pages of the *Laws*. The dialogue begins with a critique by Plato's main speaker, an Athenian visitor to Crete, of the conception of the proper goal of statecraft as preparedness for war, as is attributed by his host Cleinias to Minos and Lycurgus, traditionally regarded as authors of the Cretan and Spartan laws. The Athenian instead proposes virtue – the whole of virtue, not just courage – as the right goal. Moreover, he insists that that idea must actually have been what governed Cretan and Spartan lawgiving. This further claim is sometimes not taken very seriously by scholarship. Susan Sauvé Meyer, in her recent commentary on Books 1 and 2 of the *Laws*, is probably not atypical of many in thinking of it as a 'conceit'.[1] I shall argue on the contrary that it expresses a seriously held alternative ideological construction of Lycurgus' intentions at Sparta that Plato was not alone in championing. In short, the overarching goal of the Spartan *politeia* really was a contested issue.[2]

Xenophon's account of the laws of Lycurgus in his short work *Constitution of the Lacedaimonians* will play a key role in the development of the case I shall make.[3] The chapter has three sections. In the first, it will be shown that the view proposed by Plato's Athenian visitor that Lycurgus made virtue in its entirety the goal of his statecraft was anticipated in Xenophon's treatise. It has to be treated as an interpretation of the Spartan *politeia*, alternative to that advanced by Cleinias and accepted by (for example) Aristotle, which Plato could expect or at any rate hope to be

---

[1] Meyer 2015: 105.
[2] See Hodkinson 2005: 222–7. 'In late fifth-century Athens, in particular', he writes (p. 225), 'the Spartan *polis* was a battleground of competing imaginations.'
[3] As Vivienne Gray comments: '*Politeia* [Constitution] may not be the original title (*Lac.* uses it [sc. the word] only once, and in reference to the constitutions of other *poleis*: 15.1)' (Gray 2007: 146). As likely – I think in fact more so – is that Xenophon called it Λυκούργου νόμοι, 'The laws of Lycurgus': for that is what at the outset (*Lac. Pol.* 1.2) and throughout he makes his explicit focus. Plato's titling of his own last dialogue as simply νόμοι (*nomoi*), Laws, could then be viewed as following his own precedent of calling his Republic just πολιτεία (*politeia*).

taken seriously as such. In the second, the argument will focus on the contents of the legislative programme the Athenian says he had hoped to hear Cleinias ascribe to the Cretan and Spartan lawgivers. The case will be made that Plato can expect recognition by the reader (as by the Athenian's interlocutors) that the programme is properly Spartan and Cretan by virtue of its echoes of the programme attributed to Lycurgus by Xenophon. Finally, the third section will argue that in making law primarily concerned with fostering the proper development, conduct, and treatment of human beings at every stage of the life cycle, above all by provision for sound customary practices (ἐπιτηδεύματα, *epitêdeumata*) and the like, Plato adopts the approach to law-making taken by Xenophon's Lycurgus.[4]

Before these ideas are developed, however, something needs to be said about the Cretan system. Cleinias, the representative Cretan participant in the discussions conducted in the dialogue, is the Athenian's principal interlocutor, and his first sustained contribution to the conversation is entirely devoted to Cretan institutions, appropriately so given the question put to him (*Laws* 1.625c–626b). He is ready at once to extend his account to Sparta. But Megillus, the representative Spartan, is treated as the junior Dorian partner throughout the dialogue.[5] So one might have expected that Plato would have wanted to use an account of the Cretan *politeia* alternative to Cleinias'. Perhaps he would. But perhaps there was none, or at any rate no very substantial account that he could find.

The historical existence of such a thing as 'the Cretan *politeia*' is debatable. Plato, Aristotle, and their contemporary the historian Ephorus all speak as though there was. Yet in the fourth century BC, there were many self-governing cities on Crete (Paula Perlman documented forty-nine archaic and classical *poleis*).[6] Perlman's view was that a single template for the 'Cretan *politeia*' was created in the late classical period, probably by philosophers, which underlies the fourth-century accounts that survive.[7] Presumably its creation might have been motivated by perception of a need

---

[4] A recent study by N. Humble, 'Sparta in Plato and Xenophon', focuses 'primarily, though not exclusively, on Plato's *Republic* and Xenophon's *Spartan Constitution*' (Humble 2018: 548) but does see in Megillus' accounts of the ephorate as tyrannical in Book 4 of the *Laws* an echo of *Lac*. 8.4, and of key Spartan practices in a passage of Book 1, subsequent to the ones that most interest me, 'a succinct summary of *Lac*. 2.2–11'. She refers (at pp. 553–4 and 571) to *Laws* 4.712d (on the ephorate) and 1.633b (on habituation to endurance of pain), respectively.

[5] There was a tradition known first from Herodotus that Lycurgus actually imported his laws from Crete: Hdt. 1.65.4; cf. e.g. Arist. *Pol*. 2.10, 1271b20–32, Strabo 10.4.17–19. Polybius (6.45.1–47.6), however, thought preposterous the whole idea that Spartan arrangements bore any resemblance in their essentials to Crete's.

[6] Perlman 2004.   [7] See Perlman 2005: 282–7.

to justify the credibility of the alleged dependence of Spartan statecraft upon Cretan, particularly perhaps when (as Ephorus attests: Strabo 10.4.17) many Cretan cities were believed to be Spartan colonies (Lyktos, one of the most important, is asserted to be so by Aristotle: *Pol.* 2.10, 1271b27–30).

Two Views of Lycurgus' Lawgiving

The opening pages of the *Laws* contrast two different conceptions of what the Cretan and Spartan lawgivers (Minos and Lycurgus) were aiming to achieve in their legislation. One view is advanced by Cleinias. When asked about the communal meals, physical training, and arms bearing required of his countrymen, he relates them all to military campaigning. That in turn he relates to 'a lifelong and continuous state of war against all other cities' (*Laws* 1.625e) – 'the natural state of affairs' (626a). The lawgiver 'framed all our institutions, in the private and public spheres, with war in view' (626a.).

So far so Cretan. But when it is put to him that his position might be crystallized in a definition or defining characteristic (ὅρος, *horos*) of a well-ordered city, as one so constituted as 'to overcome the other cities in war', Cleinias is made not only to give his own assent, but also to associate with it that of the Spartan (Megillus). Megillus takes up the cue and makes his first contribution to the conversation: 'What other answer could any Lacedaemonian possibly give?' (*Laws* 1.626c). A little further on, we find him endorsing a claim by Cleinias (628e) that what he has said about Crete is true also of the Spartan lawgiver's invention of the same institutional practices: 'with war in view' (633a).

An alternative view is put by the dialogue's leading speaker, the Athenian visitor to Crete never given a name. Following his critique of Cleinias' account, we get the following passage of dialogue (630d–e):

CLEINIAS: Does that mean rejecting our Cretan lawgiver, my friend? Does it put him among lawgiving's also-rans?
ATHENIAN: Don't be offended, my friend, we are not rejecting him. But we turn ourselves into also-rans if we think Lycurgus and Minos made their legal arrangements, in Sparta and here in Crete, principally with a view to war.
CLEINIAS: What should we actually have said?
ATHENIAN: I think we should have said what was true, and what was right in a discussion of a man inspired: that he did not set about legislating with an eye to just one part of human goodness – and the least important part at that – but

with an eye to goodness as a whole (πᾶσαν ἀρετήν; alternative rendering: all of virtue).[8]

The Athenian then gives his own detailed account of how Spartan and Cretan legislation should be described on that ethical basis.[9] He concludes as follows (632d):

> That, my friends, is what I would have liked from you – what I want from you now, come to that – an explanation how all this is contained in the laws attributed to Zeus and Pythian Apollo, the work of the two lawgivers Minos and Lycurgus, and how they possess a degree of ordering which is immediately apparent to the person who has a familiarity with laws – either by formal training or by dint of some habitual practices (*ethesi*) – though it is not in the least clear to the rest of us.

It is often assumed that the Athenian's alternative has in reality nothing much to do with anything credibly attested for Cretan or Spartan legislation or otherwise believed about it. It is taken to be a purely Platonic construction. There is reason, however, to think that these opening pages of the *Laws* do reflect competing interpretations of the Spartan *politeia*, at any rate, that were espoused more widely in the fourth century BC. View A (that advanced by Cleinias and Megillus) is attributed by Aristotle to a Spartan writer he names as Thibron 'and to everyone else who has written on their *politeia*', in general with admiration (*Pol.* 7.14, 1333b11–21). Like Plato in the *Laws* (whom he has cited on the matter in Book 2 (9, 1271a41–b3)), Aristotle is highly critical of any such notion as an appropriate candidate for constituting the *telos* of a *politeia*. But unlike Plato, he takes it to be a correct construal of the basis on which the Spartan polity was constructed and has savage things to say about their legislator (*Pol.* 2.9, 1271b3–19, 7.14, 1333b21–1334a10).[10] View B (the alternative urged by the Athenian on his interlocutors) also had at least one advocate: Xenophon.

For the evidence of View B in Xenophon, we need to turn to the short work labelled in the manuscript tradition Λακεδαιμονίων πολιτεία: 'polity/political system of the Lacedaemonians'. Xenophon launches his little

---

[8] Translations from the *Laws* in this chapter are mostly those by Tom Griffith, occasionally adapted, in Schofield and Griffith 2016.
[9] In subsequent dialogue with Megillus (*Laws* 1.632e–633a), just after reiterating that 'all the things we have just been talking about have goodness as their aim', he asks: 'So tell me, these meals you have all together, and the physical training, are we saying they were an invention of the lawgiver to meet the needs of war?' Hodkinson 2005: 251 reads this implausibly, as expressing agreement on the claim on the part of the two them; better is England 1921: 1.221. 'We' is the 'we' who are at this point putting forward ideas in shared conversation for discussion and criticism by ourselves.
[10] See further my discussion in Schofield 2018: 216–20.

treatise by referring to his reflections on the 'customary practices of the Spartiates' (τὰ ἐπιτηδεύματα τῶν Σπαρτιατῶν: *Lac. Pol.* 1.1). He goes on in the ten chapters that follow that introduction to treat these as established through the *nomoi* (νόμοι) of Lycurgus, whom he regards as 'wise to the nth degree' (εἰς τὰ ἔσχατα σοφόν: 1.2). The outcome of Lycurgus' work was to make his native country an object lesson exceeding most others in *eudaimonia*, well-being or happiness (ibid.). Chapter 10 of the work provides a kind of summing up of his intent and achievement. Cultivating virtue could not be left a voluntary matter: the virtuous do not then have the capacity to strengthen (αὔξειν) their countries. So, at Sparta he compelled everyone 'to practise all the virtues' (πάσας ἀσκεῖν τὰς ἀρετάς) in public life. That is why Sparta probably surpasses all cities in virtue, because it alone practises the nobility of goodness (καλοκἀγαθίαν) in public life (10.4). People were punished for evidently not making the effort to be 'as good as possible' (ὡς βέλτιστος εἶναι: 10.5). Lycurgus made it an indispensable necessity for people 'to practise the whole of citizen virtue' (ἀσκεῖν ἅπασαν πολιτικὴν ἀρετήν: 10.7).

What has preceded this assessment has been an account that focuses almost entirely on the provisions Lycurgus made for producing children with the required natural endowment, for their subsequent upbringing and induction into the rigours of Spartan manhood, and for the communal life of the city. At the public meals, talk should be of 'whatever someone has done nobly in the city'; the accent is on mutual respect and avoidance of drunken carousing (5.6). Lycurgus' general aim was to ensure that the citizens enjoyed mutual benefit without causing harm (6.1). They must have nothing to do with making money but concentrate on activities that equip cities for freedom (7.2). Xenophon then devotes a chapter (Chapter 9) to the methods Lycurgus employed to make well-being or happiness contingent on being 'good' (ἀγαθός, *agathos*), which in context sounds more or less equivalent to 'brave' (cf. 4.6; also 4.1: ἀρετή, *aretê*) – although since the very next chapter is so insistent on the practice of the whole of citizen virtue, it may be that courage in warfare is seen only as the most important form of that virtue. Lycurgus instituted an entire concerted programme of measures ensuring that the life of the 'bad' would be thoroughly miserable.

The military ethos of the Spartan polity is therefore by no means denied or downplayed.[11] Chapters 11 to 13 will indeed go on to the organisation of

---

[11] The terms in which initial reference to the introduction of common meals is made (συσκηνούντων, συσκήνια: *Lac. Pol.* 5.2, 4) have the military associations of 'tenting together', although Xenophon

the army and to the other provisions for the conduct of war instituted by Lycurgus. But those chapters are presented as a sort of appendix to the main account Xenophon has given, which has described practices 'beneficial communally both in peace and in war' (11.1).[12] The appended chapters – conceivably a later addition (they talk of Lacedaemonians, not as hitherto Spartiates) – are provided expressly to satisfy the curiosity of someone wishing to know how Lycurgus' military dispositions for the army when on campaign were better than other systems. There is no indication that war, victory in war, and military conquest were to be the country's *telos*, as they were according to View A. Xenophon has it that Lycurgus' goal was well-being for the city and all the citizens, to be achieved by their common noble practice of the whole of virtue – all the virtues. In other words, he clearly takes View B.

A later proponent of View B was Plutarch, in the essay he devotes to the life of Lycurgus. Here is how his concluding chapter starts (*Lyc.* 31.1):

> It was not, however, the chief design of Lycurgus at that time to leave his city exercising hegemony over a great many others, but he thought that the well-being of an entire city, like that of a single individual, depended on the prevalence of virtue and concord within its own borders. The aim, therefore, of all his arrangements and adjustments was to make his people free-minded (ἐλευθέριοι), self-sufficing, and moderate in all their ways (σωφρονοῦντες), and to keep them so as long as possible.
>
> Translation by *Bernadotte Perrin* (with minor adaptations)[13]

'At that time' refers to the point at which (according to Plutarch) Lycurgus considered that he had completed the essentials of lawgiving and departed to Delphi to seek their endorsement by the oracle, where he asked 'whether the laws which he had established were good, and sufficient to promote a city's well-being and virtue'. Apollo supplied the endorsement, and Lycurgus decided this was the point at which he should put an end to his own life (*Lyc.* 29.3–4; cf. 8.5).

Plutarch was doubtless aware that View A had its advocates. 'Exercising hegemony' over other Greeks (*Lyc.* 31.1) sounds as though it might be

---

reverts to the more usual φιλίτια subsequently (*Lac. Pol.* 5.6). In fact he begins his discussion by remarking that Lycurgus had found the Spartiates 'tenting at home' (οἴκοι σκηνοῦντας: *Lac. Pol.* 5.2, i.e. lodging apart from their peers), like other Greeks.

[12] Herodotus makes Lycurgus first change all the Spartans' νόμιμα (customs) and put in place measures to ensure compliance with those he was introducing, but has him deal only subsequently with military organization and the common meals, and finally with the institution of the ephorate and γερontία, council of elders (Hdt. 1.65.5).

[13] As in the Loeb edition of Perrin 1914.

a formulation of an alternative interpretation of Lycurgus' intent incompatible with his own. 'Hegemony' (so described) was precisely what Aristotle, one of View A's proponents, thought that both Athens and Sparta had achieved and sought to use for their own advantage; and to his mind, the Spartans were only thereby carrying out the design of their lawgiver (*Pol.* 4.11, 1296a32–6; cf. 2.9, 1271b3–19, 7.14, 1333b21–1334a10). Whether Plutarch knew of that assessment we do not know; and hegemonic ambition or control was a not unfamiliar diagnosis of the realities of power in the Aegean (e.g. Isoc. *On the Peace* 30, Xen. *Hell.* 7.1.33, Dem. *Phil.* 3.23). But he does begin his whole account of Lycurgus with an acknowledgement of a kind comparatively rare among ancient Greek and Roman authors (*Lyc.* 1.1):

> Concerning Lycurgus the lawgiver, in general, nothing can be said which is not disputed, since indeed there are different accounts of his birth, his travels, his death, and above all, of his work as law-maker and statesman.

A later chapter does provide specific evidence of contrary claims about Lycurgus' involvement in warfare and its bearing on his lawgiving (*Lyc.* 23.1):

> Hippias the Sophist says that Lycurgus himself was very well versed in war and took part in many campaigns, and Philostephanus attributes to him the arrangement of the Spartan cavalry by 'oulamoi', explaining that the 'oulamos', as constituted by him, was a troop of fifty horsemen in a square formation. But Demetrius the Phalerean says he engaged in no warlike undertakings, and established his constitution in a time of peace.

Translations by *Bernadotte Perrin*

Plutarch does not come down on either side, although he gives what might be interpreted as a suggestive indication that he would prefer Demetrius to have been right.

No doubt View A and View B were both espoused in different variants. Most obviously, and most pertinently for the purposes of this article, there is divergence in the presentation of View B: Plato's Athenian takes the line that on a proper assessment of the Spartan and Cretan legislators' intentions, courage is to be conceived as 'the least important part' of virtue (*Laws* 1.630c–631d); Xenophon more plausibly and certainly less provocatively gives it an emphasis in Lycurgus' law-making that one might have expected. That said, the Athenian does begin his own substantive treatment of virtue by tackling courage first of all (*Laws* 1.632d–e; indeed, courage remains the main subject of Book 1), while on the other hand it is not accorded a central position in Xenophon's account. The chapter he devotes to the topic begins: 'This too is a provision made by Lycurgus that deserves admiration' (*Lac. Pol.* 9.1). We may contrast the more prominent focus in Book 1 of the *Laws* on the Spartan poet Tyrtaeus' verses on courage in battle with external enemies, the virtue which the Athenian gets Cleinias, a proponent of View A, to associate without hesitation with the outlook of the Cretan legislator (*Laws* 1.629a–e, 630c–d). Aristotle, likewise an advocate of View A as representing the intention of the Spartan legislator, goes further. He implies a resemblance between the Spartans and the savage peoples of the Black Sea area, who are given to mere banditry and are on his assessment entirely lacking in courage – that is, true courage (*Pol.* 8.4, 1338b19–24). Spartan success in warfare was due to their training (cf. Thuc. 2.39.1: ἐπιπόνῳ ἀσκήσει, 'oppressively strenuous physical regime', Pericles' no less dismissive assessment of their pursuit of bravery), whereas 'nobility of character rather than ferocity of disposition should play the principal part' (*Pol.* 8.4, 1338b24–30).

Plato's Debt to Xenophon

Plato and Xenophon are aligned in presenting View B as the correct interpretation of Lycurgus' intent as Spartan lawgiver. For both of them, his provisions were designed to promote 'the whole of virtue'. It would be hazardous to conjecture that Plato's espousal of View B was prompted by Xenophon's, although the *Laws* was probably composed after Xenophon's death, and certainly well after the likely circulation of the work we know as 'The polity of the Lacedaemonians'.[14] Admiration for Sparta's εὐνομία (*eunomia*), the excellence of its law-governed polity, is professed in the *Crito* by Plato's Socrates (or rather, ascribed to him by the laws of Athens that he imagines as addressing him: *Crito* 53a). There is every reason to suppose that discussion of that *eunomia* would often have occurred in Socratic circles in the fourth century. And it would not be a surprise if other Socratic authors besides Xenophon and Plato wanted to credit Lycurgus, as a wise lawgiver, with something approximating a Socratic

---

[14] All relevant dates are conjectural. The *Laws* is usually thought to be Plato's latest dialogue, mostly belonging to the late 350s BC. Xenophon's death is often dated to around 354. Dates suggested by different scholars for composition of the *Constitution of the Lacedaemonians* vary greatly, complicated by the hypothesis advanced by some that Chapter 14 (near the end), reflecting on Sparta's current condition, is a later addition composed after the Spartans' catastrophic defeat at the battle of Leuctra (371). Gray (2007: 43), favours the 360s; she argues that Chapter 14 is integral to the work as a whole: 217–21.

unity of virtue. Perhaps it was even a supposition generally entertained by those who embraced some version of Socratic philosophy.

Nonetheless, there is a specific feature of Plato's presentation of the work of the Cretan and Spartan lawgivers in the *Laws* which does argue for indebtedness on his part to Xenophon in particular, among authors for whose writing on Sparta we have evidence that might be relevant. This is the itemized programme of legislation his Athenian outlines in his account of what Cleinias *should* have attributed to Lycurgus and Minos. To see why the Xenophon treatise on Sparta discussed above (pp. 222–4) may be important here, a close look at a not altogether straightforward passage of Book 1 at the end of that account is first needed. Only then can the idea of Xenophon's silent presence be introduced.

The Athenian rounds things off by saying to Cleinias and Megillus, with words already quoted (*Laws* 1.632d):

> That, my friends, is what I would have liked from you – what I want from you now, come to that – an explanation how all this is contained in the laws attributed to Zeus and Pythian Apollo, the work of the two lawgivers Minos and Lycurgus, and how they possess a degree of ordering (τάξιν τινά), which is immediately apparent to the person who has a familiarity with laws – either by formal training or by dint of some habitual practices – though it is not in the least clear to the rest of us.

There are two dimensions distinguished here in the prescriptive presentation (*Laws* 1.631b–632c) to which the Athenian here refers back. He seems to be differentiating within it between the *content*, on the one hand, that he has been proposing to ascribe to the legislation of Minos and Lycurgus itself, as he is supposing it must truly be if it is to satisfy the prescription for good lawgiving that he has just spelled out; and its *ordering*, on the other – by which he most likely means its ranking of divine and human goods (*Laws* 1.631b–d; although some scholars have taken it to be the systematic ordering of topics of legislation for different key areas of human activity and associated points within the human lifespan which follows the ranking passage: *Laws* 1.631d–632c).[15] It is the ordering which he says is 'not in the least clear to the rest of us'. However, his own request to Cleinias and Megillus is not as clear as it might be.

---

[15] So Schöpsdau 1994: 190; Meyer 2015: 120, pointing out that the Athenian has employed this vocabulary of τάξις in concluding the introduction of his hierarchy of goods (*Laws* 1.631b–d) at 631d. The Loeb, Budé, and Penguin translations all have 'system' or 'systematic arrangement', suggesting the possibility of other forms of structuring, e.g., by topics covered in legislation. But one would not need to be a legal expert to be able to see what they are without difficulty.

He has offered an account of (a) lawgiving as it should be; the claim that (b) Minos and Lycurgus were good lawgivers; and the inference that (c) their lawgiving will therefore have satisfied the requirements of (a). When he concludes by remarking that the ordering within the legislation is 'not in the least clear to the rest of us', does that criticism relate to (a) or (c)? (a) seems very unlikely. The Athenian would then be making an odd complaint about his own presentation: odd, since for one thing he is surely including himself among 'the rest of us' (τοῖς ἄλλοις ἡμῖν), and for another his account was fullest and most specific precisely in its treatment of the hierarchy of goods.

So presumably his comment effectively relates to the idea in (c) that Dorian – that is, Cretan and Spartan – laws did meet the standards of good legislation outlined in (a). That is what the Athenian thinks will be 'immediately clear' to legal experts, but far from clear to others, himself included. The two most recent commentators on Book 1 of the dialogue both read it that way. Schöpsdau does not think Plato means to be understood as denying that some Dorian legislation actually does fit the appropriate template (although he notes that some will also soon be accused of failing to do so: *Laws* 1.634c–635b). Nor does Schöpsdau seem inclined to take very seriously the Athenian's implication that he himself does not grasp the ordering in that Dorian legislation. It is 'not without self-irony', that is, wryly insincere, because (I suppose) he has more expertise in laws and lawgiving than he pretends to Cleinias and Megillus, who are – Schöpsdau thinks – being assumed themselves to be expert.[16] Such an assumption of their expertise seems not to pay any attention to the understanding of the principles shaping the Cretan and Spartan polities that Cleinias and Megillus have advocated in the opening pages of Book 1, very different (as the Athenian has insisted) from any which *would* satisfy his own requirements for good lawgiving. Moreover, one is left wondering whether on this reading his statement of failure by non-experts to discern the ordering of Dorian legislation (rather than the content), for Schöpsdau something due simply to deficiency in them, packs much punch at all.

Meyer, on the other hand, talks of the Athenian persisting here in the 'polite fiction that the Dorian laws exemplify the highest legislative standards'. When he then says that to experts in laws their principles of ordering are 'immediately apparent', he is indeed being ironic. In actual Dorian laws, there simply is no order prioritizing divine over human goods visible

---

[16] Schöpsdau 1994: 190; cf. 198–9. England 1921: 1.219, also speaks of 'a polite irony'.

to anyone, expert or not.[17] In other words, the comments by the Athenian on who does or does not find the ordering clear are designed to puncture the entire fiction. Meyer here plausibly assumes (as does Schöpsdau) that he has in mind by 'ordering' the specific priority he has given in his own presentation (*Laws* 1.631b–d) to goods that are 'divine' (the four cardinal virtues), over those that are 'human' (health, beauty, strength, wealth). Other aspects of her interpretation are questionable. There is fiction and fiction. The Cicero and Thomas Cromwell trilogies of Robert Harris and Hilary Mantel are obviously quite different sorts of fiction from *Alice in Wonderland* or again from *The Pickwick Papers*. It is not as though evidence for historical Sparta is that plentiful or secure. The claim that Dorian laws did not prioritize divine over human goods might be regarded as debatable. For example, Cleinias has mentioned the common meals as one of the lawgiver's institutions (*Laws* 1.625e–626a). For him, the explanation of it is certainly couched primarily in terms of the protection of the army in war. But for Xenophon, Lycurgus' rationale for the same institution is exclusively ethical (*Lac. Pol.* 5.2–7).

It may be worthwhile taking an alternative approach, then, to the Athenian's treatment of the laws of Minos and Lycurgus. This is to suppose that he is assuming at least one other well-known description of the laws of Minos or Lycurgus with recognizable similarities to the sketch of how lawgiving ought to be done that he has just spelled out (*Laws* 1.631b–632d); and that it is to that sort of treatment of them that he refers in challenging Cleinias and Megillus for an explanation of how its contents and not very obvious ordering map on to his own sketch – genuinely not obvious to him, no less than to anybody else not a legal expert. If that sketch is prominently represented elsewhere as transmitting core material on Sparta and Crete, then Cleinias and Megillus will be hard put to duck the challenge.

My suggestion will be that it is an account of Lycurgus' lawgiving like Xenophon's that would, on the one hand, have provided a list of topics covered in the legislation – a *content* – similar to the Athenian's sketch. Xenophon also spells out some of the kinds of moral impact on character which Lycurgus' provisions effected that the Athenian has said he wants to see in an account of them: how it encouraged control of emotions and

---

[17] Meyer 2015: 121–2. She notes earlier (104–5) that in Book 2 the Athenian 'will not mince words in castigating their societies for being organized on exclusively military principles (666e–667a)'. But he is at pains to insist that he does not intend this as a criticism of their lawgivers – the implication being (as in Book 1) that Minos' and Lycurgus' intentions have been misunderstood and distorted by Cretans and Spartans.

appetites, how it enforced justice in the citizens' mutual transactions, and so forth. On the other hand, as to an *ordering of goods* that prioritizes divine over human, Xenophon's version of Spartan legislation does indeed indicate that only to a degree and implicitly. This would explain why the Athenian says it is not all clear to him and most other people, while indicating his acceptance that such an ordering is what the lawgivers were seeking to effect. At the same time, if we suppose that Megillus in particular might be conceived as recognizing the echoes of Xenophon's account of Lycurgus' lawgiving, then Plato might reasonably have represented the Athenian's interlocutors as raising no questions at this point about his long disquisition. Xenophon was, of course, a respected military man who had spent many years of his life in Sparta and had served the Spartans in more than one capacity.

The basic content of the Athenian's account may be broken down into four main areas, clearly demarcated in his wording of the sequence:

(1) Marriage, production and upbringing of children, both when they are young and right through their lives.
(2) Citizens' acquisition and spending, and the formation and dissolution of partnerships between them.
(3) Burial of the dead and their commemoration.
(4) Review of the legislation, and appointment of a body to ensure that it coheres and abides by the prioritization of divine over human goods.

There is an interesting difference between how (1) is mentioned and how (2), (3), and (4) are introduced. The Athenian's reference to marriage and children occurs a little way into a single sprawling sentence, on instructions to be given to the citizens (*Laws* 1.631d–632b). It is the first specific (and in this sentence only) example of such an instruction (*Laws* 1.631d–e), but it is not announced as first. Following an initial restatement for the benefit of citizens about the prioritization of divine and human goods in instructions to them, the sentence simply runs on at that point: 'both in regard to marriage unions with one another and after that in the birth and upbringing of the children'. These were not matters which were viewed in Athens as falling within the ambit of law (other than provisions for ensuring the formal legality of marriage to secure citizen status of progeny and rights of inheritance). But it is as though the reader will simply be expecting these to be listed as the first topics dealt with in Cretan and Spartan legislation – and distinctively so. By contrast, items (2), (3), and (4) are each of them explicitly introduced in sequence as topics the lawgiver must or will deal with subsequently (*Laws* 1.632b–d). Their inclusion and ordering seem to be thought to be in more need of flagging up. It is not implied that (3) will be the next topic after (2). Following completion of detail on (2), (3) is introduced with the words: 'until getting through to completion of the whole system' (*Laws* 1.632c) – which might suggest the possibility of covering other areas between (2) and (3) not actually mentioned.

One might infer that Plato expected his readers to be already well aware that marriage, childbirth, and upbringing (with continuing supervision of adult mores) were the topics first addressed in the Spartan regulative system. While we do not know how many accounts of that system may have been in circulation in the first half of the fourth century BC, from which such knowledge might have derived, Aristotle implies quite a number of writings on the Spartan *politeia* (*Pol.* 7.14, 1333b18–20); there is Xenophon's still-extant tract; and Plato at any rate is likely to have known his relative Critias' earlier treatment of the same subject. Critias' book certainly does something to support the inference. In one of the few fragments surviving from his book, he says (Fr. 32):

> I begin, you see, with the moment of a person's birth: how can he develop the best and the strongest body? The prospective father should exercise and eat healthily and impose a harsh regime on his body, and the future child's mother should exercise and strengthen her body.
>
> Translated by *M. Gagarin and P. Woodruff*[18]

Xenophon does little more than amplify Critias' account. 'To begin at the beginning', he starts (*Lac. Pol.* 1.3), 'on the production of children', continuing immediately with discussion of the need for girls of free status to exercise their bodies and engage in running races and contests of physical strength, just like boys (contrary to norms elsewhere) – if they are to be fit for their greatest responsibility: motherhood. Subsequent chapters deal with boys' education, the athletic competitions in which those who had first reached manhood should engage, and then the Spartan approach to food and drink and the institution of common public meals. For Critias we have no similar material (except for detail on drinking protocol). But it seems likely enough that the same sequence would have been found in his book too.

By contrast, the further topics of legislation to which the Athenian refers – (2), (3), and (4) above – are not mentioned in terms suggesting that they *would* usually be expected at the points in a sequential account of Lycurgus' work that he indicates. Whether there was any such general

---

[18] Gagarin and Woodruff 1995: 262–3.

ordered scheme incorporating them, we are, of course, in no position to know or perhaps even to conjecture. But there is a rough correspondence between (2), (3), and (4), in that order, and the topics of Chapters 7, 9, and 10, respectively, in Xenophon, that is, the chapters which follow those on marriage, production and upbringing of children, and regulation of eating, drinking, and other elements of lifestyle. More specifically:

- *Lac. Pol.* 7.1–4 deals with Lycurgus' prohibition of any activities on the part of the freeborn designed to make money, and the rationale for denying that they will have any need to spend money. This passage might be seen as reflected in the Athenian's reference in (2) to regulating 'the citizens' acquisition and spending' (*Laws* 1.632b2–3). He then goes on to give rather more emphasis to mutual relationships, and particularly how far they meet standards of justice, and the rewards and penalties differing conduct of them should attract, anticipating the treatment of exchange and commercial activity in Book 11 (*Laws* 11.915d–922a).
- *Lac. Pol.* 9.1–2 discusses the admiration honourable death should evoke, before dwelling at some length on Lycurgus' measures for ensuring misery and shame for the coward. In (3), the Athenian too turns to death. But here the focus is solely on burial practice and commemoration (*Laws* 1.632c; cf. 12.958c–960b).
- *Lac. Pol.* 10 overall is devoted to citizen virtue. Its first section is eloquent in its praise of the way Lycurgus encouraged its lifelong pursuit by requiring men to face a contest near the end of the normal lifespan for election to the Council of Elders (γεροντία), and the respect membership attracted because of its responsibility for judging trials on capital charges (*Lac. Pol.* 10.1–3). The Athenian's concluding reference in (4) to guardians who will ensure that all the legislation is knit together (*Laws* 1.632c4–d1) seems to adumbrate his 'nocturnal council', a body that 'exercises oversight regarding laws', where age and virtue are qualifications for membership that receive emphasis (*Laws* 12.951d–e, 961a).

There is nothing in the Athenian's summary of what he hoped to be told of lawgiving in Crete and Sparta that relates to Chapter 8 of Xenophon's book (dealing with the ways in which Spartan law and its enforcers are invested with the authority that ensures compliance). But the summary is not presented as comprehensive in coverage.

What should we make of these partial and perhaps sometimes tenuous correspondences between the sequences of topics in the two authors? They might of course be no more than the sort of thing that will quite likely happen when two writers deal with the same limited subject – if we had had more fourth-century accounts of it, we might conceivably have found similar coincidences. Or perhaps Plato may indeed be making some more specific use of Xenophon's identification and sequencing of items of Lycurgan legislation. But it might be felt hard to go beyond that without straying into arbitrary speculation: the sort of thing that in the past filled too many published pages, which we might hope serious scholarship had outgrown.

It has already been argued in broad terms here, however, that Plato needed to assume the availability of an account of Dorian lawgiving such as Xenophon's treatment of Lycurgus to give teeth to the request for explanation of how values are appropriately ordered in such a scheme that his Athenian puts to Cleinias and Megillus at *Laws* 1.632d. His reader also needed to be persuaded that his own sketch of the legislation a good lawgiver such as Lycurgus would devise had a basic content that looked Lycurgan or 'Minoan'. An obvious way of doing that would have been to make the content correspond to the main heads of some other account of it that met two conditions: (i) that comparandum must be known or readily available to Plato's likely first readership, and (ii) it must be a treatment of the subject broadly believable for most such early readers, if at all familiar with Spartan institutions or with common beliefs about them (or with Cretan law and society: but fourth-century Athenians, at any rate, may well have had only a rather sketchier sense of matters Cretan for the most part). We do not know, of course, whether either (i) or (ii) would have been true of Xenophon's little treatise. But it seems feasible that they may well have been.

The hypothesis proposed, then, is that while the initial topics of the Athenian's summary, marriage, production and upbringing of children, etc. (item (1)), are plainly 'Lycurgan', the correspondence in the summary between its items (2), (3), and (4), and the topics of Xenophon's Chapters 7, 9, and 10, is nothing coincidental. It is rather Plato's deliberate attempt to highlight in his account of Lycurgus' (and Minos') lawgiving just those elements (dealing with acquisition and spending, treatment of the dead, constitution of a senior council with specifically legal responsibilities) on which Xenophon had dwelt in the final sections of the main part of his work, particularly in the opening sections of his several chapters.[19] And the attempt is motivated by Plato's wish to lend some

---

[19] It is of course possible that one or more other fourth-century accounts of the Spartan system besides Xenophon's written prior to the *Laws* had given the same sort of prominence to Lycurgan laws or institutions that bore some degree of correspondence with items (2), (3), and (4) of the Athenian's

credibility to his suggestion that its entire content is Lycurgan. Perhaps he hoped that if the basic content could fairly readily be seen as more or less Lycurgan, the Platonic ethical preoccupations with which he invested it might similarly be accepted as Lycurgan in spirit.

Indeed, the overall requirement of ensuring that the laws give effect to arrangements that 'follow self-control and justice, not wealth or ambition' (*Laws* 1.632c–d: divine, not human goods) could well be regarded as uncontroversially Spartan even if Xenophon never spelled that out. Σωφροσύνη (*sôphrosunê*), self-control or restraint or moderation, was often seen as a pre-eminently Spartan virtue. Xenophon suggests as much when he invites his reader to judge whether it is Spartan or some other form of παιδεία (*paideia*, education) fostered in Greece that produces 'men who are more respectful and having more control over what needs to be controlled' (*Lac. Pol.* 2.14; cf. 3.4–5, where he employs the verb σωφρονεῖν). At the congress in Sparta held as the tensions which preceded the Peloponnesian War heightened, Thucydides represents the Corinthians as launching proceedings in a speech that famously begins by attributing Spartan σωφροσύνη to the trust they place in their own political and social system (Thuc. 1.68.1). And Critias for his part had eulogized Spartan sympotic practices as fostering among other things health and σωφροσύνη, 'neighbour of piety' (Fr. 6.21–2).

The Approach to Law-Making

> He [indeterminately the Cretan and/or Spartan lawgiver] did not set about legislating with an eye to just one part of human goodness – and the least important part at that – but with an eye to goodness as a whole; and he sought for the laws he gave them under categories quite different from those used by legislators nowadays. Nowadays everybody seeks to provide himself with whatever it is he personally stands in need of: for one it is Inheritances and Heiresses, for another it is Assault, and so on and so forth. What we say, by contrast, is that the search for laws – for those who approach the search correctly – should follow the procedure we have embarked upon.
>
> *Laws* 1.630e-631a

Plato's Athenian identifies a major difference between the approach to law-making taken by Lycurgus and Minos and that taken 'nowadays' – no

---

summary, perhaps in that same sequence. If that were so, then this section of the chapter might be headed 'Plato's debt to Xenophon and/or X and/or Y and/or . . . '.

doubt in contemporary Athens, but presumably elsewhere too. He is explicit about the categories most salient in contemporary legislation: inheritance, assault, and the like. Perhaps the alternatives he credits to the Cretan and Spartan lawgivers have to be inferred from the sequel (*Laws* 1.631d–632c). From that, it would seem fairly obvious what these are: marriage, birth and upbringing of children, social and economic associations, burial practices before all else (as discussed above, pp. 230–2).[20] But as the Athenian sees it, there is also a difference between what motivates the selection in each case. Nowadays, it is what the individual is in need of: presumably redress if assaulted, and a properly and fairly determined allocation of the family property if inheritance is the issue. It will be indicated in that same sequel what is the prime consideration governing choice of categories in the Cretan and Spartan systems, by contrast. It is that they should secure what is good for well-being at every stage of life, particularly in enabling citizens to cope with their appetites and emotions and the whole gamut of experiences in their relations with others. In other words: the individual's immediate need versus well-being conceived much more broadly in several dimensions – a conception already recognizable from Xenophon's account of the laws of Lycurgus.

But what form did those laws take? 'During the archaic period laws were written down and publicly displayed in cities all over Greece.'[21] Not so, it seems, in Sparta. Nor does it seem likely that the Spartan laws to which the Athenian refers had the sort of structure – which long remained typical of Greek legislation – found at Athens in Dracon's early law of homicide. There, we meet such formulations as: 'Even if a man does not kill another intentionally, he is to go into exile. The kings are to judge guilty of homicide the killer or the planner; and the *ephetai* are to decide. Reconciliation, if there is a father or brother or sons, is to be by all; or the objector is to prevail.'[22] By the fourth century, the Spartans do appear

---

[20] Main structuring topics in the Athenian's implementation of his core programme in Books 6 (last section), 7, and 8, and then passages of Books 11 and 12. The view of the categories to which the Athenian refers that is suggested above was defended a century ago by England 1921: 1.210–11. Schöpsdau 1994: 177 and Meyer 2015: 106 (cf. 123) argue however that the categories (εἴδη) the Athenian has in mind are the species (εἴδη) of virtue (identified in those terms at 632d–e). And since the first instalment of his own substantive discussion in Book 1 is devoted to the ἐπιτηδεύματα of courage, with the promise of going on from there to deal with a second (indeed he turns to σωφροσύνη at 635e) and a third species of virtue in the same way (but that never actually happens), they have a strong case (cf. Schöpsdau 1994: 190–2). This interpretation has the merit of giving the divine goods the appropriate explicit priority in the approach to legislation recommended by the Athenian. Perhaps there are elements of both sorts of structuring categories in the text. Perhaps Plato never quite chose firmly between them.
[21] Gagarin 2008: 110.   [22] As translated and cited by Gagarin 2008: 96; Greek text at 252.

to have had some written legislation which might well have taken that typical form, to judge from the Athenian orator Lycurgus' mention, in a speech of 330 BC, of a law of theirs 'covering all who refused to risk their lives for their country, which expressly stated that they should be put to death'. Lycurgus then proceeded to have the law read out to the court (*Against Leocrates* 129).[23] But Xenophon's account of the Spartan system as initiated by its legislator does not suggest either use of the kind of formulation employed in other cities for laws nor their commitment to writing.

The *Laws* does not offer much to counteract the impression left by Xenophon. We perhaps might think of a passage in Book 4, where Plato's Athenian is introducing his idea of 'double' laws (a shorter, simpler version in the typical form, and a longer, still in that same form, which however incorporates *inter alia* quite a lot of explanatory matter). Appropriately enough given the overall approach to law-making he sketched early in Book 1, he chooses an age requirement for marriage for his illustration. Megillus – who has been silent since the end of Book 3 – now intervenes. He says he would opt for the longer formulation, if it were to be enacted in his city as written prescription, despite the Spartan preference for brevity (*Laws* 4.721e–722a). His response clearly does not suggest that Sparta had any law having that structure, let alone a written law. The Athenian for his part has said nothing about writing law at this stage. But doubtless Plato can assume that Megillus is well aware of the importance attached to written law in Athens, a city with which – as he is made to stress – his family has very close connections (*Laws* 1.642b–d; the Athenian will in due course be pressing insistently for his own part the importance of written law: *Laws* 9.858c–859a; cf. 7.822d–823a, 9.870e–871a, 10.890e–891a).

It is true that at just that point in Book 9 of the dialogue, the Athenian 'refers casually' to Lycurgus as a lawgiver who, like Solon, put things in writing (*Laws* 9.858e; cf. *Phdr.* 258c).[24] Whether much can be made of this, whether as evidence for actual written laws at Sparta or as Plato's own settled view of the matter, must be doubtful. The explicit reference to Solon is in fact unique in the *Laws*. One might suspect that it is included just because mention of a lawgiver everyone knew to have put his legislation in writing was needed at this point, Lycurgus' name not being sufficiently convincing on its own.[25] As to

---

[23] See Gagarin 1986: 53 n. 9. Gagarin there and at 58 comments helpfully on the probable nature of the Spartan *rhetra* and their mode of transmission.
[24] See Lane 2013: 68.
[25] Interestingly, although both Lycurgus and Solon are mentioned in Book 10 of the *Republic* as benefactors of their cities, it is only Solon who is there described (along with Charondas) as a lawgiver (*Rep.* 10.599d–e).

the historical reliability of the Athenian's reference to written legislation in early Sparta, historians who have taken differing stances on the viability of a category of unwritten law as applicable to early Greece – such as Rosalind Thomas (for) and Michael Gagarin (against) – are agreed that (as Thomas puts it):[26]

> The 'Lycurgan laws' which supposedly governed the peculiarly Spartan way of life were the unwritten customs enforced by her educational system; the great Spartan 'rhetra', which somehow got written down, was a law about procedure, albeit important constitutional procedure.

Does that evaluation of 'Lycurgan laws' by the historians fit the account of Lycurgus's legislation presented by Xenophon (who does not mention the *rhetra*)? Certainly 'unwritten customs', enforced by the Spartan educational system and by strongly expressed social expectations (as for example in the shaming of cowards), are what much of Xenophon's text might well seem to convey.[27] On the other hand, in treating Lycurgus as a νομοθέτης (*nomothetês*, lawgiver) he places him in the context of a societal practice that from the late fifth century (when the vocabulary of νομοθετεῖν, νομοθέτης is first found in Attic prose: Antiphon, Thucydides, Andocides) is firmly tied to νόμος (*nomos*) as law, understood as an enforceable rule formally enacted by the community on some particular occasion through the agency of identified or identifiable persons. And as Vivienne Gray points out in her edition of the treatise:[28]

> Xenophon seems to differentiate ἐπιτήδευμα ('custom') from νόμος ('law') in his introduction, and then to define customs as the products of law when he says that Lycurgus 'laid down laws' that produced 'such-and-such a custom' (5.1 ἐνομοθέτησεν ... ἐπιτηδεύματα; 6.4: ἐποίησεν ἐπιτηδεύεσθαι). He also makes the laws subject to legal process, if not to specified penalties.[29]

Plato makes it clear that for his Athenian, too, Lycurgus was a lawgiver. But on the relation of law to custom at Sparta, he offers no comment. He does, however, have the Athenian reflect interestingly on that relationship as he proposes to handle it himself in his treatment of what – like Xenophon's Lycurgus – he takes to be the main business of

---

[26] Thomas 1995: 71; Gagarin 1986: 57–8; cf. Gagarin 2008: 33–8.
[27] Gray 2007: 46, says: 'Xenophon never suggests that Lycurgus' laws were unwritten'. Nor does he suggest that they were written, unless we are to assume that νομοθεσία in his usage must imply that. He might even be taken to be avoiding the question. Plutarch notoriously claims that Lycurgus decreed that written laws should not be employed (*Lyc.* 13.1–2).
[28] Gray 2007: 45.
[29] Legal procedure often remained entirely oral in Greece even when law itself was in writing: Gagarin 2008: 110–21.

lawgiving. That job is described as 'dealing with marriage, together with the birth and upbringing of children, plus of course education and the appointment of officials in the city' (*Laws* 8.842e: topics to which the whole of Books 6 and 7 and the greater part of Book 8 have been devoted). And in the course of his discussion of the earliest stages of upbringing, he says this on the subject of what are generally called 'unwritten customs' (ἄγραφα νόμιμα), to which people give the name 'ancestral laws' (793b–d):

> We should neither call these things laws, nor yet pass over them without mention. ... If they are the right customs in the first place, and have become second nature, then they envelop, and completely protect, whatever written laws exist at that point; if they are out of key, and get out of true, then ... they bring the whole thing down with them. ... Laws (νόμους), habits (ἔθη), customary practices (ἐπιτηδεύματα) – whatever anyone calls them ... we must find a place for them. Things of this kind all play a part in holding a city together, and of the two types, neither can endure without the other. Which is why it should come as no surprise if a large number of apparently unimportant customs (νόμιμα) or even habitual behaviours (ἐθίσματα) – an incoming tide of them – make our laws a bit on the long side.

Nor does that exhaust the complexity of law-making as Plato perceives it. The Athenian has already stressed the need for regulation of citizens' private lives as well as the city's public and communal life, particularly women's lives (*Laws* 6.779d–781d). But when it comes to instructing pregnant women and nurses carrying babies and infants on how to move around so as best to foster the child's development, he holds back from legislation, for fear of its being ridiculed and ignored. Instead, he decides to concentrate on persuading householders of the importance of proper control of the private sphere. Then, he says (*Laws* 7.790b):

> That may prompt the householder to adopt these rules that we have suggested for himself; and if he does adopt them, then he may make a good job of running his own household – and the city into the bargain – and in that way achieve well-being.

At the end of Book 7, when about to launch on the topic of hunting as a pursuit for the young, he recurs to the general approach there advocated (*Laws* 7.822d–e):

> The lawgiver's task seems to have to go beyond merely putting laws in place and then calling it a day; something more is called for, over and above the laws, something whose nature puts it midway between advice and actual

law – not the first time this has cropped up in our discussion, for example when we were talking about the upbringing of very young children.

What is needed is explanation, with a stress on what the lawgiver thinks fine (καλά) or the opposite in any practice – expressed in criticism and praise, which should be valued and treated as directives (*Laws* 7.823c–d).[30]

In sum, the Plato of the *Laws* endorses Lycurgus' main focus on laws dealing with the proper development, conduct, and treatment of human beings at every stage of the life cycle. If from Xenophon we form the impression that Spartan law was primarily concerned with sound customary practices (ἐπιτηδεύματα) and the like, then the *Laws* takes the same view of what should be law's emphasis. But Plato has reflected more fully and with much more conceptual sophistication both on how law *sensu stricto* is best formulated, and how it should relate to less formal kinds of advice, encouragement (and discouragement), and persuasion.

Conclusion

No reader of the *Laws* can be in doubt that it is dense with material echoing and often engaging with ideas, themes, and cultural and institutional forms given expression both in Greek writings of other provenance and in actual Greek practice past and present, as well as with reference of various kinds to Plato's own huge oeuvre. As Shorey put it, 'allusions to methods and ideas of the dialectical dialogues, and explicit solutions of problems dramatically presented in the minor dialogues, make the work almost a complete compendium of the Platonic philosophy'.[31] Often reconstruction of such engagement has to be a conjectural business, subject to obvious hazards.[32] The opening section of Book 1, together with its relationship to Xenophon's treatise on Sparta, has perhaps not previously been viewed from the angle whose fruitfulness has been suggested here. Further debate is awaited.

---

[30] Such explanations would presumably be akin to the 'preludes' the Athenian outlines in Book 4 (*Laws* 4.719e–724a; cf. pp. 184–5 above). But in Books 6 to 8 the notion of preamble is notable by its absence, except for one instance early on (dealing with choice of marriage partner: *Laws* 6.772e–773c). In general, these books seem to belong to a different stratum of composition from Book 4 and Books 9–11 (which do employ preludes so named).

[31] Shorey 1914: 347.

[32] For a previous exercise of mine in this genre that engages with different material in the *Laws*, see Schofield 2013a.

CHAPTER 12

Injury, Injustice, and the Involuntary in the Laws

Socratic Intellectualism and the Socratic Paradox

In the long monologue which takes up Book 5 of the *Laws* and constitutes the second instalment of the general prelude to the legislation that is to follow in the succeeding books, the Athenian Visitor begins by discussing the soul and the virtues. Among the virtues that he commends are a contrasting pair: passion ('noble *thumos*') and gentleness (731b–d). Where the wrongdoings of others are concerned (*adikêmata*), one should resist these and punish them relentlessly – which means being passionate (*thumoeidês*). But when people commit wrong (*adikein*), at any rate remediably so (the unrepentant and irremediable are a different story), we should recognize before anything else that everyone who is unjust (*adikos*) is not so willingly (*hekôn*). Why so? Because nobody would ever willingly have acquired any of life's greatest ills, least of all in what is most precious to him: his soul. So with the reasonable wrongdoer, there is room for restraint and gentleness. In other words, we should hate the sin but love the sinner.

In this passage of Plato's last dialogue, the Socratic paradox – here initially in the form: 'Every unjust person is not willingly unjust' – announces itself alive and well. And it soon recurs. A few pages later, the Athenian Visitor sums up his views on the choice of lives. He puts the issue primarily in terms of the contest between the temperate life (*bios sôphrôn*) and the life without restraint (*akolastos*). When you look at the issue properly, there is really no contest. By now it is clear, he says, that everyone who is *akolastos* is so involuntarily (*akôn*). If you weigh up the balance of pleasure over pain correctly, you can see that someone who wants a pleasant life will not willingly live without restraint. The only reason why the great mass of humanity live lives deficient in temperance (*sôphronein*) is either through ignorance (*amathia*) or through incontinence (*akrateia*), inability to exercise what we call 'self-control', or both (733d–734b).

In the *Protagoras*, the Platonic Socrates had defended the proposition that nobody does what is bad or disadvantageous willingly by arguing against the possibility that someone might know it to be bad but succumb to pleasure or some overpowering emotion. Quite how the argument is meant to work is notoriously a matter of controversy. But *akrateia* – recognized in the *Laws* as a viable form of explanation – is excluded from any such role by the *Protagoras*' Socrates. The key idea is that if a person knows or believes that some choice open to them is better than the alternatives, there is and can be no option to choose anything else. Succumbing to pleasure, for example, would be nothing other than knowingly choosing what one believes to be a worse alternative – and that just does not make sense.

The Socratic paradox that nobody goes wrong willingly is supported in the *Protagoras*, then, by a strong version of Socratic intellectualism. Knowingly acting against one's beliefs about what is best is some sort of impossibility. From the *Laws* passages I have summarized, it seems clear that the Athenian Visitor embraces and indeed insists upon the Socratic paradox, couched in terms of virtue and vice: nobody will willingly be an unjust person or commit wrong or injustice, or willingly live the life of self-indulgence without restraint. But there is no attempt to marshal any sort of Socratic intellectualism in its support. People do not willingly live without restraint, but among the reasons why they do *not* lead temperate lives is incontinence. By incontinence, he means the inability to master passion, pleasure, and so on. The full range of psychic motivations he has in mind is indicated when in Book 9 the Athenian gives what he calls his 'clear and uncomplicated' definition of justice and injustice: 'I call "injustice" the tyranny in the soul of passion and fear and pleasure and pain and envies and desires – whether it results in any injuries or not' (863e6–864a1).

Back in Book 3, in eking out principles of government from reflections on history, the Athenian had identified wisdom and ignorance as the crucial factors in determining success or failure in a polity. Ignorance or stupidity in its greatest form, he says, is what destroyed the power of most of the Dorian states. What does he mean by 'ignorance (*amathia*) in its greatest form'? Here is the answer (689a5–9):

> The ignorance you get when someone hates instead of loving something when he judges it fine or good, but loves and embraces what he judges evil and unjust. This discord (*diaphônia*) between rational judgement and

pleasure and pain I claim to be the ultimate form of ignorance or stupidity, and the greatest, because it inhabits the main mass of the soul.

The name the Athenian gives this condition is 'folly' (*anoia*, 689b3): 'when the soul opposes knowledge or beliefs or reasoning, the natural ruling principles', and 'when noble reasonings in the soul achieve nothing, in fact entirely their opposite'.

This might be conceived as a form of cognitive dissonance (note the expression 'discord'): you have a rational judgement (whether knowledge or belief) about what is noble or good, but your soul resists that judgement – not in the sense that it denies its truth, but because its loves and hates are at odds with what reason values.[1] Someone in this condition is not ignorant in the straightforward sense that they don't know what is good or noble. The problem is that that knowledge has no effect on how the person feels about things 'in the main mass of the soul'; or worse, that in loving or hating what they do love or hate, they reject the appeal of the values whose attractiveness their reason continues to affirm, and they are consequently 'simultaneously dragged in opposite directions' (9.863e3). This is presumably why the Athenian Visitor calls this state of mind 'folly'. It is the state not of lacking knowledge or reason, but of losing one's grip on it: *anoia*, which I've been translating 'folly', is literally 'mindlessness'. In the *Timaeus* (86b3-4) we are told that *anoia* comes in two forms: *amathia* (as here) and *mania*, madness.

So when the Athenian Visitor treats *akrateia*, incontinence, as 'the greatest ignorance or stupidity', he is not in some strange way rehabilitating an intellectualist explanation of what goes wrong in such cases. It is precisely the tyrannizing ambitions (to echo the Book 9 formulation) of passion and fear and pleasure and pain and envies and desires that puts one in a state of mindlessness worse than ordinary ignorance of the good: a condition in which there may be knowledge, but where its natural authority is rejected.

So we may reaffirm: the *Laws* upholds the Socratic paradox, but without reliance on Socratic intellectualism.

The Inconsistency Problem

In Book 9, the Athenian Visitor turns to the business of formulating criminal law. He has not got going very long when he decides he needs to tackle a theoretical problem threatening the whole enterprise. An

---

[1] I am thus rejecting the attempt in Bobonich 2002: 258–67 to deny that the *Laws* recognizes anything in the region of 'hard' *akrasia*. So far as I can find, he does not offer an interpretation of the passage at 689a.

apparent conflict is looming: between commitment to the Socratic paradox, on the one hand, and the distinction drawn 'in every city and by every legislator there has ever been between two sorts of wrongdoing (*adikēmata*), voluntary and involuntary (861b3–5)', on the other. The Athenian Visitor makes it plain that he is not going to give up on the claim that the bad or unjust person is bad or unjust involuntarily. But he is equally firm that before legislating it has to be made clear that the voluntary and involuntary acts in question *are* two separate things, and what the difference between them consists in. So he has a major problem about the consistency of his position to tackle.

The *Laws*' attempt to deal with the issue takes up a notoriously dense and tricky section of Book 9, and the commentators do not agree either on what Plato's solution is or on whether it works. One thought that often occurs to readers is that voluntary/willing and involuntary/unwilling do not mean the same thing when used in articulating the Socratic paradox and as applied in a distinction between two sorts of wrongdoing – whether or not Plato was entirely aware of that. Trevor Saunders, author of the Penguin English translation of the *Laws*, took the view that he *was* aware of it, and indeed that his resolution of the consistency problem effectively turns on exploiting the difference between two meanings or uses or interpretations of 'voluntary'. The bad or unjust person's state of mind is involuntary inasmuch as nobody *would choose* or *would have chosen* to be bad (cf. Plato's formulation at 5.731c3–4) *if they knew* that wickedness or injustice brings a person in that condition the greatest conceivable harm. An act, on the other hand, is voluntary when it *is in fact deliberately chosen* by the agent. Given this distinction, there is after all no contradiction between saying of someone that he has a bad or unjust disposition, but not willingly or voluntarily so, and saying he voluntarily or willingly committed some crime or other. And that (Saunders proposes) is how Plato solves his problem.[2]

Saunders's proposal has been rightly criticized, for example by Richard Stalley and Jean Roberts.[3] To my mind there are two obvious difficulties with the idea that Plato's solution turns on this distinction in meanings of 'voluntary'. First, he never has the Athenian Visitor draw any attention to any distinction of that sort. If something like that were the fulcrum of his approach to the question he is discussing, he would surely have needed and

---

[2] See Saunders 1968: 422–5; Saunders 1991: 142–4.
[3] See Stalley 1983: 154–5; Roberts 1987: 29–30.

wished to have indicated that more explicitly. Second, if Plato had any secure sense that there is a real difference in usage of these expressions in the different contexts identified by Saunders, or of the importance of being alert to it, he would have been keen to block the prospect of any inferences from the use of 'voluntary' as applied to the condition of the unjust soul to its use as applied to acts. But as it is, he makes no effort to do so – in fact, quite the opposite.

At the very beginning of his discussion, he asserts that if you make injustice involuntary, then you have to make unjust behaviour involuntary too. It would be illogical (*ouk ekhei logon*) to suppose otherwise (860d6). I agree, he says, that everyone performs unjust actions (*adikein*) unwillingly; and a bit later, he rejects the possibility (suggested to him by Cleinias, his main interlocutor) of opting out of commitment to the view that all unjust acts (*adikêmata*) are involuntary – I'm not prepared not to say what I think is the truth, he replies (861c–d). Nor is it that he has not seen that someone might think that there was an alternative. For he already mentioned the possibility that somebody might out of sophistry or bravado take the line that, while all are involuntarily unjust, many perform unjust actions voluntarily. If I took that line too, I'd be being inconsistent, he says (860d–e). The talk of *philoneikia* here (I have supposed eristic disputation is what he has in mind) suggests that he can see that some people *might* want to say (for example) that the involuntariness of one's disposition does not necessarily transmit to one's acts. He for his part does not want to take that route.

The distinction the Athenian Visitor actually exploits to deal with the inconsistency problem is one between the notions of injustice (*adikia*) and injury (*blabê*): that is what the legislator must look to, he says (862b). And no commentator doubts that *this* distinction is the one Plato formally makes central to his penology. The idea is that injuries may be committed either voluntarily or involuntarily, but in either case what the legislator must provide for here is not punishment, but compensation and reconciliation (862b–c). I have to compensate you for an injury to you or harm to your property whether I intended the injury or harm or not. Accordingly, once the Athenian Visitor gets back to actual legislation after this theoretical excursus, he is quickly into the rule that is to govern compensating someone for involuntary manslaughter of his slave (865b–c), although procedures for purification figure rather more largely in the discussion of an involuntary killing such as that (865a–866d). But if the harmful act committed was an unjust or wrongful act, now punishment as well as penalty enters the picture. Or rather, consideration of injustice as a disease of the soul, and of the sorts of *cure* that may be available. For here we meet immediately Plato's famous doctrine that punishing people should be conceptualized as the attempt to heal their diseased souls by some appropriate combination of instruction and compulsion (if they are curable), or (if they are incurable) putting them out of their misery and executing them, for the good of society *et pour encourager les autres* (862c–863a).

This is of course a radical and (if you are sympathetic to the Enlightenment) enlightened attempt to take the criminality out of criminal behaviour and reconfigure penal theory and practice accordingly: a complex blend of civil action (to deal with the element of injury) and medical or psychiatric intervention (including termination where for the element of disease healing is impossible). But here our questions begin. Is the foundation on which the whole superstructure of the penological system rests – the distinction between injury and injustice – robust enough to support it? Obviously there *is* a valid distinction to be made between injury and injustice, and the Athenian Visitor makes some sound points in introducing it. We can agree that nobody should count all injuries as *ipso facto* injustices, and that there is therefore no basis for thinking that because injuries may be either voluntary or involuntary there is a matching division between voluntary and involuntary injustices (861e6–862a1). When (862a2–7) he goes on to say that so far from counting an involuntary injury an involuntary act of injustice (*adikêma*), he will not count such an injury an injustice at all (a point to which he recurs at 864a1–8), that seems entirely correct – although *why* it should be correct is where the arguments might begin.

A difficulty arises, however, when we consider the category of voluntary harm. Many acts of voluntary harm – for example, defrauding with intent, burglary, murder – are also unjust acts, cases of wrongdoing. Nor is this denied by the Athenian. His initial treatment of injustice (862c–863a) is actually introduced as a consideration of unjust or wrongful injury and benefit. Injury and injustice are not treated as wholly separable dimensions of behaviour, the former a category of act, the latter a condition of soul. Although injustice is in the first instance a psychic disorder, it characterizes actions also – as a consequence of the psychological state which underlies it. So the question then arises: is an act of injustice voluntary or involuntary? The Socratic paradox dictates the answer: involuntary. But as a voluntary injury presumably known by its perpetrator to be unjust or wrongful, it begins to look as though the answer has to be: voluntary. And indeed, although the Athenian does not comment on his use of the vocabulary of the voluntary and involuntary at this point, as one might perhaps have expected him to do, he shows no hesitation in speaking of such acts as voluntary. As well as prescribing compensation (for the injury), the law must prohibit anyone who commits any unjust act, great or small, from ever *willingly* (*hekôn*) having the effrontery to do such a thing again – or at any rate, it must get them to be very much less willing to do so (in addition to the payment for the harm) (862c–d).

So – as, for example, Schöpsdau and Stalley concluded[4] – it might well look as though Plato should have acknowledged that his response to his inconsistency problem does actually add up to saying *more Aristotelico*: acts of wrongful injury are in a way voluntary, in a way involuntary. They are involuntary because they are the sorts of act nobody would choose to do if they understood the extreme harm the injustice that is their source wreaks upon their perpetrator's soul. They are voluntary because they are injuries deliberately committed against others in full knowledge that they are wrongful. In other words, the distinction between meanings of 'voluntary' which Saunders attributed to Plato is after all the one he does need to rely upon, and which he should have acknowledged explicitly as the key to resolving the inconsistency problem. It might be argued that he should have been more accommodating to those who – from sophistry or bravado, as he suggested – want to say that while all are unjust involuntarily, many perform unjust acts voluntarily (860d–e). In fact (one might be tempted to conclude), the solution is mislocated in the contrast between injury and injustice. That contrast is obviously far from irrelevant to defusing the apparent inconsistency that he highlights. But – the conclusion might be – it does not in and of itself enable us to unlock the puzzle of how to reconcile the Socratic paradox with the need legislation has to deal with voluntary acts of wrongdoing.

How far, however, need Plato concede that perpetrators of wrongful injury really do voluntarily in full knowledge commit an *injustice*? In the wording that he employs at this point, what the law must do is 'instruct and compel' them not to 'have the effrontery voluntarily to do "such a thing" again'. But he has had the Athenian Visitor state that application of the labels 'just' or 'unjust' to actions without qualification would be a mistake. The legislator needs to apply them with regard to the agent's character and way of life (862b). One could infer that unjust actions are to be reckoned as those that flow from an unjust character, and as such are committed *unwillingly* and *without* full knowledge. On that assumption, it would therefore have to be under some other description, not 'unjust', that the

---

[4] See Stalley 1983: 156; Schöpsdau 1984: 131–2.

perpetrator of an injury that is in fact unjust would have to have the effrontery to commit it willingly. 'Harm that the victim deserved' might be a false such description. The lawgivers' job would then consist in making its falsehood clear to the perpetrator, and likewise that willingly doing 'such a thing' on a false pretext is an injustice. When the Athenian Visitor says that they must compel them never willingly to do such a thing again, but to hate injustice, the rider 'or at any rate be very much less willing' admits of various interpretations. For example, he might mean 'less willing to harm someone without properly establishing the facts'. If that were the kind of thing Plato had in mind, then he need not be convicted of implicitly allowing after all that there is such a thing as voluntary injustice.

Perhaps the interesting question to ask at this point is the following. Even if Plato had ended up allowing such a category of injury or harm as voluntary injustice, would that invalidate his attempt to make injury something requiring not punishment, but compensation, purification, and reconciliation, and injustice a matter for punishment, but punishment conceptualized as cure for a disease? It depends, I suggest, on what you think is bad about committing an unjust injury (here memories of the *Gorgias* start to bite more sharply even than they will have been doing already). I suspect Plato would have said the following. Insofar as the injury is an *injury*, then its badness is appropriately treated as a loss to be compensated and as a disturbance to the good order of the community, necessitating purification of the perpetrator and reconciliation with those who have suffered the loss. Insofar as the injury is an *injustice*, the badness consists in the involuntary harm sustained by the perpetrator in his soul – for which punishment conceived as cure is what is appropriate. Wronging and being wronged is an ugly business. But from this Platonic perspective, it does not carry any evaluative charge as interpersonal transaction over and above that already carried by harming and being harmed. Wronging someone does not accordingly merit retribution or any analogue of retribution as recognition of what the perpetrator has done to their victim.

So the concession that unjustly injuring someone is under some appropriate description or other a voluntary act – and we have canvassed different options on what Plato might have considered to be 'appropriate' – does not (properly interpreted) contradict the Socratic paradox, although he does not himself make the point. And no less importantly for Plato's main penological project, it *need* not undermine the main idea that the way to deal juridically with the injustice of an unjust act is not to think of it as a form of injury, but to treat it as evidence of a disease of the soul. If that is the case, we may be able to understand better why Plato gives the lion's share of his attention to the distinction between injury and injustice, and why he neglects to pursue the issue of different applications of the expression 'voluntary'. We should conclude that the inconsistency problem is not really his main concern. Raising that issue is more a way of getting into the topic he is truly interested in: differentiating between treating crime as injury and dealing with it as the product of psychic disease – and by making that disjunction exclusive removing the possibility of a special juridical category of injury: *wrongful injury*, calling for a special kind of recompense, 'retribution'. As we have seen, Plato acknowledges that there are injuries that are wrongful. But the injury and the wrongfulness inhabit two different logical spaces. Injury is what someone does to another, and as such it never has any moral dimension. Wrong or injustice is damage people do only to themselves, and that never other than involuntarily.

At this point, someone might object that Plato does *not* expel all resort to retribution in what he says about voluntary acts of wrongdoing. When he gets down to the business of constructing his highly elaborate system of legislative provisions for dealing with the perpetrators of such acts, retribution is precisely what he talks of once he reaches the final main category: of voluntary acts committed 'in all injustice and from design, because of being overmastered by pleasures and desires and grudges' (869e). As a preface to the legislation that follows, the Athenian Visitor goes on to comment in more detail on these overmastering causes – but to this preface he appends a piece of popular religious lore: that *tisis*, probably to be understood here as 'retribution', is exacted for homicide of this kind in Hades, and that the perpetrator will suffer the same fate at the hands of others in his next reincarnated life on earth (870e). When the Athenian Visitor subsequently turns to the murder of one's own family members in particular, the 'myth or *logos*, or whatever one should call it' is spelled out further, and the retribution is now described as the work of 'Justice avenging bloodshed' (872d–e).

Here, we need to remind ourselves that the *Laws* operates at more than one discursive level and in more than one intellectual register. In the section of text we have been examining at length, Plato is doing philosophical analysis for those readers with an appetite for it, particularly for anyone puzzled by the apparent incompatibility between recognition of voluntary wrongdoing and acceptance of the Socratic paradox. Philosophical analysis leaves no logical space for the notion of retribution. In the later passages to which we have just been referring, by contrast, Plato is engaged on something quite different: building into his legislation persuasive considerations which, through the fear they inspire, will induce those to whom it is to be addressed – viz. the inhabitants of Magnesia, representing human beings in general – to refrain from wrongdoing of the kind in question (870e, 872d, 873a). He does not endorse the truth of the *logos* of divine retribution that he invokes but is clearly prepared to put it to use as an effective tool for shaping a political community and its members. We might judge it a sort of Noble Lie.

Farewell to Socratic Intellectualism

In the final part of his theoretical excursus in Book 9, the Athenian Visitor starts with an analysis of different ways in which behaviour can go wrong or constitute error – a classification of what he calls *hamartêmata* (863b–e). But its centrepiece is a summing up of his view of justice and injustice. I earlier reproduced the account of injustice in this passage (863e6–864a1): 'The tyranny in the soul of passion and fear and pleasure and pain and envies and desires – whether it results in any injuries or not.' The interesting thing about this definition relative to the discussion of error that has immediately preceded is what is omitted.

There is no reference to ignorance of any of the three sorts that were mentioned as causes of error alongside pleasure and pain (863c–d). In particular, the Athenian Visitor does not include among the sources of injustice ignorance in the form of the false conceit of wisdom, even though he has told us that in a physically strong person it can be the cause of great and gross (*amousa*) errors. In other words, the principal shortcoming the early Platonic Socrates had detected in many of his interlocutors, however appalling the behaviour to which it might lead (one thinks of the strong young Oedipus' murder of Laius at the crossroads), is no longer to be identified as ignorance. Injustice is now getting from Plato a radically *anti*-intellectualist interpretation.

What about justice? The Athenian Visitor's account of this, too, strikes a radical note and is only indirectly prepared for in the preceding discussion (864a):

> If there is 'the opinion of what is best', however a city or particular individuals think they will attain it; and if that opinion is in control of the soul and governs every man; then everything done on that basis must be declared just, and the same must be said of subjection to that kind of principle as operative in individuals, provided also that it is best for human life as a whole. That is so even if there are mistakes, resulting in the sort of injury people in general take to be involuntary injustice.

With most recent interpreters, I take it that when Plato speaks of 'the opinion of what is best', he means us to take this to be *true* or at least well-considered opinion. Otherwise, the further condition that action done on that basis must be best for human life as a whole would be difficult to satisfy. The meaning of the rider 'however a city or particular individuals think they will attain it [i.e. what is best]' is hard to fathom – if indeed Plato wrote anything resembling that (the text seems to be corrupt). But the overall impression is that, provided my motivation is right, and provided that my plan of action within the sphere of the community does indeed conform with what is best for human life as a whole, then even though I get things wrong sometimes (here the relevance of the discussion of error becomes apparent) my action counts as just.

In other words, not only is ignorance not the explanation of badness and injustice, it is in fact compatible with justice and just behaviour. For example, suppose I am a judge working within a good legal system, well designed for promoting what is best for human life as a whole (thoughts about a well-ordered political community seem to be uppermost in Plato's mind at this point: note the reference to the city's idea of what is best, and the assumption that by virtue of internalization it 'governs' or 'sets the pattern for' (*diakosmêi*) *every* man). Suppose further that through some error of judgement I wrongly convict an innocent person, or wrongly acquit someone who is guilty. Then that is not a breach of justice. It is not even an involuntary injustice.

Convicting the innocent is an injury all right, but if the conditions the Athenian Visitor specifies are satisfied it may still be an act of justice. Once again, and in this sense the previous discussion about error *has* prepared the ground, what matters is the state of mind of the individual in question. What matters, too, is the contrast with injustice. Injustice is allowing passion or pleasure or desire to take over your mind. Justice is putting reason in control – to the extent that we are to be governed by right opinion (no mention at this point of the knowledge so prominent in Socratic discourse, and infallibility is expressly not insisted upon). Here, presumably, is where the voluntary comes into its own, although that is not a point Plato is intent on making here.

CHAPTER 13

Plato's Marionette

One thing Plato is always remembered for is his banishment of the poets in Book 10 of the *Republic*. He has been attacking their appeal to emotion, not to reason (we shall incidentally be looking at an extract from that section of text), and their over-reliance on images, not real knowledge of truth. But of course, the *Republic* is at the same time a work itself full of images (cf. *Rep*. 6.487e–488a), from the ship of state to the cave, which has been described as 'the most famous metaphor in the history of philosophy'.[1] And striking images are littered throughout the corpus: the torpedo fish of the *Meno*, the dying swan of the *Phaedo*, the midwife of the *Theaetetus*, for example, all in description or self-description of Socrates. Early in Book 1 of the *Laws*, a dialogue in which uniquely there is no Socrates, Plato created another image that was to resonate down the centuries:[2] the comparison of human beings to marionettes, constructed as playthings for the gods or perhaps for some more serious purpose of theirs.

Here is how he introduces the idea (644d–e):[3]

> Let's take the view that each of us living creatures is a puppet belonging to the gods, put together either as their toy or for some serious reason – that being something we don't know. What we do know is that these feelings [πάθη][4] we have are like tendons or strings inside us, drawing [σπῶσιν] us but pulling

---

[1] Blackburn 2006: 101; also quoted p. 163 above.
[2] Perhaps its most recent appearance, inspired by an essay of 1810 by Heinrich von Kleist, is in Gray 2015.
[3] Translations of passages in the *Laws* are by Tom Griffith (with occasional adaptation): see Schofield and Griffith 2016.
[4] Meyer 2015: 40, 179 renders πάθη as 'experiences', suggesting (cf. Bobonich 2002: 539–40 n. 77) that the term here covers 'calculation' too (cf. 644d1–2), and noting that Megillus has just referred to his puzzlement as a πάθος (644d6; but puzzlement is much more obviously a feeling, which is how she translates the word there, than is calculation). The parallel with *Rep*. 10.604a–d suggests rather that the pull of active calculation or deliberation is to be understood as distinguished from the pull of πάθη. I take it that when the Athenian here speaks of the opposite directions in which we are pulled by string-like πάθη, he has in mind principally the 'opposed' advice of pleasure and pain (644c6). It will be the job of calculation to make sure we respond to these in the right way: achieving the correct 'demarcation'.

[ἀνθέλκουσιν] in opposite directions, towards opposite actions, and in fact the demarcation line between human goodness and badness lies here.

And the meaning? Seemingly that, as E. B. England put it in his notes to the *Laws*:[5] 'We answer to the tug of passion or to other motives just in the way that the marionettes answer to the pull of the wires.' Or in other words, we might think we humans are in control of our own behaviour, but in fact much of the time we are not: we are controlled by the pull of pleasure or pain. To use a term of art applied to Plato by Myles Burnyeat, he deploys here an 'alienating description',[6] to get us to see ourselves as behaving not like living thinking beings ('living creatures though we are'),[7] but like artefacts operated by strings or cords and devised by a higher being for what purpose we can only guess – but we fear it might be comparable to the amusement that a child gets from a marionette show: a very small child, so a passage on puppets in Book 2 of the *Laws* suggests (658b–d).

There has been a great deal of valuable discussion of the *Laws*' marionette passage in recent years, with notable contributions from Christopher Bobonich, Susan Sauvé Mayer, Joshua Wilburn, and Leslie Kurke, among several others.[8] However, I shall argue that the subtlety and complexity of the dense sequence of thought Plato constructs are not adequately captured in recent scholarship on the dialogue, particularly his treatment of the role of law in enabling self-rule (in this connection, I make considerable use of a pertinent passage in Book 10 of the *Republic* (603e–604d)). One little explored puzzle is the relationship between the opening sketch of human psychology (644c–d) and the account of the marionette image itself (644d–645b). The diagnosis I shall offer suggests a kind of Hegelian-style dialectic, which will give the chapter its structure. (1) The reader of the passage is first offered a cognitive model of a unitary self, presided over by reasoning – which prompts bafflement in the Athenian Visitor's interlocutors. (2) The marionette image then in effect undermines that model, by portraying humans as passive subjects of contrary controlling impulses determining their behaviour. (3) Finally, the image is complicated, and in the end transcended, by reintroduction of reasoning as a special kind of divinely inspired impulse, with which one must actively cooperate if animal impulses are to be mastered. I examine the way Plato's reference at this point to law (where there is a key translation problem) should be understood to bear upon the nature of the reasoning in question. In conclusion,

---

[5] England 1921: 1.256. [6] Burnyeat 1999a: 306–7. [7] England 1921: 1.255.
[8] See Bobonich 2002; Meyer 2012, 2015; Wilburn 2012; Kurke 2013.

The Initial Sketch of Human Psychology

I comment on what light we may suppose to be thrown by the marionette passage on self-rule, as we are promised it will.

The Initial Sketch of Human Psychology

At 644b–c, the Athenian visitor returns to the idea introduced early in Book 1 (626e–627b) that the good are those able to exercise self-rule, the bad those unable to do so. He then indicates that he will employ an image (εἰκών, *eikôn*) to make clearer what we mean when we talk like that. But in fact, first he provides a bare list of the basic psychological factors that are to figure in the approach to understanding self-rule that introduction of the image will make possible. What he says is this (644c–d):

> ATHENIAN: Can we assume, then, that each of us is a single entity?
> CLEINIAS: Yes.
> ATHENIAN: But possessing, within himself, a pair of mindless and opposed advisers – to which we give the names pleasure and pain.
> CLEINIAS: That is so.
> ATHENIAN: And in addition to these two, there are also opinions about what is going to happen, to which we give the general name 'expectation', but the particular name 'fear' for expectation of pain, and 'confidence' for expectation of the opposite. Presiding over all this – deciding which of them is better or worse – is 'calculation'; and when this is made a common enactment of a city,[9] it is called 'law'.
> CLEINIAS: I'm having a bit of difficulty following this. Still, take it that I am following, and tell us what comes next.
> MEGILLUS: That goes for me too. That's exactly how I'm feeling.

That listing does not correspond exactly with any of the other itemizations of elements of the soul to be found in the dialogues. But there are significant affinities with a passage in the *Timaeus*.

Indeed, in many respects, as Susan Sauvé Mayer in her 2012 article on our *Laws* material observed, the *Laws*' list is its doublet. The *Timaeus* passage presents 'an enumeration of the sorts of "affections" (παθήματα) that arise in the soul as a necessary consequence of its embodiment'.[10] This is how they are listed there (*Ti.* 69d):

> First of all pleasure, the greatest enticement to evil, next pains that drive us away from the good, and further those mindless advisers, confidence

---

[9] At this point, Griffith has 'when this is enacted by the city as a whole': I render the Greek more literally.
[10] Meyer 2012: 323.

and fear, as well as anger, hard to assuage, and expectation easily led astray.

Timaeus goes on to add:

> These they mixed together with sense perception, incapable of reasoning and ready to attempt any and every sort of passionate desire (ἔρως, *erôs*), and so inevitably they composed the mortal species [of soul].

The *Timaeus* passage offers something a bit fuller and more fine-grained and nuanced than the *Laws* account.[11] The main emphasis, however, falls on how incapable of sound thought is any of these affections (where – as in expectation – thought occurs), the moral danger they constitute, and their motivational force. By striking contrast, the *Laws* designations focus more, and in less ethically charged and less prejudicial terms, on the input some at least of the items it mentions contribute to the way we think about what to do.

No wonder that Cleinias and Megillus are baffled. They were expecting an explanation of the phenomenon of self-rule and its failure. But so far, the Athenian has done nothing that directly engages with how we do or do not succeed in controlling ourselves. Why does his account of the matter begin in this apparently unhelpful manner? The obvious answer is that its sketch of human psychology establishes a framework for what follows: a structure of key concepts we shall need to bear in mind as we engage with the nature of self-rule, and indeed as we pursue the broader agenda of education for virtue – and in the first instance for courage – to which the treatment of self-rule is designed to contribute.[12] As sometimes elsewhere in the dialogue, however, Plato leaves it to the reader to work out what the point is, and in this case (as we shall see) then to apply the conceptual framework to the subsequent discussion that it has served to introduce. Despite or perhaps because of its skeletal character, a full treatment of what is implicit in it would be a lengthy business. I shall restrict myself to a few mostly brief observations on each of its elements in turn, however deferring a fuller discussion of fear and confidence – which are relevant mostly not to the presentation of the marionette but to the passage that follows it – to an Appendix.

---

[11] One particular difference is its identification, not of pleasure and pain, but of fear and confidence, as the 'mindless advisers' (and not as forms of expectation).

[12] This explanation is worked out in detail (much of which however I find debatable) in Meyer 2012; see also Meyer 2015: 175.

Each of Us a Single Entity

Commentators have rightly registered this initial stress on the individual as a unitary subject.[13] In the development of the marionette comparison it will prove important that, as well as the different factors represented within the imagery, there is a key role for 'us'. And of course, the passage as a whole is offered as an attempt to clarify the idea of 'self-rule'. So the emphasis on the unitary subject or agent at the outset looks as though it is intended to carry weight. I shall suggest that it does indeed shape Plato's approach to self-rule in the passage.

Pleasure and Pain

'Pretty well the whole enquiry' into laws, the Athenian has said (636d), 'is to do with pleasure and pain – whether in cities or in the behaviour of individuals.' He calls them 'nature's two well-springs'. Drawing on them in the right way on the right occasion is key to happiness. Doing so without knowledge makes for a life of misery (636d–e). Sometimes, he will treat pleasure and pain in a relatively specific way, as affections comparable with (for example) anger, fear, envy, or the appetites (e.g. 645d, 9.863e). But often they will work as much more generic designations, each presumably covering a range of feelings and emotions that could in other contexts be given more specific identification (as e.g. at 9.864b, where 'pain' is explained as a term there used to embrace anger and fear).

As we have noted, the discussion of self-rule proposed by the Athenian is offered as a contribution to understanding the development of courage in a person. Coping with pleasure as well as pain has been identified as a job for courage. The Athenian had asked (633c–d):

> Now, what about courage? How are we to define that? Is it perfectly straightforward, simply a struggle against fear and pain, or do we include desires, pleasures, and those allurements, so terribly enticing, which, no matter how full of their own importance people may be, can still turn their hearts to putty?

Megillus proved ready – perhaps surprisingly – to widen his notion of courage beyond the exclusively martial sphere he and Cleinias originally had in view and agreed that it needs to be 'a struggle against all those things'. So a focus on both pleasure and pain has special point within the agenda of this part of Book 1.

---

[13] See especially Bobonich 2002: 261; Meyer 2015: 172.

'Calculation' (λογισμός) Presiding over All These

Griffith's 'presiding over all these' (cf. Budé: 'par-dessus tout', Pangle: 'over all these') renders ἐπί + dative (LSJ s.v. B.III.6). Meyer has 'against all these' (cf. Saunders's Penguin: 'above and against all these'; LSJ s.v. ἐπί B.I.I.c), perhaps anticipating her interpretation of the role of calculation in the marionette image. But 'deciding which of them [pain, pleasure, etc.] is better or worse' does not suggest that its role is primarily one of opposition.[14] The Loeb has the minimalist 'in addition' (cf. Schöpsdau: 'zu diesen allen kommt noch'; LSJ s.v. ἐπί B.I.I.e). But calculation is the culminating item, no mere addition. And its role, as the Athenian indicates, is to make a judgement on what all the other factors may be saying to a person. If it needs assistance to achieve an authority over them when it does so, effective in how we then act (as Schöpsdau objects, looking ahead to the marionette analogy),[15] or if the person fails to engage in calculation at all, that does not negate the fact that calculation's job is to preside as adjudicator.

As to what exactly Plato means by 'calculation' here, and the function he sees it as exercising, I do not have much to say at this stage, reserving discussion to pp. 262–8 below. Meyer has an excellent note.[16] She begins by observing that it need not be understood as indicating anything like a hedonistic calculus of short- and long-term pleasures and pains and concludes with the verdict that the formulation here is not to be supposed to constitute a complete characterization of calculation, nor even to be preparing the ground for anything more theorized. It becomes clear in the subsequent treatment of the fear that is shame, in particular, that a range of other values are there in play. It would be odd to suppose that they are excluded here, where the Athenian is offering not a theory, but nothing more than a quick sketch of factors at work in human psychology that is presumably intended to be pretty uncontroversial – up to this point, at any rate.

Does 'calculation' mean 'correct calculation'? If so, the Athenian would only be assuming something like the treatment of the faculty of calculation offered in the *Republic* (e.g. 4.441e, 9.591b). It will be apparent from what he goes on to say in developing the marionette image that correct calculation must be what is meant. But it is already suggested by the interpretation of 'law' that he immediately goes on to offer.

---

[14] Cf. also p. 251 n. 4 above: the opposing the Athenian refers to seems primarily that between pleasure and pain.
[15] Schöpsdau 1993: 236. [16] Meyer 2015: 176–7.

'Law' as an Enactment of Calculation Common to a City

While readers might have had little reason to question the way the Athenian has characterized the psychic factors he has just listed, his definition of law here no longer remains undisputed territory. Thrasymachus, for example, would have found it inadequate (*Rep.* 1.338c–339a), and the *Laws* remains well aware of the Thrasymachean alternative, which is briefly summarized and dismissed later in the dialogue (4.714b–715e). Later in the dialogue the idea that right reason is the essence of law will be given ambitious theoretical weight (4.713e–715e). But even if the idea itself is being introduced here, that fuller development is still to come. More intriguing than the definition in itself is the problem – seldom posed by commentators – why the topic of law is introduced at all at this juncture. A mention of it at this point looks at first blush quite extraneous to a context dealing with self-mastery and the soul. The puzzlement now expressed by Cleinias and Megillus might understandably be compounded.

All in all, the simplicity of the brief listing of factors at work in the human psyche that the Athenian offers in the passage we have just worked through has proved deceptive. How they might figure in a discussion of self-rule remains quite unclear. The significance of the prominence among them of fear and confidence will emerge only in the further treatment of courage in the closing pages of Book 1. And I will be arguing below (pp. 262–8) that the rationale of the final clause – on law – becomes clear only with the proper understanding of the further reference to law in the marionette passage. So no wonder if by now we need an image to get some understanding of self-rule. To that image I shall now turn.

The Marionette

The first reference we have to marionettes in Greek literature appears to be a passage in Book 2 of Herodotus' *Histories*, which clearly indicates such an artefact (Hdt. 2.48.2):

> The rest of the festival of Dionysus is observed by the Egyptians much as it is by the Greeks, except for the dances; but in place of the phallus, they have invented the use of images two feet high pulled by strings, the private part nodding and nearly as big as the rest of the body, which are carried about the villages by women; a reed-pipe leads the way, and the women follow behind singing of Dionysus.

'Images pulled by strings' renders the Greek ἀγάλματα νευρόσπαστα (*agalmata neurospasta*): the expression νευρόσπαστα, 'pulled by strings', used as a substantive was to become the standard term for 'marionettes', although Plato talks of θαύματα (*thaumata*), 'marvels' or 'prodigies', with this very specific denotation intended.[17] That Plato's term can carry such a particular meaning without further explanation might surprise one, and indeed Aristotle prefers to speak of τὰ αὐτόματα as a subset of such θαύματα ('automatic marvels': *Metaph.* A.3.983a14, *GA* 2.1, 734b10, 2.5, 741b7–8; cf. *MA* 7, 701b2–10). But θαύματα without such amplification clearly means 'puppets' in the cave analogy of the *Republic* (7.514b). Here, Socrates compares the wall above which people carry the statues whose shadows are seen by the chained prisoners, with the screens used by the puppeteers, above which the people show their puppets (θαύματα) – 'as in a Punch and Judy show', Adam says in his note.[18] More generally 'θαύματα embraces puppet-shows, juggling, circuses and other kinds of popular entertainment', as James Diggle comments à propos of an instance in Theophrastus' *Characters* (*Char.* 6.4), noting also that songs are mentioned in such a context at a further point (*Char.* 27.7).[19]

I suspect that Plato in our *Laws* passage says 'tendons *or strings*', νεῦρα ἢ σμήρινθοί τινες, to help clarify what particular sort of puppet he is referring to there, since σμήρινθος (*smêrinthos*) or μήρινθος (*mêrinthos*) can be used to mean a fishing line, as in a proverbial expression in Aristophanes (*Th.* 928). He could thus indicate that the puppet in question operates by strings manipulated from top down – that is, marionettes.[20] Some marionettes were no doubt fairly simple artefacts, operated by puppeteers skilful in the manipulation of whichever limbs they wished to activate. When Philo of Alexandria wants to illustrate the way the intellect or ἡγεμονικόν (*hêgêmonikon*) employs the different sensory faculties, his comparison with a puppeteer suggests something of that nature (*Opif.* 117, *Abr.* 73). Perhaps that is what Plato has in mind in the *Laws* passage. On the other hand, the marionettes Aristotle, his commentators, and some later Greek and Roman authors are thinking of were evidently quite complicated mechanical systems, whose coordinated operation might indeed suggest an automaton and was such as might well particularly evoke wonder in those who (in Aristotle's words) 'have not yet

---

[17] On marionettes as νευρόσπαστα, see in particular Herzog-Hanser 1936; Schröder 1983.
[18] Adam 1963 [1902]: 89–90.   [19] Diggle 2004: 254.
[20] μήρινθος is the word used for marionette string in a comparison of the control of the cosmos with the functioning of a marionette in the pseudo-Aristotelian περὶ κόσμου (*On the Cosmos*) (6.398b17), usually dated to the first century BC. But Plato's use of the term here, as an alternative to the untechnical νεῦρον, perhaps suggests that it had not yet become a standard usage in this context.

studied the cause' (*Metaph.* A.3, 983a14–15).²¹ In a useful review of the evidence about the device he may have had in mind, Martha Nussbaum in an early article summed it up like this:²²

> The picture which emerges from all these passages is the following: the puppets were attached, marionette-fashion, to strings at each separate limb or joint. A complex mechanism of cables, pegs, or both ensured that, given an initial action of the puppeteer (the untying of a cable, or the freeing of a peg), the puppet performed various complex motions without further direction.

Perhaps the nicest illustration of the sort of outcome that would result is to be found in Apuleius' *De Mundo* 27:

> Think about it! Even the people who set in motion gestures in wooden puppets [what in Greek would be termed more economically of expression οἱ νευροσπάσται, 'the tendon-pullers', or in short 'the puppeteers'], when they pull the string for the limb they want to get activated, then the neck will turn, the head will nod, the eyes will roll, and the hands present themselves for service – and the creature as a whole will appear to be alive.

Such images are standardly referred to as wooden. Consequently, it is not surprising that – so far as I can discover – the archaeological record is only doubtfully informative (what are sometimes claimed to be terracotta marionettes are mostly more plausibly interpreted as particular variants on the jointed doll, which survives in numbers).²³ Nor have I been able to discover any pictorial representation. Marionette shows were perhaps regarded as too juvenile in their appeal or too much of a low-life entertainment to be the sort of things the elite wanted much represented on their pots or their walls. However, it may well be thanks ultimately to Plato that in Greek and Latin literature there are a considerable number of passages exploiting the image of the marionette, not all of them glum reflections on the human condition.²⁴ Thus Apuleius, here apparently recycling

---

²¹ Frede 2010: 116, uniquely among translators, editors, and commentators, suggests that, because Plato's θαύματα in our *Laws* passage are plainly not manipulated by the gods, but are controlled by their internal workings, we should think of them not as puppets but as wind-up automata (presumably somewhat like the toy carts with which Aristotle compares what are usually taken to be puppets at *MA* 7.701b2–10). This interpretation seems to me to press the image further than is warranted. Plato's focus is on the strings that tug at us, not on what initially activates them: whether that is something internal or external to the artefact is not a question he is inviting us to ask.
²² Nussbaum 1976: 148.
²³ That said, there do survive jointed human clay images in which a hole has been made in the top of the head, which might indicate suspension enabling the figure's manipulation as a simple type of marionette.
²⁴ It was a particular glum favourite with Marcus Aurelius, invariably commenting on ordinary unenlightened humanity. For discussion of the mechanism he had in mind, see Berryman 2010.

material in the pseudo-Aristotelian *On the Cosmos* (6.398b16–20), sees the single control governing the marionette's various interconnected movements as an analogue of divine control of the cosmos and its parts (not unlike Philo's representation of the ἡγεμονικόν). Nonetheless, as a vehicle for comment on human helplessness the image had obvious potential, realized for example by Horace (*Sat.* 2.7.82), making a slave suggest that his master too is a slave to other things, just as a marionette must dance to strings not his own (he goes on to ask: is it only the sage who is free?); or by Aulus Gellius, reporting Favorinus' argument that the fatalism of astrology leaves humans no longer λογικὰ ζῷα (*logica zôia*), rational animals, but *ludicra et ridenda quaedam neurospasta*, just marionettes, playthings designed to prompt laughter (*Noct. Att.* 14.1.23).

The example from Gellius prompts the question: so is Plato's marionette likewise deterministically conceived? Can we do no other than yield to whichever tug – the string of pleasure, the string of pain – pulls the harder on a given occasion? I think there is no entirely straightforward answer to the question. At first blush, it might look as though we can reply without more ado: 'No, not deterministically.' Our condition and behaviour as humans may be designed by the gods for whatever their amusement. But there is no suggestion that they are the puppeteers: as Christopher Bobonich says, 'Plato makes no use of the idea that some external agent is pulling the strings'.[25] When the Athenian Visitor introduces the topic of self-rule that the marionette image is meant to illuminate, as we have seen he starts with the assumption that each of us humans is 'a single entity'. He immediately elaborates on this with the suggestion that we each possess, within ourselves, 'a pair of mindless and opposed advisers – to which we give the names "pleasure" and "pain"' (644c). The implication is that, far from simply reacting to the pull of pleasure or pain as the case may be, we treat them as counsellors, whose advice presumably we may or may not accept.

The Athenian goes on to make 'calculation', deciding which of them is better or worse, exercise the function of presiding over all the other inputs he mentions – 'fear' and 'confidence' as well as pleasure and pain (644c-d). The marionette image is itself developed accordingly. In the extract I shall reproduce shortly (pp. 262–3), it will transpire that as well as 'hard, iron' pulls exerted by some of the strings (which certainly include those representing the insistent demands of pleasure and pain in particular), there is a 'pliant, golden' pull from calculation which is 'gentle and non-violent' (645a). And the narrative as a whole makes *us* – the single entity that each of us is – responsible

[25] Bobonich 2002: 266.

for our choices, and for deciding which of the pulls upon us we follow. We are presumably to understand that that is what self-rule – which the marionette image was meant to illuminate – consists in.

This is not in the end the picture of a deterministic system. But nor is it anything very recognizable as a marionette. If the golden pull from the string representing calculation is what *we* make guide our behaviour, whether in general or in some particular instance, the marionette is not a marionette at all: the very idea that we are puppets is subverted, from within, one might say. As commentators from England to Bobonich have well brought out, from being passive spectacles we turn into actors. The best discussion is provided by Julia Annas, in a beautifully nuanced couple of pages in *Platonic Ethics, Old and New*. As she puts it:[26] 'The moral of the image seems, then, to be not that human action is always at the mercy of intractable internal forces, but rather the opposite, that it is open to us to control and direct forces that might have appeared to be intractable.'

Nonetheless, two later passages suggest that the marionette analogy actually gets much of its force from occasions when what we do is dictated by whichever turns out to be the stronger of the opposing pulls of pleasure and pain. It is then that we are most marionette-like, devised by the gods for their amusement – in other words, when 'we' are not in control, judging by λογισμός (*logismos*, calculation) which of them is better, which is worse. One such passage comes in Book 7, the other in Book 5. I take the Book 7 passage first, since here the puppet image is explicitly reintroduced, in the general context of a sustained discussion of upbringing and education. We meet it at the end of the Athenian's main set of reflections on how music should be performed – which in fact turn into a meditation on how life itself should be lived, and how we should conceive of the serious and the playful in it. He says of humans that they are 'puppets for the most part, yet with a small kernel of truth (*alêtheia*)' (804b: σμικρὰ ἀληθείας ἄττα μετέχοντες). The point is presumably that human psychology is mostly dominated by the mindless tuggings of pleasure and pain. But there is an element in us – the 'small kernel of truth' – that can grasp something more elevated, and that makes us *un*like the marionettes we mostly otherwise resemble.[27]

The Book 5 passage comes at a point where the Athenian has reached the end of his exposition of the true values which should guide the life of the citizen: 'all those that are divine', as he puts it; and where he now turns to

---

[26] Annas 1999: 144.
[27] A more complete consideration of the *Laws*' marionette image would need to include exploration of the rich material in this Book 7 passage. Kurke 2013: 132–8 offers interesting suggestions.

'things human' (732d–e). This marks the transition from ethics done from a theologically informed perspective to one taking human nature just as human. 'Human', he says (in Tom Griffith's translation), 'by its nature essentially means pleasures and pains and desires; these are, quite simply, the strings from which every mortal creature dangles, like it or not, dancing to their powerful influence.' A more literal translation would retain the dangling but make no explicit mention of strings, which is doubtless why few commentators – Leslie Kurke is an honourable exception[28] – seem to have noticed the reprise of the marionette image from Book 1. For my argument, it provides two key points of support. First, there is the suggestion that it is above all our susceptibility to pleasure, pain, and desire that makes us marionette-like: something characteristically human, to be contrasted with something better; something we should think of as divine. Second, the Athenian is emphatic that such susceptibility is in fact not unique to humans, but something we share with 'every mortal creature' – an emphasis reminding us that in the Book 1 passage it was in fact living creatures generally that were treated as puppets.[29]

I conclude from this Book 5 passage that it is principally insofar as our psychology is dominated, like that of the other animals, by pain, pleasure, and desire that we are taken to be marionettes; and from the Book 7 treatment of the puppet that Plato implies that that is how we function most of the time. Both passages suggest that our capacity for reason and reasoning and our ability to take control of our behaviour as 'single entities' are limited. The Athenian's picture seems mostly a bleak one. His Spartan interlocutor, Megillus, would agree (804b): 'You really don't have much time for the human race, do you, my friend?' Insofar as we are merely human animals, we are pleasure and pain machines: we might as well be marionettes.

Reasoning and the Appeal to Law

But that is not the whole story. It is now time to take a closer look at the way Plato tries to incorporate something less mechanistic within that basically mechanistic framework of the μύθος (*muthos*) itself. Here is the relevant section of text (644e–645b):

> There is one of the pulls [ἕλξεων] which each of us must always follow, never letting go of that string, and resisting [ἀνθέλκειν] the other tendons; this pull

---

[28] Kurke 2013: 163 n. 18.
[29] Presumably the golden pull of calculation is a factor only in human make-up, although a factor more divine than human.

[ἀγωγή], golden and sacred, comes from calculation [λογισμός], and it calls in aid the law common to the city [τῆς πόλεως κοινὸν νομόν]; the other pulls are hard, of iron – where this one is pliant, being golden – but resembling various kinds of things; and we must always cooperate with the finest pull [ἀγωγή, *agôgê*], which is from the law, since calculation, fine as it is, is also gentle and non-violent, and therefore its pull [ἀγωγή] needs helpers, to make sure that within us the golden type overcomes the other types.[30]

Key here is evidently the idea of a different kind of marionette string: one effecting 'the golden and sacred drawing of calculation'. 'Sacred' intimates that this is an influence within us that we should not conceive of in solely human terms, and 'golden' that there is a different order of value associated with it from the iron pulls of pleasure, pain, and the like: calculation is something 'fine', καλόν (*kalon*). The Athenian also exploits another implication of 'golden': the relative softness of gold, taken to indicate that the pull this string exerts upon us is 'gentle and non-violent'. That being so, the pull of calculation needs assistance if it is to win out over the forcible pulls of pleasure, pain, fear, and comparable appetites and emotions.

All published translations prior to Tom Griffith's known to me tell us something else about the drawing exerted by calculation: that it is *called* common law of the city. Such a reading of the Greek is problematical. A little earlier, in first introducing 'calculation', the Athenian has stated that when made into a common enactment of a city it is named 'law' (644d) – although why it was thought relevant to have him do so is (as we noted) difficult at that juncture to work out. Plato is usually taken to be essentially repeating the same point about naming in his comment here on the golden pull of calculation. But calculation as it is now being discussed is reasoning as a process figuring in the psychology of the individual, not in the public sphere.[31] It would be odd for Plato to suggest that the pull it exercises on our minds is as such given the name 'common law' of the city, to all intents and purposes assimilating private calculation and public law, treating them now as one and the same. That difficulty is avoided by a translation such as Trevor Saunders's: '"calculation", a power which in a state is called the public law'. But there are in any case further problems. Plato was content before to speak simply of 'law' as the right name. Why now change that name to '*common* law', an expression that never recurs in this enormous work on the subject (we get it in Stoicism, as for example in Cleanthes' *Hymn to Zeus*, but pointfully, as *god*'s common law – law

---

[30] I make a number of adjustments to Griffith's translation, to achieve greater literalness.
[31] A point made by Kathryn Morgan: see Nightingale 1999: 104 n. 12.

common to all humanity, not to one particular city)? Indeed, why reintroduce the topic of nomenclature at all?

More likely – as Andrea Nightingale has proposed[32] – is that the participle ἐπικαλουμένην (*epikaloumenên*) is intended here in its more common middle voice usage, 'calling in aid'. The Athenian's suggestion at this juncture will then be that the pull exercised by reasoning will *call in aid* law as something common to the city, indeed precisely as 'the common enactment of a city' with which law as calculation was initially identified at 644d.[33] There will be real fresh bite now to 'common': the individual need not rely solely on his own ratiocination but can draw on a common resource, which will then be the finest influence pulling within his deliberations. The point of introducing 'law' as a term a few lines earlier, as a city's enactment of calculation, now becomes evident; and we have avoided the redundancy involved in the standard translation's repetition of its naming.

Plato evidently sees the need for a supplementary comment at this juncture. With law, the Athenian next says, we must always cooperate. I take it that he means we must each of us do so: the law needs a citizen's active compliance if it is to be not merely 'finest', but also effective as 'guidance' (ἀγωγή (*agôgê*) in the other sense of the word, as at 2.659d) for that individual's reasonings. Otherwise much of the point of calling law in aid – or as 'the ally (σύμμαχος) of all those in the city' (*Rep.* 9.590e) – will be lost. It is that concern with effectiveness which the Athenian makes explicit by adding in explanation that the golden pull of calculation, fine as it is, is gentle and non-violent, so needs us as helpers (ὑπηρετῶν) if it is to overcome the other pulls on a person's mind.

Plato's writing at this point is extremely compressed, which is no doubt a main reason why he has – as I see it – been misread (another being that the political dimensions of the passage have not been thought about hard enough). Compression of this nature, not always but sometimes, is a notable characteristic of the prose of the *Laws*. I want to suggest that for elucidation we can get help from the *Republic* and the *Statesman*. Readers of the *Republic* will recall the treatment of psychological conflict presented in Book 10 of that dialogue, where he has Socrates repair what he represents as an

---

[32] Nightingale 1999: 104, with n. 13, where she observes: 'In general, the verb ἐπικαλεῖν means "take as a surname or nickname" when it is used in the passive; in the middle it means "call in as a helper or ally".'

[33] My thanks to René Brouwer for this observation.

omission in the initial discussion of the topic in Book 4.[34] I reproduce the relevant part of the passage in question (603e–604d):

> 'When a good and reasonable man', said I, 'experiences such a stroke of fortune as the loss of a son or anything else that he holds most dear, we said, I believe, then too, that he will bear it more easily than the other sort.'
> 'Assuredly.'
> 'But now let us consider this: Will he feel no pain, or, since that is impossible, shall we say that he will in some sort be moderate in his grief [λύπην]?'
> 'That', he said, 'is rather the truth.'
> 'Tell me now this about him: Do you think he will be more likely to resist [ἀντιτείνειν] and fight against his grief when he is observed by his equals or when he is in solitude alone by himself?'
> 'He will be much more restrained', he said, 'when he is on view.'
> 'But when left alone, I fancy, he will permit himself many utterances which, if heard by another, would put him to shame, and will do many things which he would not consent to have another see him doing.'
> 'So it is', he said.
> 'Now is it not reason and law [λόγος καὶ νόμος] that exhorts him to resist [ἀντιτείνειν], while that which urges [or pulls: ἕλκον] him to give way to his grief [λύπας] is the bare feeling itself [αὐτὸ τὸ πάθος]?'
> 'True.'
> 'And where there are two opposite impulses [ἀγωγῆς] in a man at the same time about the same thing we say that there must needs be two things in him.'
> 'Of course.'
> 'And is not the one prepared to follow the guidance of the law as the law leads and directs?'
> 'How so?'
> 'The law, I suppose, declares that it is best [κάλλιστον] to keep quiet as far as possible in calamity and not to chafe and repine, because we cannot know what is really good and evil in such things and it advantages us nothing to take them hard, and nothing in mortal life is worthy of great concern, and our grieving checks the very thing we need to come to our aid as quickly as possible in such case.'
> 'What thing', he said, 'do you mean?'
> 'To deliberate [βουλεύεσθαι]', I said, 'about what has happened to us, and, as it were in the fall of the dice, to determine the movements of our affairs with reference to the numbers that turn up, in the way that reason indicates would be the best, and, instead of stumbling like children,

---

[34] I refer to *Rep.* 10.602c–606d. This passage has received much discussion in recent years: see for example Lorenz 2006: 59–73; Singpurwalla 2011; and Shields 2014, which includes a fairly extensive bibliography. But I have not discovered any treatment that approaches the material with the particular focus I shall be adopting.

clapping one's hands to the stricken spot and wasting the time in wailing, ever to accustom the soul to devote itself at once to the curing of the hurt and the raising up of what has fallen, banishing threnody by therapy.'[35]

'That certainly', he said, 'would be the best way to face misfortune and deal with it.'

'Then, we say, the best part of us is willing to conform to these precepts of reason [τούτῳ τῷ λογισμῷ ἐθέλει ἕπεσθαι].'

'Obviously.'

'And shall we not say that the part of us that leads us to dwell in memory on our suffering and impels us to lamentation, and cannot get enough of that sort of thing, is the irrational and idle part of us, the associate of cowardice?'

'Yes, we will say that.'

At one point, Shorey, whose translation this is,[36] has a footnote referring to the *Laws* passage we are primarily concerned with. But the close parallels in language and thought throughout are striking, and I might add that the stress Socrates here puts on shame is something echoed in the immediate sequel to our *Laws* passage, as a fear of public disgrace to which the lawgiver will attach high importance (646e–647b). One thing absolutely clear is that in this *Republic* text, too (cf. also *Rep.* 9.590c–591a), reason or reasoning and law are treated as having a common voice, with the two elements intimately related – but not assimilated to each other, no more than is the case (on my account) in the *Laws*. What the *Republic* passage communicates particularly interestingly and importantly is a degree of clarification about just how law and reasoning relate to each other.

It brings out the way law presents to the mind ready-made, as it were, reflections pertinent to feelings which may be getting out of control: reflections not unlike those the *Laws* might make use of in one of its persuasive legislative preambles expressing the 'common enactment' of reasoning. Needless to say, this is a highly idealized conception of law. But the *Republic* passage also emphasizes our need to get ourselves in a frame of mind when we can actually do what we need to engage in as quickly as possible: deliberation – our own reasoning or calculation (λογισμός again) – about what in practice we should do to remedy our suffering. Thus, calculation or rational deliberation on our own account, here as in the *Laws*, is what we end up being enjoined to follow, with law invoked as the weighty authority endorsing its credentials and setting a framework in which it ought to operate.

---

[35] The alliteration of 'banishing threnody by therapy' is Shorey's, not Plato's. The Greek reads: ἰατρικῇ θρηνῳδίαν ἀφανίζοντα, 'through medicine making lamentation vanish'.

[36] Cited from Shorey 1935.

Joshua Wilburn, who does treat law and reasoning as assimilated in the *Laws* passage, takes it accordingly that the string of calculation 'represents the collective pull of all the correct laws and principles' as promoting the individual's good – but not deliberation about specific actions we should perform in the light of this. That, he thinks, is the thing for which our assistance as helpers is needed.[37] As will by now be clear, I reject his premise, in light of the translation of ἐπικαλουμένην for which I have argued: reasoning is not assimilated to law. And Wilburn's conclusion – that the 'calculation' associated with the golden pull is not focused on specific actions – is hard to sustain in light of the parallel treatment of deliberation in the *Republic* text. There the focus is clearly on deliberating about how to deal practically with some particular 'stroke of fortune'. Our assistance as helpers, as the *Laws* passage puts it, is best understood, accordingly, as what is required to ensure that we actually act upon that rational deliberation, not succumbing to 'bare feeling'.

Reading the marionette passage in the light of this extract from Book 10 of the *Republic* reinforces some other things I have already suggested about the notion of reasoning that the Athenian associates with the string with the golden pull. First, if we reflect on the example Socrates gives of the grief someone feels at the loss of a son, then certainly the deliberation in question makes pain the focus of its attention. But the range of considerations he expects it to take into account, like those identified as concerns of the law within whose framework he sees it as operating, are articulated in terms that do not sound much like those the *Protagoras* employs in presenting the hedonistic calculus. Second, the detail the *Republic* supplies about law and deliberation as they need to be brought to bear on our emotions and feelings brings out something else in the notion of reasoning or calculation or deliberation in play in the *Laws* too. This is not ratiocination conceived in ethically neutral terms, but the reasoning of wise understanding. The same must be true of the *Laws*: otherwise its talk of a 'golden and sacred' pull would be out of place. As Christopher Rowe observes to me, both these two points are further reinforced by the moral psychology indicated in the closing pages of the *Statesman*. There, the job of the statesman and legislator in developing virtue in citizens is said to need to begin in the following way (*Plt.* 309c, in Rowe's translation):[38]

> First, by fitting together that part of their soul that is eternal with a divine bond, in accordance with its kinship with the divine, and after the divine, in turn fitting together their mortal aspect with human bonds.

---

[37] Wilburn 2012: 32–7. [38] Cited from Rowe 1995.

In response to a request for clarification he continues (ibid.):

> I call divine, when it comes to souls, that opinion about what is fine, just and good, and the opposites of these, which is really true and is guaranteed; it belongs to the class of the more than merely human.

A third point of comparison is also worth emphasizing. In the *Republic* 10 passage, Socrates begins his remarks about law's role in psychological conflict by suggesting that reason 'is prepared to follow the guidance of the law as the law leads and directs (ἐξηγεῖται)'. 'Follow the guidance' is Shorey's rendering here of πείθεσθαι, which would more literally translate as 'be persuaded'. And as we have just noted, the guidance Socrates then illustrates by way of explanation proves to be a matter of broad reflections on human life, very much in the vein of some of the persuasive preambles that are theorized, illustrated, and frequently prefaced to particular laws proposed in the *Laws* by the Athenian Visitor. So the emphasis is on the persuasion law offers as authoritative guidance. This reinforces the view that in the *Laws* the pull (ἀγωγή, *agôgê*) of law called in aid of the 'gentle and non-violent' golden pull of calculation is not the force of threat or coercion, but reasonable and thoughtful guidance (ἀγωγή) validated by its authority as the communal voice of the entire city and accepted and indeed implemented by us as its helpers or servants.

Further support for this interpretation comes in the next book of the *Laws* itself. In the course of its further exploration of education for virtue, Book 2 supplies a succinct reprise of the conception of virtue that is emerging ('for the third or fourth time' the discussion has now reached the same point, we are told), incorporating reference to the pull of law on which the marionette's golden string relies, and to its expression of the voice of the community – and making it clear enough that the accent is not on coercion (659d): 'Education is the process of attracting and guiding (ὁλκή τε καὶ ἀγωγή) children towards correct reason, as defined by the law (τὸν ὑπὸ τοῦ νόμου λόγον ὀρθὸν εἰρημένον), and ratified – as genuinely correct – by the experience of those who are most advanced in age and moral qualities.'

Conclusion

Following his exposition of the μῦθος (*muthos*) of the marionette, the Athenian Visitor sums up as follows (645b–c):

> In this way our story of human goodness, about us being puppets, would turn out to have achieved its effect, and the meaning of being 'more than a match for himself' or 'less than a match for himself'

would become somewhat clearer, and the city and the individual – well, the individual needs to take the story of the pull of the puppet-strings to heart, as something true, and follow it in his life; and the city, receiving the story from one of the gods, or from this individual with knowledge of these things, should make it into a law for itself and other cities to live by. In this way, the distinction between badness and goodness, we would find, would be more clearly articulated.

Precisely what the implications are for understanding self-rule or the failure to exercise it, and why they are what they are, are not spelled out. But key to the Athenian's claim to have made the matter clearer must be an assumption about the relation between calculation and the self. Calculation or rational deliberation is not a force pulling at us like pleasure or pain. Its pull is the pull of persuasion, 'gentle and non-violent' – or rather the self-persuasion of reflection. If the 'I' assists it to prevail, then a person 'prevails over himself' or 'is a match for himself'.

At this point a pressing question about the notion of 'self' in play is unavoidable. Is Plato envisaging a division within the human individual between a higher, rational, active self and a lower, feeling, passive self? I suggest that this is a case of the dog that did not bark. We have considered some salient similarities between the marionette passage of the *Laws* and a similar treatment of the roles of reason and law in dealing with pain and grief in Book 10 of the *Republic*. Here is a striking difference between them. The marionette passage contrasts simply the different pulls to which we feel ourselves subject. It does not articulate any inferences to different parts of our nature or different elements within us. When the Athenian speaks of the factors he identifies and the pulls they exert upon us as 'within oneself' or 'within us' (644c, e, 645a), he does not invest the identification of what is 'in' with any contestable ontological assumptions. From separate pulls or impulses, however, Socrates in the *Republic* had argued for separate things (604b):

> 'And where there are two opposite impulses [ἀγωγῆς] in a man at the same time about the same thing we say that there must needs be two things in him.'[39]
> 'Of course.'

---

[39] Note however that, while the final 'in him' in Shorey's translation is not there in the Greek, he was no doubt right in thinking it implicit. So also with 'part of us' (or some similar expression) in the next extract.

These were then identified as something better and something worse, the one leading us to follow reasoning, the other to lamentation (604d):

> 'Then, we say, the best part of us is willing to conform to these precepts of reason [τούτῳ τῷ λογισμῷ ἐθέλει ἕπεσθαι].'
> 'Obviously.'
> 'And shall we not say that the part of us that leads us [ἄγον] to dwell in memory on our suffering and impels us to lamentation, and cannot get enough of that sort of thing, is the irrational and idle part of us, the associate of cowardice?'
> 'Yes, we will say that.'

Quite what Plato's Socrates might be committing himself to, in making the inferences from impulses to psychological elements of some presumably different kind, is a fiercely disputed issue (usually discussed primarily in connection with the more elaborate argument for parts or elements in the soul in Book 4). But whatever stance one might take on that question, it cannot reasonably be doubted that he makes those inferences – and thereby posits opposed items within the mind over and above the existence of the impulses that prompt the positing. It must surely then be significant that the marionette passage avoids making any comparable inference. No further psychological elements are assumed, other than the impulses or pulls associated with talk of the different kinds of strings: bronze, iron, golden. And in contrast with the *Republic* passage, the Athenian lays stress on what 'each of us' (ἕκαστον: 644e) or the 'individual' (ἰδιώτην: 645b) must do. So it looks as though we should dismiss any thought that the Athenian's talk of 'prevailing over' and 'being overpowered by' oneself is meant to imply any distinction between a higher and a lower self. The assumption made so prominently at the very start of the initial sketch of the soul – that 'each of us is a single entity' (644c) – created a presumption against any such distinction. The avoidance of the kind of inference made by Socrates in the *Republic* confirms the presumption.

How in that case is the marionette image supposed to have made 'the meaning of being "more than a match for himself" or "less than a match for himself"' somewhat clearer'? If my reading of the passage is on the right lines, there are two related strands to an answer. First, the Athenian is effectively deflating or rendering ontologically harmless our propensity to talk in those terms. We are not to take talk of this kind as committing us to any such notion as the idea that in one case the higher self inflicts defeat on the lower, in the other it is defeated by it.[40] Second, a more ontologically parsimonious and perfectly coherent way to read these expressions is indicated. An individual who prevails over, or is more than a match for, himself is simply someone who translates into action the deliberation that he has himself engaged in (represented by the pull of the golden string). Conversely, the person who is no match for himself is one who fails to resist where appropriate the pull of the pleasures or pains (represented by the other strings) that he feels.[41]

These morals are implicit, not spelled out by Plato. We may suppose that they escape Cleinias and Megillus pretty much entirely. But Plato's practised reader, recalling the *Republic*, will take the point.[42] That point is not, I suggest, the one that Christopher Bobonich argued at length in *Plato's Utopia Recast*, where Plato was interpreted as simply abandoning the division of the soul into agent-like parts or elements, in the interests of a more unified psychology that would better guarantee that each of us really is conceptualized as a 'single entity'.[43] In the first instance, it is rather that for the purposes of the project he is engaged on in the *Laws*, of explaining the challenge a programme of education for virtue must tackle, what matters is to stress the responsibility we as 'single entities' have for our choices and our lives. And for that no highly theoretical analysis of the human soul is needed.

At the same time, Plato's tacit defusing of the language of 'more than a match for himself' and 'less than a match for himself' does seem to have its place within a different kind of theoretical agenda. As Susan Sauvé Meyer well explains in her commentary, Books 1 and 2 of the *Laws* identify two paradigms of virtue: what she calls the 'victory' and the 'agreement' models.[44] The idea that virtue is a matter of victory over oneself was introduced at the beginning of the dialogue by Cleinias (626e) and reflects the preoccupation with victory in war as the proper goal of legislation that

---

[40] So far as I can find, there is no further similar use of expressions such as 'self-ruling' or 'prevailing over oneself' in the *Laws*. (Meyer 2015: 170, notes an instance with a different force at 2.671b.) Elsewhere, Plato resorts to other vocabulary to deal with the phenomenon here identified in such terms. Wilburn 2012: 26 n. 3 supplies a useful summary of the relevant terminology; cf. also Meyer 2015: 168–71.

[41] Interestingly, the Athenian speaks of being 'no match for' pleasure or anger when he talks in that vein in Book 9 (9.863d, 869e), as earlier at e.g. 1. 633e.

[42] For the notion of the practised reader of the *Laws*, see Chapter 9 above, pp. 193–8.

[43] See Bobonich 2002 (especially with reference to the marionette: pp. 261–2).

[44] Christopher Gill suggests to me a comparison with Christine Korsgaard's distinction between a 'combat' model of the soul and the 'constitutional' model she finds in the *Republic* (Korsgaard 2009: 133–58).

Plato diagnoses as characteristic of the Cretan and Spartan mentality (625c–626c). But his Athenian will move at the end of Book 1 and through Book 2 towards development of a view of education for virtue that sets the premium on achieving consonance between our feelings of pleasure and pain and what reason would judge that they should love or hate (2.653b–c).[45] In our present passage, it already transpires that the 'winning' Cleinias talked of, and the 'self-rule' the marionette image is introduced to elucidate, occur not because calculation somehow acquires more force of the same kind as the iron pulls of our feelings, but because it changes the rules of the game – so that the language of victory is in effect in the process of being rendered obsolete.[46] Calculation exercises a different kind of power: persuasion. Or rather, we persuade ourselves. And with effective persuasion comes decision by the 'single entity' that each of us is.

APPENDIX: FEAR AND CONFIDENCE

'Fear' as Expectation of Pain, 'Confidence' as Expectation of the Opposite

The specification of fear and confidence as species of expectation is something of a recurrence to the analysis of courage in the earlier dialogues *Laches* and *Protagoras*. In the *Laches*, Socrates and Nicias reach a point where courage is characterized as 'knowledge of what induces fear and confidence', in the light of their agreement that such things can be identified as 'future goods and future evils' (*Lach*. 198b–199b). What does the Athenian mean by 'fear' here? In the sequel, it will transpire that, in order to understand how courage can confront pleasure as well as pain, he gets us to broaden our grasp of the range of prospects that are proper objects of fear.

Thus we fear not merely bad things we anticipate happening to us, but the prospect of being badly thought of if we do something that is not right: this is not terror but shame (646e–647c). Shame is treated as opposed not just to pain and fears of the other sort (shame makes one fear being seen to

---

[45] Meyer 2015: 161–3.
[46] My interpretation follows that offered by Annas 1999: 143–4. Meyer 2015: 181–2 objects that to see the victory model as being deconstructed here is to anticipate the next instalment of the agenda: the education of feeling and emotion (645c). But calculation's job of 'deciding which of them [pain, pleasure, etc.] is better or worse', as noted above (p. 256), does not point to opposition or struggle. And Annas explicitly distinguishes between reasoning's judgement of struggles between pleasure and pain, from which it maintains independence (the immediate concern of the marionette passage), and their being led and manipulated by or in accordance with reasoning (not its concern).

give into them), but to 'the most numerous and powerful pleasures' (surrendering to them, too, induces shame) – and therefore to the confidence or boldness that results in shamelessness. So in effect it is courage that is here presented as doing the job of moderation or self-control, since handling fear is the job of courage.[47] Moreover, confidence, paired in our present passage with fear, is very much an emotion associated like it with courage, not moderation, as is clear from (for example) the final section of the *Protagoras* or from Aristotle's discussion in the *Nicomachean Ethics*.

The Athenian calls fear and confidence 'expectations' and identifies expectations as 'opinions about what is going to happen'. As William Fortenbaugh pointed out years ago, the stress is on the thought-like properties of fear and confidence: their incorporation of propositional attitudes.[48] The reason for that should already be clear. If both terror and shame are forms of fear, the obvious way to indicate the way they differ is by talking of their different objects. And that requires an understanding of fear as an intentional mental state incorporating propositional attitudes.[49] I therefore follow Griffith in translating θάρρος, *tharros*, as 'confidence' here. Sauvé Meyer opts for 'daring', Pangle for 'boldness'. But the Athenian is treating θάρρος as a species of opinion. 'Confident' is an expression that can be used to convey the kind of propositional attitude – 'confident that so and so' – which is needed to make an opinion an opinion. 'Bold' and 'daring' are not.[50]

---

[47] For the most part σωφροσύνη (*sôphrosunê*, 'moderation' or 'self-control') or etymologically related vocabulary is not employed. It is reintroduced just twice, towards the end of a discussion couched otherwise in very different vocabulary (647d, 648e). Meyer's commentary does not sufficiently bring out the way that in the latter part of Book 1 the Athenian makes courage do the work of what he does initially call moderation (σωφροσύνη: 635e). Wilburn 2012: 28 n. 4 provides an excellent brief treatment of Plato's strategy.

[48] Fortenbaugh 1975: 24–5.

[49] Of course, the Athenian's initial emphasis on the thought-like properties of the psychic elements he lists does not imply that he does not also conceive them as feelings or impulses. Fear and confidence could hardly count as fear or confidence if they were not so viewed. And throughout the *Laws*, pleasure and pain are treated as such. To give just one of countless examples, a passage in Book 5 discussed above (pp. 261–2) speaks of 'the very great forms of urgency (σπουδαί) exercised by pleasures, pains, and appetites' (5.732e). Dorothea Frede, commenting on the Book 1 list, suggests that only expectations provide 'incentives to *act* in one way or another, while affections concerning the present and past do not' (Frede 2010: 117). Leaving aside the point that 'pleasure and pain' may be meant here to embrace passions and desires (cf. 645d), as Frede herself recognizes (Frede 2010: 119–20), this claim is unfortunately just false. If I have an immediate acute and persistent pain in my side, I have the most urgent conceivable incentive to seek immediate medical attention. Which should remind us that pleasure and pain may be mindless and inarticulate as advisers (as their description in the *Laws* list puts it), but the advice, even if it comes in the form of a bare imperative, may nonetheless sometimes be sound.

[50] To be sure, in subsequent sections of argument the interest is in the behaviour that will flow from the state of mind as well as in that state of mind itself. It must be significant, however, that in

The proposal that confidence is expectation of the 'opposite' of pain is I think not to be understood as equivalent to the assertion that it is expectation of pleasure.[51] In the sequel, the main focus is on fear and the different forms it takes. When the Athenian there reintroduces treatment of confidence, he talks of it as fear*lessness*, that is, the opposite of fear as its negation. He identifies two varieties corresponding to fear as terror and fear as shame: shamelessness, considered a very great evil by the legislator he imagines; and fearlessness in the face of danger, such as is required for victory in military conflict (647a–c). Presumably, the expectation at stake in confidence so conceived would have to be the thought that one will not experience pain, or not pain sufficient to deter one. The shameless person will be confident that no disapproval he will attract will much trouble him; the brave that whatever pain he might suffer will not outweigh the value of the action he proposes to take.

The treatment of confidence in terms of fearlessness is apparent again on the last page or so of Book 1, when the Athenian puts the following question to the lawgiver (649a):

> For fear there is, broadly speaking, no such medicine [i.e. a fear-inducing drug], neither given by god to humans nor one we have devised ourselves – but for fearlessness, overconfidence or misplaced confidence, is there a potion for that?

Here 'fearlessness' is again the term used in contrast with 'fear'. At this point in the conversation, the overall question being tackled is whether there is any device that will make people 'afraid of daring to say, undergo, or do anything shameful at all' (649d) and test whether they have become so in situations 'where naturally we are all particularly confident and bold' (649c).

---

a passage at 649c Plato writes θαρράλεοι τ' ... καὶ θράσεις. We should not take this as mere redundant repetition. Plato wants to refer to *both* the state of mind *and* the behaviour ('confident and bold'), as is indicated by the contrast he then makes with ἀναισχύντους τε καὶ θρασύτητος γέμοντας, 'both shameless and full of effrontery' (or as LSJ renders it – following Aristotle in the *Rhetoric* – 'over-boldness').

[51] As is often supposed, e.g., by Stalley 1983: 60–1; Bobonich 2010: 151. Meyer 2012 also accepts the supposition, while recognizing difficulties in it. But she works out a solution that ends up giving an unlikely account of Plato's understanding of the expectation in question. Meyer 2015 appears to have abandoned the supposition.

CHAPTER 14

Paradoxes of Childhood and Play in Heraclitus and Plato

In 1938, the Dutch cultural historian Johan Huizinga, author most famously of *The Waning of the Middle Ages* (1919), published a more theoretical work entitled *Homo Ludens*. In this book, which proved to be his last, he proposed the thesis that in application of the concept of play lies the route to understanding not only children's games and the place of sport in the lives of adults, but all of what he regarded as the higher forms of culture, from philosophy, poetry, and the arts to the conduct of war (at any rate until the invention of total war), the law, and above all religion and religious ritual. In his first chapter, 'Nature and significance of play as a cultural phenomenon', we find him describing what he understands by play in general terms, as follows:[1]

> Summing up the formal characteristics of play, we might call it a free activity standing quite consciously outside 'ordinary' life as being not 'serious', but at the same time absorbing the player intensely and utterly.

Huizinga's summary continues, and I shall shortly be quoting a further sentence from it. But for the moment I want to pause over his contrast between the ordinary and the serious.

'Ordinary' and 'serious' here are in scare quotes, because Huizinga has already made quite a bit of the point that 'the contrast between play and seriousness' is always fluid. He had elaborated it as follows:[2]

> The inferiority of play is continually being offset by the corresponding superiority of its seriousness. Play turns to seriousness and seriousness to play. Play may rise to heights of beauty and sublimity that leave seriousness far beneath.

---

[1] Huizinga 1949: 13. I cite this book in the first published edition of the English translation, which was prepared from two sources: the German translation of the Dutch original of 1944 and an English version of the original made by Huizinga himself.
[2] Huizinga 1949: 8.

No name figures more frequently in the index to *Homo Ludens* than Plato's. And its first Plato quotation is from a passage in Book 7 of Plato's *Laws* to which I shall be turning at the end of this chapter, a passage precisely preoccupied with seriousness, play, and ritual, or what Huizinga calls 'the *sacra*'. Many strands of learning and reflection over a lifetime clearly fed into Huizinga's notion of play and his theorizing about it. But in Plato he had found a kindred spirit, and it is to Plato and to Book 7 of the *Laws* that he returns again in the last couple of pages of his own book, where we also get a reference to Heraclitus.

Huizinga quotes there Iamblichus' remark that according to Heraclitus, human opinions were 'child's play'.[3] The Greek is παίδων ἀθύρματα, *paidôn athurmata* (Fr. 70), perhaps better rendered 'children's playthings'.[4] So far as I can find, however, that was his only reference to Heraclitus. That is a bit surprising, given that the continuation of his short summary account of what play is includes the statement:[5] 'It proceeds within its own proper boundaries of time and space according to fixed rules and in an orderly manner.' Afficionados of Heraclitus would at this point remember Fr. 52: αἰὼν παῖς ἐστι παίζων, πεσσεύων· παιδὸς ἡ βασιληίη, 'A life lived through is a child playing, moving the pieces: a child's is the kingship.' The commentators point out that the word πεσσεύων indicates a board game resembling draughts or backgammon, with highly determinate rules: just the sort of quotation that might have been grist to Huizinga's mill. What fascinated Huizinga about play and its cultural significance as a paradigm of order and intense seriousness was precisely what intrigued Heraclitus in this saying, and Plato, too.

The importance of childhood and play in Heraclitus' thought must already have been recognized in antiquity, since it gets converted into an anecdote about his lifestyle in the biographical tradition. Diogenes Laertius's Heraclitus section retails this story (D. L. 9.3):

> He would withdraw to the temple of Artemis and play at knucklebones with the boys; and when the Ephesians came and stood round, 'Why, you rascals', he said, 'are you so amazed? Isn't doing this better than engaging along with you people in the public life of the city [πολιτεύεσθαι; perhaps more dismissively still, "in politics"]?'

We have surviving to us quite a number of sayings about children that are thought to be authentically Heraclitean. All of them in one way or another

---

[3] Huizinga 1949: 211. [4] On ἀθύρματα (*athurmata*), see Kidd 2019: 97–121.
[5] Huizinga 1949: 13.

exploit opposition of childhood to the life of adults in the same kind of way as does the knucklebones anecdote. Children show up the inadequacies of adults – 'the many' (Fr. 2, 29), 'the rest of humanity' (Fr. 1). It is often suggested in remarks on Heraclitus' treatment of childhood that he takes what is sometimes referred to as the 'deficit' view of the child: the Aristotelian assumption that the main thing to grasp about a child is what it is not – a creature that has not yet reached the age of reason – rather than what it is and what it *can* do. Such an interpretation has only to be voiced for its remarkably one-dimensional and therefore unHeraclitean cast to impress itself upon one. Heraclitus does indeed exploit the 'deficit' assumption, if not explicitly then as a subtext, in all his childhood sayings. But the assumption as he handles it serves only to point up the opposite and unexpected moral: children are often wiser and cleverer than adults.

Nowhere is this agenda more up front than in Fr. 79 (from Origen): ἀνὴρ νήπιος ἤκουσε πρὸς δαίμονος ὅκωσπερ παῖς πρὸς ἀνδρός, 'The man is called infantile by his guardian spirit, just as the child is by the man.' Heraclitus is not here *endorsing* the view that children *are* infantile, silly, child*ish*, although he is not contradicting it either. His point is that grown men often talk as though that is the case, but from another perspective – that of his guardian spirit – it is the grown man himself who is regarded as infantile, and with no less reason. Δαίμονος (*daimonos*) here is usually translated 'divinity' or the like. But when Heraclitus wants to talk of divinity, he speaks of θέος (*theos*), 'god', or τὸ θεῖον (*to theion*), 'the divine'. I think that, as often with Plato's references to δαίμονες (*daimones*), a famous passage of Hesiod's *Works and Days* helps to shape his usage: the lines in which the poet says of the men of the golden age that when they die, they are called δαίμονες, and considered φύλακες (*phylakes*), 'guardians', of mortal men (*Op.* 121–2), echoed by Heraclitus in Fr. 63. In Fr. 119, we get a demythologized, rationalized version of the idea of a δαίμων (*daimôn*) as guardian spirit: ἦθος ἀνθρώπῳ δαίμων, 'His character is a human's *daimôn*'. The implication of Fr. 79 is not just that we humans have available to us the protection of a guardian spirit, but that because of our failure to use our intelligence as we should, we *need* such protection, just as much the children we regard as infantile are in need of it.

Something very similar to that implication is the point we are meant to take away from Heraclitus' saying on drunkenness, Fr. 117 (from Stobaeus):

ἀνὴρ ὁκόταν μεθυσθῆι ἄγεται ὑπὸ παιδὸς ἀνήβου, σφαλλόμενος, οὐκ ἐπαίων ὅκη βαίνει, ὑγρὴν τὴν ψυχὴν ἔχων.

> A man when he is drunk is guided by a beardless boy: stumbling, not knowing where he is stepping, with his soul drenched.

In the iconography of Greek vases, a child never leads an adult man by the hand. Ordinarily, it is men who are doing the leading, of old men, women, and children. The role reversal of Fr. 117 signifies the reversal of our normal expectations that grown men will be more intelligent, prudent, in control of their behaviour than children. But the boy is now the superior intelligence, more alert, more sensible, more in control. Heraclitus likes to heap the unexpected on the unexpected. And there is a fresh twist in the final clause. The drunk's physical system is drenched, to be sure. But what is said here to take the drenching is the soul: the seat of intelligence and rational control over behaviour. For Heraclitus, there could be no final opposition between mental and physical. It is as though he were saying: if none of my other sayings on the soul convinced you of its essentially physical identity, just look at my drunk – he is the clincher.

In the next fragment we consider, there are several more layers of paradoxical complexity than we have been confronted with so far. I shall have to cut a lot of corners. Fr. 56 goes like this:

> People are thoroughly deceived, he says, when it comes to recognition of what is obvious – like Homer, who was wiser than all the Greeks. For it was him that 'boys who were killing lice thoroughly deceived, when they said: "What we see and catch, we leave behind; what we neither see nor catch, we carry away"'.

These lines occur in Bishop Hippolytus' sequence of quotations from Heraclitus. First, I take it, comes his own summary of the point Heraclitus was making, in reproducing a well-known incident in ancient story telling about the life of Homer. It was him, as Heraclitus put it (Hippolytus now quotes verbatim, I suppose), that 'boys who were killing lice thoroughly deceived, when they said: "What we see and catch, we leave behind; what we neither see nor catch, we carry away"'. The moral Heraclitus draws (according to Hippolytus) is that the wise Homer's celebrated bafflement is symptomatic of how quite generally people grasp the wrong end of the stick (or fail to grasp the right end) when it comes to understanding what is obvious.

Homer is in the intellectual plight he is in for two particular reasons, which are not made explicit, but which are presumably taken by Heraclitus to be salient, because known to everybody who might be reading or listening to him. The boys had been fishing, so Homer comes to interpretation of the catch they refer to with already formed but quite mistaken expectations; and he is blind, so cannot *see* what would be evident to other observers: that they are picking lice out of their hair. So he is quite unable to connect his exceptional wisdom and intelligence with what to those who use the relevant sense of sight would be obvious. What Heraclitus wants us to extract from his situation, I am supposing, is the moral: people in general are as good as blind, and as misled by false expectations, as was Homer, when it comes to using their minds to interpret what their senses are telling them.

And what of the children who catch Homer out? Their very articulation of the riddle shows that they *are* aware that the obvious may not be obvious, and that what is not obvious may be obvious. The trickiness of the negotiations of the mind with the senses is not lost on them. So once again we have children more alert and more in control than adults: in this specific case, and for very particular reasons, Homer, but more generally because – well, Heraclitus of course does not tell us why, but perhaps he recognizes that children's minds may be sharper and more open because not dulled by habit.

Childhood is nowhere more ambitiously characterized than in what Charles Kahn, in his edition and commentary, rightly described as the 'most enigmatic of Heraclitean riddles':[6] the αἰών saying (Fr. 52, again from Hippolytus) that I have already referred to. It looks as though that is what the ancients thought, too. Here is Heraclitus' sales pitch in Lucian's *Sale of Lives* (of philosophers and their recommendations). When asked by the potential buyer why he is weeping, he replies with a wonderful concoction of Heraclitean echoes (*Sale of Lives* 14):

> Because, my friend, I consider that the human condition is woeful and a matter for tears, and there is nothing in it that is not grimly fated. So I pity and bewail them. Their present difficulties I do not consider great, but those to come in future will be completely devastating: I mean the ultimate conflagrations and the collapse of the universe. That is what I bewail, and because nothing is stable, but everything compressed into a porridge, and joy and joylessness, knowledge and ignorance, big and little the same in identity, rotating up and down and interchanging in the play of αἰών [*aiôn*].
> And what is *aiôn*?
> A child playing, moving the pieces, in discord, in concord.

After a little more of this sort of thing the buyer concludes that with riddles and conundrums like these, he might just as well be consulting the Delphic oracle.

---

[6] Kahn 1979: 227.

By Lucian's time, αἰών had come to carry the regular connotation of eternity, as in Plato or Aristotle. But in early Greek literature, it refers to human life, especially its vitality and dynamism, and often also its duration. I have rendered its occurrence in Fr. 52 as 'a life lived through', but 'the vitality of a life lived through' might capture more of the appropriate associations. So Heraclitus' proposal is that we can understand the dynamism that propels and sustains us through life if we picture it – I take it playfully – as a child at play: παίζων (*paizôn*), which is of course an etymological play on παῖς (*pais*), and could be rendered 'to do child' – to do the thing a child does, to live out what a child is. But then παίζων (*paizôn*) is itself glossed as πεσσεύων (*pesseuôn*). Πεσσεύων (*pesseuôn*) sounds just a bit like παίζων (*paizôn*), but the point is that it's very different. The game of πέσσοι (*pessoi*) was a form of board game played with counters (pebbles), which seems to have taken several variant forms, and was probably (as I have already remarked) fairly close to draughts or backgammon. It involved the throwing of dice, but it is thought that that was the only element of chance in an otherwise rule-governed game. Not least it was typically *not* played by children, but as backgammon has been in modern Greece by adult men, often older men. Children, by contrast, as well as aristocrats at a symposium, would play ἀστράγαλοι (*astragaloi*), knucklebones, as in the story of Heraclitus' withdrawal to the temple of Artemis in Ephesus: a simpler game predominantly of chance.[7]

παῖς παίζων πεσσεύων (*pais paizôn pesseuôn*) therefore implies – as so often in Heraclitus – a conjunction of opposites.[8] We have a child playing, presumably with all the spontaneity you might expect of a child, like the boy in Homer building sandcastles as ἀθύρματα (*athurmata*, playthings) and then knocking them down (*Iliad* 15.362-4).[9] But in the case of Heraclitus' child, that disorderly spontaneity has to be seen as the same thing as the planning of moves like those of the adult backgammon player. *That* is how we plan and sustain the moves that constitute our lives: by childish spontaneity. We might think that as adults we could do better than that, but in truth things are otherwise, as the concluding element in Heraclitus' saying confirms: 'A child's is the kingship.' 'Kingship' must here be some kind of metaphor. Scholarship has guessed that Heraclitus is trading on its application to command of the controlling piece or (rather

---

[7] On ancient Greek board games, see in general Kurke 1999.
[8] Kahn 1979: 228 agrees, comparing with Fr. 88. But I see little basis for his interpretation of the game as 'a cosmic one'.
[9] See Kidd 2019: 105–6.

more likely) to the decisive move in the game the child is playing.[10] So that final assertion tells us explicitly that it is the child in us controlling the board on which we make our moves in life and throughout our life. Which does not mean that our lives are just an arbitrary mess. The rhythm of that clause suggests quite the opposite. As Karl Deichgräber pointed out many years ago, παιδὸς ἡ βασιληίη (*paidos hê basilêiê*) is metrically a Glyconic, conveying the ordered lightness of a dance, and contrasting with the heavy spondee-dominated vowels of the words that make up the characterization of αἰών (*aiôn*), a life lived through, which has preceded, and that are given particular final emphasis by the three long syllables of πεσσεύων (*pesseuôn*).[11] The strongly diverging rhythms of the prose of the two parts of Heraclitus' saying themselves reinforce the *contradictio in adiecto* already adumbrated in the opening words αἰών παῖς (*aiôn pais*). The overall upshot? Life does have an order, but not at all the kind of order we ordinarily think of as order. It makes a pattern, but a pattern made up of spontaneous moves no one would ever have predicted.

Childhood – the counterpoint of childhood and adulthood – emerges as a theme of major significance in Heraclitus' thought, and children's playing and riddling are introduced in part to help develop that theme. In Plato, it is the idea of play itself, together with the toys, riddles, games, and so forth that are involved in play, which most engages him.[12] Not that play and childhood can easily be kept apart, whether in Plato or anywhere else. And much of what he has to say about play comes from noticing the activity of children with an acute and sympathetic eye. Well, often sympathetic: 'of all wild things', he says at one juncture, 'the child is the most unmanageable' (*Laws* 7.808d). This is because of children's unchannelled power of thinking, which makes them scheming, sly, and extremely insolent. So they need to be fettered – with bridles, as it were. On the other hand, Plato is rather keen on play as the way to get children's minds working on the right lines. He has an eloquent passage on the way the

---

[10] Kurke 1999: 257 n. 28 refers particularly to lines from the early Lyric poet Alcaeus (Fr. 351 v) for evidence of a controlling piece as 'king': but the control language there (ἐπικρέτει, prevails) is verbal, applied not to a piece on the board, but to the move in question, nor does Alcaeus actually speak of a king – for that she has to appeal to a doubtfully relevant and conceivably confused scholium on Theocritus. Bollack and Wismann 1972: 184 cite the king throw (*basilicum*) Curculio claims to have made (in Plautus' comedy of that name: *Curc.* 359 = 2.3.80), a royal flush (as it were), defeating the miserable 'four vultures' thrown by the pimp Cappadox; but that was in a game of chance (*alea*) with knucklebones (*tali*), not a board game. Perhaps the notion of the king move was a generic one, with different forms of realization in different specific types of game.

[11] Deichgräber 1962: 37.

[12] A good brief treatment of the idea of play in Plato is Guthrie 1975: 56–65. A recent monograph, which devotes much attention to Plato, is Kidd 2019.

Egyptians teach children arithmetic and geometry through play of various sorts (with apples or more complicatedly with bowls of gold and silver and bronze), and the way they succeed in making people alert and useful to themselves that way (*Laws* 7.819a–d). And he thinks the right way to develop an aptitude for building or carpentry or indeed any skill is to get children playing with miniature tools or measuring and estimating or whatever is appropriate (*Laws* 1.643b–d).

Let me recommend at this point a short article entitled 'Plato and children's games', published in 1984 by Rosamond Kent Sprague, an American scholar from South Carolina who often used to visit Cambridge in my early years in the Faculty of Classics.[13] Sprague had had a particular Cambridge philosophical hero in the person of Arthur Peck, author of some excellent and still serviceable Loeb editions of Aristotle's biological works. I imagine he is pretty much forgotten now, although one can find a useful brief account of him by Richard Sorabji in Todd's *Dictionary of British Classicists*.[14] In his time, he was quite a Cambridge figure, indeed Cambridge born and bred, and a pupil of W. H. D. Rouse at the Perse School, where eventually he became Chair of Governors. Among other things, he was principal choreographer at the church of Little St Mary's, notable there we are told for his singing of the *Exultet*; founder of the Cambridge Morris Men and for a period Squire of the national Ring; and owner of a fine growing collection of vintage lampposts which graced his keeping room in Christ's College. Peck was Huizinga man.

What interested Rosamond Kent Sprague was Plato's use of children's play and its paraphernalia to illustrate, and make more arresting and memorable for the reader, some of his key philosophical ideas. Take the notably playful *Euthydemus*, a favourite dialogue of hers, and one to which Huizinga devoted a whole appreciative page in his chapter on the importance of the play of sophistry for Greek philosophy, something that was a Peck speciality too. In the *Euthydemus*, the continually frustrated attempt to specify the knowledge that constitutes the art of kingship is compared with the way children run after crested larks (*Euthd.* 291c; while larks were caught for consumption, children's pet birds are as it happens a prominent motif in the iconography of Greek vases). The pages of the *Republic* are particularly dense with images and analogies of many sorts. I will mention a toy, a riddle, and a game.

---

[13] Sprague 1984. See also Kidd 2019: 97–121.   [14] Sorabji 2004.

The toy is the spinning top of Book 4. Plato has Socrates introduce it in service of his argument for the thesis that the soul must have parts, quite distinct and opposed sources of motivation (*Rep.* 4.436c–437a). It illustrates the principle that one and the same thing cannot undergo opposite processes in one and the same respect at one and the same time. You might think that the spinning top was a counter-example, moving while stationary. But no: it is stationary with respect to its pivot, in motion with respect to the periphery. At the end of *Republic* 5, we get the famous argument to the effect that any object of opinion (as opposed to knowledge) is in an ambiguous state of both being and not-being. It will be just as much ugly as it is beautiful, small as much as it is large, and so on. Glaucon comments that this sounds like the children's riddle about a man who wasn't a man hitting with a stone that wasn't a stone a bird that wasn't a bird sitting on a tree that wasn't a tree (*Rep.* 5.479a–d). (We are not given the answer in the text, but at risk of spoiling the fun let me explain that a eunuch hits with a piece of pumice a bat sitting on a reed.) Sprague's prize specimen was the reference to the game of *ostrakinda* in *Republic* 7 (*Rep.* 7.521b–d). Here, Plato's Socrates compares the conversion of the soul through philosophy with the game in which a shell is whirled or spun: like the spinning of a coin to set up play in a football or cricket match. Instead of heads or tails, it was 'night' if the shell fell showing its dark outside, or 'day', if it was its light inner side; and the chance would determine which of two teams or gangs of boys would chase the other. What needs to happen to the soul, Socrates says, is something less intuitively straightforward than flipping the shell. It has to be converted from a day whose light is really intellectual darkness to the true day of what is really there to be understood.

These comparisons share a common feature: they all occur at points of crucial significance for the development of major theories of the dialogue. They tend to be ignored in modern exegetical pedagogy of the philosophy of the *Republic*, except perhaps for the top, more familiar and so more readily intelligible to the contemporary student as well as more deeply embedded in the argument. Plato must have hoped that all of them would through their vividness and homeliness help the reader he envisaged to grasp and fix the philosophical point.

Although Sprague in her article talked quite a bit about the *Laws*, she made only a brief allusion at the very end to its image of the marionette.[15] The comparison of human beings to marionettes is introduced in Book 1 (*Laws* 1.644d–645a), but Plato refers to it once more in an extended passage

---

[15] On which see Chapter 13 above.

of Book 7, which had exercised its fascination on Huizinga, and to which I now want to devote attention. The issue Plato's Athenian Visitor addresses here (*Laws* 7. 803a–804c) is the big question: how – with what mode of living – we are best advised to navigate our journey through life. In response, he develops a pretty compressed and complex argument which plays with the polarity of the serious and the playful and radically destabilizes and recasts both these concepts.[16]

That contrast – playful versus serious – is a favourite Platonic trope, deployed in a variety of contexts. He often categorizes as playful, not serious, activities whose value he wants to call in question: the trick questions of Sophists (*Euthd.* 278b), for example, or mimetic paining and poetry (*Rep.* 10.602b). More challengingly, he can describe as play (mere play) his own writing or practice of philosophy, most notoriously in the *Phaedrus*. There he has Socrates ending with the remark (278b): 'Let us regard our play with the question of λόγοι [speeches, modes of discourse] as appropriately [μετρίως] accomplished'. But there is similar talk in other dialogues. In the *Timaeus* at one point, he makes Timaeus speak of someone, who for the sake of relief puts aside discussion of eternal realities and gets innocent pleasure from a thorough study of reasonable accounts of how things come into existence, as making for themselves a 'form of play appropriate [μέτριον] in life and wisely considered' (*Ti.* 59c–d).[17]

It is only in our passage of Book 7 of the *Laws*, however, that the polarity of play and seriousness is explicitly deconstructed (cf. *Epinom.* 992b). The reader of the dialogue has been given some preparation in earlier books for the shock to be administered there. Back in Book 3, the Athenian had spoken of the discussion of laws as 'an appropriately sober game for old men to be playing' (3.685a), recapitulated in Book 4 as the activity of 'elderly children' (4.712b). But Cleinias makes an interestingly pointed response to a remark by the Visitor in Book 6 about their entire discussion prior to the actual legislation that will occupy the rest of the work (6.769a): 'So far so good, then – in this our intellectual game for the elderly.' Cleinias replies: 'It looks to me as though you are explaining the sort of noble pursuit which men in their prime ought to make their serious occupation.' He gets a non-committal reply in turn ('I dare say'). What is serious and what is playful is already well and truly flagged as an issue.

In the key passage in Book 7 (7. 803a–804c), the contrast between the serious and the playful is set up at the outset and given focus through

---

[16] This topic in the *Laws* is the focus of an entire monograph: Jouët-Pastré 2006.
[17] See further Guthrie 1975: 59–64.

application to a further polarity: the human and divine. The initial moves go like this:

(1) *Human* affairs are not as such worthy of serious engagement – but we humans do need to be serious, in the appropriate (προσήκοντος) way: that would be what is 'commensurate' (σύμμετρον, *symmetron*) for us (as humans).
(2) We have to be serious about god.
(3) We are only something god contrives for play: for his own play, but it will transpire that it is *our* playing that is the play that in this context Plato will be primarily exploring – as our way of being serious. That play, however it is to be envisaged, is said to be the best thing about us.
(4) The conclusion (which follows only if our play is somehow at the same time the relevant play of the gods) is that we 'need to live our whole lives through in play of the finest possible sort, every man and woman' amongst us: παίζοντα ὅτι καλλίστας παιδιὰς πάντ' ἄνδρα καὶ γυναῖκα οὕτω διαβιῶναι.

With that fourth point – which constitutes the upshot of the opening sequence of thought in the passage – Plato articulates the claim that he will now go on to flesh out and elaborate. But before he can get on and do that, he decides he needs to go back and say more about the categories of the serious and the playful which in steps (1), (2) and (3) he has been applying very differently from the way they work in ordinary usage, or indeed in much of his own writing both in the *Laws* and elsewhere.

To persuade us to shift our understanding of the playful and the serious, Plato introduces a third polarity besides the two with which he has so far been operating. He starts his clarification with what he represents as the common view that war needs to be properly conducted for the sake of peace (he himself agrees with that: he put the case for thinking so way back at the start of Book 1). But people ordinarily reckon that war is a serious business. Therefore in effect, he suggests, they think that the serious is to be done for the sake of the playful. But (his Athenian Visitor is made to object) in war there is nothing of what *we* count as really serious – neither play (παιδιά, *paidia*) nor education (παιδεία, *paideia*): the intimate affinity between those two ideas, whose near identity is disclosed (as Plato thinks) by their etymological relationship.[18] So if we want to engage in truly serious activity, we should live the life not of war but of peace, and do that as well

---

[18] A favourite motif in the *Laws*: see again 1.643cb–d; also 2.656c, 8.832d.

as we can, given that it is only in peace that we can achieve our objective: play, or rather the right kind of play.

The Athenian has now therefore explained the logic yielding his initial conclusion: that we should live out our lives in play. The serious and the playful are one and the same thing; and it is a mistake to think as most people do that the one is to be pursued as a means to the other. The playful in life is the one truly serious thing about us.

The next thing on the agenda is to specify what sort of play should be regarded as the right kind, 'commensurate' for us. The answer: playing one's whole life through in the particular activities of sacrificing, singing, and dancing – singing and dancing being key dimensions of the religious practice central to the operation of the ideal political community envisaged in the *Laws*. The singing and dancing Plato has in mind was identified back in Book 2 as ritual choral performance, celebrating and sharing the life of the gods. The rhythm and harmonies of dance and song express the rational order that he takes to be divine, educating the emotions, and enabling us to transcend ordinary human limitations.

His immediate focus at this juncture in our Book 7 argument, however, is not on the city and the community, but on the individual (ἕκαστον, *hekaston*). And what he promises the individual is that engagement in the activity he has specified will – besides the key thing, its intrinsic importance as play – bring other benefits in its train. It will attract divine favour – and it will make it possible to see off one's own enemies (ἐχθρούς, *ekhthrous*) and defeat them in battle. So war and victory in war re-enter the picture, albeit subordinated to the true seriousness of play, and apparently in consequence of the right kind of play (perhaps the appropriate sort of martial music, shaping character as such music is meant to do: cf. *Rep.* 3.399a–b).

Whatever we make of this perhaps unexpectedly utilitarian consequence, and its consideration of merely human advantage, Plato has certainly by now made intelligible his claims of seriousness for play at its finest. He is talking about a form of play designed to celebrate the divine, and (as the Athenian puts it in the opening stage of the argument: (2) above) 'in the nature of things it is god who is worth treating with complete (and truly rewarding) seriousness'. In a sense, his argument is now complete. Nonetheless, it is given a final further brief section. At the end of the whole discussion, Plato comes back once again to the idea of human beings as playthings of the gods – as puppets.

I take it that his purpose in doing so must among other things be that of reinforcing a point I extracted from the opening sequence. The play he has been describing – as what we must devote ourselves to as the most serious activity available to us – is to be conceived not just as our play, but much more importantly as the gods' play. Here we should recall a passage from the beginning of Book 2 of the dialogue, where Plato refers to the gods as 'our companions in the dance' (*Laws* 2.653c–654a). But there looks to be a problem with that idea. Our human kind of dance, in which body as well as soul, emotion as well as reason, are at work, is something geared specifically to our nature, not theirs. So we need to try and work out the sense in which the gods could be our companions in it, as engaging in their own play.

I think the starting point has to be Plato's assessment of human nature: his observation first of children's initially disordered pleasurable or painful movement of body and voice, and then his reflection that song and dance for us have the capacity to bring order to those movements. The observation is what presumably suggested to him the marionette image itself in the first place. In particular, Plato must have noticed the marionette-like jerkiness with which our bodies and voices respond to the pulls of pleasure and pain. But I take it that it was the reflection about dance and song that prompted the further idea that humans must be conceived as a rather special sort of marionette. We would have been ill fitted to serve as the sorts of playthings of the gods he is envisaging unless we had been contrived as marionettes not limited in our repertoire to responses to pleasure and pain.

We had to be equipped with what in the Book 1 account of the marionette is called the ability to respond to the pull of the golden string of reason, as well as to the inflexible and peremptory tugs of pleasure and pain. By giving us (alone among animals) reason, in its primitive form perception of order and disorder, the gods contrived us as creatures able to engage in a kind of play in which – according to Plato – they themselves could participate, along with us as their playthings. Quite how that is possible the *Laws* does not attempt to say. One might suppose that insofar as choral singing and dancing are forms of rational order, they constitute a kind of activity in which gods too can share – and at the same time open up for us too the possibility of a bit of sharing in truth, making us more than the puppets we are for the most part.

Plato makes the Athenian's Spartan interlocutor Megillus interpret his account of humanity as thoroughly contemptuous: 'You really don't have much time for the human race, do you, my friend?' And many modern commentators too have seen the puppet image as an indication of a deeply pessimistic view of human nature. But we should not fail to notice a closing reference to 'the small kernel of truth', nor miss the possibility of salvation though play that Plato envisages, in the joy of singing and dancing with and for the gods.

Had he been reflecting on Heraclitus and the αἰών saying (Fr. 52) as he came to write the passage we have just been trying to understand?[19] Heraclitus' saying is a commentary on how any life lived is bound to be: a child playing. Plato, by contrast, sees the life of play as the truly serious alternative to the one most people actually lead. Nonetheless, Heraclitus' assertion of the control over our lives exerted by the child in us is given expression in words that have something of a dance-like rhythm to them. In Plato, song and dance are said quite explicitly to be the form that play should take. Moreover, the idea of living through the whole of one's life in play is a theme common to the two of them. And there is something else about Plato's treatment of the topic that seems particularly Heraclitean in spirit. I am not thinking of its preoccupation with polarities of god and man and of war and peace, although there is another affinity there too, but rather of the paradoxical abolition of the distinction between the serious and the playful, and the radical transformation of the two concepts in the process. What is serious is given specific shape as a kind of play, and play is recast as something not in the least spontaneous or arbitrary, but as a highly organized activity with the most solemn of purposes. That kind of paradoxical manoeuvre is of course particularly characteristic of Heraclitus.

Yet more generally, Heraclitus and Plato are both philosophers who use shock rhetorical tactics to get us to transform the way we think and what we value. Perhaps like Aristotle we may be predisposed to think of children as mere potential for adulthood. Perhaps we are inclined to think of play as amusing and often trivial diversion from what really most matters in life. Heraclitus however wants to puncture humanity's self-esteem. Prompting unconventional thoughts about childhood gives him one ideal lever for carrying through that enterprise. Plato is himself often into the Socratic business of unsettling the unexamined life. In the *Laws*, he is mostly in rather more expository style working through an ideal alternative to current political forms and conventional lifestyles. But now and again in the dialogue, he wants to be more disconcerting, by challenging the presuppositions of the vocabulary and the conceptual schemes that underpin current assumptions about what is or is not important. In other words,

---

[19] Plato very likely had Fr. 52 in mind when composing the eschatological myth of Book 10. There he speaks of 'him who cares for the universe' as the πεττευτής (*petteutês*, draughts player) moving good and bad souls to their appropriate destinies (i.e. like pieces on the games board), and shortly thereafter calls him 'the king' (ὁ βασιλεύς, *ho basileus*) (*Laws* 10.903d–904a). See further Saunders 1973: 241–4.

he wants to call in question the whole framework of conventional assumptions which might still be imprisoning us, however attracted we might be in theory to the ideal alternative he has been sketching. The passage from Book 7 we have just been working through is a case in point: a surprise in an expository sequence that is otherwise more straightforwardly articulated. It breaks in upon the reader suddenly, inviting us to take several steps back and ask ourselves about our very notions of the important and the unimportant, and so to look at the whole of our lives quite differently. Play is for him a concept that promises the elasticity he needs to do that work of unsettling, and to open up a vision – almost a mystical vision – of how things might be and look different.

I think Plato has here put his finger on something central to religion – virtually any religion – and the way ritual, as Huizinga expressed it in his general characterization of play, is 'a free activity standing quite consciously outside "ordinary" life as being not "serious", but at the same time absorbing the player intensely and utterly' (with the scare quotes round "ordinary" and "serious" duly registered).[20] Not every reader of this book will be particularly if at all religious. But most of us engage in activities that share those features of Platonic serious play: activities which release us into freedom by taking us out of ourselves and ordinary human concerns into something that so long as we are absorbed in it – whether it be singing or playing or listening to music, or our research, or carpentry, or any comparable activity – has a focus and an order and rhythm more worthwhile, yet still in a way engaged in playfully, than pretty well anything else we do.

---

[20] Huizinga 1949: 13. For a contemporary approach to the seriousness of ritual, see Xygalatas 2022.

References

Abbott, E., and Campbell, L. (1897). *The Life and Letters of Benjamin Jowett*. London: John Murray.
Abbott, E., and Campbell, L. (1899). *Letters of Benjamin Jowett*. London: John Murray.
Adam, J. (1963 [1902]). *The Republic of Plato: Edited with Critical Notes, Commentary, and Appendices*. 2 vols. Cambridge: Cambridge University Press.
Ademollo, F. (2011). *The Cratylus of Plato: A Commentary*. Cambridge: Cambridge University Press.
Adomenas, M. (2006). 'Plato, Presocratics, and the question of genre', in M. M. Sassi (ed.), *La costruzione del discorso nell'età dei Presocratici*. Pisa: Edizioni della Normale, pp. 329–53.
Allan, D. J. (1954). 'The problem of Cratylus', *American Journal of Philology* 75: 271–87.
Allen, R. E. (1983). *Plato's Parmenides: Translation and Analysis*. Minneapolis: University of Minnesota Press.
Annas, J. (1976). *Aristotle's Metaphysics, Books M and N*. Oxford: Clarendon Press.
Annas, J. (1978). 'Plato and common morality', *Classical Quarterly* 28: 437–51.
Annas, J. (1981). *An Introduction to Plato's Republic*. Oxford: Clarendon Press.
Annas, J. (1999). *Platonic Ethics, Old and New*. Ithaca: Cornell University Press.
Annas, J. (2010). 'Virtue and law in Plato', in C. Bobonich (ed.), *Plato's Laws: A Critical Guide*. Cambridge: Cambridge University Press, pp. 71–91.
Arendt, H. (1968). 'Truth and politics', in her *Between Past and Future: Eight Exercises in Political Thought*. New York: Viking Press, pp. 223–59, with notes at pp. 290–2.
Atkins, E. M. (2018). 'Sorting out lies: the eight categories of St Augustine's *De Mendacio*', *Augustinianum* 58: 441–68.
Barker, E. (1918). *Greek Political Theory: Plato and His Predecessors*. London: Methuen.
Barker, E. (trans.) (1995). *Aristotle: The Politics*, rev. R. F. Stalley. Oxford: Oxford University Press.
Barney, R. (2001). *Names and Nature in Plato's Cratylus*. New York: Routledge.
Barney, R. (2006) 'The Sophistic movement', in M. L. Gill and P. Pellegrin (eds.), *A Companion to Ancient Philosophy*. Malden, MA: Blackwell, pp. 77–97.

Bartels, M. (2017). *Plato's Pragmatic Project: A Reading of Plato's* Laws. Stuttgart: Franz Steiner Verlag.
Barton, J. (2005). 'Hippocratic explanations', in P. J. van der Eijk (ed.), *Hippocrates in Context*. Leiden: Brill, pp. 29–47.
Berryman, S. (2010). 'The puppet and the sage: Images of the self in Marcus Aurelius', *Oxford Studies in Ancient Philosophy* 38: 187–209.
Bestor, T. W. (1980). 'Plato's semantics and Plato's *Parmenides*', *Phronesis* 25: 38–75.
Blackburn, S. (2006). *Plato's Republic: A Biography*. London: Atlantic.
Blank, D. L. (1985). 'Socratics versus Sophists on payment for teaching', *California Studies in Classical Antiquity* 1: 1–49.
Bobonich, C. (1991). 'Persuasion, compulsion and freedom in Plato's *Laws*', *Classical Quarterly* 41: 365–87.
Bobonich, C. (1996). "Reading the *Laws*', in C. Gill and M. M. McCabe (eds.), *Form and Argument in Late Plato*. Oxford: Clarendon Press, pp. 249–82.
Bobonich, C. (2002). *Plato's Utopia Recast: His Later Ethics and Politics*. Oxford: Clarendon Press.
Bobonich, C. (2010). 'Images of irrationality', in C. Bobonich (ed.), *Plato's Laws: A Critical Guide*. Cambridge: Cambridge University Press, pp. 149–71.
Bobzien, S. (1998). *Determinism and Freedom in Stoic Philosophy*. Oxford: Clarendon Press.
Bok, S. (1978). *Lying: Moral Choice in Public and Private Life*. New York: Pantheon Books.
Bollack, J., and Wismann, H. (1972). *Héraclite ou la séparation*. Paris: Les Éditions de minuit.
Bouchet, C., and Giovanelli, P. (eds.) (2015). *Isocrate: entre jeu rhétorique et enjeux politiques*. Lyons: Centre d'étude et de la recherche sur l'Occident romain.
Boys-Stones, G. (2004). 'Phaedo of Elis and Plato on the soul', *Phronesis* 49: 1–23.
Brock, R. (2021). 'In search of Socrates' voiceprint', in E. Dimauro (ed.), μεταβολή: *Studi di storia antica offerti a Umberto Bultrighini*. Lanciano: Carabba, pp. 309–26.
Brown, E. (2000). 'Justice and compulsion for Plato's philosopher-rulers', *Ancient Philosophy* 20: 1–17.
Brunschwig, J. (2003). 'Revisiting Plato's Cave', *Proceedings of the Boston Area Colloquium in Ancient Philosophy* 19: 145–77.
Brunt, P. A. (1997). 'Plato's Academy and politics', in his *Studies in Greek History and Thought*. Oxford: Clarendon Press, pp. 282–342.
Burkert, W. (1972). *Lore and Science in Ancient Pythagoreanism*. Cambridge, MA: Harvard University Press.
Burnyeat, M. F. (1987). 'Platonism and mathematics: A prelude to discussion', in A. Graeser (ed.), *Mathematics and Metaphysics in Aristotle*. Bern: Haupt, pp. 213–40.
Burnyeat, M. F. (1990). *The Theaetetus of Plato*, trans. M. J. Levett, rev. and introd. Myles Burnyeat. Indianapolis: Hackett.

Burnyeat, M. F. (1997). 'Plato's first words', *Proceedings of the Cambridge Philological Society* 43: 1–20.
Burnyeat, M. F. (1998). 'The past in the present: Plato as educator of nineteenth-century Britain', in A. O. Rorty (ed.), *Philosophers on Education: Historical Perspectives*. London: Routledge, pp. 353–73.
Burnyeat, M. F. (1999a). 'Utopia and fantasy: The practicability of Plato's ideally just city', in G. Fine (ed.), *Plato 2: Ethics, Politics, Religion, and the Soul*. Oxford: Oxford University Press, pp. 297–308.
Burnyeat, M. F. (1999b). 'Culture and society in Plato's *Republic*', *The Tanner Lectures on Human Values* 20: 215–324.
Burnyeat, M. F. (2000). 'Plato on why mathematics is good for the soul', in T. Smiley (ed.), *Mathematics and Necessity* (Proceedings of the British Academy 103). Oxford: Oxford University Press, pp. 1–81.
Burnyeat, M. F. (2001). 'What was the "common arrangement"? An inquiry into John Stuart Mill's boyhood reading of Plato', *Utilitas* 13: 1–32.
Burnyeat, M. F. (2002). 'Plato on how not to speak of what is not: *Euthydemus* 283a–288a', in M. Canto-Sperber and P. Pellegrin (eds.), *Le Style de la pensée: Receuil de textes en homage à Jacques Brunschwig*. Paris: Belles Lettres, pp. 40–66.
Burnyeat, M. F. (2003). 'By the Dog', review of Ruby Blondell, *The Play of Characters in Plato's Dialogues*, *London Review of Books* (7 August 2003): 23–4.
Burnyeat, M. F. (2005). 'Platonism in the Bible: Numenius of Apamea on *Exodus* and eternity', in R. Salles (ed.), *Metaphysics, Soul, and Ethics: Themes from the Work of Richard Sorabji*. Oxford: Clarendon Press, pp. 143–69.
Burnyeat, M. F. (2013). 'Justice writ large and small in *Republic* 4', in V. Harte and M. Lane (eds.), *Politeia in Greek and Roman Philosophy*. Cambridge: Cambridge University Press, pp. 212–30.
Bury, R. G. (trans. and ed.) (1926). *Plato: Laws*. 2 vols. London: Heinemann; New York: G. P. Putnam's Sons.
Caird, E. (1865). 'Grote's *Plato*', *North British Review* 99: 351–84.
Caird, E. (1897–8). 'Professor Jowett', *International Journal of Ethics* 8: 42–8.
Campbell, L. (1866). Review of Grote's *Plato*, *Quarterly Review* 119: 108–53.
Campbell, L. (1867). *The Sophistes and Politicus of Plato*. Oxford: Clarendon Press.
Canto-Sperber, M. (2001). *Éthiques grecques*. Paris: Presses Universitaires de France.
Capra, A. (2003). 'Dialoghi narrati e dialoghi drammatici in Platone', in M. Bonazzi and F. Trabattoni (eds.), *Platone e la tradizione platonica*. Milan: Cisalpino La Goliardica, pp. 3–30.
Cherniss, H. (1944). *Aristotle's Criticism of Plato and the Academy*. Baltimore: Johns Hopkins University Press.
Cherniss, H. (1945). *The Riddle of the Early Academy*. Berkeley: University of California Press.
Cherniss, H. (1957). 'The relation of the *Timaeus* to Plato's later dialogues', *American Journal of Philology* 78: 225–66.
Clarke, M. L. (1962). *George Grote: A Biography*. London: The Athlone Press, University of London.

Cohen, M. (1971). 'The logic of the Third Man', *Philosophical Review* 80: 448–75.
Cooper, J. M. (1999). 'Socrates and Plato in Plato's Gorgias', in his *Reason and Emotion: Essays on Ancient Moral Psychology and Ethical Theory*. Princeton: Princeton University Press, pp. 29–75.
Cornford, F. M. (1939). *Plato and Parmenides*. London: Routledge and Kegan Paul.
Cornford, F. M. (trans.) (1941). *The Republic of Plato*. Oxford: Oxford University Press.
Coxon, A. H. (1986). *The Fragments of Parmenides*. Assen: van Gorcum. Revised and expanded edition Las Vegas: Parmenides Publishing, 2009.
Cross, R. C., and Woozley, A. D. (1964) *Plato's Republic: A Philosophical Commentary*. London: Macmillan.
Crossman, R. H. S. (1937). *Plato Today*. London: G. Allen and Unwin.
Crystal, I. (1996). 'Parmenidean allusion in Republic V', *Ancient Philosophy* 16: 351–63.
Curd, P. K. (1998). *The Legacy of Parmenides: Eleatic Monism and Later Presocratic Thought*. Princeton: Princeton University Press.
Dahl, N. O. (1991). 'Plato's defence of justice', *Philosophy and Phenomenological Research* 51: 809–34.
Dancy, R. M. (1991). *Two Studies in the Early Academy*. Albany: State University of New York Press.
Deichgräber, K. (1962). *Rhythmische Elemente im Logos des Heraklit*, in *Akademie der Wissenschaften und der Literatur. Abhandlungen der Geistes- und Sozialwissenschaftliche Klasse* 9. Wiesbaden.
Demetriou, K. N. (1998). 'George Grote and the Platonic revival in Victorian Britain', *Quaderni di storia* 47: 17–59. Reprinted as Essay VI in Demetriou (2011).
Demetriou, K. N. (1999) *George Grote on Plato and Athenian Democracy: A Study in Classical Reception*. Frankfurt am Main: Peter Lang.
Demetriou, K. N. (2004). *The Reception of Grote's Philosophical Works*. Bristol: Thoemmes Continuum.
Demetriou, K. N. (2011). *Studies in the Reception of Plato and Greek Political Thought in Victorian Britain*. Farnham: Ashgate.
Détienne, M., and Vernant, J.-P. (1978). *Cunning Intelligence in Greek Culture and Society*. London: The Harvester Press.
Diggle, J. (2004). *Theophrastus: Characters. Edited with Introduction, Translation and Commentary*. Cambridge: Cambridge University Press.
Dillon, J. (2003). *The Heirs of Plato*. Oxford: Clarendon Press.
Dimas, P. (2015). 'Wanting to do what is just in the Gorgias', in Ø. Rabbas, E. Emilsson, H. Fossheim, and M. Tuominen (eds.), *The Quest for the Good Life. Ancient Philosophers on Happiness*. New York: Oxford University Press, pp. 66–87.
Dodds, E. R. (ed.) (1959). *Plato: Gorgias*. Oxford: Clarendon Press.

Döring, K. (2011). 'The students of Socrates', in D. Morrison (ed.), *The Cambridge Companion to Socrates*. Cambridge: Cambridge University Press, pp. 24–47.
Dorion, L.-A. (2011). 'The rise and fall of the Socratic problem', in D. Morrison (ed.), *The Cambridge Companion to Socrates*. Cambridge: Cambridge University Press, pp. 1–23.
Doyle, J. (2006). 'The fundamental conflict in Plato's Gorgias', *Oxford Studies in Ancient Philosophy* 30: 87–100.
Dunn, J. (1979). *Western Political Theory in the Face of the Future*. Cambridge: Cambridge University Press.
Dunn, P. (2005). '*On Ancient Medicine* and its intellectual context', in P. J. van der Eijk (ed.), *Hippocrates in Context*. Leiden: Brill, pp. 49–67.
England, E. B. (1921). *The Laws of Plato: The Text Edited with Introduction, Notes, etc.* 2 vols. Manchester: Manchester University Press.
Eucken, C. (1983). *Isokrates: Seine Positionen in der Auseinandersetzung mit den zeitgenössischen Philosophen*. Berlin: De Gruyter.
Faber, G. (1957). *Jowett: A Portrait with Background*. London: Faber & Faber.
Ferrari, G. R. F. (1989). 'Plato on poetry', in G. A. Kennedy (ed.), *The Cambridge History of Literary Criticism*, vol. 1. Cambridge: Cambridge University Press, pp. 92–148.
Ferrari, G. R. F. (ed.) and Griffith, T. (trans.) (2000). *Plato: The Republic*. Cambridge: Cambridge University Press.
Field, G. C. (1930). *Plato and His Contemporaries*. London: Methuen.
Fine, G. (1986). 'Immanence', *Oxford Studies in Ancient Philosophy* 4: 71–97.
Fine, G. (1993). *On Ideas: Aristotle's Criticism of Plato's Theory of Forms*. Oxford: Clarendon Press.
Folch, M. (2015). *The City and the Stage: Performance, Genre, and Gender in Plato's Laws*. New York: Oxford University Press.
Ford, A. (2001). 'Sophists without rhetoric: The arts of speech in fifth-century Athens', in Y. L. Too (ed.), *Education in Greek and Roman Antiquity*. Leiden: Brill, pp. 85–109.
Fortenbaugh, W. W. (1975). *Aristotle on Emotion*. London: Duckworth.
Frede, D. (2010). 'Puppets on strings: moral psychology in *Laws* Books 1 and 2', in C. Bobonich (ed.), *Plato's Laws: A Critical Guide*. Cambridge: Cambridge University Press, pp. 108–26.
Furley, D. J. (1989). *Cosmic Problems*. Cambridge: Cambridge University Press.
Furley, W. D. (1996). *Andokides and the Herms: A Study of Crisis in Fifth-Century Athenian Religion*. London: Institute of Classical Studies.
Gagarin, M. (1986). *Early Greek Law*. Berkeley: University of California Press.
Gagarin, M. (2008). *Writing Greek Law*. Cambridge: Cambridge University Press.
Gagarin, M., and Woodruff, P. (trans.) (1995). *Early Greek Political Thought from Homer to the Sophists*. Cambridge: Cambridge University Press.
Gifford, M. (2001). 'Dramatic dialectic in *Republic* Book 1', *Oxford Studies in Ancient Philosophy* 20: 35–106.

Gill, C. (1996). *Personality in Greek Epic, Tragedy, and Philosophy: The Self in Dialogue*. Oxford: Clarendon Press.
Gill, C., and McCabe, M. M. (eds.) (1996). *Form and Argument in Late Plato*. Oxford: Clarendon Press.
Gill, M. L., and Ryan, P. (trans.) (1996). *Plato: Parmenides*. Indianapolis: Hackett.
Glucker, J. (1987). 'Plato in England: the nineteenth century and after', in H. Funke (ed.), *Utopie und Tradition: Platons Lehre vom Staat in der Moderne*. Würzburg: Königshausen & Neumann, pp. 149–210.
Glucker, J. (1996). 'The two Platos of Victorian Britain', in K. A. Algra, P. W. van der Horst, and D. Runia (eds.), *Polyhistor: Studies in the History and Historiography of Ancient Philosophy*. Leiden: E. J. Brill, pp. 385–406.
Grant, A. (1857, 1858). *The Ethics of Aristotle, Illustrated with Essays and Notes*. London: John W. Parker and Son.
Grant, A. (1871). 'Professor Jowett's translation of Plato', *Edinburgh Review* 134: 303–42.
Gray, J. (2015). *The Soul of the Marionette: A Short Enquiry into Human Freedom*. London: Allen Lane.
Gray, V. J. (2007). *Xenophon on Government*. Cambridge: Cambridge University Press.
Griffith, M. (1977). *The Authenticity of Prometheus Bound*. Cambridge: Cambridge University Press.
Grote, G. (1826). 'Institutions of ancient Greece', *Westminster Review* 5: 269–331.
Grote, G. (1850). *A History of Greece*, vol. 8. London: John Murray.
Grote, G. (1865). *Plato and the Other Companions of Socrates*. London: John Murray.
Grote, H. (1873). *The Personal Life of George Grote*. London: John Murray.
Guthrie, W. K. C. (1969). *A History of Greek Philosophy*, vol. 3, *The Fifth-Century Enlightenment*. Cambridge: Cambridge University Press.
Guthrie, W. K. C. (1975). *A History of Greek Philosophy*, vol. 4, *Plato: The Man and His Dialogues, Earlier Period*. Cambridge: Cambridge University Press.
Guthrie, W. K. C. (1978). *A History of Greek Philosophy*, vol. 5, *The Later Plato and the Academy*. Cambridge: Cambridge University Press.
Hackforth, R. (1936). 'Plato's theism', *Classical Quarterly* 30: 4–9.
Hahm, D. E. (1969). 'Plato's "Noble Lie" and political brotherhood', *Classica et Mediaevalia* 30: 211–27.
Halperin, D. (1992). 'Plato and the erotics of narrativity', in J. C. Klagge and N. D. Smith (eds.), *Methods of Interpreting Plato and His Dialogues*, Oxford Studies in Ancient Philosophy, Supplementary Volume, pp. 93–129.
Harte, V. (2007). 'Language in the Cave', in D. Scott (ed.), *Maieusis: Essays in Ancient Philosophy in Honour of Myles Burnyeat*. Oxford: Oxford University Press, pp. 195–215.
Harte, V. (2013). 'Plato's politics of ignorance', in V. Harte and M. Lane (eds.), *Politeia in Greek and Roman Philosophy*. Cambridge: Cambridge University Press, pp. 139–54.

Heidel, W. A. (1940). 'The Pythagoreans and Greek mathematics', *American Journal of Philology* 61: 1–33.
Herzog-Hanser, G. (1936). 'Νευρόσπαστα, *neurospasta*, Marionetten', in G. Wissowa and W. Kroll (eds.), *Paulys Realencyclopädie der classischen Altertumswissenschaft*, vol. 17.1. Stuttgart: J B Mettlersche Verlagsbuchhandlung, cols. 161–3.
Hesk, J. (2000). *Deception and Democracy in Classical Athens*. Cambridge: Cambridge University Press.
Hinchcliff, P. (1987). *Benjamin Jowett and the Christian Religion*. Oxford: Clarendon Press.
Hodkinson, S. (2005). 'The imaginary Spartan politeia', in M. H. Hansen (ed.), *The Imaginary Polis*. Copenhagen: The Royal Danish Academy of Arts and Sciences, pp. 222–81.
Horky, P. S. (2013). *Plato and Pythagoreanism*. Oxford: Oxford University Press.
Hornblower, S. (2003). *The Greek World 479–323 BC*, 3rd ed. London: Routledge.
Hornblower, S., and Spawforth, A. (eds.) (2012). *The Oxford Classical Dictionary*, 4th ed. Oxford: Oxford University Press.
Huffman, C. A. (1993). *Philolaus of Croton: Pythagorean and Presocratic*. Cambridge: Cambridge University Press.
Huffman, C. A. (2005). *Archytas of Tarentum: Pythagorean, Philosopher and Mathematician King*. Cambridge: Cambridge University Press.
Huffman, C. A. (2016). 'Archytas', in E. N. Zalta (ed.), *The Stanford Encyclopedia of Philosophy*. https://plato.stanford.edu/archives/fall2016/entries/archytas/.
Huizinga, J. (1949). *Homo Ludens: A Study of the Play-Element in Culture*. London: Routledge and Kegan Paul.
Humble, N. (2018). 'Sparta in Plato and Xenophon', in G. Danzig, D. Johnson, and D. Morrison (eds.), *Plato and Xenophon: Comparative Studies*. Leiden: Brill, pp. 547–75.
Irwin, T. (1979). *Plato Gorgias: Translated with Notes*. Oxford: Clarendon Press.
Irwin, T. H. (1999). 'The theory of Forms', in G. Fine (ed.), *Plato 1: Metaphysics and Epistemology*. Oxford: Oxford University Press.
Isnardi Parente, M. (1982). *Frammenti: Senocrate, Ermippo*. Naples: Bibliopolis.
Jackson, H. (1882). 'Plato's later theory of Ideas, II: the *Parmenides*', *Journal of Philology* 11: 287–331.
Jenkyns, R. (1980). *The Victorians and Ancient Greece*. Oxford: Blackwell.
Johnson, R. (1959). 'Isocrates' methods of teaching', *American Journal of Philology* 80: 25–36.
Johnson, W. A. (1998). 'Dramatic form and philosophic idea', *American Journal of Philology* 119: 577–98.
Jouanna, J. (1999). *Hippocrates*. Baltimore: Johns Hopkins University Press.
Jouët-Pastré, E. (2006). *Le jeu et le serieux dans les Lois de Platon*. Sankt Augustin: Academia Verlag.
Jowett, B. (1871). *The Dialogues of Plato*, 1st ed. Oxford: Clarendon Press.
Jowett, B. (1875). *The Dialogues of Plato*, 2nd ed. Oxford: Clarendon Press
Jowett, B. (1892). *The Dialogues of Plato*, 3rd ed. Oxford: Clarendon Press

Jowett, B. (1899). *Sermons: Biographical and Miscellaneous*, ed. W. H. Fremantle. London: John Murray.
Jowett, B. (1987). *Dear Miss Nightingale. A Selection of Benjamin Jowett's Letters to Florence Nightingale*, ed. V. Quinn and J. Prest. Oxford: Clarendon Press.
Kagan, D. (2003). *The Peloponnesian War: Athens and Sparta in Savage Conflict, 431–404 BC*. London: HarperCollins.
Kahn, C. H. (1963). 'Plato's funeral oration: the motive of the *Menexenus*', *Classical Philology* 58: 220–34.
Kahn, C. H. (1979). *The Art and Thought of Heraclitus*. Cambridge: Cambridge University Press.
Kahn, C. H. (1983). 'Drama and dialectic in Plato's Gorgias', *Oxford Studies in Ancient Philosophy* 1: 75–121.
Kahn, C. H. (1988a). 'Plato and Socrates in the *Protagoras*', *Methexis* 1: 33–52.
Kahn, C. H. (1988b). 'On the relative date of the *Gorgias* and the *Protagoras*', *Oxford Studies in Ancient Philosophy* 6: 69–102.
Kahn, C. H. (1995). 'The place of the *Statesman* in Plato's later work', in C. J. Rowe (ed.), *Reading the Statesman*. Sankt Augustin: Academia Verlag, pp. 49–60.
Kahn, C. H. (1996). *Plato and the Socratic Dialogue*. Cambridge: Cambridge University Press.
Kahn, C. H. (2001). *Pythagoras and the Pythagoreans: A Brief History*. Indianapolis: Hackett.
Kamtekar, R. (2005). 'The profession of friendship: Callicles, democratic politics, and rhetorical education in Plato's Gorgias', *Ancient Philosophy* 25: 319–39.
Kennedy, G. (1963). *The Art of Persuasion in Greece*. Princeton: Princeton University Press.
Kerferd, G. B. (1981). *The Sophistic Movement*. Cambridge: Cambridge University Press.
Kidd, S. E. (2019). *Play and Aesthetics in Ancient Greece*. Cambridge: Cambridge University Press.
Kirk, G. S. (1951). 'The problem of Cratylus', *American Journal of Philology* 72: 225–53.
Kirk, G. S. (1954). *Heraclitus: The Cosmic Fragments*. Cambridge: Cambridge University Press.
Kirk, G. S., Raven, J. E., and Schofield, M. (1983). *The Presocratic Philosophers*, 2nd ed. Cambridge: Cambridge University Press.
Kirwan, C. A. (1989). *Augustine*. London: Routledge.
Knorr, W. R. (1981). 'On the early history of axiomatics: The interaction of mathematics and philosophy in Greek antiquity', in J. Hintikka, D. Gruender, and A. Agazzi (eds.), *Theory Change, Ancient Axiomatics and Galileo's Methodology*. Dordrecht: Reidel, pp. 145–86.
Knorr, W. R. (1986). *The Ancient Tradition of Geometric Problems*. Boston: Birkhäuser.
Korsgaard, C. M. (2009). *Self-Constitution: Agency, Identity, and Integrity*. Oxford: Oxford University Press.

Kurke, L. (1999). 'Ancient Greek board games and how to play them', *Classical Philology* 94: 247–67.
Kurke, L. (2013). 'Imagining chorality: Wonder, Plato's puppets, and moving statues', in A.-E. Peponi (ed.), *Performance and Culture in Plato's Laws*. New York: Cambridge University Press, pp. 123–70.
Laks, A. (1990). 'Legislation and demiurgy: On the relationship between Plato's *Republic* and *Laws*', *Classical Antiquity* 9: 209–29.
Laks, A. (1991). 'L'utopie législative de Platon', *Revue Philosophique* 4: 417–28.
Laks, A. (2000). 'The *Laws*', in C. Rowe and M. Schofield (eds.), *The Cambridge History of Greek Political Thought*. Cambridge: Cambridge University Press, pp. 258–92.
Lane, M. (1995). 'A new angle on utopia: The political theory of the *Politicus*', in C. J. Rowe (ed.), *Reading the Statesman*. Sankt Augustin: Academia Verlag, pp. 276–91.
Lane, M. (1998). *Method and Politics in Plato's Statesman*. Cambridge: Cambridge University Press.
Lane, M. (2013). 'Platonizing the Spartan politeia in Plutarch's Lycurgus', in V. Harte and M. Lane (eds.), *Politeia in Greek and Roman Philosophy*. Cambridge: Cambridge University Press, pp. 57–77.
Lee, E. N. (1966). 'On the metaphysics of the image in Plato's *Timaeus*', *The Monist* 50: 341–68.
Lee, E. N. (1973). 'The second "Third Man": an interpretation', in J. M. E. Moravcsik (ed.), *Patterns in Plato's Thought*. Dordrecht: D. Reidel, pp. 101–22.
Livingstone, N. (2001). *A Commentary on Isocrates' Busiris*. Leiden: Brill.
Lloyd, G. E. R. (1979). *Magic, Reason and Experience*. Cambridge: Cambridge University Press.
Lloyd, G. E. R. (1990). *Demystifying Mentalities*. Cambridge: Cambridge University Press.
Lloyd, G. E. R. (ed.) (1978). *Hippocratic Writings*. Harmondsworth: Penguin.
Loraux, N. (1993). *The Children of Athena: Athenian Ideas about Citizenship and the Division between the Sexes*. Princeton: Princeton University Press.
Lorenz, H. (2006). *The Brute Within: Appetitive Desire in Plato and Aristotle*. Oxford: Clarendon Press.
Mackenzie, M. M. (1986). 'Putting the *Cratylus* in its place', *Classical Quarterly* 36: 124–50.
McCabe, M. M. (2000). *Plato and His Predecessors*. Cambridge: Cambridge University Press.
McCabe, M. M. (2015). *Platonic Conversations*. Oxford: Oxford University Press.
Menn, S. (1995). *Plato on God as Nous*. Carbondale: Southern Illinois University Press.
Meyer, S. S. (2012). 'Pleasure, pain and "anticipation" in *Laws*, Book I', in R. Patterson, V. Karasmanis, and A. Hermann (eds.), *Presocratics and Plato: Festschrift at Delphi in Honor of Charles Kahn*. Las Vegas: Parmenides Publishing, pp. 311–28.

Meyer, S. S. (2015). *Plato: Laws 1 & 2: Translated with an Introduction and Commentary*. Oxford: Oxford University Press.
Mill, J. S. (1969). *Essays on Ethics, Religion and Society: Collected Works*, vol. 10, ed. J. M. Robson. Toronto: University of Toronto Press and London: Routledge & Kegan Paul.
Mill, J. S. (1978). *Essays on Philosophy and the Classics: Collected Works*, vol. 11, ed. J. M. Robson, introd. F. E. Sparshott. Toronto: University of Toronto Press and London: Routledge & Kegan Paul.
Mill, J. S. (1981). *Autobiography and Literary Essays: Collected Works*, vol. 1, ed. J. M. Robson and J. Stillinger. Toronto: University of Toronto Press and London: Routledge & Kegan Paul.
Mirhady, D., and Too, Y. L. (trans.) (2000), *Isocrates I*. Austin: University of Texas Press.
Momigliano, A. (1994). 'George Grote and the study of Greek history', in his *Studies on Modern Scholarship*, ed. G. W. Bowersock and T. J. Cornell. Berkeley: University of California Press, pp. 15–31.
Monro, D. B. (1871). 'Jowett's *Plato*', *Quarterly Review* 131: 492–522.
Morrow, G. R. (1960). *Plato's Cretan City: A Historical Interpretation of the Laws*. Princeton: Princeton University Press.
Morrow, G. R. and Dillon, J. M. (trans.) (1987). *Proclus' Commentary on Plato's Parmenides*. Princeton: Princeton University Press.
Nails, D. (2002). *The People of Plato*. Indianapolis: Hackett.
Nightingale, A. W. (1993). 'Writing/reading a sacred text: A literary interpretation of Plato's *Laws*', *Classical Philology* 88: 269–300.
Nightingale, A. W. (1995). *Genres in Dialogue: Plato and the Construct of Philosophy*. Cambridge: Cambridge University Press.
Nightingale, A. W. (1999). 'Plato's lawcode in context: Rule by written law in Athens and Magnesia', *Classical Quarterly* 49: 100–22.
Nightingale, A. W. (2004). *Spectacles of Truth in Classical Greek Philosophy*. Cambridge: Cambridge University Press.
Norlin, G. (ed.) (1928 and 1929). *Isocrates*, vols. 1 and 2. London: Heinemann.
Nussbaum, M. C. (1976). 'The text of Aristotle's *De Motu Animalium*', *Harvard Studies in Classical Philology* 80: 111–59.
O'Brien, M. J. (1967). *The Socratic Paradoxes and the Greek Mind*. Chapel Hill: University of North Carolina Press.
Ober, J. (1989) *Mass and Elite in Democratic Athens*. Princeton: Princeton University Press.
Ober, J. (1998). *Political Dissent in Democratic Athens: Intellectual Critics of Popular Rule*. Princeton: Princeton University Press.
Ostwald, M. and Lynch, J. P. (1994). 'The growth of schools and the advance of knowledge', in D. M. Lewis, J. Boardman, S. Hornblower, and M. Ostwald (eds.), *The Cambridge Ancient History*, vol. 6, 2nd ed. Cambridge: Cambridge University Press.
Owen, G. E. L. (1953). 'The place of the *Timaeus* in Plato's dialogues', *Classical Quarterly* 3: 79–95.

Owen, G. E. L. (1960). 'Eleatic questions', *Classical Quarterly* 10: 84–102.
Owen, G. E. L. (1986). 'Notes on Ryle's Plato', in G. E. L. Owen (ed.), *Logic, Science and Dialectic*. London: Duckworth, pp. 85–103.
Page, C. (1991). 'The truth about lies in Plato's *Republic*', *Ancient Philosophy* 11: 1–33.
Palmer, J. A. (1999). *Plato's Reception of Parmenides*. Oxford: Oxford University Press.
Palmer, J. A. (2009). *Parmenides and Presocratic Philosophy*. Oxford: Oxford University Press.
Papillon, T. L. (trans.) (2005). *Isocrates II*. Austin: University of Texas Press.
Perlman, P. (1992). 'One hundred-citied Crete and the "Cretan πολιτεία"', *Classical Philology* 87: 193–205.
Perlman, P. (2004). 'Crete', in M. H. Hansen and T. H. Nielsen (eds.), *An Inventory of Archaic and Classical Poleis*. Oxford: Oxford University Press, pp. 1144–95.
Perlman, P. (2005). 'Imagining Crete', in M. H. Hansen (ed.), *The Imaginary Polis*. Copenhagen: The Royal Danish Academy of Arts and Sciences, pp. 282–334.
Perrin, B. (ed. and trans.) (1914). *Plutarch's Lives*, vol. 1. London: W. Heinemann and Cambridge, MA: Harvard University Press.
Popper, K. R. (1945). *The Open Society and Its Enemies*, vol. 1: *The Spell of Plato*. London: Routledge & Kegan Paul.
Prauscello, L. (2014). *Performing Citizenship in Plato's Laws*. Cambridge: Cambridge University Press.
Price, S. (1999). *Religions of the Ancient Greeks*. Cambridge: Cambridge University Press.
Prior, W. J. (1985). *Unity and Development in Plato's Metaphysics*. London: Croom Helm.
Redfield, J. M. (2003). *The Locrian Maidens: Love and Death in Greek Italy*. Princeton: Princeton University Press.
Rhodes, P. J. (2006). *A History of the Classical Greek World 478–323 BC*. Oxford: Oxford University Press.
Richter, M. (1956). 'T.H. Green and his audience: Liberalism as a surrogate faith', *The Review of Politics* 18: 444–72.
Riginos, A. (1976). *Platonica: The Anecdotes Concerning the Life and Writings of Plato*. Leiden: Brill.
Roberts, J. (1987). 'Plato on the causes of wrongdoing in the *Laws*', *Ancient Philosophy* 7: 23–37.
Ross, W. D. (1951). *Plato's Theory of Ideas*. Oxford: Clarendon Press.
Rowe, C. J. (ed. and trans.) (1995). *Plato: Statesman*. Warminster: Aris and Phillips.
Rowe, C. J. (2007). 'Plato and the Persian Wars', in E. Bridges, E. Hall, and P. J. Rhodes (eds.), *Cultural Responses to the Persian Wars*. Oxford: Oxford University Press, pp. 85–104.
Rowett, C. (2016). 'Why the philosopher kings will believe the Noble Lie', *Oxford Studies in Ancient Philosophy* 50: 80–110.

Samaras, T. (2002). *Plato on Democracy*. New York: Peter Lang.
Sansone, D. (ed.) (2020). *Plato: Menexenus*. Cambridge: Cambridge University Press.
Saunders, T. J. (1968). 'The Socratic paradox in Plato's *Laws*', *Hermes* 96: 421–34.
Saunders, T. J. (trans.) (1970). *Plato: The Laws*. Harmondsworth: Penguin.
Saunders, T. J. (1973). 'Penology and eschatology in Plato's *Timaeus* and *Laws*', *Classical Quarterly* 23: 232–44.
Saunders, T. J. (1986). '"The RAND Corporation in antiquity?" Plato's Academy and Greek politics', in J. H. Betts, J. T. Hooker, and J. R. Green (eds.), *Studies in Honour of T. B. L. Webster*. Bristol: Bristol Classical Press, vol. 1, pp. 200–10.
Saunders, T. J. (1991). *Plato's Penal Code*. Oxford: Clarendon Press.
Saunders, T. J. (trans. and comm.) (1995). *Aristotle: Books 1 and 2*. Oxford: Clarendon Press.
Schiefsky, M. J. (2005). *Hippocrates On Ancient Medicine*. Leiden: Brill.
Schöpsdau, K. (1984). 'Zum Strafrechtsexkurs in Platons *Nomoi*', *Rheinisches Museum für Philologie* 127: 97–132.
Schöpsdau, K. (1994). *Platon: Nomoi (Gesetze). Übersetzung und Kommentar*, vol. 1. Göttingen: Vandenhoeck & Ruprecht.
Schöpsdau, K. (2003). *Platon: Nomoi (Gesetze). Übersetzung und Kommentar*, vol. 2. Göttingen: Vandenhoeck & Ruprecht.
Schöpsdau, K. (2011). *Platon: Nomoi (Gesetze). Übersetzung und Kommentar*, vol. 3. Göttingen: Vandenhoeck & Ruprecht.
Schofield, M. (1971). 'Who were οἱ Δυσχερεῖς in Plato, *Philebus* 44Aff?', *Museum Helveticum* 28: 2–20, 181.
Schofield, M. (1973). 'Eudoxus in the *Parmenides*', *Museum Helveticum* 30: 1–19.
Schofield, M. (1998). 'Antisthenes', in E. Craig (ed.), *Routledge Encyclopedia of Philosophy*. London: Routledge, vol. 1, pp. 314–17.
Schofield, M. (1999a). *The Stoic Idea of the City*, rev. ed. Chicago: Chicago University Press.
Schofield, M. (1999b). 'The disappearing philosopher-king', in his *Saving the City*. London: Routledge, pp. 31–50.
Schofield, M. (2000). 'Plato and practical politics', in C. J. Rowe and M. Schofield (eds.), *The Cambridge History of Greek and Roman Political Thought*. Cambridge: Cambridge University Press, pp. 293–302.
Schofield, M. (2006). *Plato: Political Philosophy*. Oxford: Oxford University Press.
Schofield, M. (2009). 'Fraternité, inégalité, la parole de Dieu: Plato's authoritarian myth of political legitimation', in C. Partenie (ed.), *Plato's Myths*. Cambridge: Cambridge University Press, pp. 101–15.
Schofield, M. (2013a). 'Friendship and justice in the *Laws*', in G. Boys-Stones, D. El Murr, and C. Gill (eds.), *The Platonic Art of Philosophy*. Cambridge: Cambridge University Press, pp. 283–97.
Schofield, M. (2013b). Review of F. Ademollo, *The Cratylus of Plato*, *Gnomon* 85: 489–95.

Schofield, M. (2018). 'Aristotle's critique of Spartan imperialism', in P. Cartledge and A. Powell (eds.), *The Greek Superpower: Sparta in the Self-Definition of Athenians*. Swansea: The Classical Press of Wales, pp. 215–34.
Schofield, M. (2019). 'Plato in his time and place', in G. Fine (ed.), *The Oxford Handbook of Plato*, 2nd ed. New York: Oxford University Press, pp. 41–67.
Schofield, M. (2021). 'Plato, Xenophon, and the laws of Lycurgus', *Polis* 38: 450–72.
Schofield, M. (ed.), and Griffith, T. (trans.) (2010). *Plato: Gorgias, Menexenus, Protagoras*. Cambridge: Cambridge University Press.
Schofield, M. (ed.), and Griffith, T. (trans.) (2016). *Plato: Laws*. Cambridge: Cambridge University Press.
Schröder, H. O. (1983). 'Marionetten', *Rheinisches Museum* 126: 1–24.
Scott, D. (2015). *Levels of Argument*. Oxford: Oxford University Press.
Sedley, D. (1998). 'Parmenides', in E. Craig (ed.), *Routledge Encyclopedia of Philosophy*. London: Routledge, vol. 7, pp. 229–35.
Sedley, D. (2003). *Plato's Cratylus*. Cambridge: Cambridge University Press.
Sedley, D. (2004). *The Midwife of Platonism: Text and Subtext in Plato's Theaetetus*. Oxford: Clarendon Press.
Sedley, D. (2007). 'Philosophy, the Forms, and the art of ruling', in G. R. F. Ferrari (ed.), *The Cambridge Companion to Plato's Republic*. Cambridge: Cambridge University Press, pp. 256–83.
Sedley, D. (2009). 'Myth, punishment, and politics in the Gorgias', in C. Partenie (ed.), *Plato's Myths*. Cambridge: Cambridge University Press, pp. 51–76.
Sheffield, F. C. C. (2021). 'Moral motivation in Plato's *Republic*', *Oxford Studies in Ancient Philosophy* 59: 79–131.
Shields, C. (2014). 'Plato's divided soul', in K. Corcilius and D. Perler (eds.), *Partitioning the Soul: Debates from Plato to Leibniz*. Berlin: Walter de Gruyter, pp. 15–38.
Shorey, P. (1903). *The Unity of Plato's Thought*. Chicago: University of Chicago Press.
Shorey, P. (1914). 'Plato's Laws and the unity of Plato's thought', *Classical Philology* 9: 345–69.
Shorey, P. (ed. and trans.) (1930 and 1935). *Plato: The Republic*, 2 vols. London: W. Heinemann and Cambridge, MA: Harvard University Press.
Shorey, P. (1938). *Platonism Ancient and Modern*. Berkeley: University of California Press.
Singpurwalla, R. (2011). 'Soul division and mimesis in *Republic* X', in P. Destree and F.-G. Herrmann (eds.), *Plato and the Poets*. Leiden: Brill, pp. 283–98.
Smith, N. (1997). 'How the prisoners in Plato's Cave are "like us"', *Proceedings of the Boston Area Colloquium in Ancient Philosophy* 13: 187–204.
Sorabji, R. (2004). 'A L Peck', in R. B. Todd (ed.), *The Dictionary of British Classicists*. Bristol: Thoemmes Continuum, pp. 756–7.

Sprague, R. K. (1984). 'Plato and children's games', in D. E. Gerber (ed.), *Greek Poetry and Philosophy. Studies in Honour of Leonard Woodbury*. Chico, CA: Scholars Press, pp. 275–84.
Stalley, R. F. (1983). *An Introduction to Plato's Laws*. Oxford: Basil Blackwell.
Stopper, M. R. (1981). 'Greek philosophy and the Victorians', *Phronesis* 26: 267–85. [This article is attributed to J. Barnes in the catalogue of his publications in B. Morison and K. Ierodiakonou (eds.), *Episteme, etc.: Essays in honour of Jonathan Barnes*. Oxford: Oxford University Press, 2011.]
Strauss, L. (1975). *The Argument and the Action of Plato's Laws*. Chicago: Chicago University Press.
Tarán, L. (1981). *Speusippus of Athens*. Leiden: Brill.
Tarrant, H. (2013). 'Narrative and dramatic presentation in *Republic* III: Theory and practice', in N. Notomi and L. Brisson (eds.), *Dialogues on Plato's Politeia (Republic)*. Sankt Augustin: Academia Verlag, pp. 309–13.
Taylor, C. C. W. (2019). 'Plato's epistemology', in G. Fine (ed.), *The Oxford Handbook of Plato*, 2nd ed. New York: Oxford University Press, pp. 429–54.
Taylor, C. C. W. and Lee, Mi-Kyoung (2016). 'The Sophists', in E. N. Zalta (ed.), *The Stanford Encyclopedia of Philosophy*. https://plato.stanford.edu/archives/wi n2016/entries/sophists/.
Thomas, R. (1995). 'Written in stone? Liberty, equality, orality and the codification of law', *Bulletin of the Institute of Classical Studies* 40: 59–74.
Thompson, W. H. (1868). *The Phaedrus of Plato*. London: Whittaker and London: George Bell.
Too, Y. L. (1995). *The Rhetoric of Identity in Isocrates: Text, Power, Pedagogy*. Cambridge: Cambridge University Press.
Turnbull, R. G. (1989). 'The third man argument and the text of the *Parmenides*', in J. Anton and G. Preus (eds.), *Essays in Ancient Greek Philosophy*, vol. 3. Albany: State University of New York Press, pp. 203–26.
Turner, F. M. (1981). *The Greek Heritage in Victorian Britain*. New Haven: Yale University Press.
Vaio, J. (1996). 'George Grote and James Mill: How to write history', in W. M. Calder III and S. Trzaskoma (eds.), *George Grote Reconsidered*. Hildesheim: Weidmann, pp. 59–74.
van Harten, A. (2003). 'Creating happiness: The moral of the myth of Kronos in Plato's *Laws* (*Laws* 4, 713b–714a)', in S. Scolnicov and L. Brisson (eds.), *Plato's Laws: From Theory to Practice*. Sankt Augustin: Academis Verlag, pp. 128–38.
van Hook, L. (1945). *Isocrates*, vol. 3. London: Heinemann.
Vlastos, G. (1954). 'The third man argument in the *Parmenides*', *Philosophical Review* 63: 319–49.
Vlastos, G. (1969). 'Plato's "Third Man" argument (*Parm.* 132A1–B2): text and logic', *Philosophical Quarterly* 19: 289–301.
Vlastos, G. (1973). 'Socratic knowledge and Platonic "pessimism"', in his *Platonic Studies*. Princeton: Princeton University Press, pp. 204–17.
Vlastos, G. (1991). *Socrates: Ironist and Moral Philosopher*. Cambridge: Cambridge University Press.

Wardy, R. (1996). *The Birth of Rhetoric*. London: Routledge.
Wardy, R. (2013). 'The Platonic manufacture of ideology, or how to assemble awkward truth and wholesome falsehood', in V. Harte and M. Lane (eds.), *Politeia in Greek and Roman Philosophy*. Cambridge: Cambridge University Press, pp. 119–38.
Wilberding, J. (2004). 'Prisoners and puppeteers in the cave', *Oxford Studies in Ancient Philosophy* 27: 117–39.
Wilburn, J. (2012). '*Akrasia* and self-rule in Plato's *Laws*', *Oxford Studies in Ancient Philosophy* 43: 25–53.
Williams, B. (1982). 'Cratylus' theory of names and its refutation', in M. Schofield and M. C. Nussbaum (eds.), *Language and Logos*. Cambridge: Cambridge University Press, pp. 83–93.
Williams, B. (2002). *Truth and Truthfulness*. Princeton: Princeton University Press.
Wilson, J. R. S. (1976). 'The contents of the cave', in R. A. Shiner and J. King-Farlow (eds.), *New Essays on Plato and the Pre-Socratics*. Guelph, ON: Canadian Association for Publishing in Philosophy, pp. 117–27.
Wohl, V. (2002). *Love among the Ruins: The Erotics of Democracy in Classical Athens*. Princeton: Princeton University Press.
Woolf, R. (2000). 'Callicles and Socrates: psychic (dis)harmony in the Gorgias', *Oxford Studies in Ancient Philosophy* 18: 1–40.
Xygalatas, D. (2022). *Ritual: How Seemingly Senseless Acts Make Life Worth Living*. London: Profile Books.
Zeyl, D. (ed.) (1997). *Encyclopedia of Ancient Philosophy*. Westport, CT: Greenwood Press.
Zuntz, G. (1971). *Persephone*. Oxford: Clarendon Press.

Index

Academy, 30–1, 32, 36–9
Ademollo, F., 119
Aeschines of Sphettos, 15, 45
akrateia, 241
allegory, 8, 164, 179
Antisthenes, 8, 15, 31, 130–3
Archytas, 24, 26–7
Arendt, H., 149
argument, 2, 6, 91–3, 96–116
    second TMA, 104–12
    Third Man regress, 7, 96–7
aristocratic values, 83–5, 86, 93
Aristophanes, 28
Aristotle, 32–4, 37–8, 122–5, 197, 202, 214, 222, 225, 226, 277, 288
    *Politic*s, 203–8
assimilation, 77, 82, 85, 87–90, 94
atheism, 199
Athens, 4, 6, 10, 19, 20–3, 28–9, 39–41, 87–90, 94, 141–2, 160, 170, 186, 208–11, 215
Augustine, 146

Barney, R., 118
Burnyeat, M., 2–3, 185, 252

calculation, 256, 260, 263–7, 269, 272
Callicles, 6, 28, 73–95
Canto-Sperber, M., 53
Cave, 9, 21, 143, 156, 161, 163–79
    narration vs. commentary, 165
child, 11, 20, 153, 230–2, 235, 238, 252, 276–83, 287–8
citizens, 39, 84, 92, 140, 142, 150, 158, 215, 261, 264
citizenship, 94
city, 19, 39, 92, 150–4, 162, 169, 172, 257, 263–4, 268
    divinely governed, 192
    ideal, 139
    second-best, 205
cognitive dissonance, 242
communism, 206

confidence, 253, 272–4
courage, 219, 223, 225, 254, 255, 272
Cratylus, 7, 32–6, 119–35
Crete, 10, 186, 187–90, 219–22, 233
criminality, 245
Critias, 22, 231, 234
Cronos, 193–8
culture, 144, 173, 176, 177
customary practices, 220, 223, 238, 239
Cyrus, 40, 211

dance, 287
death, 76, 82, 83, 93, 230, 232, 235
deception, 139–50
democracy, 6, 20, 21–2, 23, 40, 87–90, 94, 140–2, 164, 169, 171, 211, 214, 217
dialectic, 29, 167
dialogue, 2, 7, 9, 97, 119, 184
    erotic, 45–6
    expository, 56
    fictiveness, 47–50
    frame, 43, 44, 47, 48
    late style, 36
    narrated, 5, 42–51
    sceptical, 56
    scripted, 5, 43, 51
    unity vs. development, 55, 196–8
Dracon, 235
Dunn, J., 140

economic activity, 230, 232, 235
economy, 206
education, 179, 190, 285
    Academy's programme, 30
    Antisthenes' treatise, 132
    children, 153, 161
    citizens, 206, 216
    for virtue, 268, 271
    guards, 143
    laws, 10
    mistaken conception, 16

education (cont.)
  philosophers, 9, 164, 165–8, 179
  Protagoras's manifesto, 19
  protreptic, 45
  Spartan, 238
Ephorus, 220
equality, 206, 209, 214
error, 249–50
ethics, 33, 37, 59, 140
Eucleides, 15, 43, 44, 48
Eudoxus, 37, 100
evil, 75–8, 94
Experience philosophy, 61, 66

falsehood, 8, 31, 130, 133, 139–50
fear, 241, 253, 266, 272–4
Forms, 7, 32, 34–6, 37, 148
  immanentism, 100–1
  original–copy model, 99–104
  paradigmatism, 116–17
freedom, 209, 210, 211, 215–16, 217
friends, 31, 147
friendship, 28, 80–1, 94, 206, 209, 210, 212, 217

games, 11, 276, 279–83
Glucker, J., 53, 66–7
god, 11, 143, 144, 187, 189, 192–200, 251, 261, 277, 284–8
good, 16, 69, 79, 86, 146, 155, 161, 165, 179, 235, 242, 250
  communal, 140, 142, 153, 155, 193, 197
  divine vs. human goods, 228–30, 234
Gorgias, 28, 124
Grote, G., 5, 18, 52–70

Hackforth, R., 200
happiness, 212, 216, 223
harm, 11, 76, 85, 244–7
Hegelianism, 62–4, 66–7
Heracliteanism, 32–6, 122–4, 125, 126, 129, 133
Heraclitus, 11, 125, 276–81, 288
hermeneutic atomism, 55, 58
Hermogenes, 119, 121
Hippias, 18, 225
historiography
  Benthamite vs. Hegelian, 61–5
history, 6, 15, 53, 60–1, 64–5, 208–11, 214
Homer, 278
homicide, 235
honest perplexity, 97, 98
Huizinga, J., 11, 275, 282, 289
human nature, 211–13, 217

idealism, 6, 57, 65–7
identity, 139, 154–8, 162

ideology, 156
ignorance, 240, 241–2, 249
individual, 269, 270, 286
injury, 244–50
injustice, 6, 11, 27, 75–85, 93, 195, 240–50
involuntary, 11, 240–50
Isocrates, 4, 29–32, 40, 47
Italy, 4, 23–6

Jackson, H., 107
Jowett, B., 5, 52–70, 118
justice, 16, 17, 21, 27, 89, 156, 157, 170, 173, 178, 195, 199, 234, 248, 249–50

Kant, I., 140, 147
knowledge, 16, 32–6, 38, 69, 129, 133, 140, 162, 242, 250
  political, 196

law, 10, 39, 193, 194–8, 202, 203, 215–16, 252, 257, 262–9, 275
  approaches to law-making, 234–9, 243
  general prelude, 240
  prelude, 184, 198, 213, 266, 268
lawgiver, legislator, 202, 209, 219–39
lawlessness, 209
laws, 157, 188, 219–39
  review, 230
legal code, 212
legislation
  dual nature, 213, 216, 217, 236
  written, 236
lie, 8–9, 139–62, 249
  medicinal, 142, 144, 146
  useful, 147, 149
life, 11, 16, 250, 280, 284–6, 288–9
  choice of lives, 240
  life cycle, 220, 235, 239
like, Likeness, 7, 109–17
Line, 164
linguistic naturalism, 118–35
logic, 44, 62, 65, 96
love, 89–90, 94, 151
Lucian, 279
Lycurgus, 10, 209, 219–20, 221–39

marionette, 11, 251–3, 257–63, 269–72, 283
marriage, 230–1, 235, 236, 238
mathematics, 4, 9, 17, 24, 25, 26, 31, 47, 165, 166–7
McCabe, M. M., 131, 135
medicine, 16, 18, 216
metaphysics, 32, 36, 37, 65, 97
metaspeleology, 163
methodology, 37, 60, 98, 113, 190
Meyer, S. S., 228, 271

Mill, J. S., 53, 55, 58–60, 61, 68, 70
Minos, 221–2, 227
modern applications, 68–70
monarchy, 215, 217
moral character, 167–8, 177, 229
morality, 139–50, 229
music, 27, 287
myth, 8, 24, 27, 139, 144, 146, 153–5, 158–62, 193, 198, 248

Nietzsche, F., 150
Nightingale, A., 184, 264
Nightingale, F., 69
nomos, 19, 175, 190, 192, 194
Nussbaum, M., 259

Old Oligarch, 220
old vs. young, 187–90, 192
oligarchy, 214
ontology, 37, 129, 130
opinion, 250, 253, 268, 273

pain, 240, 249, 252, 255, 260–2, 272–4
paradox, 8–9, 10, 11, 31, 153
    Heraclitean, 276–81
    serious vs. playful, 284–8
    Socratic, 240–2, 245, 247
Parmenides, 35–6, 130
patriotic devotion, 150–4, 156
Peck, A. L., 282
Peloponnesian War, 22, 234
penology, 212, 244–9
Pericles, 21, 22, 26, 28, 84, 90, 92, 141, 211, 226
Persia, 40, 208–11
persuasion vs. coercion, 213, 272
Phaedo, 15, 50
philosopher, 20–1, 24, 41, 144, 148, 156, 175, 195
philosophical history, 61, 69–70
Philosophical Radicals, 53, 61, 70
philosophy, 16, 20, 24, 30, 32, 45, 166, 177, 184, 185, 189, 190–2, 200
    history of, 60–7
    system, 5, 52, 55–7, 62
Plato
    Charmides, 45–7
    Cratylus, 7, 34, 118–35
    Euthydemus, 29–30, 47, 130, 282
    Gorgias, 6, 27–9, 73–95, 247
    Laches, 272
    Laws, 38–41, 161, 183–201, 202–18, 219–39, 240–50, 251–74, 281, 283–9
    Parmenides, 7, 37, 48, 96–117
    Phaedo, 50
    Phaedrus, 186
    Philebus, 37

    Protagoras, 19, 241, 267
    Republic, 8–9, 41, 50–1, 67–8, 139–62, 163–79, 191, 195, 204, 205–7, 264–7, 269–70, 282–3
    Seventh Letter, 23, 28, 41
    Sophist, 66, 130
    Statesman, 194–8, 267
    Symposium, 48
    Theaetetus, 43, 48, 125, 126, 131, 170
    Timaeus, 48, 49, 253
play, 11, 275–89
pleasure, 240, 249, 252, 255, 260–2, 272–4
Plutarch, 224
politeia, 190, 192, 199, 203, 208
    as book title, 220
    Cretan, 220
    Spartan, 221–6
politics, 20–3, 24, 28–30, 60, 87–90, 91–3, 94, 139–44, 188, 207
    political obligation, 154–8, 162
    political system, 203–18
Popper, K. R., 140, 144
power, 28, 41, 77–82, 85, 93, 140, 171, 195, 197
Proclus, 98, 100, 102, 104, 112, 185
Prodicus, 18, 130
projects, 9–10
    idealizing vs. pragmatic, 212–14
    main vs. subsidiary, 216–18
property, 214
Protagoras, 18–19, 125, 130, 199
psychology, 253–7, 261, 263
punishment, 10, 201, 244, 247
puppet. *See* marionette
Pythagoras, 18, 26–7
Pythagoreanism, 24, 31, 32, 37, 38, 199, 212
Pythagoreans, 24–7, 32

rationality, 195
readerships, 9, 185, 193–8, 201, 271
reality, 174–7
reason, 11, 140, 193, 194, 197, 215, 250, 268, 269, 272
reasoning, 242, 252, 253, 262, 263, 266
religion, 10, 25, 191–4, 198–201, 275, 289
retribution, 247–9
rhetoric, 4, 28–32, 82, 84, 86, 88, 92, 94, 157, 170, 186, 201
ritual, 206, 275, 289
ruler, 79–81, 87, 142–3, 149, 150–3, 165, 193, 195, 215

Saunders, T. J., 183, 243
Schleiermacher, F., 55, 57
Schöpsdau, K., 228
security, 75–87, 93
Sedley, D., 118

self, 10, 11, 252, 269–72
   self-rule, 252, 254, 257, 260, 268–72
   unitary, 255, 271
seriousness, 275, 284–9
shame, 265, 266, 272
Shorey, P., 53, 55, 59, 239
Sicily, 4, 23–5, 41
slavery, 215
social organization, 216
Socrates, 6, 10, 15–17, 20–3, 47, 170, 178, 187, 190, 203, 226
   Socratic circle, 15, 45, 226
   Socratic discourses, 15, 46
   Socratic intellectualism, 240–2, 249
   Socratic paradox. *See* paradox
Solon, 10, 18, 40, 210, 236
Sophists, 18–20, 92
sôphrosunê, 45, 224, 234, 240, 273
soul, 4, 24, 25, 26, 45, 82, 94, 166, 240–2, 253, 267, 278
   psychic disease, 244–8
Sparta, 10, 23, 40, 186, 187–90, 208–11, 219–39
Sprague, R. K., 282
Stoicism, 45, 145, 263
Strauss, L., 185, 189

technê, 16–18, 29, 31, 121
Themistocles, 21, 28, 84, 92, 171

theocracy, 192
theology, 189, 191, 199–200
Thirty Tyrants, 22
Thrasymachus, 195, 257
Thucydides, 22, 28, 170, 234
truth, 8, 58, 64–5, 69, 133, 139–50, 162, 172, 177, 261, 287
tyranny, 4, 28, 209, 216, 241
tyrant, 28, 41, 79–84, 89

utilitarianism, 6, 57, 62

virtue, 10, 19, 31, 38, 143, 211–15, 216, 219, 222, 223–4, 227, 232, 240–1, 252, 253, 254, 267–8, 271
Vlastos, G., 6, 96–7
voluntary, 11, 215–16, 240–50

war, 190, 219, 221, 224, 225, 229, 271, 275, 285, 288
well-being. *See* happiness
Williams, B., 133, 147
wisdom, 30, 209, 210, 211, 215, 217, 241
women, 207, 238
wrongdoing, 240–50

Xenophon, 10, 219–20, 222–4, 226–7, 229–39

Zeno of Elea, 113

For EU product safety concerns, contact us at Calle de José Abascal, 56–1º,
28003 Madrid, Spain or eugpsr@cambridge.org.

www.ingramcontent.com/pod-product-compliance
Lightning Source LLC
LaVergne TN
LVHW020000160426
836326LV00066B/38